Emerging Business Opportunities in Africa:

Market Entry, Competitive Strategy, and the Promotion of Foreign Direct Investments

Christopher O. Gekonge
Doing Business in Africa Inc., USA

BUSINESS SCIENCE
Reference
An Imprint of IGI Global

Managing Director: Lindsay Johnston
Production Manager: Jennifer Yoder
Publishing Systems Analyst: Adrienne Freeland
Development Editor: Austin DeMarco
Acquisitions Editor: Kayla Wolfe
Typesetter: Travis Gundrum
Cover Design: Jason Mull

Published in the United States of America by
Business Science Reference (an imprint of IGI Global)
701 E. Chocolate Avenue
Hershey PA 17033
Tel: 717-533-8845
Fax: 717-533-8661
E-mail: cust@igi-global.com
Web site: http://www.igi-global.com

Library of Congress Cataloging-in-Publication Data

Gekonge, Christopher O., 1943-
Emerging business opportunities in Africa : market entry, competitive strategy, and the promotion of foreign direct investments / by Christopher O. Gekonge.
pages cm
Includes bibliographical references and index.
Summary: "This book presents the basic business modeling for developing appropriate strategies in exploiting business opportunities in the emerging economy in Africa"-- Provided by publisher.
ISBN 978-1-4666-4570-7 (hardcover) -- ISBN 978-1-4666-4571-4 (ebook) -- ISBN 978-1-4666-4572-1 (print & perpetual access) 1. Investments, Foreign--Africa. 2. Industries--Africa. 3. Africa--Commerce. 4. Africa--Economic conditions--1960- I. Title.
HG5822.G45 2014
330.96--dc23

2013020597

British Cataloguing in Publication Data
A Cataloguing in Publication record for this book is available from the British Library.

This work is dedicated to Consolata Moraa, my grandmother, and Kate Oser, a dear family friend, two great women who lived their lives in full, going to the Lord in their 90s, the former a peasant farmer in rural Kenya, the later a social worker in Central New York, USA. The two women came from two totally different cultural and national backgrounds, but both women had a similar and radiant spirit of a scholar that enthusiastically inspired all that were lucky and fortunate enough to meet them. I was fortunate enough, not only to know them both well, but grew up with one—my grandmother, Moraa—and she phenomenally shaped my life. The two women immensely inspired my intellectual curiosity and gave me a strong sense of adventure to passionately, enthusiastically, and rigorously pursue scholarly work with penchant curiosity, vigor, and rigor.

Table of Contents

Chapter 10

Chapter 11

Foreword

Christopher Gekonge is a man with considerable business experience in Africa and a scholar on how to undertake doing business. He has written this book on how and why to do business in Africa, calling upon both his practical side and his scholarship to meld these two together in a volume of great worth in understanding the business climate in Africa.

Why is this important? This has been well summed up by the Secretary of State Hilary Clinton who stated, "I want all of my Fellow America citizens, particularly our business community to hear this: Africa offers the highest rate of return on foreign direct investment of any developing region in the world today" (Clinton, 2012).

This book lays out the social and political background of the African continent, looks at history, and documents why the future looks bright for this part of the globe. Political and economic challenges face the entire world, including Africa, but the potential for great gains seems greatest on this continent. While it may not have done all that well in the past, the future looks especially good. This book addresses the possible difficulties and prepares the reader for what to expect when moving businesses into this part of the world. The insights are not given from afar, but represent important lessons learned on the ground, with an overall view of making all the region stronger, not just benefiting a few.

As someone who has traveled extensively, I learned a great deal from reading this book and find it would be suitable for several audiences. Anyone wishing to do business in Africa or wanting to learn how to apply modern business techniques in a developing part of the world would benefit greatly from reading this volume.

Arthur L. Frank
Drexel University, USA

Arthur L. Frank *is a physician and educator who practices occupational medicine. He also holds a Ph.D. degree and has done extensive work on occupational lung diseases and agricultural safety and health. He has traveled widely and lectured in Africa, Asia, Europe, and elsewhere, and has seen major changes occur in several parts of the world. He has served as a consultant to U.S. and international governments, corporations, and labor groups. He currently serves as Professor of Public Health and Chair of the Department of Environmental and Occupational Health at Drexel University School of Public Health and is also a professor of Medicine at the College of Medicine. He has carried out research in several countries and lectures widely.*

REFERENCES

Clinton, H. (2012, June 14). *Remarks at the African growth and opportunity act forum to mark global economic statecraft day*. Retrieved from http://www.state.gov/secretary/rm/2012/06/192327.htm

Preface

Writing a book on Africa, its emerging business opportunities, and Foreign Direct Investment in Africa is like embarking on a long journey fraught with obstacles and a slippery road full of road-blocks. It has been especially challenging to find reliable and current empirical evidence to support assertions because little materials of value have been written on the area the book is focusing on: doing business in Africa. However, the journey has been successful despite the formidable hardships. This book is about Africa, the third largest continent in land mass and population, and its emerging business opportunities. It elucidates Africa and its emerging business opportunities in the context of the global economy.

This book is about doing business in Africa, about exploiting the business opportunities Africa offers to African entrepreneurs, global corporations, and institutions. It highlights the hospitality of the African people, giving one a preview of how interesting, exciting, and thrilling it is to work with them in business and in other human endeavors. The book will be a guide for modifying attitudes, thinking patterns, and behaviors on Africa. The book will expand the understanding of the African people's entrepreneurial spirit and capacity, the emerging and exciting business opportunities in Africa, and Africa in the diversity and complexity of today's global business and economic environment that is integrating and changing rapidly.

Diamond (1998) asserts that no matter how much one has read about Africa beforehand, one's first impressions, from actually being there, are overwhelmingly interesting and exciting. It is awesome to be in Africa. No other continent is as amazing or has the diversity that Africa does. African's diversity is in natural resources, human divisions, in spoken languages, the number of countries, and the great business opportunities.

Interestingly enough, Africa harbors five of the six major divisions of humanity—except the Aborigines of Australia—namely, Blacks, Whites, Pygmies, Khoisans, and Asians (Diamond, 1998). One quarter of the world's languages are indigenous and spoken only in Africa. However, English, Arabic, Portuguese, and French are the major business languages in the continent. Africa is also well endowed, as mentioned above, with an abundance of environmental resources of different kinds that await exploitation.

The continent is made of 54 countries of different sizes and at different levels of development. This book presents them and a model on how to enter and do business in Africa. It is meant to persuade global companies to do more business in Africa and be a source book for students of business and a basis for further research on doing business in Africa. The book describes Africa as a rich and vibrant emerging continent with rapidly expanding regional markets at different levels of the regional integration process.

Despite the many positive elements on Africa, it remains a continent still in crisis, and the beginning of the new millennium appears to have accentuated its gravity. Violent conflicts, human rights violations, economic mismanagement that often stems from foreign advice, incompetent governance, and flawed development policies are among the manifestations of this crisis. However, Africa can easily and quickly overcome all these constraints through effective and targeted reforms and the use of indigenized strategies and policies, some of which are postulated in this book, to speedily develop the continent.

The book is divided into eleven chapters: Chapter one defines Africa and its place in human history. It describes Africa as a continent filled with abundant natural resources, people, and current economies poised and ready to advance to the next stage of economic development. Chapter two anecdotally describes several perspectives of African history including the African slavery period, the colonial period, the post independence period, the structural adjustments and reforms period, and the impact of what happened during each of these periods on Africa today. Chapter three describes globalization generally and explains Africa's current and future position in the global economy. Chapter four identifies and describes the rising and compelling imperatives of doing business in Africa, Africa's market attractiveness, and the GDP and Purchasing Power Parity (PPP) as measures of market size and market intensity in Africa.

Chapter five, perhaps the most important chapter in the book considering the great importance of increasing regional integration and trade globally, focuses on the perspectives of international trade, regional integration schemes and processes, the African regional integration, and its regional trading blocs meant to enlarge African markets and as a foundation and building blocks of the African economic community. The seven major trading blocs cover the Eastern, Central, Southern, Northern, and the Western African regions for both Francophone and Anglophone countries.

Chapter six describes enabling opportunities of doing business in Africa and specific business opportunities covering several industries and business sectors. The enabling opportunities include a market of about 1 billion people and approximately 2 trillion dollars at the Purchasing Power Parity level growing at an average of 7.5 percent annually, abundant natural resources, a good demographic profile, regional integration, cheap but literate labor, generally speaking English or French and ensuring low business costs, linkages and several USA, European, Indian, Brazilian, and Chinese institutions focusing on promoting African trade and business, convertible currencies, readily available banking services, growing Stock Exchange Markets, and increasingly reformed institutions to improve the business climate and to make it easy to do business in Africa.

The specific opportunities include strong and increasing demand for IT services and IT-based technologies, back office service (outsourcing), fertilizer, cement, and textile manufacturing, natural resources exploitation, water resources management, electricity generation, coffee and tea processing, manufacture and marketing of health care products and services, tourism, art, entertainment, and educational and training services, among others.

Chapter seven looks at sites and market entry evaluation criterion and global and African markets entry strategies to do business in Africa. These strategies include opening up regional hubs, exporting to selling agents, franchises, leveraging host government's goals, joint ventures, acquisitions, turnkey projects, contractual agreements, and greenhouse operations. Chapter eight focuses on developing a business model to do business in Africa including corporate-level and competitive strategies that firms need to develop to successfully create a sustainable competitive advantage in the industries and market segments they will compete in Africa.

Chapter nine enumerates and discusses the challenges of doing business in Africa. These challenges include poor perceptions others have of Africa, persistently poor leadership, poverty, institutional voids, corruption, poor infrastructure, global competition, disease pandemics, and lack of indigenous corporations to create business pathways in Africa. Chapter ten presents a framework and suggests specific strategies to eliminate or minimize the impact of challenges in doing business in Africa. Chapter eleven summarizes the book and makes concluding remarks on doing business in Africa.

The book also compares Africa with other commonly discussed and important emerging markets in Brazil, Russia, India, and China (BRIC countries). It is hoped that the book will generate interest and help global companies, universities, students of business, social entrepreneurs, and company executives to perceive

Africa positively, to encourage more research, and to encourage corporations and entrepreneurs to seek African business opportunities and to develop appropriate strategies to competitively exploit these opportunities in order to create value for their increasingly demanding stakeholders.

Christopher O. Gekonge
Doing Business in Africa, Inc., USA

REFERENCES

Diamond, J. (1998). *Guns, germs, and steel: The fates of human societies.* New York: W. W. Norton and Company.

Acknowledgment

This book has been a project spanning more than two decades. Notwithstanding that, nobody writes and publishes a book by his or her own efforts alone. I am indebted to very many people and institutions that supported me during the research and writing of the book.

I am thankful to my family. Here, I wish to name Truphosa Gekonge, Dr. Eunice Omanga, and Dr. Bethsebah Gekonge for special mention. My family has always been a great source of inspiration, enthusiasm, and hope. They were particularly so during the research and writing of this book. I am extremely grateful for the support, fellowship, and prayers from Leverington Presbyterian Church in Roxborough, PA, USA. I am also very grateful to Mr. Yaron Bluevise for his generous financial support during the book development. I am grateful to Dr. Yeetey Enuameh. Dr. Enuameh did not only help me with gathering research data, but he also introduced me to Prof. Emmanuel Koku of Drexel University. Prof. Koku went through the first draft of the manuscript and made valuable comments that helped me set the tone of the book.

I am thankful to Dr. Martin Ogutu of the University of Nairobi in Kenya. Dr. Ogutu thoroughly went through the manuscript and made insightful and helpful changes. My gratitude goes to Prof. Arthur Frank of Drexel University. Prof. Frank gave the book the rigor it deserved. I am very thankful to Prof. Frank for writing a foreword for the book.

I am thankful to three knowledgeable and experienced African authors, who became my role models and guiding stars when researching and writing this book. These resourceful African talents are Prof. John Mbaku, Prof. Calestous Juma, and Dr. Dambisa Moyo. I have also been inspired by and benefited from—in my research and writing this book—the works of four great American authors, namely Mr. Thomas Friedman, Prof. Paul Krugman, Nicholas D. Kristof, and President Bill Clinton.

I am grateful for the insightful ideas I gained from the various people I worked with as a manager, consultant, and business counselor over the years. In this group, I wish to single out one person for special thanks: Mr. Julius Okara Barare. Mr. Barare was once my chief executive officer and mentor. He profoundly influenced my persistent character of pursuing an issue. He always had faith in me and expected the best out of me and often gave me the opportunity to prove it. He taught me that success was falling down and getting up one more time without end. I am eternally thankful to my editor, Austin DeMarco, and the two book reviewers he engaged for their thorough reviews and comments that helped to considerably improve the flow, cohesion, and readability of the book.

Lastly, but definitely not least, I am ever thankful to both Prof. Clint Tankersley and Prof. Peter Koveos, both of the Whitman School of Management, Syracuse University. They gave me unwavering support when I needed support most. Furthermore, they gave me an opportunity to teach a course on doing business on the global scene and enabled me to participate in the department's outreach program to the Chamber of Commerce of Central New York. At this time, I met Prof. Pierre Yourougou, from Ivory Coast, and a Clinical Associate Professor of Finance, Syracuse University, who previously worked with the IMF. Prof. Yourourgou and Prof. Peter Oslon, formerly a professor of management at Utica College, NY, critiqued various articles I wrote on management and "doing business in Africa." These articles became the foundation of the various chapters of this book.

Finally, as an anonymous person once stated, "*to err is human.*" Any error of grammar, prose, fact, flow, and reference in this book is entirely mine alone and not of any of those persons, groups, and institutions that greatly helped me to research and successfully write this book.

Christopher O. Gekonge
Doing Business in Africa, Inc., USA

Introduction

I was born in a polygamous home in Kenya. My father, albeit illiterate, was a wise, knowledgeable, and skilled man, held in great esteem and high regard by the community in which we lived. He was an effective colonial judge on the social, economic, political, and cultural issues that affected African communities during colonial Kenya. My mother was his 7th wife and she was known—in our Kisii culture—as my father's "Omoriakari" (latest wife). She bore him nine children, six boys, of whom I am the oldest, and three girls. In total, my father had forty-two children, twenty-four boys and eighteen girls from all his seven wives.

In a polygamous home—and with such a large number of children—things were very tough and children usually learnt survival skills and tactics early in life. A lot of times, we had to fend for ourselves. Oftentimes, children were cared for and brought up by their maternal grandmothers. My maternal grandmother brought me up. My grandmother was a virtuous woman and was intensely intimate and keenly familiar with life knowledge and the survival skills of her ancestors. She lived, I believe, an enjoyable life. She intimated to me often that her great grandmother was sold, as a little girl, to her people by the Suba, a sub-tribe of the Luo people of Kenya for corn during one of the hunger episodes that afflicted people in Kenya.

Although without formal education, my grandmother was convincingly and definitely virtuous, wise, and scholarly. She was well skilled in the affairs of life and events that affected the community. She knew about hunger and how to forestall it, various strategies of food management, community dispute resolutions, child-rearing skills, and the knowledge and skills that should be instilled into young children to make them useful and effective community members and leaders later in life that continued the community traditions and values.

She informally instilled in me the skills of observation and analysis, respect, inquiry, rigor, effective communication, persistency, curiosity, passion, and toughness in tackling problems, be they intellectual, physical, or otherwise. As a consequence, I developed a keen interest and did very well in mathematics, geography, and history in high school, which formed the foundation in my pursuit of economics and business later in college and doing real business in the real world. I also developed respect for the old as the custodians of wisdom, knowledge, security, stability, and long-term survival of the community. These are some of the skills and knowledge Mark McCormack calls "street smart" which he describes in his seminal book, *What They Do Not Teach You at Harvard Business School: Notes from a Street Smart Executive* (Bantam, 1984).

After successful completion of high school, I earned a full scholarship—from the United States Agency for International Development (USAID)—to study in Liberia, where I studied economics and earned a BA (Economics) degree in 1970. In Liberia, I met students from virtually every African country. While in college in Liberia, the African students formed a mock Organization of African Unity (OAU). The real OAU, formed in 1963, later changed to African Union (AU) in 2001. At one time, I had the honor and privilege of serving as a senior official of the mock OAU, the Liberian branch. We annually held a conference in various African countries, particularly in the western African region. We planned our meetings to coincide with the real OAU conference going on in Addis Ababa, Ethiopia. Our meetings discussed solutions to problems from our perspectives at that time of the newly independent African countries. The issues included full liberation of Africa, African unity, poverty, education, healthcare, and economic development.

In those years, OAU heads of state and government met exclusively in Addis Ababa, Ethiopia, unlike today when they move from one country to the other annually. The head of state in the country where the meeting is held becomes the chairperson of AU in the coming year. During the head of state's tenure, he or she represents Africa in international forums. As it were, we were the pioneers of moving the mock OAU from one country to another annually. For example, the 2009 annual conference was held in Libya and Muammar Gadhafi became the Chairman of AU.

Because of our annual mock OAU conferences, I traveled extensively in Africa. I was to do even more traveling on business later on in life as an airline executive and as a management consultant. During my travels in Africa, I became intimately aware of Africa's economic, social, political, and business opportunities as well as problems. This is the genesis and grounding of this book.

After my studies in Liberia—I later studied in Britain, Canada, and Kenya—I went back to Kenya and worked in various positions and industries including the sugar industry, the airline industry, management consultancy, and small and micro enterprises business counseling. I moved to the USA in 2005. In 1975, I married my best friend, Truphosah, and God has blessed us with five children. We have five grandchildren.

Another key element of this book is my wife's guarded and pragmatic approach to issues in life. My wife believes that one should take and look at issues cautiously until all their merits, demerits, and implications are known and understood and that statements should be checked thoroughly before confirmed as statements of fact and reality. This book bears a lot of that. My wife worked as an executive legal secretary for 24 years and then went back to college to study nursing becoming a Registered Nurse (RN) in 2005.

The economic development, prosperity, and participation of Africa in global business has fascinated me and held my interest for decades. Therefore, this book is a consequence of my thoughts and deliberations on that over the years. This book is also about travels in Africa. It is an observation of the African economic and business experiences firsthand.

To create jobs and hence wealth to eradicate poverty in Africa, we believe that Africa needs vibrant businesses, both by indigenous entrepreneurs and investments by global companies or Foreign Direct Investments. These investments will enable Africa to eliminate the pervasive and degrading poverty that afflicts many of its people. We are acutely aware that poverty is not purely an African problem but a global problem that needs concrete and concerted international effort to solve. In my observations, there are many countries—in other regions of the world—that are poorer than many African countries, but they do not come on the international radar for scrutiny as Africa does. India for example, has some of the poorest people in the world, but being a nuclear power, it is treated with golden gloves and often mentioned more positively in the Western world than Africa (Wong et al., 2008).

In this book, I have set out to make my contribution to understanding Africa and what must be done for Africa to grow and prosper in order to participate in world affairs as an equal partner with other regions of the world rather than being seen as a charity case and marginalized from the global economy. At the core of my thoughts, arguments, and presentations are African history, African business opportunities, challenges of doing business in Africa and how to overcome them, regional integration and trade, and how Africa is viewed worldwide today and its implications for African institutions and its people.

My aim is not to write a book about one African country, but instead, to write one about the entire continent and its ability to integrate and regionalize to accelerate economic development in the continent because, in my opinion, it will be difficult for one African country to succeed in isolation. I understand that my knowledge of any one African country cannot approach that of an expert. Furthermore, I do not claim a comprehensive understanding of all the complexities of political, economic, and social problems in each African country or region that guide their policy formulation and implementation, particularly on business and trade policies. Furthermore, to summarize the economic underpinnings of a continent of more than 50 countries is difficult, especially one as diverse and complex as Africa. In an effort to present my views on Africa's potential, I look at and describe in detail some of the major economic opportunities and challenges Africa faces and how to overcome these challenges to exploit the African economic opportunities and great potential to create value for the African people and people of the world.

The point here is not only an attempt, as much as possible, to provide authoritative detailed recommendations for doing business in Africa. It is also to discuss general issues and relevant problems and illustrate useful ways that can enhance doing business in Africa successfully for indigenous entrepreneurs and global firms. This would lead to creation of value for their stakeholders and creation of wealth for the African people and hence eradication of pervasive poverty in the continent. My hope is that readers, with their various perspectives and interests, can draw from the book useful implications in their area of interest and for their organizations, individual needs, and the African countries' needs.

Some people may find some views expressed in the book controversial. My objective has not been to avoid controversy, but instead to develop a vibrant and robust argument about doing business in Africa in simple terms backed by as much authoritative evidence as possible. While I suspect that some readers will be happy with what I have done, I hope that a lot of people will be persuaded and excited to look into the issues reviewed and discussed more critically and positively for the good of Africa and its people now and in the future.

Other than my thorough understanding of Africa through my extensive readings and business travels in the continent, I have taught "Doing Business in Africa" as a course at graduate school level, done business outreach to industry on doing business in Africa, consulted and counseled businesses, studied and researched on African business extensively, and read the following materials: books and journal articles on the history of Africa, annual reports of international organizations and agencies, international trade, regional integration and trade globally and specifically in Africa, and principles of management and strategic management.

Furthermore, I have thoroughly, constantly, and extensively read weekly and monthly issues of *Business Week*, *Time*, the *Economist*, *Fortune*, and daily papers including the *New York Times*, the *Wall Street Journal*, the *Philadelphia Enquirer*, the *Daily Nation*, the *Standard*, the *East African*, the *Nigerian Guardian*, the *Ghanaian Observer*, and *Time of London*, as well as visiting different Websites. One difficulty in writing a book like this is getting evidence and statistical information to support the assumptions and assertions one makes. Despite the constraints, I got a lot of help from many people in advancing the African business opportunities and the discussions in the book.

In addition, my inspiration to do this book was further elevated by reading seminal work on Africa by four prominent authors: John Mbaku, V. Mahajan, Ndabisa Moyo, and Calestous Juma, who have done extensive studies and written on the various aspects of the African situation. John Mbaku has written on the role of institutions in doing business in Africa, African regional integration schemes to expand African markets, and the role of economic freedoms in economic development in Africa. V. Mahajan has written on the marketing opportunities in Africa in the rising and emerging African market. Dambisa Moyo has written on the failure of financial aid to develop Africa in the last fifty years and how there is a better way to finance African development. Finally, Calestous Juma has written on the role of technological innovations and innovation systems in developing African agriculture in order to deal with African hunger and poverty. All these great works have immensely inspired my work.

The book is targeted at African policy makers, global entrepreneurs and managers, African entrepreneurs, teachers of global business and strategy, corporate managers, researchers, and students of business and management. It is, therefore, hoped that the book will generate more interest in organizations to perceive and seek African business opportunities and to develop appropriate strategies to competitively exploit these opportunities, and through that, enable entrepreneurs and corporate managers to create value for their stakeholders and wealth for the African people and thus help in eradicating chronic poverty in Africa. It is hoped too that the book will provoke interest in scholars and researchers to carry out further research on "Doing Business in Africa."

Christopher O. Gekonge
Doing Business in Africa, Inc., USA

REFERENCES

McCormark, M. H. (1984). *What they don't teach you at Harvard Business School: Notes from a street smart executive*. New York: Book Views Inc..

Wong, E. (2009, December 20). China's export of labor faces scorn. *New York Times*.

Chapter 1
Africa

ABSTRACT

This book is divided into eleven chapters that explain business opportunities in Africa and strategies to exploit them for the benefit of humanity. This chapter is the foundation of the book and it defines Africa and its place in human history. It describes Africa as a continent endowed with abundant natural resources, people, and economies poised and ready to advance to the next level of economic development. The continent is made up of 54 countries of different geographic and demographic sizes and at different levels of economic development. This chapter presents these countries, their market sizes, and a model on how to enter and do business in them. The chapter also describes Africa as a rich and vibrant continent, with rapidly expanding regional markets at different levels of the regional integration process. It explains clearly the source of the continent's business potential and how to enhance it. Generally, the whole book is meant to persuade global companies to invest more in Africa. It is also a source book for policy makers, corporate managers, students of global business, and a basis for further research on "doing business in Africa."

1. AFRICA DEFINED

Africa is a blessed and attractive continent with abundant natural resources; friendly people; a beautiful landscape, inhabited by exotic wildlife; and a complex ecosystem. Africa is the second largest of the five continents. The continent's natural resources include plenty of underground water in shallow aquifers, oil and gas, various metals,

DOI: 10.4018/978-1-4666-4570-7.ch001

exotic wildlife, and exciting and friendly people. African has emerging economies poised and ready to advance to the next level of economic development, as their GDP grows at an average of 5 percent pa (Wang et al., 2008).

Africa's western most borders are about five thousand miles away from the continental United States and a mere eight miles separate Europe from North Africa through the Straits of Gibraltar. The shores of South East Asia are connected to Africa by the Indian Ocean, and the Southern Atlantic links Africa with Latin America. The Mediterranean and the Red Seas, and the Gulf of Eden separate Africa from southern Europe and the Middle East respectively (The Africa Guide, 2005).

With South Sudan becoming a new nation in July 2011, the Africa continent is made up of fifty four countries. The fifty four countries constitute the African Union (AU); originally the Organization of African Unity (OAU) whose foundations were pioneered and developed by Ghana, Morocco, Algeria, and Ethiopia in 1963 (OAU Charter, 1963). The other key original members of OAU are Liberia, Guinea, and Egypt.

The OAU became the African Union in 2001, currently buttressed with seven economic regions and trading blocs at the various stages of regional integration levels. These economic regions are the East African Community (EAC); Common Market of Eastern and Southern Africa States (COMESA); Economic Community of West African States (ECOWAS); the Arab Maghreb Union (AMU), in North Africa; Western African Economic and Monetary Union (WAEMU); Southern Africa Development Community (SADC); and the Community of Central African States (ECCAS). These trading blocs are discussed in more details in chapter five below. They are anticipated to be pillars and building blocks for the envisaged "the African Economic Union" in the coming years (Mbaku, 1998; Juma, 2011).

The African population is currently estimated to be over 1 billion people, which is about 15 percent of the world population. The African population is also currently estimated to grow at an average rate of 2.5 percent annually (EIU, 2009; ERA, 2010). Africa is the only region of the world today where birthrates are above the population replacement rates. African population is also the fastest growing of all the continents and it has the youngest, reasonably well-educated, work force in the world today. What these people need is more education, good healthcare, and employment to provide a large market for goods and services (Straziuso, 2012).

Today, Nigeria has the largest population in Africa-162.5 million people-followed by Ethiopia 85 million, and Egypt with 82.5 million people (ERA 2010). Several of the island nations have the smallest populations of about 1 million people each. A majority of the other larger African nations have population numbers averaging 30 million people, with the continental life expectancy averaging 52 years (Mahajan, 2009).

Although the average HIV/AIDS prevalence rate has reduced from 14 percent to 5 percent in recent years in many African nations, the HIV/AIDS pandemic has negatively impacted the African life expectancy (ERA 2010). This trend is expected to reduce further given the major preventive measures African governments have instituted to deal with the pandemic in recent years.

The archeological studies and discoveries have often confirmed that man originated in Africa over several million years ago, before spreading throughout the world (Diamond 1998). The Rift Valley, in East Africa, has provided an almost unbroken history of the earliest development and evolution of humans. It is now accepted as the earliest identified location for the human species (Diamond 1998). Diamond (1998) further asserts that no matter how much one has read about Africa, beforehand, one's first impressions from actually being there are awesomely and overwhelmingly interesting and exciting.

However, aside from the ancient Egyptian culture of the rich and fertile Nile Valley-one of the most highly developed, enduring, and lasting empires in human history–and probably the Ashanti empire of Gold Coast, the remainder of the African continent has not yet produced enduring influence on the rest of the world despite of the spread and presence of Africans in many parts of the world and despite of its enormous wealth in natural resources. Many Africans spread across the world, as slaves, centuries ago. However and due to cycles of civil wars and poverty, many Africans have migrated to other parts of the world in recent years where they are referred to as the African Diaspora. It is estimated that there are forty million Africans in the Diaspora.

The lack of developed transportation and communication systems; limited trade among African countries; poor leadership and weak governance leading to the persistent record of elections resulting in governments with no pretence of honesty, existing simply to enrich the rulers as long as possible; weak economic and political institutions; corruption; the colonial residue of debilitating ethnicity based on divide and rule strategy throughout sub-Saharan Africa; horizontal inequalities; warring factions in the commodity-rich regions; chronic hunger due to low agricultural productivity; poorly funded education and research; and the absence of basic healthcare and social services for the growing population have all conspired to contribute to the persistently low level of economic development in the African countries leading to poverty and deprivation as the order of the day (Deng et al, 2002; Schuster et al, 2006).

Africa harbors five of the six major divisions of humanity-except the Aborigines of Australia-namely, the Blacks, the Whites, the Pygmies, the Khoisans, and the Asians. One quarter of the world's languages is indigenous and spoken only in Africa. However, English, Arabic, Portuguese, and French are the major business languages in the continent. Africa is also well endowed, as mentioned above, with an abundance of environmental resources of different kinds that await exploitation.

For examples, ranging from large quantities of oil in Nigeria, Libya, and Angola to diamonds and gold in Botswana, South Africa, and Congo DR, fertile land, to rich equatorial forests across the continent, to beautiful plains and savannas inhabited by exotic and tantalizing to see wild life in Kenya/Tanzania/South Africa/Botswana, Africa is exceptionally rich. No other continent is as amazing and approaches this level of environmental resource abundance and human diversity as Africa does (Diamond, 1998).

As mentioned above, Africa is the world's second-largest continent by landmass and contains more than 15% of the world's population. Sub-Saharan Africa (SSA) itself is unique in that it has the largest number of countries per square area of any developing region. A large portion of SSA's population lives in landlocked countries compared to other regions; for example, it is 40% landlocked versus 23% for Eastern Europe. The region is also unique for its low population density, which accentuates internal transport and communication costs.

Sub-Saharan Africa remains one of the world's poorest regions. In a region where the basic needs of much of the population remain unmet and a major part of it is under civil unrest, opportunities in the consumer sectors are limited for now. The consumption potential in the longer-term, however, could be considerable and substantial as the region has favorable demographic trends and its economic growth and incomes per capita are increasing. The African Development Bank estimates that most of Africa will grow at 7.5 percent–from 5 percent today-in the next decade, which means an African middle class is developing fast (ERA, 2010).

All African countries, except Liberia and Ethiopia, were colonized, at one time or other, in their long, chequered, and amazing history. The main colonizing nations were Britain, France, Portugal, and Belgium, although there was a limited German presence before the First World War; in Namibia, Cameroon, and Tanzania (Deng et al., 2002; Schuster et al., 2006).

Given the assimilation policies used by these colonizing countries, African countries today are mainly Anglophone, Francophone, or Portuguese speaking, with the mixture of Arabic mostly in the North. However, English is spoken well virtually and generally all over Africa. The major indigenous languages are Kiswahili in East and Central Africa, Arabic in the North, and Hausa in Nigeria and neighboring countries in West Africa (Schuster et al, 2006).

A majority of the African countries gained their independence in the early 1960's, with Sudan and Ghana, being the first, having attained their independent in 1956 and 1957 respectively. Liberia and Ethiopia were not colonized, although Ethiopia was temporarily occupied by Italy for a short time during and after World War II (Denge et al., 2002; Schuster et al., 2006).

The European colonial legacies left behind, in Africa, an infrastructure, business culture, an institutional context, and legal framework and systems that were geared toward serving the colonial governments. This was true, too, with the educational system that was meant to produce clerical staff and other lower-level employees for the colonialists, both government administrators and business employers. Africans were hardly allowed to do commercial businesses except being peasant farmers in designated areas for each ethnic group and lowly paid laborers for the colonial large-scale farmers and commercial enterprises. They were not even allowed to grow certain high value cash crops like tea until near independence times in countries like Kenya in East Africa (Moyo 2009).

The colonial governments pursued the policies of indirect rule, in some countries, such as Nigeria and Uganda; total control in others, such as Kenya, Zimbabwe, and many of the French and Portuguese speaking countries, and a divide and rule policy in all cases. The divide and rule policies–such between the Kikuyus versus Luos (Kenya), Ndembele versus Shona (Zimbabwe), Ibo versus Yoruba/Hausa (Nigeria), Tutsi versus Hutu (Rwanda), and Shiites versus Sunnis in the Arab Africa—kept Africans separated and suspicious of each other and it was even used to assist and encourage tribes and groups to develop differently in different countries (Deng et al., 2002).

Map of Africa

The divide and rule strategy promoted negative diversity that emphasized differences and weaknesses among people rather than similarities and strengths that exist among the African people. The policies stressed the negatives and weaknesses of different communities instead of positives and strengths that could enable them to work together with synergy and coherence to develop the country (Figure 1).

These destructive colonial governing arrangements and development policies have almost wholeheartedly and greatly contributed to the African social and political instability, insecurity, and disorder today. The long-term effects of these policies have been responsible, almost single handedly, to the decreased chances of accelerated economic development in Africa. The consequences of underdevelopment show up, today, in persistence poverty and chronic hunger in most of the continent (Deng et al., 2002; Gudrun, 2004; Moyo, 2009).

Sometimes, the churches, particularly the Catholic and Anglican churches provided some degree of a unifying force in the African countries during colonial times. This unifying force was provided through their educational systems whereby, at least in some countries like Kenya, admitted students from all parts of the country in their schools, particularly in high schools. These schools were truly national schools. Students from such schools grew up having a national view of life despite the surrounding forces against it.

Figure 1. Map of Africa

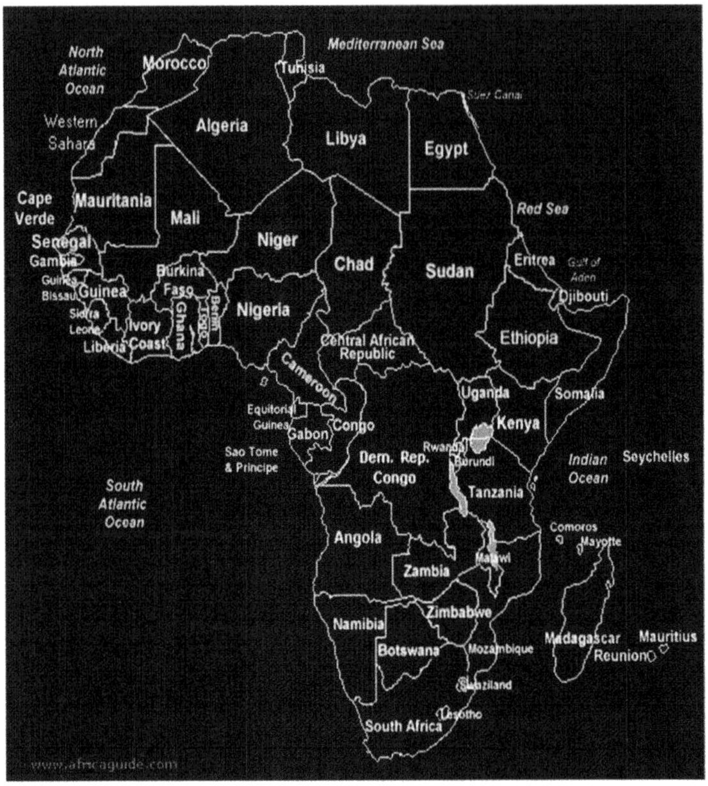

The consequences and usefulness of this unifying educational system became very important later when the Africans started agitating for independence. It enabled them to work together somewhat in seeking freedom from the colonial powers. However, many of them got highly and ethnically divided immediately they gained independence. A lot of the differences arose from their disagreements on how to share the national wealth and not how to build it. Each wanted the whole cake for their families, relatives, friends, and tribe (Deng et al., 2002). They took over private companies and agricultural farms–that they shared among themselves-that were doing well before and at independence and made them public or government property and agencies that did very poorly in the poisoned political climate.

Still, the overall colonial divide and rule policies came to haunt Africa later during and after independence. The policies were a challenge to the new African leaders as they made it difficult to unite the African people on one national cause and to create viable, stable, and cohesive nation states at and after independence, a situation that has persisted, to date, in almost all African countries.

2. AFRICAN TRADE AND CO-OPERATION

As discussed later in the book, colonial countries' trade was strictly with the metropolitan countries that colonized Africa for decades. Therefore, post-colonial African trade has continued to be mostly with the former colonial powers. The situation has changed, albeit slowly, in the last two decades or so. With increasing globalization and regional integration among African countries, inter-Africa trade is growing significantly. Although it is still dismally low–at 10 percent of their world trade-compared to their total world trade and trade of regions the size of Africa. Africa is also increasingly trading with China and India–a recent phenomenon–and the USA.

As mentioned above, the inter-African trade is currently is very low of its total global trade (Wilde et al., 2008). It is very low indeed when compared, for example, with inter-northern American trade that is 56 percent of its total world trade and inter-European trade that is 74 percent of its total world trade (Wild et al., 2008,). And, of course, these are the wealthiest regions of the world.

Empirical data indicate further that Africa is the poorest continent today largely because of its low inter-African trade and too much dependence on global aid (Moyo, 2009). Inter-regional trade improves and successfully promotes economic development and results in better standards of living of the people involved (Ghemawat 2005). Africa must accelerate trade within itself for it to prosper economically to alleviate pervasive poverty and perennial hunger in the continent.

African regional integration has increased substantially during the last two decades. Consequently, Africa can be classified into seven active regional trading blocs, including several non-trading organizations–the New Partnership for African Development (NEPAD)–meant for mobilizing resources for African development, enhancing African cohesion, and improving governance in the continent. There are also the African Leadership Forum (ALF) and the Conference on Stability, Security, Development, and Corporation in Africa. The goal of these institutions is to promote security and stability through effective leadership and strong governance as contexts for African cooperation and development (Deng et al., 2002).

Furthermore, there is the United Nations Economic Commission for Africa (ECA) established by the United Nations Social and Economic Council in 1958 to encourage economic corporation among African countries. ECA promotes economic development in Africa by gathering and disseminating statistics necessary for economic planning and development. It also provides advice to national governments on issues that are important in increasing African integration, trade, and development (ERA, 2010).

Through NEPAD and Mo Ibrahim's commission–in order to promote good governance in Africa-African presidents are evaluated against each other, annually, on a specified criterion, which includes, among other factors, effective governance in their countries, provided and sustained by them. The evaluation is done through a process called "Peer Review Mechanism," which means the review is done by fellow presidents who wish to participate in the annual review. African private Corporations, including Mo Ibrahim's Commission, have set up a commission that eventually evaluates the former presidents or a retiring president and gives awards to the best-assessed former president that including a onetime award of US $5m and $200,000 annually (The East African, 2010).

These awards have great implications for effective leadership and good and strong governance in Africa. The first president to win the US $5 m award-in 2007-is former president Joaquin Chisano of the Republic of Mozambique. The second recipient is former president Festus Mogae of Botswana, in 2008. There was no award in 2009 and 2010 for various reasons as discussed by the Commission (The East African, 2010). The 2011 award was received by the president of Cape Verde.

Furthermore, Imo Mohamed's Commission and the East African News Paper, annually, evaluate sitting African presidents and award them a grading raging from A to F based on their performance in governance in the year under consideration. In the 2011, evaluation, the presidents of Ghana, Botswana, Mauritius, and Cape Verde, obtained the A grade.

As discussed in Chapter five below, the seven African trading blocks are: the East African Community (EAC); the Southern African Development Community (SADC); the COmmon Market of Eastern and Southern Africa (COMESA); the Economic COmmunity of Western African States (ECOWAS); the Maghreb Economic Union, in Northern Africa; and the two Francophone economic communities of the West Africa Economic and Monetary Union; and the Central Africa Economic and Monetary Union. There are also several smaller unions that pursue narrower and limited objectives such as the Western African Monetary Zone, in West Africa, and the Inter-Governmental Authority on Development (IGAD) in the Horn of Africa.

There are overlaps in these regional trading blocs in the sense that some countries are in more than one trade region, at the same time; for instance Tanzania, in East Africa, is within the East African Community and the Southern African Development Community. Furthermore, Kenya and Uganda, also in East Africa, are in the East African Community and in COMESA, at the same time, and Zambia and Zimbabwe are in both COMESA and SADC at the same time. Eight of the Western African francophone countries are in ECOWAS and in their separate trade region of the West Africa Economic and Monetary Union at the same time.

It is anticipated that these regions will eventually, as they increasingly become fully operational, form the building blocks of the African Economic Community formed by the African heads of state and government in 1991, in Abuja, Nigeria. The trade regions, several of which are at the customs union level of economic integration process, will stimulate inter African trade and therefore create business opportunities in the continent by enlarging African markets (Mbaku, 1998).

However, it is important to note that the East African Community is at the Common market level and the Francophone trading blocs are at the monetary union level of regional integration process. Both Francophone trading blocs have regional central banks and growing stock market exchanges, with a common currency, the French Franc, managed by the regional Central Banks based in Senegal and Cameroon, respectfully. The currency is tied to the Euro and the French Treasury assures its stability by holding foreign exchange reserves, of the francophone countries, in the French Central Bank as discussed further in chapter three below (Mbaku, 1998; The East African, 2010).

3. A MANAGER'S NOTE

Africa is a large continent and one is expected to encounter difficulties and complexities in doing business in Africa. But despite the many challenges of doing business in Africa–disease, hunger, poverty, institutional voids, poor governance, corruption, poor perception of Africa by others, and poor infrastructure–the continent's macroeconomic factors and business climate are improving rapidly creating opportunities for savvy executives and corporations to do business (EIU, 2009). The continent is increasingly becoming small as it were, in business terms through regional integration, that is enlarging markets and standardizing business climate and practices.

Furthermore, the African countries are well endowed with environmental resources. Its literacy levels are rising fast, as per the Millennium Development Goals, and therefore there are well-educated young people for employment at low wages. Placement of industry in Africa to utilize these resources will give corporations a competitive advantage in Africa and globally. With these high value endowments, Africa will be the last frontier for global wealth creation for mankind today and in the coming years as it was the credo of civilization and origin of mankind many centuries ago (Diamond, 1998). It is a region to enter now and to do business today to create a first-mover and incumbency advantages for the global corporations and the African entrepreneurs. First-mover and incumbency advantages are barriers to entry of late comers (Wang et al., 2008).

REFERENCES

Diamond, J. (1998). *Guns, germs, and steel: The fates of human societies*. New York: W. W. Norton and Company.

EIU. (2009). African economic report. *The Economist Intelligence Unit*. Retrieved from http://viewswire.eiu.com/index.asp.

ERA. (2010). *Economic report on africa. AU Commission*. Addis Ababa, Ethiopia: ERA.

Ghemawat, P. (2005). Regional strategies for global leadership. *Harvard Business Review*. PMID:16334585.

Juma, C. (2011). *The new harvest: Agricultural innovation in africa*. Oxford, UK: Oxford University Press.

Mahajan, V. (2009). *Africa rising: How 900 million african consumers offer more than you think*. Upper Saddle River, NJ: Pearson Prentice Hall.

Mbaku, J. M. (1998). Emerging trade blocks and the fortune of african participation in the world economy. *Journal of Economic Integration, 10*(2).

Mbaku, J. M. (2004). *Institutions and development in africa*. Tranton, NJ: Africa World Press.

Moyo, D. (2009). *Dead aid, Why Aid is not working and how there is a better way for Africa*. New York: Farrar, Straus, and Giroux.

OAU. (1963). *Organization of african union charter*. Addis Ababa, Ethiopia: OAU.

Ostby, G. (2004). Horizontal inequalities and civil conflict. In *Proceedings of the 13th Annual National Political Science Conference*. Hurdalsjoen, Norway: SEAS Press.

Schuster, C. P., & Copeland, M. J. (2006). *Global business practices: Adapting for success*. Atlanta, GA: Thomson.

Straziuso, J. (2012). Africa sees hotels rise with its economic gains. *The Philadelphia Inquirer*. Retrieved from http://www.philly.com/philly/opinion/inquirer/.

The Africa Guide. (2005). Map of Africa, 2005. Retrieved from www.africaguide.com.

The East African. (2010) Retrieved from www.nationmedia.com.

Wang, M., Garner, J. F., & Silver, V. (2008). GEMs equity strategy: Sub-saharan africa: Improved fundamentals priced near term. *Morgan Stanley*. Retrieved from http://www.morganstanley.com/.

Wild, J. J., Wild, K. L., & Han, J. C. Y. (2008). *International Business* (4th ed.). Upper Saddle River, NJ: Pearson.

Chapter 2
The Perspectives of African History

ABSTRACT

Anecdotally this chapter describes several perspectives of African history. These historical perspectives include the slavery period, the colonial period, the post-independence period, and the so called structural adjustments and reforms period. The consequences and impact of what happened, during each of these periods, on Africa, are analyzed. Therefore, the chapter gives the origins of the continent's current social, economic, political, and business circumstances. Moreover, a discussion is developed on how to overcome the negative effects of these circumstances in order to create more and enhance existing economic and business opportunities in the continent.

1. INTRODUCTION

The perspectives of African history give the background and context of African economic and business situation today. African history is an interesting and amazing panorama of ever changing events. It is a tortuous history (Mbaku 2004).

Based on living memory, and from a business perspective, one can broadly divide African history into four distinct periods. The occurrences, during these four periods, mostly happening out of the control of the African people, have had a tremendous and long lasting and many-a-time devastating impact, particularly,

DOI: 10.4018/978-1-4666-4570-7.ch002

on the continent's low social, political, technological, and economic development over the years. These periods form the background and the context of the African social, economic, political, and technological conditions today.

It is oftentimes stated by scholars that the events during these periods created and perpetuated the state of social and political instability, technological backwardness, slow economic development, innovative and entrepreneurial challenges that have dogged Africa during the last sixty years of independence of many African countries (Denge et al., 2002; Mbaku, 2004; Moyo, 2009). The four periods can be described as the slave trade; the colonial; the independence; and immediately post independence, the structural adjustment, and the rising of the effective governance periods.

2. THE SLAVE TRADE PERIOD

The main African slave trade age ran approximately from about the middle of the 16th century to the second half of the 19th century (Larson, 2004). Slavery was a savage act that became illegal in Great Britain in 1807/8 and officially ended in the USA in the middle of the 1860's, after having wreaked havoc on the African continent, particularly the Western African countries of Ghana, the Guineas, Benin, Togo, and Senegambia (Horton et al., 1999; Larson, 2004).

Acemoglu et al. (2012), assert that "the more intense areas or countries of slavery such as Angola, Benin, Ghana, and Togo, total cumulative slave exports amounted to more than the population of the countries in 1400".These countries were the main sources of slaves to the New World and Europe and there has never been compensation or payment of reparations for the human destruction of these counties. The slave trade left un-healing human wounds to the slaves themselves and to the countries of their origin.

The East African countries are said to have been sources of slaves to the Middle East, where there is no legacy of slaves because men were castrated immediately they arrived as slaves. Available literature further indicates that slaves were badly treated and ill managed like chattel, despite their good behavior, hard work, and considerable ability to contribute to the economic advancement and wealth of the slaveholders particularly those in the USA (Horton et al., 1999; Larson, 2004).

Although there is no early evidence of developed institutions to support development in Africa, the institution of slavery robbed Africa some of the best and brightest people. Perhaps, the strongest and most creative African people, who could have made a difference in the social, political, economic, and technological advancement of the continent, were targeted and taken away through slavery (Larson 2004).

The first slaves arrived in Virginia, USA, in 1619, and in the next almost two hundred years, over 10 million Africans were forcibly taken as slaves in the most inhuman and intolerable fashion to unfamiliar lands (Acemoglu et al., 2012; Horton et al., 1999; Brown et al., 1996), where they worked hard and skillfully for propertied Europeans and Americans without compensation. While on board the slave ships, the sick, the weak, those who were not subdued, and those who continually resisted being taken into slavery were thrown into the sea during the long voyage to the New World and other destinations (Larson, 2004).

Crowder (2011) sadly states that in the International Slavery Museum in Liverpool, England, the devastation of generations of enslaved men, women, and children is remembered. The price innocent people have paid–without their immense contribution to development in the West recognized in modern times-for the greed of others is horrific–but theirs is not the only cost. Engraved in a wall of the museum is a profound and poignant observation made by Frederick Douglass, former slave and crusader for human rights, which reads, "No man can put a chain about the ankle of his fellow man without at last finding the other end fastened about his own neck. In the act of dehumanizing others, we dehumanize ourselves."

St. Paul put it even more poignantly, in another way, when he wrote in the book of Galatians, "Do not be deceived, God is not mocked; for whatever a man sows, that he will also reap" (Galatians 6:7). Paul's words form a stark reminder to us that our choices have consequences–and that includes how we choose to treat others. When we choose to hate, that hate can return to us in the form of consequences we can never fully prepare for. We can find ourselves alienated from others, angry with ourselves, and hamstrung in our ability to serve Christ and others effectively. Instead, let's choose "not to grow weary while doing good, for in due season we shall reap….As we have the opportunity, let us do good to all" (Galatians 6: 9–10).

Larson (2004) asserts that although prone to revolt, the Asante–the greatest source of slaves from West Africa to Europe, West Indies, and America–were highly prized by slaveholders in the USA particularly because of their strong physical and creative abilities and high flexibility in performing different work tasks. They were the first multitasking workers in human history. They brought their farming, landscaping, land management, and timber harvesting and curing techniques and skills that were later adopted and used by farmers and timber harvesting merchants in the USA. These were the knowledge, creative skills, and techniques that created the foundation of the American industrial and economic revolution of early years that made America the great Nation it is today. The Asante enormously contributed–without acknowledgement and appreciation-to this development and industrial base (Larson, 2004).

The Asante became adept at clearing densely forested land-in West Africa-for small farms, establishing specific timetables for altering fallow land and crop production. And they knew how and they were keenly aware of the need to protect the newly cleared land from the disastrous effects of soil erosion, particularly near rivers and streams. The visiting Europeans and observers noted the well-ordered and fenced farms of the Asante people–in present day Ghana-producing abundant crops of yams, corn, nuts, cassava, and plantains. It was these skills associated with forest clearing, agriculture, and timber harvesting and curing that made the Asante and the related peoples of western Africa very attractive as slave labor in the USA particularly (Larson, 2004).

The Asante and Akan developed social, cultural imperatives, and paradigms that placed a high value on fruitfulness, increase, maximization, and abundance (Larson 2004). New World planters very well may have detected these principles of accumulation among the Asante and Akan people. Therefore, the enslaved Africans from western Africa brought an acute understanding of the role and significance of land use-present day agriculture-with them to the New World. The slaves were the foundation of the American economy and their contribution to the early economic development of the West, particularly to the USA, is immense (Larson, 2004). They planted the first seeds of industrial development of this great country and tended them to maturity; the tremendous maturity we see today as the USA.

For example, by the 1740s, enslaved Africans had become the dominant labor resource for the expanding American agricultural and timber economy. African slave's imports rose steadily between 1720 and 1770, culminating in several thousand slaves disembarking during the decade prior to the American Revolution (Larson 2004). Looking for fresh sources of labor for the rapidly expanding economies of Maryland, Alabama, Mississippi, Louisiana, Florida, Georgia, and Texas, buying and selling slaves expanded rapidly and extensively during this period (Horton et al., 1999; Brown et al., 1996).

During this period, too, many white southerners believed in slavery as a cultural, economic, and institutional foundation of southern economy and society (Larson 2004). This is also the time America laid down the firm foundation of its economic development, the greatness of which we see and marvel at today. The slaves made that foundation firm, strong and everlasting (Horton et al., 1999; Brown et al., 1996).

The slaves built canals, shipyards, waterways, ships, later the railroads, and the slaves were central and participated fully in major American economic development activities of the time. Anecdotal data and even general observations indicate that the African-American's contribution in the industrial and economic development of the USA, particularly in the 18th and 19th centuries, is what the Jewish-Americans came to build on in the 20th century America, especially in finance and accounting, law, academia, sciences, and information technology. And the anecdotal and press data further indicate that the 21th century may be the Asian century in the USA (Pappas, 2011; Friedman, 2011). They are leading in mathematics and science. Asian immigration is a boon to American science and math, a new report asserts, noting that 70 percent of the finalists in a recent prestigious science competition are the children of Asian immigrants. The report by the National Foundation for American Policy, a nonprofit research group, in Arlington, Va., states that many Asian immigrant parents emphasize hard science and math education for their children, viewing those fields as paths to success and of course technological advancement of a country like the USA (Pappas, 2011).

The slaves increasingly became the replacements for indentured servants who dominated the American economy in the early 17th century to the middle of the 18th century (Moraley et al., 2005). The Indentured Servants, in colonial America were, for the most part, adult white persons who were bound to labor for a period of 4-7 years. There were three indentured classes: the free-willets, or redemptioners; then there were those who were enticed to leave their home country out of poverty or who were kidnapped for political or religious reasons; and lastly the convicts.

The first class represented those who chose to bind themselves to labor for a definite time to pay for their passage to America. The best known of these were Germans and Irish, but many English and Scottish men and women came in the same way. The second class, those who came to escape poverty or were forcibly brought to the colonies, was the largest group because of the scarcity of labor in America. Their services were profitably sold to plantation owners or farmers, who indentured them for a period of 4-7 years. The third class or convicts were sentenced to deportation and on arrival in America were indentured unless they had personal funds to maintain themselves. Seven years was a common term of such indentured services. The West Indies and Maryland appear to have received the largest number of immigrants of the third class (Moraley et al., 2005).

Indentured servants made up a large portion of the population of the Chesapeake region, especially during the seventeenth century, when they accounted for 80 to 90 percent of European immigrants. The middle colonies of Pennsylvania, Delaware, and New Jersey also relied heavily on indentured servants and in the eighteenth century more lived in these colonies than in any other region in the USA (Gordon et al., 2005).

When the prospects for upward mobility dimmed, as they did in the late seventeenth century Chesapeake region, indentured servants proved willing and ready to participate in violent rebellions and to demand wealthier colonists' property. The threat posed by great numbers of angry indentured servants might have been one of the reasons this type of servitude diminished over the course of the eighteenth century, with many farmers and plantation owners coming to heavily rely instead on the labor of enslaved Africans (Larson, 2004).

Africans, on the other hand, were disciplined, excellent, enthusiastic, and reliable workers: they often had skills and experience in agriculture, keeping cattle, and timber harvesting and curing, which land owners and farmers did not have at the time.

They also planned well and worked very hard and conscientiously in the plantations and in the mines without much supervision which the indentured laborers could not do (Gordon et al., 2005). That reality made the institution of slavery last for many years and it had to take a civil war to end it and intense hate and racial discrimination followed which has virtually and covertly existed up to today (Larson, 2004).

Slavery robbed Africa the foundation and building blocks of its social, political, and economic development. Acemoglu et al. (2012), asserts that probably the most obvious impact of this massive extraction of human beings was demographic. It is difficult to know with any certitude what the population of Africa was before the modern period, but scholars have made various plausible estimates of the impact of slave trade on the population.

The historian Patrick Manning (1990), for example, estimates that the population of those areas of West and West-Central Africa that provided most slaves for export was around twenty two to twenty five million in the early eighteenth century. On the conservative assumption that during the eighteenth and early nineteenth centuries these areas would have experienced a rate of population growth of about half a percent a year without the slave trade, Manning estimated that the population of this region in 1850 ought to have been at least forty six to fifty three million. In fact, it was about one half of this during this period.

This massive difference was not only due to about eight million people being exported as slaves from this region from 1700 to 1850, but the millions likely killed by continual internal warfare aimed at capturing slaves. Slavery and the slave trade in Africa further disrupted family and marriage structures and therefore may also have reduced fertility. These events or slave trade factors would ultimately shape the path of development in Africa not only before but also after1807/8 when slavery ended in Britain. Therefore, given these extractive economic and political institutions based on the slave trade, industrialization did not spread to Africa, which stagnated and even experienced economic retardation, resulting in severe and pervasive poverty and hunger up to date, as other parts of the world were greatly transforming their economies and achieving high economic growth rates.

But the slaves' enormous contribution to American development, for example, is generally unrecognized in the county and the African still suffers racial discrimination. For example, one hardly sees much of African statues and monuments in the city of Philadelphia, one of the biggest cities in the USA, as compared to those of other American heroes, particularly whites, who made an immense contribution to American history. There is an African-American museum in the city of Philadelphia.

Moreover, Africans are still discriminated against in the USA and racial attitudes against Africans have not changed over the years, even the election of an African as a president in 2008 did not help. An August/September, 2012, survey by the Associated Press with researchers from Stanford University, the University of Michigan, and the University of Chicago, has established that racial attitudes have not changed in the USA even after electing a black president in 2008. The poll finds that a majority of white Americans now express prejudice toward African-Americans whether they recognize those feelings or not.

Racial prejudice has increased slightly since 2008 whether those feelings were expressed or measured using questions that explicitly asked respondents about racist attitudes, or through an experimental test that measured implicit views toward race without asking questions about that topic directly.

In all, 51 percent of Americans now express explicit anti-black attitudes, compared with 48 percent in a similar 2008 survey. When measured by an implicit racial-attitude test, the number of white Americans with anti-black sentiments jumped to 56 percent, up from 49 percent during the last presidential elections. In both tests, the share of white Americans expressing pro-black attitudes fell considerably (Ross et al., 2012). Hopefully one day someone will think of compensating Africa for its destruction by slavery and pay liberations to Africa and ex-slave Africans and thus contribute to African development.

Brazil is the only country in the world, I am aware of, that seems to seriously acknowledge the tremendous role Africans made in building the foundation of that country. As such, President Lula of Brazil (2004 to 2012) made Africa a priority in his foreign policy. The Brazilian leader made improving links with Africa a vital part of his foreign policy, which emphasizes "South-South" relations. He has toured the continent at least ten times, visiting 25 different countries. "Brazil is committed to help Africa build a future of stability and development", President Lula has said in Africa recently. "Brazil could never repay its historic debt to the continent."

"Today we are united for the future," President Lula told a summit of the West African regional grouping, ECOWAS, in Santa Maria, Cape Verde recently. "Brazil-not just me-took a political decision to make a re-encounter with the African continent." He said that Brazil could never repay its "historic debt" to Africa-a reference to the millions of Brazilians who are descended from African slaves. "Brazil would not be what it is today without the participation of hard working millions of Africans who helped to build our country." He said that Brazil was determined to help eliminate hunger and poverty in Africa through trade, investment, and the transfer of technology, particularly in agriculture, which is a mainstay of the African economies. "Whoever comes after me has the moral, political, and ethical obligations to do much more "Trade between Brazil and Africa grew from $6 billion to $24 billion under President Lula. Press reports indicate that Brazil also wrote off $ 900 million African debt to Brazil. This was during the AU 50th anniversary celebrations in in May, 2013, in Addis Ababa, Ethiopia.

Furthermore, Brazilian companies have invested heavily in oil and mining, and have taken on big infrastructure projects in Africa, particularly in Angola and Mozambique. Lula has also promoted cooperation in agricultural development and bio fuels, and launched an international television station - TV Brasil Internacional - that broadcasts to African nations (BBC, 2010).

In increasing its cooperation with African countries in agriculture and other technical fields, the country has also established a branch of the Brazilian Agricultural Research Corporation (EMBAPA) in Ghana. And the country has also created a tropical agricultural research institute at home to foster cooperation and research and development with African countries (Juma, 2011).

3. THE COLONIAL PERIOD

Africa was colonized almost immediately after slavery. Today, the African population has broad and complex diversity with many tribes, languages, beliefs, and ethnicities sharpened by colonialism. Many of these tribes cannot work together today as a result of the divide and rule policies of the colonial powers and hence a source of political tension and instability in many African countries today.

In an effort to find Silk Routes by sea, many European countries' explorers landed on and colonized locations along the coast of Africa before moving inland. From about the sixteenth century to the second half of the twentieth century, the Portuguese, Belgians, French, Dutch, Germans, Italians, Spanish, and British developed colonies throughout Africa, which became the basis for the current cluttered political map of Africa (Schuster et al., 2006).

The colonialists also created a paradigm of a dual economy in Africa by dispossessing African farmers their fertile land that led to their mass impoverishment. It created not only the institutional foundations of a backward economy, but the poor people to stock it. This duality has persisted up to date. Therefore, the dual economy paradigm, originally proposed in 1955 by Sir Arthur Lewis, still shapes the way that most social scientists think about the economic problems of less-developed countries including those of Africa.

According to Lewis, many less-developed or under-develop economies have dual structures and are divided into a modern sector and a traditional sector. The modern sector, which corresponds to the more developed part of the economy, is associated with urban life, modern industry, and the use of advanced technologies, while, the traditional sector is associated with rural life, agriculture, and "backward" institutions and technologies and the majority of Africans live in the traditional sector.

Backward agricultural institutions included communal ownership of land, which implies the absence of private property rights on land. Labor is used so inefficiently in the traditional sector that it could be reallocated to the modern sector without reducing the amount the rural sector can produces. For generations of development economists building on Lewis's insights, the problem of development has come to mean moving people and resources out of the traditional sector into industry and cities.

Furthermore, when the colonizers claimed or conquered a new territory, they established an administrative structure and system in that country. The indigenous people were not usually consulted or welcomed by the colonialists into the government arrangements and elite circle of society. Operating within the government, educational, and social systems created by the colonial power, the members of the local population learned to adapt to this overlaid culture just to survive and, in most cases, to provide cheap labor to the modern sector of the economy (Schuster et al., 2006).

The large number of tribes-whose differences were accentuated by colonial rule-in Africa and the number of foreign countries influencing different tribes differently resulted in a diverse cultural milieu and a mosaic of influences that came to haunt Africa later at independence. Unlike colonial India, for example, where over 80 percent of the population consider themselves Hindu; the majority of Africans do not follow a common religion or belief system or nationalistic ideals.

Unlike colonial India, again, colonized as a single geographic region by the British, different countries and regions of Africa were colonized by different countries whose methodology and approach to the population and its needs varied considerably, and later, at independence, producing a mosaic of small African nations, unrelated national governments, and small limited markets for products and services. These administrative arrangements also made it difficult for Africans to cohere–at independence-and work together in trade, innovation, and other essential developmental initiatives and priorities leading to Africa's inability to sufficiently tackle pervasive and degrading poverty today and in a lot of cases persistent hunger in many African countries in the continent.

Specifically, the colonial period ran from the second half of the 19th century, in fact twenty years after the end of slavery in the USA in 1965–from the infamous and iniquitous 1885 Berlin Conference that shared Africa, as if it were chattel, among European powers-to the second half of the 20th century. Colonization destroyed African culture, in all its respects, and any little creativity and innovative ability left by the slave trade. The colonial powers partitioned Africa into segments that did not fit together as nation states later at their independence in the 1950's and 1960's. They even promoted the negative aspects of African diversity among these segments–making it difficult for them to unite for common causes-resulting in the harmful consequences of insecurity and instability that are felt across most of Africa today

Africa was left hemorrhaging after the colonial governments pillaged its environmental and creative resources. The divide and rule policies pursued by the colonial governments left Africa a parchment of tribes that were put together as countries with no national identity. This condition served as the genesis and propelled the continent into persistent civil strives that have sadly characterized most of Africa for the last five decades; the continuous quarrels and lack of national cohesion in the Congo DR, Ivory Coast, Mali, Zimbabwe, Sudan, Guinea, Niger, Somalia, and increasingly Kenya being cases in point.

However, the situation is changing, albeit slowly, as the various ethnic groups have realized the folly of the divide and rule policy and they have accepted their situation of nationhood as it is today. African leaders are also building appropriate and unifying national institutions, and making tribes learn to co-exist peacefully. This is improving the chances of enhancing nationhood and national cohesion of the African countries. Democratic institutions, including new constitutional dispensations, holding regular democratic elections are also increasing to support further social development, sustainable economic growth, national identities, and unity.

Still, during the colonial period, the African economies and trade were structured and conducted to serve as suppliers of low cost labor and non-value added raw materials to the metropolitan economies and as markets for manufactured and value-added products. The economies were fully integrated to the metropolitan economies and in the process created a one-sided dependency that has, in many cases, lasted to this day. Therefore, the colonial economies and trade generated benefits primarily for the metropolitan nations and marginalized and impoverished African countries (Wild et al., 2008).

The colonial governments pursued the same policies in colonies in other parts of the world even to an extent of destroying those colonies' industrial capacity in order to make them sources of cheap labor, raw materials, and markets of manufactured products as they did in Africa. For example, Britain pursued an aggressive industrial policy to topple India's predominance in the textile trade in order to make India a source of cheap labor and raw materials and a market for its manufactured British textile products. It also sent Indians to other colonies as cheap labor to build infrastructure in those countries (Sachs, 2005). In Africa, the Indian laborers eventually became traders and entrepreneurs suppressing the emergence and development of African entrepreneurship.

The current geographic trade patterns of Africa still reinforce the continent's one-sided dependency on the developed market economies, especially its former colonial powers. Inter-Africa trade – only 10 percent of its world trade - has been dismally low as a percentage of its total global trade! For example, it is estimated that 56 percent of Francophone countries' global trade is currently with France and 48 percent of non-oil products of Anglophone countries' trade are with Britain

(AFDB, 2008). The rest of the trade is mostly with the USA, Canada, India, and increasingly with China. Trade with China grew tenfold between 2003 and 2008 to reach $107 billion in 2008 (ERA, 2010). However, with increasing African regional integration, the trend is changing and African countries are increasingly trading with each other as African regional integration schemes intensify and thus expanding African market.

Regarding China, anecdotal and press data indicate that currently the country has a US$2.2 trillion sovereignty wealth fund, accumulated from trade surpluses, to invest in Africa and other developing and emerging markets, while America had $ 1.7 trillion deficit in its international trade account in 2009 and a national debt of $ 14 trillion (Business Week, 2009). China is the biggest exporter of goods in the world today. In 2009, it surpassed Germany as the number one exporter of goods and services when it exported $ 1.2 trillion of goods and services versus Germany's $ 1.17 trillion of exports and USA had $ 0.9 trillion exports of goods and services in the same year.

However, anecdotal data indicate that the USA leads in the export of services–with the USA being competitive in 21 of the 22 services traded categories–having increasingly huge surpluses in this account over the years. Specifically, the surpluses increased from $ 58 billion in 1992 to $144 billion in 2008. But, currently services are only 20% of the value of international trade, although growing faster than trading in goods due to overseas sales increasingly being delivered in person or sent across the Internet. Since 2000, exports in services worldwide have jumped up by 84 percent as compared to 66 percent for goods but still being a small share of merchandise trade (Wild et al., 2008; Cox, 2010).

Still, China became the second largest economy in 2010 in the world, after the USA, as it passed Japan in that position through its phenomenal economic growth rates. Early data for 2009 indicate that China accounted for 66% of the global growth in GDP–excluding countries with negative growth rates-and India accounted for 11%, with Indonesia taking third place with 4% (Ghemawat, 2010).

Furthermore, available data indicate that the economic clout of big emerging markets, particularly China and India, is likely to increase over the next few decades, not just the next few years. According to the World Bank projections, by the year 2050, China and India will together account for 50% of global GDP–about the same size of the G7 countries' current share–whose share is expected to decline to 25% in 2050. And since per capita incomes in China and India are projected to be only one-half to one-third the size of those in advanced economies, by 2050, there is room for even higher growth rates in these markets after 2050. The same holds true in many other emerging markets as well including those of Africa (Ghemawat, 2010).

The Chinese focus in African is to obtain cheap raw materials and oil for its growing industrial complex, developing African infrastructure, and creating markets for its industrial products. Many observers, however, wonder whether the concerted and high profile penetration by China into Africa, is, in a sense, re-colonizing Africa all over again in the 21st century (Stanley, 2008).

Ironically, China is currently popular in Africa because of its approach to African development. Its approach focuses mostly in tackling bread and butter issues that are at the heart of most of the African people. The issues include hard infrastructure constructing: roads and bridges, rails, airports, oil and gas pipelines, schools, agricultural research institutions, hospitals and dispensaries, power lines, and water projects (Shambaugh, 2013). These are things African people can see and directly relate within their daily lives and in their communities; they resonate with them and therefore make a real difference in their daily lives. Therefore, the Chinese create value for the Africans, which makes a difference for them now and for their children and grand children in the future; an important life aspect for an African. Africans are respectful to; they appreciate, and are grateful to anybody who helps them to build a strong economic future for their extended families and descendants.

Furthermore, the latest press reports indicate that China is currently undertaking to build one of the largest infrastructure projects being undertaken in Africa today, involving South Sudan, Kenya, and Ethiopia. China plans to build, together with the three governments, an oil pipeline, a railway line, and a highway from Juba, South Sudan, to Lamu, a port in North Coast, in Kenya, at a cost of $ 24 billion. At Isiolo, Central Kenya, the project will branch off and extend to Addis Ababa, Ethiopia and an oil refinery will also be built at Isiolo. The project is mainly intended to help South Sudan, a landlocked country; to have access to the world markets for its exports, particularly oil. Uganda is expected to join the project in the future. The project will also include building the largest water dam in East Africa. The 165 square kilometers dam will provide water for drinking in the area and Lamu town, generating electricity, and irrigation (Kanga'ru & Mureithi, 2013).

At the Africa-Chinese cooperation Forum in Cairo, Egypt, in November 2009, the Chinese Prime minister declared: "We will help Africa build up its financing, institutional, agricultural, and infrastructure capacities; we will provide $10 billion in concessional loans, over and above the $ 5 billion provided in 2006, in the next two years, to enable the African countries to meet that goal." China is seriously contributing to African development and may not only repair and cure the wounds and damage inflicted on Africa by slavery and colonialism, but may also enable Africa to proudly move forward and to robustly participate in the global economy in the 21st century.

The irony of Chinese financing projects in Africa, however, is that Chinese contractors bring a large number of cheap laborers from China for the projects instead of largely employing local people from the African communities where the projects are situated. There are over 740,000 Chinese workers–with 58 percent sent out in 2008 alone-working on various Chinese financed projects in Africa, the Middle East, and Asia (Wong, 2009).

The exporting of cheap labor from China to developing countries is causing serious tension and resentment from the local communities in some countries. In recent years, there have been flare-ups against Chinese workers–in Chinese funded projects-in countries as far apart as Vietnam and Angola. This is despite of the belief–even among the local contractors–that Chinese workers are better workers in that they work hard, are dedicated, they work passionately and conscientiously, exercising a sense of responsibility and discipline; all which ensure that the projects they undertake are completed on schedule and within budget (Wong, 2009).

4. THE INDEPENDENCE AND IMMEDIATELY POST INDEPENDENCE PERIOD

The third African period is the period starting at independence and several decades thereafter. This period runs approximately from the late 1950's–Sudan and Ghana, the first independent African states gained independence in 1956 and 1957 respectively-to the late 1980's (Deng et al., 2002). Except for the Republic of South Africa, all African countries were virtually independent by the beginning of the 1980's. South Africa gained her independence, from an awfully abominable system of apartheid in 1994.

The period immediately after African independence–the late 1950's and early1960's onwards-and up to the late 1980's, was mostly characterized by poor economic performance, political instability, civil strives, military coups, and violent eruptions among many African countries, particularly in West Africa. Virtually every western African country, except Senegal, has been under a military dictatorship of one kind or other in the last fifty years. Some of the countries, such as Nigeria and Ghana had military dictorships several times over. The turmoil extended to Central Africa, and to the Great Lakes region, including the Congo's, Uganda, Sudan, Ethiopia, and Somalia. Somalia, in the horn of Africa, is where the political turmoil and an undignified failed state status have persisted for over two decades and often the country is ravaged with severe hunger claiming the lives of almost a whole generation of Somalis.

In explaining the African state after independence, Zartman (2002) asserts that the sobering fact was that most of the hopes and aspirations that had provided the spur for independence were not realized. African nations seeking self-determination only reached half their goals. They are characterized by poor economic development and social and political instability. Since the passage of power from foreign rule to national rule had left nationalists firmly ensconced with seats of power in the name of the people but without the obligation of turning to their people for authorization and accountability in order to legitimize themselves in power and whenever they supposedly turned to the people for legitimacy, they did it corruptly and dishonestly by rigging the elections and changing the constitutional order in order to remain in power longer than stipulated by the law.

Many other reasons have been offered to account for why African countries have not worked well, both economically and politically, since the 1960's. Most common explanations have been geographic, historical, cultural, tribal, racial, and institutional factors. While each of them is plausible and convincing in explaining Africa's poor showing, they do not tell the whole story (Moyo, 2009).

One argument, advanced by the geographical determinists such as Jared Diamond in *Guns, Germs, and Steel* (1998), is that a country's wealth and success depends on its geographical environment and topography. Certain environments are easier to manipulate for economic growth than others. For example, societies that can domesticate plants and animals, in their environment, with relative ease, are likely to be more prosperous.

At a minimum, a country's climate, location, flora, fauna, and terrain affect the ability of its people to provide food for consumption and for export, which ultimately has an impact on a country's economic growth. Diamond notes that all societies and cultures have had approximately similar abilities to manipulate nature, but the raw materials with which they had to start with were different and hence differences in growth levels and success in creating wealth and hence eradicating poverty sustainably.

There is also a largely unspoken and insidious view that the problem with Africa is Africans themselves–that culturally, mentally, and physically Africans are innately different. That, somehow, deeply embedded in their psyche is an inability to embrace development and improve their own lot in life without foreign and outside guidance and help (Moyo, 2009)!

Furthermore, McClelland (1953, 1987), developed an achievement motivation paradigm, which envisions that people in a community have three interrelated needs–affiliation, power, and achievement-that are influenced by the environment the people are born and grow in. The gravitation in an attempt to meet these needs eventually affect the people's behavior and their success. Their accomplishments are demonstrated by material accumulation and general well being.

It is stated that McClelland carried out extensive and awesome research in the Americas, Europe, and Asia, although not in Africa. He bases his conclusions from these studies to the effect that achievement motivation–and of course the other two motivational needs-is influenced by the environment of the individual, both distant and immediate environments. The environmental factors include land, natural resources, and the immediate family. He concludes that success and economic development have been certainly with those societies in supportive physical and immediate environments.

However, and despite of Diamond's and McClelland's assertions, Africa's broad economic experience shows that the abundance of land and natural resources do not guarantee economic success. In fact, many observers think that natural resources dependence has proved to be a developmental curse rather than a blessing in Africa (Moyo, 2009).

Furthermore, research data indicate that Africans are not innately impervious to development and unable to better their lot without outside help. They can better their lot like everybody else in the world with correct leadership and governance systems. In fact, Africans have been known to plan well what they want to do and execute those plans conscientiously with rigor, passion, and discipline (Larson, 2004).

Instead, a lot of social and political insecurity, instability, and poor economic performance in Africa–after independence-have been attributed to poor leadership of those who took over power from the colonial administrations at independence (Deng et al., 2002). It was the kind of leadership that had little education and experience required to effectively govern a modern state that is ethnically and culturally diverse (Deng et al., 2002).

Leadership is the capacity and ability to establish the organizational and/or national direction. It is to influence and align others toward a common goal, mobilizing, motivating, and committing them to action to move toward that direction. Leadership is creating standards and milestones of performance, mobilizing resources and distributing them fairly to those who need to use them for the good of the organization or nation. And it is making the people responsible and accountable for their actions and performance (Kotler, 2001).

At independence, African political leaders should have been people of integrity, savvy in the politics of a nation and skilled in national development. They should have been visionaries that created a national vision and mobilized their people towards the national vision. And that held their followers responsible and accountable for their actions and that remained in power with the people's consent.

However and unfortunately, most of the African leaders, who captured the reins of power at independence, privatized state structures and used them as instruments of plunder to extract rent and benefits from the economy for themselves, their relatives, and those who supported them. They restricted and stunted economic growth and thus impoverished their countries (Deng et al., 2002).

Acemoglu et al. (2012), assert thus in their seminal book, *Why Nations Fail: the Origins of Power, Prosperity, and Poverty,* "the end of colonialism in the decades following the Second World War created critical junctures for many former African colonies to prosper. However, in most cases, in sub-Saharan Africa, the post independence governments and leaders simply repeated and intensified the abuses of their predecessors, often severely narrowing the distribution of political power, dismantling *institutional* constraints, and undermining the already meager incentives that economic institutions provided for investments" and economic growth leading to pervasive and chronic poverty and hunger in the continent.

Mobutu Sese Seko of Zaire and Jomo Kenyatta of Kenya exemplify this kind of low quality and poor governance leadership Africa inherited immediately at African independence. Thus: "A state-later renamed Zaire - was installed only through the efforts of Gen. Mobutu Sese Seko during his first decade in power after 1965. But in the subsequent twenty years, he privatized his creation and national resources for himself and family, alienated his population, bought off his opponents and opposition, and left a growing vacuum around his operations. He massively invested his wealth in Belgium and often hired a Concord from Air France for his private trips to Europe using an airport he built in his home village in Zaire. Furthermore, since government agencies were providing no local services and were only conducting predatory activities, communities were impoverished and forced to get by on their own inadequate resources" (Deng et al., 2002; Acemoglu et al., 2012).

It is often said too that Jomo Kenyatta, the first president of Kenya, at independence, completely ethinized the country into tribal groups fighting for national resources, which he allocated arbitrary giving his tribe the bulk of the resources especially land and public service jobs. Anecdotally, it is often said that he took, for himself, his immediate family, relatives and friends, a quarter of arable land in Kenya (Kisiang'ani, 2007; Daily Nation, 2009).

He was succeeded by President Daniel arap Moi, a manipulative character, corrupt, and kleptomaniac dictator, who brought a somewhat vibrant Kenyan economy-he inherited from Jomo Kenyatta - to its knees intensifying poverty and hunger of his people through inept leadership and massive corruption that pervaded the entire public service during his long destructive tenure of 24 years. He is often said to have been directly involved in the biggest corrupt deal in the history of the country; the "golden burg" deal which is said to have cost the country Kshs 60 billion ($1billion) over four years, in the 1990s. This scandal was a subject of a protracted judicial commission whose conclusions are not very clear to many people.

The actions of these so called founding leaders were a recipe for impaired and uneven economic development in their countries, creating horizontal inequalities. And the horizontal inequalities became the genesis and foundation of the social disorder, political instability, and insecurity, not only in Zaire and Kenya today, but characterized all parts of Africa. In Kenya, the cumulative effects of the poor leadership and weak governance is the 2007/8 post election violence that led to the death of 1,300 people and 600,000 displaced. Kenyatta's son, Uhuru, is accused as one of the masterminds of these deaths and huge displacement of people, with a case at the International Criminal Court, at The Hague, Netherlands.

Additionally, the African elites promoted highly divisive behaviors including kleptomania, corruption, nepotism, mediocrity, and negative ethnicity and other behaviors that were devoid of achievement motivation. They perpetuated and in many cases enhanced the colonial policy of divide and rule among their people. They emphasized the negative aspects of tribal diversity and emphasizing segregated, and at times, discriminatory economic and social developments such as in education, healthcare, and agricultural development. These arrangements were meant to enhance the divide and rule policies in order to remain in power, long after any little popularity they had and when their usefulness were far gone.

These governing arrangements eventually led to the creation of tribal hostilities and what scholars (Stewart, 2003; Moraa & Ostby, 2004) describe as horizontal inequalities seen in many African countries today. The occurrence of organized group conflicts has been the rule and not the exception in Africa. From South Africa to Sudan, racial and ethnic cleavages have been used by ethnically powerful elements in society to economically and politically stratify states. This unhealthy relationship, among stratified groups, often finds expression through violent and devastating conflicts that have lasted, in some cases, for decades. The causes for these conflicts have been directly associated with growing horizontal inequalities (Stewart, 2003 & Ostby, 2004).

Horizontal inequalities are systematic inequalities–created intentionally or unintentionally-between groups of people that coincide with their ethnic cleavages to bring about conflict. When studying today's civil conflicts–particularly those in ethnic-sensitive Africa-one must consider-in addition to economic inequalities-other dimensions of inequalities such as political participation, social access, and the economic situation of the people involved. Extremely entrenched horizontal inequalities led to fractionalization and polarization of communities that were antagonistic to each other already due to the colonial policy of divide and rule. The fractionalization and polarization increased tribal and racial resentment and antagonism that caused military coups, civil strife, and violence during elections, and civil wars (Stewart, 2003; Ostby, 2004).

Annan (1999) further asserts that inequality between rich and poor or vertical inequality is not enough to cause violent conflict. What is highly explosive is horizontal inequality, when power and resources are unequally distributed between groups that are also differentiated in other ways–for instance by race, religion, or language. The so-called "ethnic" conflicts occur between groups which are distinct in one or more of these ways, when one of them feels it is being discriminated against, or another enjoys privileges which it fears to lose; in their defense, conflict and civil strives ensue, a situation that has been a common feature in most of Africa in the last five decades of independence.

However, horizontal inequalities-as with other developmental problems of poverty, disease, and ethnic differences–is not an African predicament per se, but a global problem, particularly in Asia and South East Asia, in countries such as Malaysia, Indonesia, the Philippines and India. You find extreme horizontal inequalities even in the USA too, although not acknowledged as such. However, South East Asian countries, for example Malaysia–as discussed in chapter nine below–have developed appropriate national policies and strategies to deal with the phenomenon of horizontal inequalities in some of the ways that Africa can borrow and adapt to its specific context to minimize inequalities and strives (Stewart, 2004).

Empirical data further indicate that many of the post independence African leaders were completely unprepared for the challenges facing the newly independent countries (Deng 2002). They had a very narrow/tribal views of leadership, they were poorly educated, lacked the experience, the understanding, and the appreciation of the needs of diverse and complex communities that needed to come together to form an effectively working nation state.

Furthermore, these leaders lacked the vision and necessary managerial skills and personal qualities required to manage complex and ethnically diverse and divided countries with the expectation of equitably distributing the "*fruits*" of independence to all groups in the country; the groups that were already highly divided, by the "divide and rule" policies of the colonial governments, before and at independence. Oftentimes, it is said that at independence, Africa did not have the George Washington, the Thomas Jefferson, the Alexander Hamilton, and the John Adams of the USA in 1776 to lay a solid foundation for their nations at independence, hence Africa's dire and poor political and economic state today.

Despite all that, Africa has had a few iconic leaders who have had a global recognition in their outstanding contribution to African development and in uniting their countries, liberation of Africa, and promoting African unity and peace. These great and iconic leaders include Kwame Nkrumah of Ghana, Nelson Mandela of South Africa, Julius Nyerere of Tanzania, and Leopard Senghor of Senegal.

Still, unlike the majority of post independence leaders, there is a growing group of more educated, more nationalistic, visionary, democratic, and much younger leadership that is emerging in Africa today. This new group of leaders has a strong vision for Africa; Africa that is democratic, that is enthusiastically and passionately reform oriented, that supports national cohesion and fair distribution of national resources, that is staunchly anti-corruption and kleptomaniasm, which supports greater African unity and regional integration and trade, and the developing of a positive image for Africa in the world.

This leadership is also helping the continent to focus on the long-term economic and political transformation of the continent by creating inclusive institutions in their various countries and in the continent generally (Juma, 2011; Acemoglu et al., 2012).This leadership includes, among others, Paul Kagame of Rwanda, Ellen-Johnson Serif of Liberia, King Hassan of Morocco, Jakaya Kikwete of Tanzania, Raila Ondinga of Kenya, Morsi of Egypt, and Morgan Tzvangirai of Zimbabwe. They are interested in bringing about accelerated development in Africa to eradicate poverty, hunger, and increase the respect and pride of the African people in the world. Their interest and commitment in all these African issues is palpable (The East African, 2011).

These leaders further believe that one of the major causes of Africa's present economic dilemma and crisis is its failure to utilize earnings from commodity exports to diversify economic activity and invest in value-added production. They believe that a time has come for effective diversification, horizontally, by broadening the production base and vertically by processing and marketing of value-added African abundant raw materials.

Furthermore, the new African leadership believes that the diversification of both the composition of exports and of export markets is essentially important as part of the strategy for improved African competitiveness and participation in the global economy and overall economic development (Mbaku, 1998; Deng, 2002). They also believe in investment in education; agriculture; technology, particularly in agriculture; healthcare; the infrastructure; and sustainability as important sources of accelerated African development to eliminate poverty and hunger. They also believe that popular participation and equal opportunity and access by African people must be promoted and sustained as a crucial basis for the realization of development objectives and minimization of horizontal inequalities and conflict in Africa.

They further believe in the promotion of widespread entrepreneurship in their economies as an engine of economic growth through constructive destruction in the economy generated by creativity and innovation by African entrepreneurs. Finally, they believe that regional integration and trade–to enlarge the African markets-is indispensable for African's socioeconomic transformation and for its competitiveness with the rest of the world in the 21st century (Deng et al., 2002).

5. THE STRUCTURAL ADJUSTMENTS AND GOVERNANCE CHANGES PERIOD

The fourth period-in African history-runs approximately from the middle of the 1980's to date. This period is characterized by the emergence–through the insistence of local and foreign civil society, multilateral and bilateral donor agencies, and the agitation of the African people-of economic, institutional, and political reforms; democracy; and promotion of transparence; responsibility; and accountability in Africa by African leaders.

Since the middle of the 1980's, there have been concerted efforts towards economic, social, and political reforms meant to lead to the development of the African economies to create wealth to eradicate growing and pervasive poverty that is demeaning to the African people. Many African countries held multi-party elections, in the 1990's and 2000's, and started to promote the ideals of effective governance. These ideals also require and encourage responsibility, transparency, and accountability in public affairs.

In addition, there was an attempt to have proper; appropriate distribution of independence benefits, among the population; efficient and effective use of national resources; and, of course, a determined fight of one of the most debilitating "diseases" that has persistently eluded many African countries today: pervasive corruption.

Furthermore, one of the most important and key development issues in Africa–in the 1980's and 1990's-has been how to increase indigenous entrepreneurship to maximize employment and wealth creation in the continent. Therefore, from the mid-1980's throughout the 1990's, the World Bank and IMF–together with bilateral donors–prompted the promotion of a series of adjustment programs–referred to as the "Structural Adjustment Programs" (SAPs)-in Africa, intended to promote appropriate social and political changes and economic reforms. These reforms were meant to develop a business climate conducive to attracting direct foreign investments and encouraging the growth of domestic entrepreneurship. They were meant to create an ease climate of doing business in Africa.

Ssemogerere (2002) asserts that Stabilization and Structural Adjustment Policies (SAPs) have been pursued in Sub-Saharan Africa (SSA) since the middle 1980s to restore internal and external equilibrium by controlling aggregate demand, and by liberalizing markets to reinstate the role of the price mechanism and markets in efficient resource allocation and encourage the growth of indigenous entrepreneurship to promote economic growth, create employment and wealth. With increasing economic growth, these countries were expected to be able to pay huge debts - accumulated over the years - they owed western governments, bilateral and multilateral institutions.

The Structural Adjustment Program (SAPs) conceived mainly by IMF, World Bank, and the USA Treasury–under the so-called Washington Consensus-stood on three economic policy pillars: fiscal austerity, privatization of government owned companies, and financial and capital markets liberalization. It consisted of measures basically designed to help a country repay its debts by earning more hard currency, by increasing exports and decreasing imports, as well as promoting economic stability and growth through controlled government expenditure (Stiglitz, 2003).

SAPs particularly affected the countries of sub-Saharan Africa, whose economies they negatively impacted (Rickecker, 2002). African governments that implemented the SAPs usually had to: spend less on education, infrastructure, health care, and social services–key areas in fighting poverty-devalue the national currency, cut back on food subsidies, cut jobs in government institutions, thus lower the wage bill for government workers, and encourage privatization of public enterprises to local entrepreneurs and foreign investors. This was expected to stimulate national economic growth, increase government revenue to enable them pay debts they owed to western governments, bilateral, and multilateral institutions (Deng et al., 2002).

In recent years, and because of the dismal performance and failure of the SAPs, the African countries have again pursued other programs, still designed together with IMF, under various strategic plans and the most common of these programs is the Poverty Reduction and Growth Facility (PRGF) (EIU, 2009). The program defines poverty in the African context–although poverty is universal–as the deprivation of sufficient food, education, health, proper housing, water, and other necessities of life that make life more bearable (EIU, 2009).

The PRGF programs describe what needs to be done to eradicate poverty, including achieving or meeting the Millennium Development Goals (MDG's). In 2000, 189 UN member countries signed up to the Millennium Development Goals (MDG). The MDGs are a series of eight-point goals and action plan items aimed at health, education, environmental sustainability, child mortality, women empowerment, alleviating poverty, reduction of hunger, and development of a global partnership for growth and development defined by the UN in 1999 in order to focus the world on eradication of poverty (Sachs, 2005). They are evaluated regularly but their target date of reducing poverty by a half, for example, of what it was in 2000 is 2015. Specifically, the Millennium Development Goals are (Opanga, 2010):

- Eradicate extreme poverty and hunger;
- Achieve universal primary education;
- Promote gender equality and empower women;
- Reduce child mortality;
- Improve maternal health;
- Combat HIV/AIDS, malaria, tuberculosis, and other diseases;
- Ensure environmental stability;
- Develop global partnership for development.

Other hypes you hear in Africa these days and associated with the IMF and World Bank too are HIPC initiatives and Vision 2030 strategy. According to Rickecker (2002), the Heavily Indebted Poor Country (HIPC) Initiative is an agreement among official creditors, planned and managed by IMF, designed to help the poorest, most heavily indebted countries escape from unsustainable and crippling debt. It is meant to enable poor countries to focus their energies on building the policy and institutional foundation for sustainable development and poverty reduction. HIPC represents the first effort to coordinate all creditors to reduce African debt. It includes foreign debts owed to bilateral creditors (Paris Club), multilateral creditors (international financial institutions, such as the World Bank and the IMF) and commercial creditors (the London Club) (Rickecker, 2002).

Vision 2030 is an economic development strategy adopted by several governments in Africa. For example, the Kenyan Vision 2030 program is built on the development of three distinct but interdependent pillars: political, social, and economic pillars. The aim of the political pillar is to promote the development of a stable, secure, transparent, and accountable political systems. The aim of the social pillar is to create a just and cohesive society with universal access to education, healthcare, housing, food, water, and sanitation. In the education pillar alone, the goals are ambitious: Kenya hopes that by 2012 it will be able to boast an 80% adult literacy rate and a 95% school enrollment rate. The economic pillar focuses on significantly boosting economic growth at high rates to reduce poverty and hunger by half of what they were in 1999 by 2015 (Keeler, 2010).

In a majority of countries, the vision is aimed at developing several different economic zones–as engines of growth-in various parts of the countries pursuing the plans. The plan also aims to eventually achieve annual economic growth rates of 10%. Currently, GDP growth of the countries involved, like Kenya, averages 5%.

The Kenyan vision calls for a series of five-year plans, with the first one being between 2008 and 2012. The first plan calls for investments in key economic sectors–agriculture, education, tourism, horticulture, services, manufacturing, and environmental protection-with flagship projects, in each sector, meant to have the greatest impact on social and economic development of the country (Keeler 2010; Rickecker, 2002).

However, and more often than not, a lot of the programs by IMF and the World Bank, particularly the Structural Adjustment Programs of the 1980's and 1990's, were externally imposed on the African people and therefore failed and hence the current reasons and justification for the design and implementation of the new programs like the PRGF and Vision 2030. The structural adjustment programs failed to achieve their intended targets because they generalized and applied the western economic development models and democratic experiences to the African development problems, without consideration of the uniqueness and diversity of Africa (Deng, 2002 & Moyo, 2009). The designers of the programs–although supposedly well intentioned-also completely failed to involve the African people in designing and evolving these programs.

Furthermore, they failed to realize that development must be viewed as a product of the unique political, social, and historical experiences of the society in question and that indiscriminate replication of ideas, frameworks, and models, most of which have been developed outside of the African context, are not likely to foster and enhance development in the continent (Deng, 2002). The key attributes of successful development and growth strategies and policies are that they are home grown and owned, designed by people within each country, they are pragmatic, and sensitive to the needs and concerns of the people and the country.

Stiglitz (2003) has described IMF/World Bank imposition of the failed strategies and policies very succinctly,

As a member of the President of the USA's cabinet, I was well positioned not only to observe the debates and see how they were resolved but, especially in areas that touched upon economics, to participate in them. I knew that ideas mattered but so did politics, and one of my jobs was to persuade others not just that what I advocated was good economics but also that it was good politics. But as I moved to the international arena, I discovered that neither dominated the formulation of policy, especially at the International Monetary Fund. Decisions were made on the basis of what seemed a curious blend of ideology and bad economics, dogma that sometimes seemed to be thinly veiling special interests. When crises hit in any part of the world, the IMF prescribed outmoded, inappropriate, if "standard" solutions, without considering the effects they would have on the people in the countries told to follow these policies. Rarely did I see the forecasts about what the policies would do to poverty. Rarely did I see thoughtful discussions and analyses of the consequences of alternative policies. There was a single prescription for every situation. Alternative opinions were not sought. Open, frank discussion was discouraged – there was no room for it. Ideology guided policy prescriptions and countries were expected to follow the IMF guidelines without debate.

These attitudes made me cringe. It was not just that they often produced poor results; they were antidemocratic principles. In our personal lives, we would never follow ideas blindly without seeking alternative advice. Yet countries all over the world, particularly in Africa and East Asia, were instructed to do just that. The problems facing developing countries are difficult, and the IMF is often called upon in the worst of situations, when the country is facing a crisis. But its remedies failed as very often, or even more often than they worked. IMF structural adjustment policies–the policies designed to help a country adjust to crises as well as to more persistent imbalances–led to poverty, hunger, and riots in many countries; and even when results were not so dire, even when they managed to eke out some growth for a while, often the benefits went disproportionately to the better-off, with those at the bottom sometimes facing even greater poverty. What astounded me, however, was that many of the people in power in the IMF didn't question those policies, by those who were making the critical decisions. They were often questioned by people in the developing countries, but many were so afraid they might lose IMF funding, and with it funding from others, that they articulated their doubts most cautiously, if at all, and then only in private. But while no one was happy about the suffering that often accompanied the IMF programs, inside the IMF it was simply assumed that whatever suffering occurred was a necessary part of the pain countries had to experience on the way to becoming a successful market economy, and that their measurers would, in fact, reduce the pain the countries would have to face in the long run.

Undoubtedly, some pain was necessary, but in my judgment, the level of pain in developing countries created in the process of globalization and development as it has been guided by the IMF and the international economic organizations have been far greater than necessary. The backlash against globalization draws its force not only from the perceived damage done to developing countries by policies driven by ideology but also from the inequities in the global trading system. Today, few - apart from those with vested interests who benefit from keeping out the goods produced by the poor countries–defend the hypocrisy of pretending to help developing countries by forcing them to open up their markets to the goods of the advanced industrial countries while keeping their own markets protected, policies that make the rich richer and the poor more impoverished–and increasingly angry.

Inevitably and contrary to their expected positive effects, the IMF and World Bank Africa programs failed dismally. And, oftentimes, enhanced poverty that they were meant to eradicate and made the African economic conditions much worse than before the start of the programs. Per capita income and other measures of growth, well-being, and quality of life largely deteriorated during the structural adjustment period (Moyo, 2009).

In explaining the African situation after the structural adjustments, Meng et al (2002), states thus: "Generally, however, most of the states still confront the socioeconomic strains that dominated the 1980's and 1990's: economic disparities compounded by poorly implemented World Bank and IMF imposed structural adjustment programs, low domestic savings, dependence on declining and scarce foreign capital for investment, heavy debts, and weak financial and physical infrastructure. Consequently, almost all African economies–that implanted the structural adjustment programs-have witnessed increasing poverty, rising unemployment, and falling standards of living of the people the programs intended to help."

Moyo (2009), in her seminal book, 'Dead Aid', provides further evidence of the resulting economic deterioration because of the structural adjustment programs thus:

with an average per capita income of roughly US $1 a day, sub-Saharan Africa remains the poorest region in the world. Africa's real per capita income today–after the structural adjustment programs-is lower than in the 1970s, leaving many African countries at least as poor as they were forty years ago. With over half of the 900 million Africans living on less than a dollar a day, sub-Saharan Africa has the highest proportion of poor people in the world–some 50 per cent of the world's poor. Poverty instigated by IMF and World Bank.

And while the number of the world's population and proportion of the world's people in extreme poverty fell after 1980, the proportion of people in sub-Saharan Africa living in abject poverty increased to almost 50 per cent. Between 1981 and 2002, the number of people in the continent living in poverty nearly doubled, leaving the average African poorer today than just two decades ago, at the start of the structural programs. Life expectancy stagnated, and in some countries it fell to what it was in the 1950s, and adult literacy plummeted below pre-1980 levels. And between 1970 and 1998, when structural adjustment and governance policies were at their pick, poverty in African rose from 11 percent to a staggering 66 percent. That is roughly 600 million of Africa's about a billion people trapped in a quagmire of poverty–a truly shocking figure.

Despite their dismal failure, however, the structural adjustments and governance programs introduced some sense of discipline and planning in the use of national resources and imbued a degree of democratic principles and behavior in the African continent. Due to these reforms, and with a few exceptions, the countries, in which SAPs were vigorously and fully implemented–as they were in a majority of African countries-have held parliamentary elections every five years with limitation of the presidential stay in office to two equal terms, although some of the leaders, like Museveni of Uganda and Toude of Niger, have changed their constitutions in order to seek election for more than two terms. All the same, African countries have initiated more disciplined long term planning such as the much daunted and famous vision 2030 described above and introduced increasingly free trade among African countries and the regions, the hallmarks of excepted accelerated economic development in Africa.

The African leaders have also increased attempts to integrate the African continent into regional trading blocs to enlarge the markets for their products and in an effort to spur the development of increased trade among them, as opposed to concentrating their trade with their former rulers (Mbaku, 1998; Mahajan, 2009).

The trading blocs and the African Economic Community, to which they are building blocks, are enlarging African markets and therefore making Africa a 21st century economic frontier and a place to do business now and in the future. First-movers to Africa and thus future incumbents will create barriers to entry and develop sustainable competitive advantage for their products and services thus creating increasing value for their stakeholders.

6. THE MANAGER'S NOTE

The manager's note is meant to outline the implications of business opportunities from the subject matter of the chapter and describe what the practicing manager could apply and use immediately in doing business in Africa. For example, the outline of African history in this chapter is meant to help managers and policy makers to understand the origins of Africa's current social, political, and economic challenges. African history is an interesting episode and it is important to understand it fully in order to understand the African current business environment (Mbaku 2004).

Therefore, from a business perspective, one can broadly divide African history into four distinct periods. The cumulating occurrences, during these periods, variously impacted on the Africans. Moreover, these occurrences happened without the involvement of the people of Africa. They have had a lasting impact on the continent's social, political, technological, and economic development over the years. The consequences of these developments are the results of Africa's poor performance and limited participation in economic development and global business. But, these experiences could provide business opportunities for an enthusiastic business manager.

It is often stated by scholars too that the events during these periods created and perpetuated the state of social and political instability, technological backwardness, slow economic development, innovative and entrepreneurial challenges that have dogged Africa during the last sixty years of independence of many African countries (Denge et al., 2002). These conditions can also be sources of business opportunities including technological innovations and consumer products development.

The African population surpassed 1 billion people in 2010, which is about 15 percent of the world population, and growing at an average rate of 2.5 percent annually (ERA, 2010). Nigeria has the largest population, of over 162 million people, followed by Ethiopia 85 million, and Egypt with 82 million people (ERA, 2010). Several of the island nations have smallest populations of about 1 million people each. A majority of the other larger African nations have a population averaging 30 million people. The continent's life expectancy averages 52 years (Mahajan, 2009). HIV/AIDS pandemic has negatively impacted on the African population and life expectancy. But the average HIV/AIDS prevalence rate has reduced from 14 percent to 5 percent in recent years (ERA, 2010). These facts about the African population present opportunities in products and services. The diseases provide opportunities for products such as phermarseuticals, mosquito nets, hospitals, and training opportunities for doctors, nurses, and paramedical personnel.

As discussed in Chapter five below, Africa has developed seven regional trading blocs: the East African Community (EAC), the Southern African Development Community (SADC), the Common Market of Eastern and Southern Africa (COMESA), the Economic Community of Western African States (ECOWAS), the Maghreb Economic Union, in Northern Africa, and the two Francophone economic communities of the West Africa Economic and Monetary Union and the Central Africa Economic and Monetary Union. There are also several smaller unions that pursue narrower and limited objectives such as the Western African Monetary Zone, in West Africa, and the Inter-Governmental Authority on Development (IGAD) in the Horn of Africa. These trading blocs overlap in the sense that many countries are in more than one trade region at the same time, which makes it easier to invest in one region and do business in the other regions at the same time.

It is anticipated that these regions will eventually, as they increasingly become fully operational, form the building blocks of the African Economic Community formed by the African heads of state and government in 1991, in Abuja, Nigeria. The trade regions, several of which are at the customs union level of economic integration process, will stimulate inter African trade and therefore create business opportunities in the continent by enlarging African markets (Mbaku, 1998).

However, it is important to note that the East African Community is at the Common market level and the Francophone trading blocs are at the monetary union level of regional integration process. Both Francophone trading blocs have regional central banks and stock market exchanges, with a common currency, the French Franc, managed by the central banks. The currency is tied to the Euro and the French Treasury assures its stability by holding foreign exchange reserves, of the francophone countries, in the French Central Bank (Mbaku, 1998). These trading arrangements increase markets sizes in Africa. Businesses can enter into African through any of these regional trading blocs, considering the language–English, French, and Arabic-preferences of the firm.

The other reality of African business is the 1999 Millennium Development Goals whose target date is 2015. The goals are (Opanga, 2010):

- Eradicate extreme poverty and hunger;
- Achieve universal primary education;
- Promote gender equality and empower women;
- Reduce child mortality;
- Improve maternal health;

- Combat HIV/AIDS, malaria, tuberculosis, and other diseases;
- Ensure environmental stability;
- Develop global partnership for economic development.

These goals also suggest business opportunities in healthcare, education, social services, trade, and environmental protection services.

Other interesting facts about Africa and associated with the IMF and World Bank are HIPC initiatives and Vision 2030 strategy. According to Rickecker (2002), the Heavily Indebted Poor Country (HIPC) Initiative is an agreement among official creditors, planned and managed by IMF, designed to help the poorest and most heavily indebted African countries escape from unsustainable global debt. These countries include Zambia, Uganda, and Tanzania. The HIPC initiative is meant to enable the affected African countries to focus on sustainable economic development to reduce poverty as per the UN Millennium Development Goals.

HIPC represents the first effort to coordinate all creditors to reduce African debt. It includes foreign debts owed to bilateral creditors (Paris Club), multilateral creditors (international financial institutions, such as the World Bank and the IMF) and commercial creditors (the London Club) (Rickecker, 2002). The savings will hopefully be put into agriculture, education, healthcare, infrastructure, and environmental protection, creating more business opportunities in the affected countries.

Another area of interest to business, in Africa, is the Vision 2030 or Vision 2030 economic development strategy adopted by many governments in Africa. For example, the Kenyan Vision 2030 program is built on the development of three distinct but strong and interdependent national pillars: political, social, and economic pillars. The aim of the political pillar is to promote the development of a stable, secure, transparent, and a political system that is responsible and accountable. The aim of the social pillar is to create a just and cohesive society with universal access to quality education, healthcare, housing, food, water, and sanitation. In the education field alone, the goals are ambitious: Kenya hopes that by 2012 it will be able to boast an 80% adult literacy rate and a 95% school enrollment rate. The economic pillar focuses on significantly boosting economic growth at high rates to reduce poverty and hunger in the country (Keeler, 2010).

In a majority of countries, the vision is aimed at developing several different economic zones–as engines of growth-in various parts of the countries that are pursuing the strategy. The plan also aims to eventually achieve annual economic growth rates of 10%. Currently, GDP growth of the countries involved in the Vision 2030/2020, like Kenya, averages 5%.

The Kenyan vision calls for a series of five-year plans, with the first one being between 2008 and 2012. The first plan calls for investments in key economic sectors–agriculture, education, tourism, horticulture, services, manufacturing, and environmental protection-with flagship projects, in each sector, meant to have the greatest impact on social and economic development of the country (Keeler 2010). The flagship projects will create business opportunities for firms, entrepreneurs, and corporations.

It is important to note too that despite of the dismal failure of the structural adjustment programs, they introduced and created a sense of national discipline and strategic planning in the use of national resources in many of the African countries. The programs imbued democratic principles and responsible behavior in the African continent. Due to these reforms, and with a few exceptions, the African countries, in which SAPs were fully implemented–as they were in a majority of African countries–have, for example, held parliamentary elections every five years with limitation of the presidential stay in office to two equal terms, although some leaders, like Museveni of Uganda and Toude of Niger, have changed their constitutions in order to seek election for more than two terms. Furthermore, African countries have initiated more disciplined long-term economic planning such as the much daunted and famous vision 2030 described above and introduced increasingly free trade among African countries, the hallmarks of accelerated economic development in Africa to deal with poverty. These developments are sources of business opportunities in Africa. The reforms have also introduced and linked Africa into the global economy.

REFERENCES

Acemoglu & Robinson. (2012). *Why nations fail: The origins of power, prosperity, and poverty*. New York: Crown Business.

Annan, K. (1999). Peace and development: One struggle two fronts. *Address to the World Bank Staff.* Washington, DC: DANCE. Retrieved from http://www.un.org/News/Press/docs/1999/19991019.sgsm7187.doc.html.

BBC. (2010). Retrieved from www.bbc.com.

Brown, K. (1996). *Goodwives, nasty wenches, and anxious patriarchs: Gender, race, and power in colonial virginia*. Chapel Hill, NC: University of North Carolina Press.

Business Week. (2009). Retrieved from http://www.businessweek.com/.

Crowder, B. (2011). *Choices and consequences*. Our Daily Bread.

Daily Nation. (2009). Retrieved from www.nationmedia.com.

Deng, F. M., & Zartman, W. I. (2002). *A strategic vision for africa: The kampala movement*. Washington, DC: Brookings Institution.

Diamond, J. (1998). *Guns, Germs, and Steel: The Fates of Human Societies*. New York: W. W. Norton and Company.

EIU. (2009). *African economic and business report. Economist Intelligence Unit*. London: EIU.

ERA. (2010). *Economic report on africa. African Union Commission*. Addis Ababa, Ethiopia: ERA.

Friedman, T. L., & Mandelbaum, M. (2011). *That used to be us: How america fell behind in the world it invented and how we can come back*. New York: Farrar, Straus, and Giroux.

Gekonge, M. (2006). *Eliminating Horizontal Inequalities in Post Conflict Northern Uganda: Tackling the Neglected Dimensions of the Humanitarian Crisis in Northern Uganda. (Unpublished Master's Research Project)*. South Orange, NJ: Seton Hall University.

Ghemawat, P. (2010). Finding your strategy in the new landscape. *Harvard Business Review*. Retrieved from http://hbr.org/2010/03/finding-your-strategy-in-the-new-landscape/ar/1.

Horton, L. E., & Horton, J. O. (1999). *African-american history. Encarta Encyclopedia*. Redmond, WA: Microsoft.

Juma, C. (2011). *The New Harvest: Agricultural Innovation in Africa*. Oxford, UK: Oxford University Press.

Keeler, D. (2010). Kenya: Rebirth of a nation. *Global Finance*. Retrieved from http://www.globalfinance.gr/page/.

Kisiang'ani, E. (2007). The lies about jomo kenyatta and kenya. *The Standard*. Retrieved from http://www3.standard.com/net/public/Individuals.

Kotler, J. P. (1990). *A force for change. How leadership differs from management*. New York: Free Press.

Larson, K. C. (2004). *Harriet tubman: The portrait of an american hero, bound for the promised land*. New York: Random House Publishing Group.

Mahajan, V. (2009). *Africa rising: How 900 million african consumers offer more than you think*. Upper Saddle River, NJ: Pearson Prentice Hall.

Manning, P. (1990). *Slavery and african life: Occidental, oriental, and african slave trade*. New York: Cambridge University Press.

Mbaku, J. M. (1998). Emerging trade blocks and the fortune of african participation in the world economy. *Journal of economic integration, 10*(2).

Mbaku, J. M. (2004). *Institutions and development in africa*. Trenton, NJ: Africa World Press.

McClelland, D. C. (1987). *Human motivation*. New York: Cambridge University Press.

Morley, W., Klepp, S. E., & Smith, B. G. (2005). *The unfortunate: The voyage and adventures of william morley, an indentured servant*. University Park, PA: Pennsylvania State University Press.

Moyo, D. (2009). *Dead Aid, Why Aid is not working and how there is a better way for africa*. New York: Farrar, Straus, and Giroux.

Opanga, K. (2010). Millennium development goals must be achieved. *Daily Nation*. Retrieved from http://www.nation.co.ke/.

Ostby, G. (2004). Horizontal inequalities and civil conflict. In *Proceedings of the 13th Annual National Political Science Conference*. Hurdalsjoen, Norway: SEAS Press.

Ross, S., & Agiesta, J. (2012). Survey finds racial views have not improved since 2008. *The Philadelphia Inquirer.* Retrieved from http://philly.newspaperdirect.com/epaper/viewer.aspx.

Sachs, J. (2006). *End of poverty: The economic possibilities for our times*. New York: Penguin Books.

Schuster, C. P., & Copeland, M. J. (2006). *Global business practices: Adapting for success*. Atlanta, GA: Thomson.

Shambaugh, D. (2013). *China goes global: The partial power*. Oxford, UK: Oxford University Press.

Ssomogerere. (2002). Financial sector restructuring under the structural adjustment programs and economic program in uganda. *A policy paper.*

Stewart, F. (2000). *Policies towards horizontal inequalities in post-conflict reconstruction*. Oxford, UK: Queen Elizabeth House.

Stiglitz, J. (2003). *Globalization and its discontents*. New York: W. W. Norton and Company.

The Daily Bread. (2011, December). [The Daily Bread.]. *Galatians*, *6*, 9–10.

The Daily Bread. (2011, December). [The Daily Bread.]. *Galatians*, *6*, 7.

The East African. (2011). Retrieved from www.nationmedia.com.

Wachira & Mureithi. (2013). Coming soon, Kenya's greatest and largest water dam. *Daily Nation.* Retrieved from http://www.nation.co.ke/.

Wild, J. J., Wild, K. L., & Han, J. C. Y. (2008). *International Business* (4th ed.). Upper Saddle River, NJ: Pearson Hall.

Wong, E. (2009, December). China's export of labor faces scorn. *New York Times.* Retrieved from http://www.nytimes.com/.

Chapter 3
Africa in the Global Economy

ABSTRACT

This chapter describes concepts and perspectives of globalization generally and explains Africa's current and anticipated position in the global economy. The chapter further enumerates and fully explains the economic and business strategies that are necessary to increase the competitiveness of African economies in the global markets. By increasing Africa's competitiveness, the continent will become an attractive business region for the urgently needed foreign direct investments.

1. GLOBALIZATION: CONCEPTS AND PROCESS

The world is flat and more highly interconnected today than ever before (Friedman, 2005, 2011). This means that more people are suddenly competing, connecting, and collaborating with more other people from more different places around the world with less cost than ever before in the history of mankind. The flattening of the world is affecting businesses, armies, governments, and most importantly individual workers across the globe. Globalization is greatly influenced by the increasing information technology revolution (Friedman et al., 2011).

Friedman et al., 2011 assert further that globalization and Information Technology are totally intertwined, each being spurred by the other. New technologies become enablers of more globalization, erase boundaries, break down walls, and connect the previously disconnected world. Then those connected people and firms

DOI: 10.4018/978-1-4666-4570-7.ch003

and governments build up webs of trade, commerce, investment, innovation, and collaboration that create markets for, and demand for, more technologies to connect more people at even lower costs and greater speed.

Therefore, the world economy is increasingly becoming a single connected economy in which companies conduct business globally and compete anywhere and with anyone in the world. And countries trade with whatever countries they wish, most likely following rules set by the World Trade Organization (WTO). The WTO rules are bilaterally and/or multilaterally agreed on (Cullen et al., 2008). While future trends in developing countries are likely to be considerably affected by the forces of globalization, indeed the overall thesis holds high for much of Africa (Juma, 2011).

Today, globalization is a daily experience among all countries and people of the world. Individuals and companies increasingly see the entire world as a source of business opportunities. Still, globalization is a situation whereby social, commercial, political, and economic systems of the people of the world have become increasingly interdependent. It is a condition whereby decisions made in one country are, more often than not, becoming dependent on decisions made abroad or in other countries related or unrelated. In competitive business, globalization is a situation whereby large and small firms alike relocate or outsource production and services to distant, cost-effective locations like China and India to enhance their competitive advantage mostly through a low cost leadership competitive strategy (Copeland et al., 2006).

Giddens (2001) looks at globalization from the point of view of social relations where the local situation is dissolved and re-organized by global events and over time and space. He defines globalization as the intensification of worldwide social relations that connect distance locations in such a way that local relations and occurrences are shaped by events taking place in faraway lands.

Stiglizt (2003) has described globalization as fundamentally the closer integration of the countries and peoples of the world which has been brought about by the enormous reduction of the cost of transportation and communication, and the breaking down of artificial barriers to the flow of goods, services, capital, knowledge, and people across borders. Globalization has been accompanied by the creation of new institutions–such as the WTO-that have joined with existing ones to work across borders. In the arena of international civil society, new groups, like the Jubilee movement pushing for debt and poverty reduction in the poorest countries, have joined with established organizations like the International Red Cross to try and deal with poverty in many nations around the world. Globalization is mostly driven by international corporations, which move, not only capital and goods across borders, but technology and people too. Globalization has led to renewed interest and keener attention to long-established intergovernmental institutions such as the UN, the WHO, and the ILO.

However, globalization today is not working as well as it should for many of the world's poor, particularly those of Africa. It is not working for much of the environment. It is not working for the stability of the world economy (Stiglitz, 2003). Despite the sincere efforts and concerns of many people opposed to globalization, it has already happened and cannot be undone. It can only be managed efficiently and effectively for the benefit of all mankind and to minimize its negative aspects or consequences like those caused by the ideologically and self interest-focused free market ideology and promotion of free financial markets interests endorsed by the Washington Consensus. The Washington Consensus is made of the World Bank, IMF, and the USA Treasury. And they are committed to liberalizing the world economy for the benefit of Wall Street regardless of the damage it does to the developing and emerging economies and markets (Stiglitz, 2003).

The Washington Consensus, according to Stiglitz (2003), stands on three pillars: fiscal austerity by governments around the world, privatization of government enterprises, and financial and capital market liberation to achieve free market economies around the world. Therefore, they have, at times, pushed for the adoption of ruinous strategies and policies relating to fiscal austerity, privatization of government enterprises, and liberalization of financial and capital markets in developing countries including emerging markets of Russia and Eastern Europe; East Asian countries, particularly leading to the 1997 financial crisis; African countries; and Latin American countries over the years. Through their incoherent and inconsistent strategies and policies, they created economic instability, persistent unemployment, and pervasive poverty in these countries that their governments have been trying to solve in recent years (Stiglitz, 2003). These policies were described and presented as structural adjustment in Africa. They caused negative GDP growth and economic performance in many African countries leading to widespread poverty and hunger in the continent.

Moreover, in the global economy, Africa is marginalized in every conceivable way. In defining globalization and attempting to explain how Americans have not really realized the full impact of globalization in their way of life, Friedman and Mandelbaum (2011), in their seminal book, "That Used Be Us....", state thus "the essence of globalization is the free movement of people, goods, services, *ideas,* and capital across national borders. It expanded dramatically because of the remarkable economic success of the free-market economies of the West, *the* states that traded and invested heavily among themselves, *such as those in the European Union.* Other countries, observing this success, decided to follow Western patterns of *production, trade, and consumption.* China, other countries in East and Southern Asia, India, Latin America, and formerly communist Europe all entered the globalized economy. Americans did not fully grasp the implications of globalization becoming–if we can put this way–even more global, in part because we thought we had seen it all before."

However, the two leading commentators on issues of globalization do not mention Africa in the globalization process although they talk about all countries and regions of the other parts of the world. Africa does not feature on their radars of observing globalization, attesting, once again, to the marginalization of Africa in the global scene. President Clinton (2011) has also described the globalization process without mentioning any region in particular including Africa. However, he discusses the function of a government that will assist its firms to go global that will be relevant for African governments in the global economy.

President Clinton (2011), in his recent seminal book, "Back to Work, Why We Need Smart Government for a Strong Economy", implicitly on the current American economic situation and intensifying globalization and its challenges, succinctly asserts thus:

We live in the most interdependent age in history and in order to make it continue to work effectively we have to have more shared prosperity. We have to assume more shared responsibilities. People are increasingly likely to be affected by actions beyond their borders, and their borders are increasingly open to both negative and positive crossings: travelers, immigrants, money, goods, services, information, communication, and culture; disease, trafficking in drugs, weapons, and people, and acts of terrorism and violent crime.

The modern world has many attractions—scientific advances, technological breakthroughs, instant information-sharing, greater social diversity, and the empowerment of people everywhere; but challenges, most of which can be grouped into three categories. The modern world is too unequal in incomes and in access to jobs, health, and education. It is too unstable, as evidenced by the rapid spreading of the 2008/9 financial crisis, economic insecurity, political upheavals, and our shared vulnerability to terrorism. In addition, the world's growth pattern is unsustainable, because the way we produce and use energy and deplete natural resources is causing climate change and other environmental problems.

No matter what the naysayers claim, the evidence is overwhelming that the climate is changing because of human activity, and if we don't change course quickly and sharply, the consequences are going to be terrible and dire. The signs are all around us, in rising temperatures (nine of the hottest ten years on record occurred in the last thirteen years), melting ice caps, rising sea levels, more droughts, fires, floods, and severe storms. My native state of Arkansas is in America's tornado alley just South of Joplin, Missouri, which was recently devastated by an especially powerful tornado. But in 2010 and 2011, tornadoes also hit in Queens in New York City and in Massachusetts, areas in the Northeast where they're all but unheard of.

Though these problems are affecting the lives of people in every nation, responding to them effectively presents very different challenges to poor and rich nations. Poor nations have to build systems that those of us in wealthy nations take for granted—economic, financial, education, health-care, infrastructure, energy, environmental, government service, and other systems that make prosperity and security possible and provide predictable rewards to citizens for hard work and honest dealing. When poor countries succeed in building these systems, their citizens are able to rapidly increase their incomes, as Vietnam, Rwanda, and other developing nations have proven over the last fifteen years.

Wealthy countries have such systems; they were built on the road to prosperity. The challenge is to keep them working, and improving them, as times and conditions change, because at some point the people who run them and those who benefit from them inevitably become resistant to change: more committed to holding on to the past and their positions than to advancing the purposes for which they were established in the first place; more interested in holding on to or increasing present advantages than in creating greater opportunities for others and a brighter future for our children. You can see these forces at work in the politics of Washington: The status quo is represented by much more powerful lobbying groups than the future is.

Because the world is still organized around nations, the decisions national leaders make and citizens' support today determine tomorrow's possibilities. For poor countries, that means building systems that give more and more people a chance to have decent jobs and send their kids to school. For rich countries, it means reforming systems that once worked well but no longer do, so people can keep moving forward in an increasingly globalizing, complex, and competitive environment.

President Clinton (2011) has also suggested and crystallized what he thinks are key functions of an effective government in the globalized world that will ensure the competitiveness of its firms in the global markets. He asserts thus:

I think the role of government is to give people the tools and create the conditions to make the most of out of our lives. Governments should empower us to do things we need or want to do that we can only do together by pooling our resources and spending them in large enough amounts to achieve the desired objectives. Therefore, the most successful nations in the twenty-first century, including those of Africa, have both a strong economy and a strong, effective government. Here's a list of the functions of a successful and strong government covers today:

1. **National Security:** Including the military, intelligence agencies, diplomatic efforts and development assistance, homeland defense, federal law enforcement, border control, natural-disaster response, and effectively combating climate change.
2. **Assistance to Those Objectives unable to Fully Support Themselves and to Provide a Decent Retirement for Seniors:** Including Medicaid, Medicare, and Social Security, aid for the disabled, food stamps, unemployment benefits, nutrition aid for newborns and mothers, and public housing.
3. **Equal Access to Opportunity:** Including federal aid to education for low-income and disabled students, scholarships and tax credits for college tuition costs, the student loan program, work-study-payments, and job-training assistance.
4. **Economic Development:** Including trade agreements, financing for businesses to enter new markets; incentives to create new businesses and jobs in advanced manufacturing, clean energy, energy efficiency, and other high-growth areas; investments in basic research and development and incentives for private research and development to be done in the country; an adequate minimum wage and support for work and childrearing, including the Family and Medical Leave Law and the child tax credit; Small Business Administration in support of entrepreneurs as engines of the economy in terms of guaranteed microcredit, and community development loans to promising businesses that would otherwise be shut out of credit markets; financing and other support to help companies sell products made in the country to other countries; and incentives to invest in areas of high unemployment and low incomes.
5. **Oversight of Financial Markets and Institutions:** To ensure transparency and honest financial dealings, competition, and consumer choice, and to limit leverages to avoid future collapses and bailouts of companies.
6. **Protection and Advancement of Public Interests that the Market Cannot Fix:** Including clean air, clean water, safe food, safe transportation, safe workplaces, civil/human rights, access to affordable health care, housing, and preservation of natural resources for the common good, including national monuments, and national forests.
7. **Providing Investments:** Through tax or fee revenue, for projects we all need when the costs are too great or the cost recovery period too long for the private sector to finance, including highways, airports, rails, accelerated broadband connections, *schools*, a national electric grid, and critical research and development in areas from space to advanced materials to nanotechnology and biotechnology to clean energy.

8. **An Effective, Fair, and Progressive Revenue Collection System:** To collect all taxes and issue credits and deductions where applicable and/or deemed by *parliament or* congress to be in the national interest, including tax deductions for home mortgage payments, charitable giving, health-care payments, children, and many business expenses and deductions.

2. AFRICA IN THE GLOBAL ECONOMY

Africa is still marginalized in the global economic systems. The continent's merchandise trade-which is only 3.5 percent of total world merchandise trade-remains undiversified in portfolio mix and in destination. Agriculture, mining, and fuel products constitute at least 80 percent of African exports (ERA, 2010). Africa exports about $ 17.5 billion of services annually (ERA, 2010).

Therefore, Africa abundantly produces and exports cheap raw materials–mainly oil, gas, coffee, tea, cut flowers, iron ore, copper, diamond, gold, bauxite, and lumber-to the industrialized world, mostly Europe and North America, and increasingly today to China and India. These exports are converted into manufactured products and then exported back to Africa at high prices as it happened during colonial times.

In this time and age, and by and large, Africa does not add value to its primary products so it really does not receive full benefit, from the global economy, for its abundant resources. Hence, Africa's inability to generate enough financial resources to develop the continent in order that it effectively tackles pervasive poverty affecting its growing population. Still, the current African trade portfolio concentration exacerbates the vulnerability of Africa to the world economic crises (ERA, 2010).

For instance, the economic slowdown in the European Union, the USA, and China in 2008-2009, during the global economic meltdown, had a pro-cyclical effect on demand for African exports, which resulted in declining commodity prices. The abrupt fall in commodity prices caused significant terms-of-trade shocks in 2009 for African economies. The impact that has on the export sector is not likely being limited to the medium-term but could have long-term economic and social implications as new investments get curtailed and the rural sector remains suffering from unemployment and poverty. African governments can only reduce poverty in Africa when they are able to create decent and quality jobs and reduce unemployment and underemployment in their economies (ERA, 2010). This can only be done through higher and more valuable earnings from its exports. This, therefore, calls for export diversification and adding value to its exports in Africa before exporting them.

Furthermore, trade relationships developed during colonialism have persisted-exacerbating the unemployment and poverty conditions in Africa-with the former metropolitan countries. These relationships substantially govern African's global trade today. Quite often, these arrangements have been strengthened by tied aid and other development assistance programs that have been designed and managed to keep African economies as sources of cheap raw materials and markets for high value manufactured products from industrialized countries and increasingly with China and India; two of the world economies that are growing phenomenally today (Mbaku, 1998; Sachs, 2005).

For example, the French have tied their former African colonies to financial and military arrangements that are supposedly helpful to these countries over the years. They all use one currency, the Franc, whose value is controlled and regulated by the French Treasury in Paris. They also maintain their foreign earnings in the French Central Bank in Paris. But these countries are some of the poorest and politically unstable countries in Africa and the world (Wang, et al, 2008 and EIU 2009). The countries produce cotton, mined metals, oil, and gas which they export as raw materials mostly to France and import manufactured products from France. They do not add value to their exports that will enhance their economic diversification and sophistication necessary to create high value jobs to deal with pervasive poverty in these countries. The situation is almost similar in the Anglophone, the Arab north, and Portuguese speaking countries (Moyo, 2009).

Scholars (Mbaku et al., 1998) have also examined major systems of trade preferences for Africa-the Generalized System of Preferences and the African, Caribbean, and Pacific Convention-and what they are based on. These scholars have concluded that such preferences yield very little benefits to African countries. They generally have very little economic value to the African countries. They offer only marginal benefits; in fact, these arrangements retard Africa's development effort because they make Africa dependent on valueless arrangements for its development. They also hinder Africa's ability to integrate regionally to expand their markets and increase intra-Africa trade to improve its chances of being competitiveness in the global markets.

Africa should design and decide on its own development agenda and negotiate the arrangements and preferences that are beneficial to the continent like the current AGOA 2000 Act by the USA Congress. This Act allows free entry of specified items from certain African countries to the USA market. Between 2000 and 2009, African countries have earned $ 88 billion from exports to the USA under AGOA, giving a $ 64 billion surplus in favor of Africa (AGOA Report, 2009). But, many observers argue that the act needs to be extended to cover many more manufactured items including farm produce to contribute to the accelerated economic development in the frontier continent.

At the WTO Doha Round of International Trade negotiations, Africa is focusing on Agriculture and Non-agriculture market access to the European Union and American markets. African countries continue to show particular interest in these two areas given the promise they offer as pillars in their economic development strategies, emphasizing their high employment elasticity. Most employment in Africa has remained in agriculture, and the countries where manufacturing sector employment and size of the economy has become significant, the industries rely heavily on agriculture for their inputs.

Employment creation is very important for African countries, because employment is a key channel through which economic growth can result in poverty reduction in the African economies (ERA, 2010; Juma, 2011). However, in all negotiations of market access, Africa should realize that inter-regional trade is the easiest pathway by which Africa will prosper faster in the context of the global economy. Therefore, in any trade agreement–including the Economic Partnership Agreements (EPA's) being negotiated by African countries with the European Union-regional integration should take precedent and be a priority as the most important route through which Africa will achieve economic prosperity faster and on its own terms (ERA, 2010).

In explaining African economic and business development strategy, in the global context, President Julius Nyerere of Tanzania once said that Africans must be responsible for their economic development within the global economic system. He recommended what he called a "stagnationist" dependent model to African development. The model encourages investors to come to the country but the country decides what should be done; its national priorities, and areas of investment. The core tenet of this approach is that the country itself becomes the center of development instead of starting from far away from the state. Development should be "home" grown and managed rather than having the experts from far away telling the country what to do and, in most cases, what these foreign experts propose does not work well and measure to the needs of the people of the country (Stieglitz, 2003). And that multinational Corporations investing in the African extractive industries should engage in vertical integration in processing the African raw materials to create value in Africa before export.

These arrangements will create other economic linkages to create more high value employment to deal with poverty in the continent. Some international companies are already doing that as Porter (2011) states in the following case in explaining the creation of Corporate Shared Value by companies. The concept of Corporate Shared value–as opposed to Corporate Social Responsibility-is defined as the policies and operational practices that enhance competitiveness of a company while simultaneously advancing positively the economic and social conditions in the communities in which it operates. Shared value creation focuses on identifying and expanding the connection between societal and economic process in companies (Porter, 2011).

In this regard, Porter asserts that Olam International, a leading cashew producer, traditionally shipped its nuts to Asia for processing at facilities staffed by skillful and productive Asian workers. But, by opening local processing plants and training workers in Tanzania, Mozambique, Nigeria, and Cote d'Ivore, Olam has cut processing and shipping costs by as much as 25%, not to mention the fact that it has greatly reduced carbon emissions. In making this move, Olam also built preferred relationships with local farmers. Through these investments, Olam International has provided direct and high value employment to 17,000 people, 95% of whom are women-and many indirect employment opportunities-through economic linkages and externalities in rural areas where jobs otherwise were not available.

Also, in discussing Africa in the global economy and the failures of the World Bank and IMF imposed policies on African economic development, Stiglitz (2003) states that international financial markets were at the root of the problem of African underdevelopment. World Bank and IMF recommended capital market liberalization strategies, privatization of government owned companies, and fiscal austerity did not bring people of Africa the prosperity they were promised. But they brought poverty and deprivation instead partly caused by wages falling by 20% or 30% and underemployment up by the factor of two, three, four, ten, depending on the country's resilience. The former IMF managing director, Camdessus concurs and states that "I obliged those African countries seeking IMF help to submit to major macroeconomic surgery when six aspirins could have brought the same result" (Stiglitz, 2003).

African regional integration and trade should considerably reduce African dependence on these useless preferences and externally created arrangements. In fact, Intra-regional trade remains one of the crucial pillars around which Africa's trade marginalization and foreign dependence can be effectively addressed (EAR, 2010). Effective regional integration and trade will allow the African countries to trade among themselves. This will enable them to assert their political and economic independence and be able to determine their economic destiny (Mbaku, 1998). As discussed in chapter five below, regional integration will allow African countries to create larger markets that will enable them produce diversified and competitive products and services destined for global markets.

In supporting regionalism as a basis of formulating a successful global trade strategy, Ghemawat (2005) states that regions matter in trade and business and argues that much has been made of the death of distance in recent years through communication technology. But when it comes to trade and business, distance still matters. Countries and companies must sill explicitly account for it when they make decisions about international trade and global expansion respectively. Therefore, traditional country portfolio analysis needs to be tempered by a clear-eyed evaluation of the many dimensions of distance and their probable impact on trade and business opportunities.

In foreign markets and global economy, distance between two countries can manifest itself along several dimensions and the type of distance influence different businesses in different ways. One of these dimensions is geographic proximity. But, before discussing African regional integration, as an element of geographic proximity; regional trade; enlargement of African markets; and the other dimensions of proximity–administrative, cultural, political, and economic-in Africa as key elements in African economic development and foundations of doing successful business in Africa, it is important to first examine Africa's global competitiveness and secondly the rising and compelling imperatives of doing business in Africa.

3. AFRICA IN GLOBAL COMPETIVENESS

In today's tough global economic environment, African governments–to grow and create employment to deal with poverty-should focus on increasing the competitive ability of their products and services in their domestic and global markets (Juma, 2011). The World Economic Forum has gleaned through the experiences of successfully exporting economies–particularly Germany, Singapore, and China, who have been leading exporters in recent years–to develop a framework to define competitiveness, identify competitive economies, and develop pillars of competitiveness that countries can build in order to be competitive in real time in global markets.

Competitiveness is the set of institutions, policies, and factors that determine the level of productivity of a country that enables the country to produce quality, low cost, and competitive products and services. The level of productivity, in turn, sets the sustainable level of prosperity that can be earned by the economy and produces higher levels of income for the country's citizens. It also earns a high return for the other factors of production. Because the rates of return of the factors of production are the fundamental drivers of the growth rates of the economy, a more competitive economy is one that is likely to grow faster in the medium and long run and thus bring prosperity to its citizens (World Economic Forum Report; 2010-2011).

Competitive economies are those that have in place factors that are driving the productivity enhancements on which their present and future prosperity–through the successful marketing of their products and services in global markets-is built. A competitiveness-supporting economic environment can help national economies to support high incomes and ensure that the mechanisms enabling solid economic performance going into the future are in place (World Economic Forum Report, 2010-2011).

According to the authors of the World Economic Forum Report 2010-2011, there are many determinants driving productivity and competitiveness in an economy. They have described these determinants as the twelve pillars of competitiveness.

The authors further assert that many of these pillars are nurtured by an economy itself. The African countries should ensure that they nurture these pillars in their economies as a means of producing competitive products and services. These pillars – they include education, innovation, and technology - are discussed in more details in chapter ten below.

Meanwhile, Porter and Rivkin (2012) have also discussed in great details factors and/or drivers that they think underpin the competitiveness of a nation. These are some of the factors which African countries can focus on to improve their global competitiveness. Porter and Rivkin assert that a country is competitive to the extent that its companies–or their products and services-are able to compete successfully in the global economy while supporting high and rising living standards for the average citizen back home. A global competitive location produces prosperity for both companies and citizens.

Whether a nation is competitive hinges instead on its long-run productivity. That is the value of goods and services produced per unit of human, capital, and natural resources in the long-run. Only by improving their ability to transform inputs into valuable products and services can companies in a country prosper while supporting rising wages for citizens. Increasing productivity in the country and in the long-run should, therefore, be the central goals of economic policy of a government. This also requires a business environment that nurtures and supports continual innovation in products, processes, and management practice.

The set of environmental factors that support productivity and hence competitiveness of a nation include its macro and micro components of the economy. From a macro perspective, a competitive nation requires sound monetary and fiscal policies–such as manageable government debt levels, low interest rates, and appropriate government expenditure; strong human development, good healthcare, and quality K-12 education systems; and effective political institutions such as the rule of law, reduced institutional bureaucracy, property rights, and effective law making bodies led by effective leaders who are always willing to build their nation and are able to increasingly build consensus and achieve comprise around critical national issues, such increasing employment creation, security and stability of the nation, adequate economic growth rates, and sustainable development.

The macro foundations create potential for long-term productivity improvement, but actual productivity depends on the microeconomic conditions that daily affect business itself. A competitive nation exhibits a sound business environment including modern transport and communication infrastructure, high-quality research institutions, streamlined regulations, sophisticated local consumers, and effective capital markets, as well as strong clusters of firms and supporting institutions in particular fields such as information technology. Competitive nations develop national companies/champions that adopt advanced operating and management practices led by effective leadership and strong governance to increasingly produce globally competitive products and services (Williams, 1997).

Currently, African economies are not competitive in the global markets because they have not built solid drivers of competitiveness and they basically produce raw materials for the world markets with little value added (Wang et al., 2008). All African economies and their entrepreneurs have to make global competitiveness a major strategic goal. This goal can be achieved through, among other drivers of competitiveness, economic diversification and sophistication to produce high value added products from their abundant raw materials. No country, however how much raw materials it produces, can hope to survive and succeed, in the world today, unless it innovates and upgrades its business models, ads increasing value to its primary and raw materials, and it operates beyond the standards set by the leaders in their fields in the world (Drucker, 1999).

The implication here is that it is no longer possible to base a business and economic development in Africa only on cheap labor and raw materials. Higher labor productivity–through education, knowledge, and technology–is going to be critical in producing quality products and services at competitive prices-as a result of economies of scale and learning curve effects–to enable Africa to be competitive in global markets. Better education and knowledge increase the stock of human capital in the economy, improve the efficiency of the work force, and raise aggregate productivity that does not only reduce cost but also increase the quality of products and services produced making them competitive in global markets (Kamara et al., 2008).

There are world experiences Africans can learn from. Asian countries, particularly Singapore, Indonesia, China, and India, have vigorously pursued and focused on productivity improvement strategies. These countries have been phenomenally successful in global markets by producing quality and low cost products and services. Countries in Latin America, like Mexico that did not pursue this strategy–Mexico was inward looking for decades–early in its development hindered it from being a noticeable global player and suffered for it in foregone or delayed economic development, despite being a neighbor to the USA, the richest and most developed economy and strongest consumer market in the world.

In this case of Mexico, for seventy years, from 1929 to 1999, the country had a deliberate policy of building its own domestic economy independent of the outside world (Drucker, 1999). It did this not only by building high walls of protectionism to keep foreign competition out, but it also did it by practically forbidding its own companies from exporting. Such extreme protectionist measures were unique to Mexico. This attempt, however, to create a modern but purely Mexican economy failed dismally. Mexico actually became increasingly dependent on imports, both of food and manufactured products, from the outside world. It was finally forced to open itself up to the outside world since it simply could no longer pay for the needed imports. Eventually, Mexico found that a good deal of its industry could not survive, let alone compete globally. Moreover, this inward looking and protectionist policy did not assist Mexico in gaining benefits from its economically and politically strong neighbor, the United States, until the formation of the North American Free Trade Area (NAFTA) in 1994 (Wild et al., 2008).

Similarly, the Japanese tried to protect the bulk of their businesses and industry by keeping global companies out of its domestic market. However, the country created a small but exceedingly competitive number of export industries, and then provided these industries with cheap capital, thus giving them a tremendous competitive advantage in the world markets for some time. That policy failed as well. The 1990's crisis of anemic growth in Japan, which has persisted to the present day, is in large part the result of the inability of Japan to make its businesses and industry globally competitive by opening its economy to outsiders (Drucker, 1999).

These examples of successful policies and failed inward looking policies in other parts of the world serve as a stark and powerful lesson to African countries as they strive for systematic and tangible economic development and their participation in the global economy. African countries have to accept a new reality and fundamental approach that is strong on increased global competitiveness in manufacturing and technology and weak on protectionism. To be successful in tackling this challenge, African nations and their institutions have to work really hard and measure themselves against the standards set by global leaders any place in the world (Black et al., 2010). Africa's abundance of human and environmental resources will give it a competitive advantage in the global markets when these resources are applied correctly to improve its productivity and thus its global competitiveness.

REFERENCES

AGOA. (2009). *AGOA annual report*. Washington, DC: Department of Commerce.

Black, J. S., & Morrison, J. A. (2010, September). A cautionary tale for emerging market giants: How ethnocentric leadership in corporate japan knocked its companies off the world stage. *Harvard Business Review*.

Clinton, W. J. (2011). *Back to work: Why we need smart government for a strong economy*. New York: Alfred A. Knopf.

Copeland, M. J., & Schuster, C. P. (2006). *Global business practices: Adapting for success*. Washington, DC: Thomson.

Cullen, J. B., & Parboteeah, P. K. (2008). *Multinational management: A strategic approach* (4th ed.). Atlanta, GA: Thomson.

Drucker, P. F. (1999). *Management challenges for the 21st century*. New York: Harper Business.

EIU. (2009). *African economic and business report*. London: Economist Intelligent Unit.

ERA. (2010). *Economic report on africa*. Addis Ababa, Ethiopia: African Union Commission.

Friedman, T. L. (2005). *The world is flat: A brief history of the 21st century*. New York: Farrar, Straus, and Giroux.

Friedman, T. L., & Mandelbaum, M. (2011). *That used to be us: How america fell behind in the world it invented and how we can come back*. New York: Farrar, Straus, and Giroux.

Ghemawat, P. (2001, September). Distance still matters: Hard realities of global expansion. *Harvard Business Review*.

Ghemawat, P. (2005, December). Regional strategies for global leadership. *Harvard Business Review*.

Ghemawat, P. (2010, March). Finding your strategy in the new landscape. *Harvard Business Review*.

Giddens, A. (2002). *The transformation of intimacy*. Stanford, CA: Stanford University Press.

Juma, C. (2011). *The new harvest: Agricultural innovation in africa*. Oxford, UK: Oxford University Press.

Kamara, A. B., Bousrih, L., & Nyende, M. (2008). Growing a knowledge based economy: Evidence from public expenditure on education in africa. *African Development Bank Economic Research Working Paper Series*. Abidjan, Cote d'Ivoire: African Development Bank.

Mbaku, J. M. (1998). Emerging trade blocks and the fortune of african participation in the world economy. *Journal of Economic Integration, 10*(2).

Mbaku, J. M. (2004). *Institutions and development in africa*. Trenton, NJ: Africa World Press.

Moyo, D. (2008). *A small price to pay: Financing africa's infrastructure bill. Global Economics Paper No: 174*. New York: Goldman Sachs.

Moyo, D. (2009). *Dead aid, Why aid is not working and how there is a better way for africa*. New York: Farrar, Straus, and Giroux.

Porter, M. E. (1998). Novemeber). Cluster and the new economics of competition. *Harvard Business Review*.

Porter, M. E., & Kramer, M. R. (2011a, January). Capitalism is under siege. *Harvard Business Review*, (January-February): 2011.

Porter, M. E., & Kramer, M. R. (2011a, February). Business is caught in a vicious circle. *Harvard Business Review*.

Porter, M. E., & Kramer, M. R. (2011b, January). Diminished trust in business is causing political leaders to set policies that sap economic growth. *Harvard Business Review*.

Porter, M. E., & Kramer, M. R. (2011b, February). The purpose of the corporation must be redefined around creating Shared Value. *Harvard Business Review*.

Porter, M. E., & Rivkin, J. W. (2012, March). The looming challenge to U.S. competitiveness. *Harvard Business Review*.

Sachs, J. (2005). *End of poverty: The economic possibilities for our times*. New York: Penguin Books.

Stiglitz, J. (2003). *Globalization and its discontents*. New York: W. W. Norton and Company.

Wang, M., Garner, J. F., & Silver, V. (2008). *GEMs equity strategy: Sub-saharan africa. Improved Fundamentals Priced Near Term*. New York: Morgan Stanley.

WEF. (2011). *The world economic forum report*. Davos, Switzerland: The World Economic Forum.

Wild, J. J., Wild, K. L., & Han, J. C. Y. (2008). *International Business* (4th ed.). Upper Saddle River, NJ: Pearson.

Williamson, P. J. (1997, September). Asia's new competitive game. *Harvard Business Review*.

Chapter 4
The Rising and Compelling Imperatives to do Business in Africa

ABSTRACT

This chapter identifies and describes the current rising and compelling imperatives of doing business in Africa. It defines Africa's market attractiveness and the African Gross Domestic Product (GDP)—the sum of the value of goods and services that a nation produces in a year—and the Purchasing Power Parity (PPP) both as measures of market size and market intensity in the African economies. It also outlines the origins of the concept of PPP, its uses together with GDP, and the strengths and the limitations of the PPP as a currency exchange rate determinant and as a market size and market intensity measure, hence business opportunities.

1. WHY LOOK INTO AFRICA FOR BUSINESS OPPORTUNITIES?

Many people from outside Africa picture her as a continent of poor and hungry people. People over burdened by cyclic civil wars and diseases, and with subsistence farmers unable to produce enough food leading to chronic hunger and pervasive poverty. However, in reality, there is a sizable and flourishing middle class on the continent. By 2008, 16 million African households had incomes above $20,000 a year – a level that enabled them to buy houses, cars, appliances, and branded

DOI: 10.4018/978-1-4666-4570-7.ch004

products. Another 27 million households earned $10,000 to $20,000. In addition, 41 million households reported incomes of $5,000 to $10,000 – the level at which families start spending more than half of their income on non-food items.

Furthermore, it is estimated that by 2020 the total number of households in all the three segments will reach 128 million households. This trend in household income makes Africa one of the fastest growing consumer markets of this decade (Chironga et al., 2011). Therefore, there is a huge business potential in Africa that is dissipating in other parts of the world particularly in the developed world.

Meanwhile, when commenting on business and market potential for products and services in Africa, Ian Goldin, a professor of business at Oxford University, recently told a business forum in Nairobi, Kenya, that the African middle class is 300 million people today. But, by the year 2050 it will number one billion people who will represent a greatly increased purchasing power. Africa is the only region of the world today where birthrates are above the population replacement rates. Africa's population is the fastest growing of all the continents and it has the youngest well-educated work force in the world today. Notably, income inequality on the continent is going down too even as it rises in the rest of the world. Therefore, Africa is the best region to invest in and do business today (Straziuso, 2012).

Furthermore, at an African Growth Opportunity Act (AGOA)—see Chapter Six—forum in Washington, DC, recently, then US Secretary of State, Hillary Clinton, asserted that Africa was a region of great potential and growing opportunities. She vehemently continued to say: *"I want all of my fellow American citizens, particularly our business community and entrepreneurs, to hear and appreciate this fact: Africa offers the highest rate of return on foreign direct investment of any developing region in the world today"* (www.bbc.com, *June 14, 2012)*.

Kristof (2012) asserts further that generations of Americans have learned to pity Africa. It is mainly seen as a quagmire of famine, poverty, and genocide, a destination only for a sybaritic safari or a masochistic aid mission. However, I offer an alternative way to think of Africa: Africa is an economic dynamo. It is time to prepare for the African tiger economy. Six of the world's 10 fastest-growing economies between 2001 and 2010 were in Africa, according to The Economist Magazine. The International Monetary Fund says that between 2011 and 2015, African countries will account for 7 of the top 10 spots in the fasted growing economies in the world. Africa is not just a place for safaris or humanitarian aid. It is also a place to do business and make good money for stakeholders.

Some major global companies are expanding their business ventures into Africa. F*or example, Wal-Mart bought Massmart of South Africa for $2.4 billion in 2011. Massmart operates in 13 African countries and growing steadily in the continent*; Massmart will enable Wall-Market to be competitive in many African economies now and in the future. Vast deposits of oil, gas, and minerals are being discovered and converted into products and services in the domestic economy through value additions causing Goldman Sachs to recently issue a report, "Africa's Turn," comparing business opportunities in Africa with those in China in the early 1990s, when China laid down a strong foundation of its overwhelming and phenomenal growth rates in the start of the 21st century.

Still, one of the more interesting market opportunities in Africa currently resides in what the International Finance Corporation (IFC), a World Bank department that promotes private investments in developing and emerging markets, and several academics have termed the "Base of the Pyramid" (BOP). The concept of the "Base of the Pyramid" has been persuasively articulated by C.K. Prahalad (2005 and 2010), a former management and strategy professor at Michigan University.

The notion of the base of the pyramid describes those at the bottom of the consumer pyramid in every country. They are poor by any western poverty line, but by their sheer numbers—estimated to be 5 billion people, in the world today, with a purchasing power of over $ 13 trillion—still constitute a significant purchasing power and market opportunity for corporations globally (Prahalad, 2005).

Scholars (Prahalad, 2005, 2010; Porter et al., 2011) have looked at the BOP as a viable and profitable growth market. They have made it understood that targeting the BOP can lead to poverty eradication, particularly if NGOs, governments, and community groups join with Multinational Corporations and local companies as business partners by getting out of their current dominant logic of disregarding those at the bottom of the pyramid. The development of markets and effective models at the BOP can transform the poverty alleviation task from one of constant struggle with subsidies and aid to that of large and widespread entrepreneurship leading to a generation of wealth that will enhance the BOP market opportunities further.

In Sub-Saharan Africa (SSA), the IFC and the academics currently estimate the BOP market at $429 billion, representing the region's dominant consumer market segment, with 71% of the aggregate purchasing power in the region. Even in South Africa, Africa's largest and most modern economy, the BOP constitutes 75% of the economy. Other countries in the region offering even larger BOP market opportunities are Ethiopia $84 billion and Nigeria $74 billion (Moyo, 2009; AER, 2010; Prahalad, 2010; Juma, 2011).

Doing business in Africa presents unique opportunities in many other important ways. Africa is rich in natural resources, skilled and low cost labor, making it most likely cheaper to do business in the continent than in many other regions of the world (Mahajan, 2009). In the emerging markets, particularly those of Africa, there are growing and educated populations, rising incomes, more urbanization, and increasing trade. These factors and any inconveniences experienced in Africa drive the need for more products and services and every firm—domestic and global—should position itself to take advantage of them (Fortune, 2009).

The continent is aggressively reforming its institutions to make it easier to do business. The macroeconomic factors of the African countries are improving to make them better markets. The African GDP grew consistently at 6 percent, on average, as compared to 3 percent in world growth in the last five years (World Bank 2007 World Economic Growth Report). GDP growth was a positive 2 percent while it was negative in many other regions of the world in 2009, the year with the lowest world growth after the world economic meltdown. The African Development Bank estimates that the African GDP grew at 7.5 percent in 2010. Inflation rates are decreasing and are expected to remain at single digit, in many African countries, in the near future (EIU September 2009).

At the same time, African countries have made genuine progress in reining in deficits, as well as selling off bloated state enterprises to private investors – creating business opportunities for corporations in the African countries. Of course, the measures taken have been uneven and there is a long way to go in every country, but it is indisputable that Adam Smith's invisible hand philosophy is wining the day in African markets (Garten, 1997).

Therefore, Africa presents exciting business opportunities to the world. Again, outside troubled countries such as Somalia, Sudan, Congo DR, and Zimbabwe, Mali, and Chad, there is a healthy economic growth to explore and take advantage of among many African countries. In addition, according to the World Bank 2007 country report, GDP in each of the 14 sub-Saharan African countries has consistently grown by at least 5% a year since the mid-1990s as compared to 3% world growth.

Botswana and South Africa have long topped "best African business environment" charts. Since Uganda started to improve its business environment, in the early 1990s, private investment, as a share of GDP, has more than doubled (Afdb 2009 Annual Report). Some foreign investors and observers point to a drop in petty corruption and better courts in important countries such as Nigeria (EIU 2009). All these changes should make Africa an attractive business environment.

Still, in 2006/2007 alone, 24 African countries implemented 49 reforms, which have made it simpler to start and do business in these countries. They have strengthened property rights, enhanced investor protection, increased access to credit, and eased tax burdens. They are improving their infrastructure, are determined in dealing with corruption, and expedited trade while reducing costs of doing business.

In "Doing Business 2008," the fifth in an annual series of reports issued by the World Bank and the International Finance Corporation, two African countries—Ghana and Kenya—ranked among the top 10 reformers worldwide who have made the most significant advances in the aggregate ease of doing business in the world. Ghana has also made peaceful transitions in government over the years and the last one being 2008 elections.

Accelerated technological advances, in developed countries, have also substantially improved industrial productivity and have allowed suppliers to produce an unprecedented array of products and services. The result is that, in an increasing number of industries, in these countries, supply exceeds demand, with excess supply that needs new markets like those of Africa (Kim et al., 2005). The trend toward globalization also compounds the supply and demand problem, accelerating the need to open up new markets in Africa.

As trade barriers between other nations and regions of the world are dismantled and as information on products, services, and their prices become increasingly instant and globally available, niche markets and havens for monopoly continue to disappear, increasing competitive pressures in existing advanced markets. Empirical evidence indicates that the desire for emerging markets, including African markets, is similarly intensifying (Kim et al., 2005; Mahajan, 2009).

While supply is on the rise as global competition intensifies, there is no clear evidence of an increase in demand in other parts of the world, and statistics even point to declining populations in developed markets. But, in Africa, statistical evidence indicates that the population is rising and demand for products and services is increasing annually creating new and expanding markets in the continent (Mahajan, 2009).

The result of advanced technology in supply and demand has accelerated commoditization of products and services, increasing price wars, and shrinking profit margins in existing developed markets. Recent industry wide studies on major American brands confirm this trend (Kim et al., 2005). These studies reveal that for major product and service categories, brands are generally becoming more similar, and as their similarities increase, people increasingly select products and services based on price. Price competition makes survival of firms difficult creating a need for new markets, to survive, for example in Africa and elsewhere in the world. Therefore, existing developed markets, including Chinese markets, are becoming tight and congested needing opening up and developing new global markets particularly in Africa where incomes and population are rising.

Garten (1997) asserts that companies in the industrialized world depend on overseas markets for both economies of scale and increasing profits. The countries in the developed world want high value jobs at home—for their citizens—that come with expanding exports. And many pension-plan investors are banking on the high returns that result from investing in the developing world. Africa provides such opportunities to the developed world corporations, pension-plan funds, and to the developed countries themselves generally, as an economic frontier of the 21st century.

Despite its substantial natural resource endowment, it could be wrong to view Africa as simply a warrant on commodities. Even with the impact of diseases, Africa has a favorable demographic profile in the world. The share of the educated working age population in Africa is set to accelerate over the next four to five decades according to the UN, compared to a declining trend for the rest of the world. A rising working age population has some important implications for growth, consumption, and eventual development of end-user consumer markets.

Therefore, Africa has one of the fastest growing middle class populations with an increasingly strong demand for consumer goods in the world today, for both perishables and durables. As mentioned earlier, it is estimated that there are over 300 million middle class Africans within its population today growing at 2.5 percent annually (Mahajan, 2009). These people need to be supplied with goods and services hence the rising and compelling imperative to do business in Africa to satisfy this fast growing market.

Furthermore, and because of increased African regional integration and trade, that is increasing market sizes, entry into one Central, Western, and Eastern, Northern, and Southern African country often grants easy access to numerous other countries in the region, as it currently happens in the European Union. Harmonization of regulations, customs duties, banking laws, trade laws, and currencies is already in place in all these regions; changes that are enlarging and enhancing African markets and thus increasing the imperatives of doing business in Africa (Mahajan, 2009).

In 1999, Kofi Annan—the former UN Secretary General—argued that Africa's profitability is one of the best-kept secrets in today's world economy. Africa's dilapidated image acted as a protective guardian and ensured that only the most daring investors ventured south of the Sahara. But the protective guardian has now been unveiled and Africa is clearly exposed and immensely attractive to global companies and non-for-profit organizations for business (Annan, 1999).

As Annan asserts above, doing business in Africa has always been perceived as a challenging and complex undertaking. The reasons being: the numerous processes associated with conducting business, combined with a fragile investment climate, small markets, political instability, institutional voids, corruption, and inadequate infrastructure. But, with decreasing and fewer conflicts, more democratic elections, concerted institutional reforms—Rwanda, Kenya, and Ghana were described by the World Bank as the top reformers in 2007—increasing regional integration, and economic growth rates that gradually have begun to compete with those of other emerging markets—Brazil, Russia, India, and China—Africa is proving itself again as a continent of positive change and an attractive market with many business opportunities to exploit and make money for stakeholders (Mahajan, 2009).

As described in chapter five below, many African countries have growing Gross Domestic Products (GDP) and Purchasing Power Parity (PPP), both of which support the potential and opportunities of doing business in Africa. The graphical presentation below further indicates that the average African GDP and PPP per capita will grow to approximately \$ 4200 and \$ 5800 respectively by the year 2020.

Gross Domestic Product (GDP) is the total value of goods and services produced by a country in a year as opposed to Gross National Product (GNP) which is also the total value of goods and services produced by a country in a year but it includes the country's international transactions. They both indicate—particularly the GDP/GNP per capita—the economic health and development of a country and the attractiveness of the market (See Figure 1).

The Purchasing Power Parity (PPP), as described below, is also an important measure of the health and well-being of an economy in terms of market and sales potential. Total Purchasing Power Parity indicates the size and intensity of the market.

Research data further indicate that companies that choose new markets systematically often use GDP and PPP as the size of the market and the potential profit from doing business in developing countries and emerging markets like those of Africa (Khanna et al., 2005). In 2004, McKinsey Global Survey of Business Executives established that 61% of the executives in the survey said that market size and growth measured by GDP and GDP per capita income and PPP growth rates and population composition and growth rates, and the country's exchange rates, drove their firms' decisions to enter new countries. While 17% felt that political and economic stability was the most important factor in making those decisions, only 13% said that structural conditions, in other words, the institutional context, mattered most. To complete the picture, managers considered the nation's standing on the world Economic Forum's Global competitiveness index, the World Bank's governance

Figure 1. African GDP and PPP per capita 2010 – 2020
Source: http://www.africaneconomicoutlook.org and author's estimates

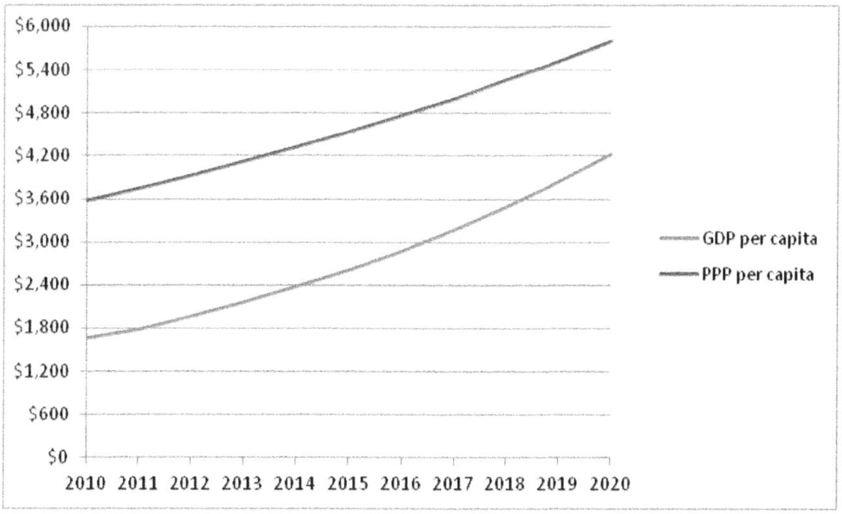

indicators, and Transparency International's corruption rating; its weight in emerging markets funds investments; and, perhaps, forecasts of its next political transition (Khannan et al., 2005).

Indeed GDP, PPP, and the population growth rates are the key measures of the market size and form the basis of the firms' market entry decisions. African Development Bank estimates that African GDP and PPP will grow at 7.5% in 2010 and thereafter—against the world economic growth rate in 2010 of 3.1%, predicted by the IMF—and that the African population will hit a billion at the end of 2009 (The East African, 2009). These facts, among other factors discussed in-here, increase the rising and compelling imperatives of doing business in Africa as a new business frontier of the 21st century. Other strategies that will allow Africa to effectively participate in the global economy and hence increase its business attractiveness and opportunities include:

- Africa should speedily develop regional trading blocs as pillars of the African economic union. These trading blocs should significantly increase the size of African markets and improve the latter's viability to allow domestic industrialization to effectively exploit technological economies of scale and add value to Africa's abundant raw materials. In addition, regional markets will increase the area within which infant industries can be provided assistance they need to develop and become competitive and thus enable the continent to participate fully in the global economy, and of course, create high value jobs and wealth to eliminate chronic poverty in the continent. Increase of wealth and elimination of poverty increase business opportunities through consumer growth;
- Africans should work together to ensure social and political stability in the whole of Africa as a foundation for successful regional integration and a suitable climate for business. On the other hand, increase the democratic process in Africa and the development of institutions that maximize popular participation of the people and businesses in the development of the continent;
- Finally, economic and human development and welfare should be the basis of regional integration than mere economic growth, which is just increase in numbers like GDP per capita that do not tell the whole story and the actual welfare of the people involved. Development, as opposed to growth, however, emphasizes poverty alleviation, the reduction of inequities in income distribution, improvements in human capital, and innovation; all these will obviously enhance African competitiveness. Some of the other important measures and indicators of economic development of a country and hence its business attractiveness include:

- Life expectance rates;
- Changes in infant mortality rates;
- Physicians per population;
- Ease of communication within the country and the region;
- School enrolment rates;
- Urbanization versus rural population ratio;
- Other income and social indicators, which can reveal the efficacy of income distribution in the country;
- To be included in all these measures are the purchasing power parity measures.

2. THE THEORY OF THE PURCHASING POWER PARITY

Purchasing Power Parity (PPP) is the idea that, in the long run, identical products and services in different countries should cost the same in those different countries. This is based on the belief that exchange rates will adjust to eliminate the arbitrage opportunity of buying a product or service in one country and selling it in another (Lafrance et al. 2002; Wild et al. 2008).

The Purchasing Power Parity (PPP) is important in understanding the size, growth, and intensity of African product and service markets. The PPP concepts—described in greater detail below and more in chapter five—can be used to estimate African market sizes and intensity hence the economic opportunities of doing business in Africa. The PPP compares what people earn and spend in real terms in their domestic economies (Wild et al., 2008).

For example, under the Purchasing Power Parity (PPP) valuation of Gross Domestic Product (GDP) of a nation, the Chinese economy will expand from $11.2 trillion this year to $19.0 trillion in 2016. Meanwhile the size of the U.S. economy will rise from $15.2 trillion this year to $18.8 trillion in 2016. That would take America's share of the world output down to 17.7%, the lowest in modern times. China's world output would reach 18% and rising and expected to overtake the USA economy by 2025 (Arends, 2011). The African economies are in toe.

2.1. Further Concepts on the Purchasing Power Parity

Purchasing power is the value of goods and services that can be purchased with one unit of a country's currency. Purchasing Power Parity is the relative ability of two countries' currencies to buy the same "basket" of goods or services in those two countries (Lafrance et al., 2002). Therefore, purchasing power parity can be used to determine the exchange rate of two countries' currencies and their market size.

Purchasing power parity is a criterion for an appropriate exchange rate between currencies. PPP is a rate such that a representative basket of goods in country A costs the same as in country B if the currencies are exchanged at that rate. It is the equality of the prices of a bundle of goods in two countries when valued at the prevailing exchange rate. It is also the economic theory linking currency exchange rates to prices paid for goods and services in any two countries (Laflance et al., 2002; Wild et al., 2008).

For example, if a basket of goods can be bought with a $1,000 in the United States or 150,000 Yen in Japan, the parity of the U.S. Dollar to the yen is 1-to-150. If either currency has greater purchasing power, the theory goes, it might be better for buyers to convert yen into dollars, for instance, and buy in the United States to sell in Japan. Another example, consider a laptop computer that costs 1,500 Euros in Germany and an exchange rate of 2 Euros to 1 US Dollar. If the same laptop costs 1,000 dollars in the United States, U S consumers would exchange dollars for Euros and buy the laptop in Germany at an equivalent of 750 dollars. If done on a large scale, the influx of U.S. dollars would drive up the price of the Euro, until it is equalized at 1.5 Euros to 1 U.S. Dollar – the same ratio of the price of the laptop in Germany to the price of the laptop in the U.S. The theory applies to tradable goods and assumes low transportation costs.

The Purchasing power parity also allows comparison of the standard of living between countries by taking into account the impact of their exchange rates. Actual exchange rates, however, vary from the PPP levels for various reasons, such as the price level of products and service, and the demand for imports or investments between countries. Yet, PPP states that economic forces will push the actual market exchange rate toward the one determined by purchasing power parity. If they do not, profitable arbitrage opportunities would arise which would make market exchange rate to be in equilibrium with PPP determined exchange rates (Laflance et al., 2002; Wild et al., 2008).

The Purchasing Power Parity (PPP) theory uses the long-term equilibrium exchange rate of two currencies to equalize their purchasing power. Developed by Gustav Cassel in 1918, it is based on the law of one price (Cassel 1918): the theory states that, in ideally efficient markets, identical goods or services should have one price in two markets. The theory further states that the exchange rate between one currency and another is in equilibrium when their domestic purchasing powers at that rate of exchange are equivalent. The theory only applies to tradable goods, not to immobile goods or local goods and services. The theory also discounts several real world factors in exchange, such as transportation costs, tariffs, and transaction costs. It also assumes that there are competitive markets for the goods and services in both countries (Kemp, 1993; Lafrance et al., 2002).

Therefore, and since the price for any one good or service should be equal across markets, the price for any combination of baskets of goods or services should be equal across markets too. It is important to note that purchasing power parity only holds true for internationally traded products and services that are not restricted by trade barriers and that entail few or no transportation costs and therefore can easily be transferred from one market to the other as economic conditions change and according to arbitrage principles (Laflance et al., 2002).

The term arbitrage refers to a trading strategy in which an investor simultaneously buys and sells the same asset – currency and commodities – in different markets at different prices to earn an instant and risk-free profit. For example, supposing a currency trader learns that in New York she can exchange $ 2 for 1 Sterling Pound, but in London 1 Sterling Pound will buy $1.90. If the investor is smart enough she will recognize that there is a profit opportunity here. She will convert Sterling Pounds into dollars in New York and buy Sterling Pounds in London (Smart et al., 2007).

2.2. Purchasing Power Parity and Baseball Bats

Another example of purchasing power parity is illustrated using the buying and selling of baseball bats between Mexico and the USA (Kemp 1993; Smart et al. 2007). Suppose that one U.S. Dollar (USD) is currently selling for ten Mexican Pesos (MXN) on the foreign exchange rate market? In the United States, wooden baseball bats sell for US$40, while in Mexico they sell for 150 pesos. Since currently 1 USD is equal to 10 MXN, then the bat costs US$40 if we buy it in the U.S. but only US$15 if we buy it in Mexico.

Clearly there is an arbitrage advantage to buying the bats in Mexico; so consumers are much better off going to Mexico to buy their bats assuming there is no transportation costs and no trade barriers between the USA and Mexico that might cause prices to go up when bats are bought in Mexico and transported to the USA. In a free market regime, if consumers decide to do this, we should expect to see four things happen:

- American consumers' desire for Mexican Pesos in order to buy baseball bats in Mexico. So they will go to an exchange rate office and sell their American Dollars and buy Mexican Pesos. This will cause the Mexican Peso to become more valuable relative to the U.S. Dollar;
- The demand for baseball bats sold in the United States decreases, so the price American retailers charge goes down;
- The demand for baseball bats sold in Mexico increases, so the price Mexican retailers charge goes up;
- This will go on until the price of bats in the United States and the ones of Mexico will eventually move to equality;

Eventually these four factors should cause the exchange rates and the prices in the two countries to change such that we have purchasing power parity. If the U.S. Dollar declines in value to 1 USD equals to 8 MXN, the price of baseball bats in the United States goes down to $30 each and the price of baseball bats in Mexico goes up to 240 pesos each, we will have purchasing power parity. This is because a consumer can spend $30 in the United States for a baseball bat, or he can take his $30, exchange it for 240 pesos (since 1 USD = 8 MXN) and buy a baseball bat in Mexico and be no better off. Purchasing power parity is also affected by changes in inflation and interest rates of the two countries, since the changes in the two elements affect the price of bats in the two countries negatively or positively depending on the direction of the change.

2.3. Purchasing Power Parity and the Long Run

Purchasing-power parity theory tells us that price differentials between countries are not sustainable in the long run as market forces will equalize prices between countries and change exchange rates in doing so (Kemp, 1993; Laflance et al., 2002; Smart et al., 2007). You might think that the example of consumers crossing the border to buy baseball bats is unrealistic, as the expense of the longer trip would wipe out any savings you get from buying the bat for a lower price.

But, it is not unrealistic to imagine an individual or company buying hundreds or thousands of the bats in Mexico then shipping them to the United States for sale. It is also not unrealistic to imagine a store like Wal-Mart purchasing bats from the lower cost manufacturer in Mexico instead of the higher cost manufacturer in Mexico. In the long run, having different prices in the United States and Mexico is not sustainable because an individual or company will be able to gain an arbitrage profit by buying the goods cheaply in one market and selling it for a higher price in the other more expensive market, all things being the same.

2.4. Purchasing Power Parity Applications

It is attempted, here; to give the applications of the PPP concepts because PPP is one of those ideas that will constantly appear throughout the book. PPP has three main applications: as a theory of exchange rate determination, as a means to compare living standards across countries, and as a means to measure and compare the sophistication of consumers among countries and hence the intensity and potential of a market in a country or a region. A living standard, in this case, is a quality of life or the fulfillment of life one experiences in a certain country through his ability to buy a basket of goods or services using that country's one unity of its currency (Wild et al., 2008).

Concerning exchange rate determination, PPP is mainly useful as a reminder that monetary policy has no long-run impact on the real exchange rate, since the exchange rate can deviate persistently from its PPP value in response to real shocks in the product and service markets. To compare living standards, the intensity of the market, and sophistication of consumers across countries, Purchasing Power Parity exchange rates constructed by comparing the prices of national consumption baskets of goods are used to translate per capita national incomes into a common currency and its purchasing power (Laflance et al., 2002).

2.5. Weaknesses of the Purchasing Power Parity Concepts

The purchasing power parity rates are useful because they offset differences in national price levels to obtain comparable measures of purchasing power and hence living standards, sophistication of consumers and market intensity. These measures can be translated into market opportunities for products and services. Many estimates have it that PPP in Africa is expected to grow at 5.2 percent per annum and therefore making the continent potentially attractive to global companies particularly as African regional integration intensifies too that enlarges the markets (Afdb 2010).

The main reasons why PPP measures may not perfectly reflect standards of living, exchange rates, and market intensity are: PPP numbers can vary with the specific basket of goods used, making it a rough estimate of these elements. Differences in the quality of goods are hard to measure and thereby reflect in PPP. It is only applicable to internationally traded goods and services. Therefore, it may not exactly and appropriately measure the cost of products between countries and accurately reflect the exchange rates between currencies particularly if non-internationally tradable goods are a large proportion of goods consumed in a country. Furthermore, cost of transportation, transaction costs, and tariffs are ignored or minimized in PPP analysis, which removes realism from the analysis. PPP also assumes that there are competitive markets for the basket of goods and services used in PPP analysis in both countries, which may not always be the case (Wild et al., 2008). However, PPP is one of the best tools or measures we have to compare the economic performance of countries including African countries and their business potential.

REFERENCES

AFDB. (2009). *African development bank annual economic report*. Tunis, Tunisia: AFDB.

AFDB. (2010). *African development bank (AFDB) annual economic report*. Tunis, Tunisia: AFDB.

Calestous, J. (2011). *The new harvest: Agricultural innovation in Africa*. Oxford, UK: Oxford University Press.

Chan, K. W., & Renee, M. (2005). *Blue ocean strategy: How to create uncontested market space and make the competition irrelevant*. Boston: Harvard Business School Press.

EIU. (2009). *African economic and business report*. London: The Economic Intelligence Unit.

Garter, J. (1997, September-October). Troubles ahead in emerging markets. *Harvard Business Review*.

IFC. (2009). *The bottom of the pyramid (BOP) report, 2009*. Washington, DC: IFC.

ILO. (2009). *Global employment trends*. Geneva, Switzerland: ILO.

IMF. (2009). *2009 regional economic outlook, Sub-Saharan Africa*. Washington, DC: IMF.

Kempe, R. H. (1997). Development structures for Africa: The need for policy reform and good governance. *Journal of Opinion*, *25*(1).

Kristof, N. D. (2012, June 30). Africa on the rise. *New York Times*.

Lafrance, R., & Schembri, L. (2002). *Purchasing-power parity: Definition, measurement, and interpretation*. Ottawa, Canada: International Department, Bank of Canada.

Mahajan, V. (2009). *Africa rising: How 900 million African consumers offer more than you think*. Amazon Kindle.

Manning, P. (1990). *Slavery and African life: Occidental, oriental, and African slave trades*. New York: Cambridge University Press.

Moyo, D. (2009). *Dead aid: Why aid is not working and how there is a better way for Africa*. New York: Farrar, Straus, and Giroux.

Mutsa, C., Acha, L., & van Wamelen, A. (2011). *Checking the next growth market: Africa*. Boston: Harvard Business School Publishing.

Porter, M. E., & Kramer, M. R. (2011, January-February). Capitalism is under siege: Diminished trust in business is causing political leaders to set policies that sap economic growth: Business is caught in a vicious circle: The purpose of the corporation must be redefined around creating shared value. *Harvard Business Review*.

Prahalad, C. K. (2005). *The fortune at the bottom of the pyramid (BOP): Eradicating poverty through profits: Enabling dignity and choice through markets*. Philadelphia: Wharton School Publishing.

Prahalad, C. K., & Meshelkar, R. A. (2010, July-August). Innovation's holy grail. *Harvard Business Review*. PMID:20648874.

Smart, S. B., Megginson, W. L., & Gitman, L. J. (2007). *Corporate finance* (2nd ed.). Thomson Western.

Straziuso, J. (2012, October 7). Africa sees hotels rise with its economic gains. *The Philadelphia Inquirer*.

Tarun, K., & Krishna, P. G. (2005, May). Strategies for emerging markets. *Harvard Business Review*.

Wild, J. J., Wild, K. L., & Han, J. C. Y. (2008). *International business* (4th ed.). Englewood Cliffs, NJ: Pearson.

World Bank. (2007). *World economic report, report by the world, 2007*. Retrieved from www.bbc.com

Chapter 5
The African Regional Integration and Trading Blocs

ABSTRACT

This chapter is perhaps the most important and significant chapter in the book. This is because of the great importance attached to increasing regional integration and trade as an enlargement of regional markets. The chapter focuses on the perspectives of international trade as a foundation for regional integration, regional integration schemes and their processes, and the African regional integration and its regional trading blocs. The trading blocs are meant to enlarge African markets and to be pillars and building blocks of the African economic community. The chapter also examines the importance of proximities—geographic, economic, political, and administrative—in helping to promote regional trade. Regional trade has grown faster than international trade in the last five decades, and successful regional trading countries are the wealthiest in the world today. Those with low or limited regional trade—like countries in the African and the Middle East regions—are the poorest countries today. The seven major African trading blocs are fully described in the chapter.

DOI: 10.4018/978-1-4666-4570-7.ch005

1. INTERNATIONAL TRADE THEORY AND PERSPECTIVES AS A BASIS FOR REGIONAL INTEGRATION IN AFRICA

Regional integration and regional trade agreements—meant to create regional trading blocs and bigger markets—are accelerating and changing the landscape of the global marketplace today (Han et al., 2008). The process whereby countries, in a geographic region, cooperate to eliminate barriers to engagement, the flow of products, services, people, and capital, among themselves, is called regional integration and trade (Wild et al., 2008).

A group of nations in a geographic region undertaking regional integration is called a regional trading bloc. The goal of regional integration and trade is not only to increase markets and cross-border trade, flow of people, increased employment, and investment, but also to considerably improve the living standards of the people of the countries involved in the integration and the trade process through creation of high value jobs (Wild et al., 2008).

Geography helps in creating greater regional integration and bigger markets. Cluster theory, for instance, suggests that geography will continue to matter regardless of new forms of communication. Groups that are closer physically, culturally, administratively, economically, and socially are more likely to trust one another, easily exchange information and assets and enter into trade agreements, engage in complex competitive production processing, financing, marketing, and export/import arrangements (Porter 1998; Juma 2011). Geography increases the potential of African regional integration and trade because all African countries are neighborhood states through the African Union.

1.1. Classical Theories of International Trade

The rationale of economic integration and regional trade originates from the application, to regional trade, of the classical and contemporary theories of international trade. These theories attempt to explain why trade occurs in the first place and how trade can benefit both parties to an exchange or trade agreement. Over the years, scholars have postulated many such theories of international trade. Wild et al. (2008) have described the following as the major theories in international trade to date. These theories are listed and discussed below in the order of their postulation, from the 16th century to date:

1.1.1. Mercantilism

Mercantilism is the international trade theory that describes the position that a nation should accumulate financial wealth, usually in the form of gold, by encouraging exports and discouraging imports. The measure of a nation's wealth is its accumulated wealth in gold and not the people's well-being including high living standards and increased human development. This theory ran approximately from the mid 1500s to the late 1700s. The most prominent mercantilist nations included Britain, France, the Netherlands, Portugal, and Spain, who were, unfortunately, some of the great dealers in African slave trade and later savagely colonized Africa for almost one hundred years (Horton, 1999). The building blocks of Mercantilism theory and practices were:

- The trade policies that supported trade surpluses by encouraging exports, paid for in gold, and discouraging imports;
- Government intervention in trade to ensure compliance to its trade policies;
- Colonization to obtain low-cost raw materials and labor and create markets for high value manufactured products exported to the colonies.

Therefore, a major drawback of colonization was paying colonies little for their raw materials exports, but charging them higher prices for their usually manufactured imports. These trade policies and arrangements are some of the great impairments of African economic development, the impact of which is still being felt in Africa today. Furthermore and anecdotally, this policy, among others, has been attributed by scholars (Mbaku, 1998) to the genesis of African political and social instability and poverty being seen and felt in the continent today.

1.1.2. Absolute Advantage

Adam Smith first put forth the trade theory of absolute advantage in 1776. This is the ability of a nation to produce a good more efficiently and effectively than any other nation and trading the good for goods produced more efficiently and effectively by other nations. Therefore, trade should not be banned or restricted by tariffs and quotas, but allowed to flow according to market forces – the invisible hand.

1.1.3. Comparative Advantage

David Ricardo developed the theory of comparative advantage in 1817. He proposed that if one country held absolute advantage in the production of two products, specialization and trade could still benefit the two countries involved in the production of the two products. A country has a comparative advantage when it is unable to produce a good more efficiently than other nations, but produces the good more efficiently than it does any other goods. In other words, trade is still beneficial even if one country is less efficient in the production of two goods, as long as it is more efficient in the production of one of the goods than the other good. With economies of scale and learning curve effects, the country will be even more efficient in producing the good it has a comparative advantage in.

1.1.4. Factor Proportions Theory a.k.a. Heckscher-Ohlin Theory

Eli Heckscher and Bertil Ohlin developed the factor proportions theory in early 1900s. The theory states that a country will produce and export goods that require resources or factors of production that are abundant in the country and import goods that require resources or factors of production that are in short supply in the country. In other words, a country will produce and export goods and services that use most the resources—labor, land, technology, and capital—it has in abundance and import goods and services that require resources that are scarce in the country. However, scholars have found that despite its intellectual and conceptual appeal, the Factor Proportions Theory is not supported by studies that examine trade flows of nations.

In the 1950s, for example, Professor Leontief, a Russian economist, tested the theory with world trade and despite expectations that US exports would be capital intensive and imported goods would be labor intensive, the opposite was true. Therefore, contrary to the predictions of the Factor Proportions theory, the findings were that US exports require more labor-intensive production than its imports. This apparent contradiction between the predictions using the Factor Proportions theory and the actual American trade flows has been described as the Leontief Paradox. Leontief's findings are supported by more recent research on trade data of a large number of countries including China.

1.2. Contemporary Theories of International Trade

The development and postulation of international trade theories has continued unabated and in earnest. The theories postulated in later years include the product life cycle theory, the new theory, and the National Competitive Advantage theory by Michael Porter in 1990. These new theories are related or closer to the absolute and comparative advantage theories. They focus on the productivity and cost efficiency of a nation when participating in trade with other nations. These theories include:

1.2.1. Product Life Cycle Theory

The international product life cycle theory of international trade was put forth by Raymond Vernon in the 1960s. This theory states that a company will begin by exporting its products and later undertake direct foreign investment, in foreign markets, as the product moves through its life cycle. The theory further states that, for a number of reasons—such as production costs—a country's exports eventually becomes its imports. A good example today is China and the rest of the world. Many countries—America and Europe—are importing from China what were their exports to China a few decades ago. According to this theory, it is possible China will import from Africa in the future what it is exporting to the world and Africa today.

1.2.2. The New Theory

This theory emerged during the 1970s and 1980s. It states that:

- There are gains to be made from specialization and increasing economies of scale;
- The company that is first to enter a market can create considerable first-mover and incumbency advantages and barriers to entry of new entrants;
- Government may play a role in assisting its home-based companies to be competitive globally. Japan has helped its companies to be competitive in global markets over the years;
- The New Theory also states that a country may dominate in the export of certain products because it has a firm that has acquired a first-mover advantage in certain global markets and industries.

The first-mover and incumbency advantages are the economic and strategic advantages gained by being the first to enter an industry or a country. This first-mover and incumbency advantages can create a formidable barrier to entry for potential rivals and competitors who want to enter the market later.

1.2.3. Competitive Advantage of a Nation Theory

Michael Porter (1990) postulated the National Competitive Advantage theory in 1990 to explain why certain countries are leaders in the production of certain products and services. He asserts that a nation's competitiveness in an industry depends on the capacity of its firms and industries to innovate and upgrade. He identified four elements present to varying degree in every nation that form the basis of national competitiveness. These elements are described in what has come to known as the Porter's Diamond model (1990).

The term diamond is used to reflect the dynamic nature of the elements. That is any change in one element creates changes in one or all the other elements. Overall, government support and chance events such as earthquakes and tsunamis—both domestic and global—will also influence the dynamism of the diamond. The government can increase the competitiveness of its firms and even the industries through

Figure 1. Porter's diamond model for the competitive advantage of nations
Source: *www.valuebasedmanagement.com*

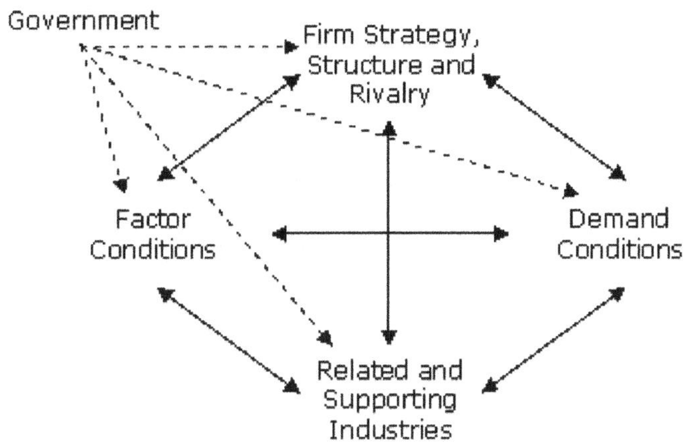

creating the level playing ground and a predictable business climate conducive to doing successful business. The government can further improve the competitiveness of its firms in global markets through provision of quality education to its citizens and support of research and development in the country in collaboration with its corporations.

Chance events include occurrences outside the control of the county and its firms such discovery of a major natural resource like oil, or events like draughts, natural disasters like floods, tornados and hurricanes, and outbreak of human and animal diseases that make it difficult for firms to obtain production resources at acceptable cost. Anecdotal data indicate that the USA, for example, is losing international competitiveness because of its inability to upgrade particularly in its basic and advanced factors and related and supporting industries due to failing educational standards and firms outsourcing their key operations to cheaper emerging markets like India, China, and Brazil hence having upgrading transferred to these countries. Specifically, the national diamond elements are (See Figure 1):

- Factor conditions both basic and advanced factors;
- Demand conditions;
- Related and supporting industries including clusters;
- Firm strategy, structure, and rivalry;
- Chance events; and Government support.

The international trade theories have a definite relevance to the process of regional integration and doing business in Africa. Every significantly successful action or practice in human endeavor is preceded by a sound and robustly constructed theory that becomes a basis for rigorous policy formulation and the practice. Therefore, international trade theories provide a foundation, framework, and context on which the strategies and plans to enter and do business in Africa are constructed and implemented. More so, these theories are critically important as a basis in the creation of African trade regions, in the regional integration schemes, in the promotion and sustainability of inter-African trade, and the understanding of the competitive advantage of national companies in the global markets, and in expanding African markets.

2. THE POTENTIAL AND NEED FOR REGIONAL INTEGRATION AND TRADE IN AFRICA

Considering international trade theories, it is widely acknowledged that there is a greater potential for increasing intra-African trade and enlargement of African markets. This will create wider economic space and enhancing economic development in the continent through greater regional integration and trade (UNCTAD 2003 Report). Therefore, in seeking new opportunities to develop their economies, and enhance the well being of their peoples, African leaders have, for a long time, undertaken great strides to create bigger markets through the creation of economic regions and trading blocs, in the continent, albeit with slow success.

At the present time, African countries are not able to produce goods and services that are competitive globally (Lynch, 2008). Regional economic integration should help African countries to develop bigger markets and thus the capacity and ability to become competitive internationally and therefore benefit from global trade. Regional integration will provide the African countries larger, viable, and more vibrant markets that they need to more efficiently and effectively exploit technological economies of scale and as a result accentuate and improve their ability to produce competitive products and services for global markets (Mbaku, 1998; Juma, 2011).

Many observers and policy makers on the African continent have looked to regional integration and cooperation as the most important and effective way to develop Africa (Mbaku 1995). The interest in economic integration as the most important and effective way for development in the continent is based on the fact that most national economies in Africa are small and not particularly viable, and the belief that over the long term, the prices of most primary products tend to decline in relationship to those of industrial goods. It is also difficult to maintain international commodity agreements at acceptable prices.

It is generally believed that if the effective size of each African country's economy is increased through regional integration, domestic production can benefit significantly from a better exploitation of technological economies of scale. In addition, the larger markets should attract more foreign direct investments. And allow domestic infant industries to seek and get the assistance they need to grow and eventually become competitive companies and even regional champions.

Indeed, in recent years, efforts, at sub-regional and regional economic integration have been stepped up, substantially, including the relaunching of the African Economic Community (AEC) in 2012 and the New Partnership for African Development (NEPAD) (Mukhisa, 2012) meant to source and obtain resources for African development. These efforts include the launch of the Conference on Security, Stability, Development, and Cooperation in Africa (CSSDA). The goal of CSSDA is to create a supportive context for accelerated African economic development through regional integration and other viable means (Deng et al., 2002).

All these arrangements are meant to promote and accelerate inter-African trade and investments and hence economic development in the continent. Inter-regional trade is known to be an important engine for high value job creation in many countries. For example, the USA Department of Commerce estimates that for every US$1 billion increase in exports, mostly to Mexico and Canada, over 22,800 jobs are created in the United States and that these jobs pay wages that are, on average, from 13 to 18 percent more than those not related to international and regional trade (Wild et al., 2008).

Poor infrastructure has been the impediment to intra-African trade which, in 2010, accounted for only 10 percent of Africa's overall trade. Africa's share of global trade also declined from 6 percent in 1980 to less than 3 percent in 2008. This is due to the uncompetitive nature of the African products and services. It is also due to Africa's reliance on commodity exports with low value addition and protectionist practices such as technical and non-technical barriers to trade with trading partners' markets. This urgently and strongly calls for increased intra-African trade by eliminating barriers and impediments to intra-African trade and cooperation (AU Commission 2009 – 2012 Strategic Plan).

Expanded African trade will most likely benefit African countries considerably. Further, increased regional trade will assist African countries to produce more manufactured products. Manufacturing will add value to primary products and increase the knowledge and skills of the people. Increased knowledge and skills will not only improve the productivity of the people of Africa but they will also enable them to be more competitive globally through productivity improvement. These investments will also stimulate more trade and economic developments thus improve the living standards and quality of life in the long run.

However, the full potential of intra-African trade has yet to be fully exploited through greater coordination of efforts aimed at harmonizing customs procedures and eliminating tariff and non-tariff barriers among African countries. And as well as improving transport and communication links through greater investments in developing regional infrastructure (AFDB 2008) to enhance regional trade. Still, it is generally agreed by scholars and policy makers that Africa will surely develop faster and more qualitatively through increased and accelerated regional integration and increased inter-African trade (Ghemawat, 2005).

Nevertheless, Africa faces the greatest challenges of addressing issues of peace, security, chronic food shortages, and peaceful change of governments, political and social stability. These conditions are conspicuously lacking today across most of the continent (Deng et al., 2002). The lack of these conditions also contributes to deep levels of underdevelopment and poverty. Furthermore, these challenges hinder greater and deeper regional integration because where there is instability and insecurity, for example, leaders will find it difficult to successfully negotiate to cooperate and integrate.

Despite these challenges, however, there has been a more determined and remarkable move towards regional integration in Africa. These efforts are fostering closer cooperation among small and fragmented economies and markets so as to achieve greater African development through increased trade. SADC, in Southern Africa, for example, has recently pronounced itself as a Free Trade Area. COMESA, in Eastern and Central Africa, has also recently announced a customs union agreement among its members. The East African Community has been a customs union for sometimes now and it has recently announced a protocol to move it on to a common market level. It actually became a common market in June 2010 (Daily Nation May 30, 2010). Still, the other challenges that face the African regions and Africa in general are the improvements of their respective macroeconomic frameworks for development, upgrading a dilapidated infrastructure, and elimination of institutional voids to enhance deeper regional integration.

It is vital too for Africa to recognize that successful nations and regions are built on the foundation of common purpose and implementation of novel ideas to development. It is also important to hold true the Latin saying, *"Ex Africa semper aliquid novi!"* – Something new and exciting always comes out of Africa (Anan, 1999). In order to attain these successes, Africa must succeed in rebuilding and reconstructing her economies, achieve sustained high rates of growth, reduce unemployment and poverty, and enhance the process of governance. The dawning of the season of hope is held hostage by Africans and it is they themselves who can enhance it through greater African cooperation, regional integration, and trade to benefit the entire continent (Sachs, 2005).

The role of political commitment in regional integration is critically important. Therefore, the right political commitment and political will by African political leaders to integrate the continent is imperative and can help considerably to overcome obstacles to integration. Most proponents of regional and economic integration in Africa argue in view of the current move toward regional integration in the world, that Africa's chance to gainfully participate in the global economy may be dependent on its ability and the willingness of its political leaders to form effective regional trading blocs (Mbaku, 1998, 2004).

But, it is important to note that the eagerness and enthusiasm to achieve greater regional integration and creating regional trading blocs, enlarging markets, are real palpable with many African leaders. For example and representative of many African leaders, when commenting on the importance of regional integration and trade in East Africa and Africa in general, the Rwandan president, Paul Kagame, in a Kenyan Nation Newspapers May 30, 2009, interview and later in the EastAfican on July 5, 2010, asserted that:

...greater integration of East Africa will benefit Rwanda and I'm sure it will benefit other countries in the East African Community. Integration is the way to go if Africa is to develop. We need people to pool their resources, countries to bring their resources together, to cooperate, to trade together, and to solve the different problems they face. Africans really have common problems. It's about poverty, it's about disease, it's about conflict, it's about governance, it's about institutional reforms, it is about political and social stability, it's about development, and there is a lot we can achieve by working together. But we are also realistic. We know that integration is a complex process, but higher level integrations are necessary. There are hurdles that we have to overcome however. But as long as we move along with people of this region, the five countries in the East African region, for example, positive things will start happening to achieve full integration and be a model for all Africa.

He later stated, in the EastAfrican:

As we celebrate the 10th anniversary of the revival of the East African Treaty, 130 million East Africans are watching closely and judging every step. They know and understand the benefits from the coming together of nations united by history, culture, and trade. There can be no doubt that a new era is dawning for our region. We now have a historic opportunity to create a new, prosperous East Africa that lifts our people out of poverty. Together, our countries can more effectively try to tackle our common challenges than we can as individual nations.

It will take courage, consensus building, and compromise from the East Africa's leaders – the road ahead will be challenging, but rewards in terms of prosperity for our people are even greater. We have made considerable progress in the past 10 years since the EAC recommitted to regional integration. This means progressive removal of internal tariffs on goods from EAC partner states and the application of the Common External Tariff on goods from non-EAC Countries. Since we committed to the Customs Union, trade within the region has grown significantly. We accelerated consultations leading up to the creation of a Common Market, which has become a reality with the formal signing of the Common Market Protocol to become effective in June 2010.

Furthermore, scholars have strongly established that the best way for countries, in similar regions, to develop fast and qualitatively are through regional integration and trade. And that global trade has grown most, in the last fifty years, through inter-regional trade rather than through trade across-regions. It also turns out that regions whose internal trade flows are the lowest relative to trade flows with other regions—Africa, the Middle East, and some of the Eastern European transition economies—are also the poorest economic performers, globally, today (Mbaku, 1998; Ghewamat, 2005).

Economists too have often relied on the gravity theory of trade flows to predict trade between nations and thus encourage regional integration. The gravity theory states that there is a positive relationship between economic size and trade and a negative relationship between distance and trade. Models based on this theory explain up to two-thirds of the observed variations in trade flows between pairs of countries. Using such a model, some economists have predicted how much distance variables affect trade between nations, such that a common border increases trade by 80 percent, a common trade policy increases trade by 300 percent and a common language increase trade by 200 percent (Frankel et al., 2000).

Still, country-level numbers also suggest that foreign direct investment is quite regionalized and companies do much better financially in their regions than globally (Ghemawat, 2005). This is because of cost savings and risk minimization due to proximities or distance to or from home operations. Research data further indicate that a common membership and currency in a region increases trade by 330% and 340% respectively. Distance—physical and otherwise—between two or more countries in a region can manifest itself along four dimensions: cultural, administrative, geographic, and economic dimensions.

The types of distance or proximity influence different businesses in different ways. Geographic distance, for instance, affects the cost of transportation and communications, so it is of particular importance to companies that deal with heavy or bulky products, or whose operations require a high degree of coordination among highly dispersed people or activities. Cultural distance, by contrast, affects consumers' product preferences. It is a crucial consideration for a consumer product company, particularly if the distance is far from home operations. The other distances—administrative, political, and economic—will have different effects on the business depending on their actual distance from the home operations. In the African context, all these distance impact on businesses support, increased rationalization, and thus increased regionalization and trade within the African regions.

According to anecdotal data, African countries have this peculiar trait of trading more with the outside world than they do between themselves. Therefore, they are not able to take advantage of close distances. The trade barriers between them are often the biggest obstacles to building competitive economies of scale in the continent. For example, trade between African countries is only 10 percent of their total export, while trade between the highly developed regions of North American countries is 56 percent of their global trade and that in the European Union is 74 percent of their world trade (Wild et al., 2008). These regions are - at the same time - the most developed regions in the world today, with per capita income raging between $26,000 and $45,000, while African per capita income averages $1,000 (Moyo, 2009).

Regional integration also proved to be a key strength in the ASEAN countries of South East Asia in the 1997 financial crisis and even in the 2008 economic and financial meltdowns. Despite continuing concerns about corruption, red tape, and political instability, the region suffered far less than other parts of the world in these crises. The region has cheap labor, natural resources, strong finances, and a low trade barrier that has enhanced trade in the region, which has somewhat, insulated it from world economic and financial turbulences (Balfour, 2009). Trade among these countries is over 50 percent of their total global trade and their per capita income averages $ 6000, growing at an average over 7 percent per annum (Wild et al., 2008; Balfour, 2009).

Ghewamat (2005) further asserts that the extent and persistence of regional integration, trade and increase in economic activity, at the regional level, reflects the continuing importance, not only of geographic proximity of the members, but also cultural, administrative, and, to some extent, economic proximity, in helping trade to occur easily and eventually economic development. These four dimensions are interrelated: Countries that are relatively close to one another geographically are also likely to share commonalities along the other three dimensions—economic, administrative, and cultural proximities—that help trade to grow and accelerate as well as economic development.

What is more important is that, those similarities—proximities—will intensify, through free trade agreements, regional trade preferences, tax treaties, and even currency unifications, with the European Union and North America Free Trade

Area (NAFTA) supplying most obvious examples (Wild et al., 2008). For example, although NAFTA is at the lowest level of regional integration—the free trade area—it has generated considerable and beneficial trade among its neighboring members. The trade rose from $120 billion at inception of the regional integration process, in 1994, to over $1trillion today. This is a large and beneficial increase in trade by any measure, most likely, accompanied by improved living standards of the people in the countries involved in the process (Wild et al., 2008).

The European Union is another example where the four dimensions of proximity have contributed to a large growth of trade among the EU members, which currently stands at US$ 3 trillion (Wild et al., 2008). African, too, can benefit from its proximities at the regional and sub-regional levels to enhance inter-Africa trade leading to increased economic development and improved living standards of the African people.

3. SCHEMES AND LEVELS OF REGIONAL INTEGRATION PROCESS

Since the development of theories demonstrating the potential gains available from international trade, nations have tried to reap these benefits in a variety of ways including through regional integration and trade. There are five potential schemes and levels of economic and regional integration namely a free-trade area, a customs union, a common market, an economic union, and a political union (Han et al., 2008). Each regional integration level deepens the regional integration process. Scholars (Mbaku, 1998; Wild et al., 2008) have briefly described these schemes and levels of regional integration that occur sequentially:

Free-Trade Area: This is a regional integration level whereby countries seek to remove all barriers to trade between or among them, but each country determines its own trade policies and barriers against non-members. It has helped to increase trade among Northern American countries—Canada, Mexico, and USA—from $120 billion at inception of the agreement in 1994 to over one trillion dollars by 2008 (Han, et al., 2008). Most of the African regional organizations have gone through this level of integration (AFDB 2008).

Customs Union: This is a regional integration level whereby countries agree to remove all trade barriers among them, and erect a common trade policy against non-members. A Customs Union may also be defined as a merger of two or more customs territories into a single customs territory, in which customs duties and other measures that restrict trade are eliminated for substantially all trade between the merged territories. The territories, in turn apply the same duties and measures in their trade with third parties. Countries in the customs union might also negotiate as a single bloc with other supranational organizations, such as the World Trade Organization or other regional trading blocs such as the European Union. COMESA and ECOWAS are at this level of regional integration.

Common Market: This is the economic integration level whereby countries remove all trade barriers and allow the free movement of factors of production—capital and labor—among them but erect trade barriers and a common trade policy against non-members. Countries in the common market might also negotiate as a single block with other supranational organizations, such as the World Trade Organization or other regional trading blocs like the European Union. Because it requires at least some cooperation in economic—monetary and fiscal—and labor policies, this level of regional integration is oftentimes very difficult to attain.

Furthermore, the benefits to individual countries can be uneven because skilled labor may move to countries where wages are higher, and investment capital may flow to where returns are greater and costs are low hence creating uneven development. However, effective and targeted policies, by members of the union, can eliminate these anomalies. The East African Community is at this level of regional integration since June 2010 when the members signed the common market protocol to be fully effective in five years.

Economic Union: This is the economic integration level or scheme whereby countries remove the barriers to trade and the movement of labor and capital, erect a common trade policy against non-members, and coordinate their economic policies including fiscal and monetary policies, and the creation of a common currency like it is currently with 17 countries in the European Union. They also have a central bank to direct their monetary policy and other institutions are also created to direct particular areas of policy in the union. The European Union has two important institutions in this regard; the European Parliament and European Commission. The Parliament formulates Europe-wide policies and the Commission implements these policies.

In an economic union level, member countries give up a certain amount of their national autonomy to the union to which they are members. That makes the economic union one of the hardest levels to achieve because countries love their sovereignty and like protecting it hard despite the benefits that are generated by regional integration at this level. African economic regions are still aspiring to reach this level of regional integration. Economic union level has been achieved at the European Union only the world.

Political Union: This is the highest level of regional integration level. It is an integration level whereby countries coordinate all aspects of their economic and political systems. A political union requires member countries to surrender a lot of their sovereignty to the union and to accept a common stance on economic, foreign, military, and political policies regarding non-member nations. Nations are, however, allowed some degree of autonomy and freedom in setting up certain political and economic policies within their territories.

This level of regional integration has not been achieved anywhere in the world to date. The European Union has made several attempts to reach this level of regional integration but with limited success to date. However, scholars (Han et al, 2008 and Mbaku, 1998) have described the USA and Canada as political unions, suggesting and assuming that the 50 American states and 13 Canadian provinces and territories are individual countries that have entered into their unions for the good of the states, provinces, and territories.

4. MAJOR WORLD REGIONAL INTEGRATIONS AND TRADING BLOCS

The success of Europe at economic and regional integration spurred other regions of the world to consider the benefits of forming their associations and unions. Therefore, there are, currently, 130 regional trading blocs of which thirteen are major regional trading blocs worldwide (Wild et al., 2008). The regional trading blocs include the seven African regional trading blocs. The most advanced examples of these regional integrations that African can learn from to deepen their integration and trading among themselves include (Wild et al., 2008):

- The European Union (EU) currently with 27 members, with 17 of these members being members of the monetary union, The Euro zone. It is the oldest and arguably the most advanced and sophisticated union in the world today. It is at the economic union level and trade within the union is estimated to be over $ 3 trillion annually;
- The North America Free Trade Agreement with three members: Canada, USA, and Mexico. It is at the free trade area level since 1994 and has had tremendous increase in trade among the three countries. However, in recent years, American political leaders at the state and federal levels have been criticizing the agreement and they feel that NAFTA has not been beneficial to the American economy. This thinking apparently is not entirely correct considering the increase in trade among the member countries exceeding 120 percent increase mostly in favor of the USA. This large increase in the volume of trade in NAFTA must have created good paying jobs in the USA over the years;

- The Southern Common Market established in 1988 between Argentina and Brazil, but expanded to include Paraguay and Uruguay in 1991 and Venezuela in 2006. Peru, Bolivia, and Chile are associate members and Mexico has observer status;
- The Association of Southeast Asian Nations (ASEAN) with ten member countries—Burma, Philippines, Indonesia, Thailand, Vietnam, Malaysia, Singapore, Brunei, Cambodia, and Laos—with advanced trade among the members and to the rest of the world. Southeast Asia is a low cost area and has been described by many as the factory of the world, with world multinationals outsourcing their manufacturing operations and services from many of the countries in the region.

Africa can learn the process and benefits of regional integration from these regional arrangements, particularly the European Union; including challenges at every level of integration and how to deal with them in order to intensify and accelerate regional integration in Africa and hence increase inter-Africa trade. African regional integration will also expand African markets and thus attract more direct foreign investments to the continent.

5. ADVANTAGES AND DISADVANTAGES OF REGIONAL INTEGRATION AND TRADING BLOCS

Scholars (Mbaku, 1998; Wild et al., 2008) have established that trade can liberate the entrepreneurial spirit of a country and bring about economic development of a nation and improved living standards of its people. Research data further indicates that regional integration and trading blocs—as they stimulate trade among the participating members—can generate great benefits for member countries. These benefits include:

- **Trade Creation:** Integration removes trade barriers and hence increases trade among member countries enhancing their economic development;
- **Greater Consensus:** The trade agreements generate understanding among members and hence it becomes easier to define and solve common problems;
- **Political Cooperation:** It makes it easier to negotiate whenever there are conflicts among members and even with other supranational bodies like the UN and World Trade Organization (WTO). African regional groupings are regularly solving political conflicts in their member countries;

- **Creates Employment Opportunities:** Regional integration can also expand employment opportunities as it makes it easier for people to move from one country to another whenever there is work and they even earn better wages;
- **Expands Markets:** Regional integration expands regional markets making them attractive to global corporations and even for local entrepreneurs. This is particularly true in African where national markets are tiny and therefore not attractive to foreign investors.

However, regional integration can generate drawbacks too. Although scholars and policy makers see integration as an investment in the future of the African continents, for example, the resources required to make the integration schemes operational are quite significant and represent an important obstacle to rapid economic integration in Africa and other regions (Mbaku, 1998). The general consensus is that the cost of integration can be grouped into four categories. Therefore, the drawbacks of regional integration and trading blocs may include:

- Trade diversion to members from non-members who might be more efficient than members;
- Unequal distribution of benefits and cost of regional integration;
- Shift in employment to low wages members causing unemployment in high wages members;
- Loss of national sovereignty particularly at the political union level of the integration process;
- Loss of flexibility to formulate and implement national economic and financial policies, particularly when regional integration is at the economic and political union levels. Difficulties and inflexibility in tackling the European Union's member-countries fiscal crises have emerged as major disadvantages of regional integration at the economic union level. Member countries cannot develop independent policies and strategies to deal with their economic problems.

These drawbacks, however, can be mitigated by greater and deeper integration in regional trading blocs and increased cooperation with regional blocs in other parts of the world, like it is with NAFTA and the European Union where trade between the different countries has expanded since the formation of NAFTA and increased integration in Europe and as it is with ASEAN and the rest of the world (Wild et al., 2008). Trade among the ASEAN members has grown considerably in the last few decades but too with the rest of the world as the world's factory of manufactured products (Wild et al., 2008). African regional integration will also benefit in the same way with increased trading within Africa and partners outside Africa.

6. REGIONAL INTEGRATION IN AFRICA AND AFRICAN REGIONAL TRADING BLOCS

There has been a high causality and correlation between increased aid to Africa, African underdevelopment, and extreme poverty in the last sixty years (Moyo, 2009). Aid to Africa, with its weak and ineffective conditionality, promoted debilitating corruption and considerable misallocation of resources over the years. Scholars and policy makers have, therefore, criticized the African heavy reliance on aid—both multilateral and bilateral—as means for African economic development. They instead recommend a greater reliance on direct foreign investments; trade, particularly inter-African trade; and private debt as alternatives for financing African development.

In a recent interview of the Liberian president and in her response to the question whether Africa is better without aid, she responded thus:

...no, Africa can still use structured and focused aid that is fully accounted for. The problem is that aid should be used properly, without corruption and misallocation. It must support the government's agenda; it must leverage trade with other African countries, and not be relied on solely as a tool for development. And the country itself should use its own resources well, responsibly, and with a high degree of accountability. I think in a few places in Africa, this is already happening (Time May 11, 2009).

The president's conclusion is in agreement with what scholars are saying that aid per se cannot develop Africa particularly where it engenders corruption and leads to poor allocation of scarce resources, as it happened in Africa in the last sixty years. The aid should be used to leverage local and other resources (Moyo, 2009). Therefore, aid alone will not develop Africa, particularly when most of it is abused and stolen through misallocations and corruption. As such, Africa needs a new paradigm in the way it does things and a new development model that minimizes the role of aid in African economic development.

Moyo (2009) has proposed a new development model, which includes a development finance portfolio of five percent aid; 30 percent trade, mainly with China; 30 percent Foreign Direct Investment (FDI); 10 percent micro-finance; and 25 percent remittances from the African Diaspora. She estimates that there are about 40 million Africans in the Diaspora who remit more than $40 billion to Africa annually.

The portfolio has given little attention to inter-African trade as a development strategy and too much reliance on distance trade particularly with China. Empirical evidence—by scholars—shows that the best way for countries—in similar regions—to develop is through regional trade and that global trade has grown most, in the last fifty years, through inter-regional trade than through trade across-regions and it turns out that regions whose internal trade flows are the lowest relative to trade flows with other regions—Africa, the Middle East, and some of the Eastern European transition economies—are also the poorest economic performers, globally, today (Ghewamat, 2005).

Accordingly, and in addition to the four financing strategies, suggested by Moyo (2009), Africa can most develop by increasing inter-Africa trade from its current level of 10 percent of its total trade to at least 50 percent of its total trade through increased regional integration rather than relying heavily on trade with China, or Europe, or USA for that matter. Africa must enhance its current regionalization schemes, at least to the common market level, in at least three of its regions—ECOWAS, COMESA, and SACD, which are strategic regions—to enhance intra-Africa trade and hence further its economic development through largely on its own efforts to eradicate African poverty. Of course, the countries of Africa should try to use aid to leverage other more effective development financing methods recommended by Moyo (2009), such as issuing government debt and promoting increasing inter-Africa trade through greater regional integration schemes.

6.1. African Trading Blocs

Since the early 1980's, there has been a renewed interest in regional economic co-operation in Africa. Therefore, African countries have, over the years, attempted to form regional trading blocs. This is meant to reduce its dependence on the industrialized economies for a greater part of their international trade. Regional integration and trading blocs have also been suggested as schemes that can be used by African countries to improve their participation in the global economy.

It is also argued that at the present moment, most African economies are small and not particularly viable markets. Through regional integration, however, these economies can increase their effective market sizes and allow them to benefit significantly from a more enhanced exploitation of technological economies of scale. Larger markets, made possible by integration, are also expected to impact on infant industries as these markets provide a more enabling environment for growth and eventually becoming competitive in global markets (Mbaku, 1998).

The urge for African regional integration and trading blocs has always been strongly expressed by scholars, politicians, policy makers, and even non-Africans of good will, among them the French minister of cooperation and development. At a conference in the Ivory Coast in 1989, he urged Africa to establish regional markets along the lines planned in Europe, asserting that, "the changes in Europe are, to my mind, a model. Without a regional market, sub-Saharan Africa, for example, will not be organized on a sufficient scale to become an area of economic growth and attractive to foreign investment. Without political coordination in all areas—economic, fiscal, social, and legal—it will remain too weak in the face of the large groupings which are being established everywhere in the world" (Deng et al., 2002). Similarly, Sadig Rasheed argues that "in a world where trade blocs and barriers are increasingly being erected and fortified, Africa has little chance of survival outside an integration and trade framework of its own" (Deng et al., 2002).

However, long before the establishment of the OAU, African leaders had recognized that cooperation and integration among African countries in the economic, social, and cultural fields are indispensable to the accelerated transformation and sustained development of the African continent. This thinking was concretized in 1963 in the objectives of the OAU Charter, as well as in the OAU Summits of 1973 and 1976, and in the Monrovia Declaration of 1979 (Deng et al., 2002).

The 1980 OAU Extraordinary Summit adopted the Lagos Plan of Action, as a major step towards regional integration and trade. During that Summit, the African leaders stated their commitment, individually and collectively, to promote the economic integration of Africa, in order to facilitate and reinforce social and economic intercourse in the continent. They also committed themselves to promoting the economic and social development and integration of their economies and, to that end, to establish national, regional, and sub-regional institutions leading to a dynamic and interdependent African economy, for the eventual establishment of the African Economic Community (Mbaku, 1998). Mbaku (1998) further states that in 1980, the OAU specifically advocated for trade integration as part of its strategic agenda for the development of Africa:

- Through the production of competitive products and services;
- De-emphasize the export of cheap raw materials and emphasize the diversification in the production and export of knowledge intensive products produced cheaply in Africa.

The commitments in the Lagos Plan of Action and the Final Act of Lagos were translated into concrete form, in Abuja, Nigeria, in June 1991 when the OAU Heads of State and Government signed the Treaty establishing the African Economic Community (AEC), which envisaged and encouraged the formation of African regional trading blocs as its foundation (Mbaku, 1998). The AEC Treaty has been in operation since May 1994 when the required number of instruments of ratification for its coming into force was deposited with the Secretary General of the OAU/AEC in Addis Ababa. But, so far it has had limited impact on intra-Africa trade hence and since its inception. Therefore, there is a strong need to accelerate the regional integration process to increase inter-African trade and as the building blocks of the African Economic Community (Deng et al., 2002).

As such and in recent times, at the regional and sub-regional levels, African countries have embarked on various programs for the promotion of integration, and have established organizations and institutions to support their effort. So far, the AEC has established direct working relations with the Economic Community of West African States (ECOWAS) in the West African region, the East African Community (EAC) in East Africa, the Economic Community of Central African States (ECCAS) in the Central African region, and in the East and Southern region, the Common Market for East and Southern Africa (COMESA). In the Southern Region, the AEC has dealings with the Southern African Development Community (SADC). In North Africa, there is the Arab Maghreb Union (UMA), which, presently, it is said, has no much direct contact with the AEC. All these efforts are geared toward the strengthening of the eventual establishment and growth of the AEC (BW May 2009). The following is the detailed description and analysis of the seven, in many cases overlapping, African economic regional trading blocs that are currently at different levels of regional integration.

6.1.1. The East African Community (EAC)

The East African Community (EAC) is one of the oldest regional integration bodies, not only in Africa, but probably in the world. It initially comprised of Kenya, Uganda, and Tanzania. Rwanda and Burundi joined in the 2000's. The initial East African Community developed out of the East African High Commission that ran the East African Common Services Organization. The Commission was created during the colonial period in 1947. It used a common currency, the shilling, in the initial three East African countries of Uganda, Kenya, and Tanzania. The common services managed by the organization included the railways, airports, courts, seaports and harbors, telecommunications services, airways, and several research institutes (Mbaku, 1998).

The new community has made significant advances on the social, cultural, economic, and political fronts. It has judicial and legislative organs and aspires to create a federal state with a single president in the future. Currently, the community is made up of Kenya, Uganda, Tanzania, Rwanda, and Burundi. It may include South Sudan, Ethiopia, Djibouti, and Somalia in the near future. But, currently, Somalia is a failed state without a viable central government so joining the community may be delayed.

To enhance the community's integration process, the countries implemented the protocol for the actual Common Market of East Africa in June 30, 2010. The member countries opened up their markets to each other and allowed the free flow of trade, people, labor, capital, and investments. In fact, the largest number of investors in Tanzania and Uganda are currently Kenyans.

As Table 1 indicates, the community brings together almost 142 million people, with a GDP of approximately $90 billion with an average GDP per capita of $536 and a Purchasing Power Parity of over $1280. The region's GDP is currently growing at an average of 5.8 percent per annum improving the consumer market. However, inflation is rather high in this region at 11.7 percent that will affect the prices of products and services produced in this region making them less competitive.

Furthermore, the Eastern African countries have a common language – Kiswahili. Although the official language in Rwanda and Burundi is French, English and Kiswahili are generally well spoken and understood in all the five EA countries. The currencies—the shilling—of the three original member countries—Kenya, Uganda, and Tanzania—are convertible at freely set market exchange rates. But, Rwanda and Burundi use the Franc as their currency with market convertibility with the currencies of the other three countries. There are also flourishing stock exchange markets in all these countries with the Nairobi Stock Exchange, in Kenya, being the most advanced and most robust exchange with over 50 companies listed, at any one time, with an increasing foreign participation (See Figure 2).

The legal and judicial systems of the three initial member countries are similar. Rwanda and Burundi are rationalizing their legal and judicial systems to match the other systems. The countries are also well linked with a reasonable air and road network and the telephone system within and between these countries are of reasonable standard. Furthermore, the mobile phone system is growing exponentially in these countries, with the current ownership of over 30 million. These nations also enjoy Internet services in their major cities and towns.

Table 1. Key macroeconomic factors for the East African community

Country	Population (Millions)	GDP ($ Billions)	GDP Growth Rate (%)	GDP per Capita ($)	PPP per Capita ($)	Annual Inflation (%)
Burundi	8.6	2.3	4.8	271	610	9.7
Kenya	41.6	41.9	5.2	808	1,710	14.0
Tanzania	46.2	25.6	6.8	532	1,500	12.7
Rwanda	10.9	6.1	7.6	583	1,270	6.0
Uganda	34.5	18.9	4.5	487	1,310	16.0
Total	141.8	94.8				
Average			5.8	536	1,280	11.7

Source 1: http://www.afdb.org: 2010.
Source 2: http://www.africaneconomicoutlook.org: 2010.
Source 3: http://data.worldbank.org: 2010.

Figure 2. East African community with possible new members

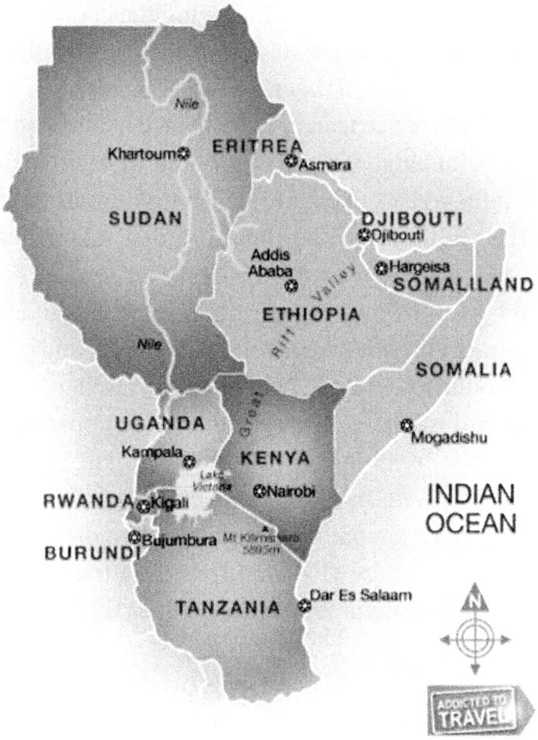

The EA countries, except Tanzania, are also members of COMESA, which is a larger and wider regional organization, in East and Central Africa. They are also, except Tanzania, Burundi, and Rwanda, members of a moribund organization called the Intergovernmental Authority for Development (IGAD). IGAD brings together countries in the horn of Africa, including Djibouti, Somalia, Ethiopia, Uganda, Kenya, Sudan, and Eritrea to tackle common political and economic development problems.

IGAD specifically aims at the promotion of joint environmental protection, peace, and stability in the region. It also aims at promoting strategies to enhance economic development and harmonization of national priorities in many other areas including livestock development and the migration of people and livestock among the member countries (FAO 2003). The total Eastern African and IGAD population is over 271 million. This is a large market indeed, and as the regional GDP per capita and Purchasing Power Parity per capita incomes rise, except in Somalia, which is currently a failed state, it is an attractive and important region to do business.

Kenya is the economic powerhouse in this region, with a population of almost 42 million people. The Kenyan GDP is US$41.9, which is almost 50 percent of the region's total GDP. Currently, Kenya's per capita income is US$ 808 and its Purchasing power parity per capita of US$1710, both the highest in the region.

Kenya can also be a business hub for the region. It has well-developed air and sea links, a good education system, a viable telecommunication and road infrastructure, and an effective financial services system that includes a well-functioning stock exchange market in Nairobi and a good system of financial services including banking, liberalized foreign exchange market, and insurance services. However, today, Kenya faces a myriad of investment climate problems. The major problems include perennial eruptions of violence during general elections, corruption, and high inflation rate. The Kenyan inflation rate currently is 14 percent compared with a regional average of about 12 percent. These problems create unpredictability in the market (Deng et al., 2002) (See Table 2).

6.1.2. COMESA

With its current 19 member states, a population of over 436 million, a GDP of over US$ 487 billion, and annual import bill of US$95 billion and an export bill of US$107 billion, the Common Market of East and Central African States (COMESA) is a potentially big and vibrant market. The COMESA region encompasses a much broader area, than the East African Community and IGAD countries and their membership overlap. Currently, COMESA is the largest and most dynamic trade

Table 2. Key macroeconomic factors for the IGAD countries

Country	Population (Millions)	GDP ($ Billions)	GDP Growth Rate (%)	GDP per Capita ($)	PPP per Capita ($)	Annual Inflation (%)
Djibouti	0.9	1.2	4.8		1,311	2.1
Ethiopia	84.7	34.6	7.0	357	1,110	29.3
Eritrea	5.4	2.6	6.3	482	580	12.5
Somalia	9.6					
Sudan	44.6	63.3				19.8
Total	145.2	101.7				
Average			6.0	419.5	1,000.3	15.9

Source 1: http://www.afdb.org: 2010.

Source 2: http://www.africaneconomicoutlook.org: 2010.

Source 3: http://data.worldbank.org: 2010.

region in Africa in terms of population and geographic area – covering an area of 12 million square kilometers. COMESA is also considered, by integration experts, as one of the most effective regional organizations in Africa today.

As shown in Figure 3, the region covers most of the Eastern and Central African countries. It became a customs union in June 2009. The meaning of the launch of the COMESA Customs Union is that:

- The flow of goods and services will be improved and firms will have a larger market for their products and services by enhanced regional trade;
- Harmonization of taxes on production inputs—raw materials, intermediate goods, and capital equipment—will level the playing field in the region and will result in increased efficiency in production leading to competitiveness in the region (See Table 3);
- Common policy formulation leads to deeper integration and more inter-dependence increasing cross-border investments thereby generating employment as well as promoting backward linkages particularly in agro businesses in the region;

Figure 3. COMESA region

- It is expected that there will be welfare gains through lower prices, wider choice, and improved quality of goods and services and thus improved living standards and quality of life of the people of COMESA region.

COMESA is based in Lusaka, Zambia. As mentioned earlier, the COMESA agreement overlaps several countries and regions. Kenya, Burundi, Rwanda, and Uganda are in the EAC and in COMESA, Malawi, Zimbabwe, and Zambia are SADC members. Tanzania is in SADC and EAC at the same time (See Table 4).

The overlaps make it possible and easier to negotiate to have joint agreements to bring the EAC, COMESA, and SADC together into a larger regional trading bloc. The three regional bodies have the same goals of promoting trade, investments, and eventually free flow of people among the member countries. Already, as expected, trade among the member countries is growing steadily. For example and according to recent press reports, 30 percent—US$ 30 billion—of Kenya's total trade, today, is within the COMESA region.

Table 3. Key macroeconomic factors for the COMESA region

Country	Population (Millions)	GDP $ (Billions)	GDP Growth Rate (%)	GDP per Capita ($)	PPP per Capita ($)	Annual Inflation (%)
Comoros	0.8	0.63	3.1	810	1,110	4.6
Egypt	82.5	229	0.8	2,781	6,120	10.8
Malawi	15.4	5.9	5.0	365	870	7.8
Madagascar	21.3	9.5	2.4	465	950	8.3
Mauritius	1.3	11.3	4.0	8,755	14,330	3.7
Seychelles	0.9	1.1	4.0	11,711	25,140	3.5
Swaziland	1.2	3.9	0.6	3,725	5,930	6.5
Zimbabwe	12.8	6.4	4.4	757		
Zambia	13.5	23.4	6.9	1,425	1,490	8.0
EAC Countries	141.8	94.8	5.8	2,681	6,400	11.7
IGAD Countries	145.2	101.7	6.0	839	3,001	15.9
Total	436.7	487.6				
Average			3.9	3077	5805	7.3

Source 1: http://www.afdb.org: 2010.
Source 2: http://www.africaneconomicoutlook.org: 2010.
Source 3: http://data.worldbank.org: 2010.

Table 4. Key macroeconomic factors for countries both in COMESA and SADC

Country	Population (Millions)	GDP $ (Billions)	GDP Growth Rate (%)	GDP per Capita ($)	PPP per Capita ($)	Inflation Rate (%)
DRC	67.8	15.2	5.1	231	340	15.1
Madagascar	21.3	9.5	2.4	465	950	8.3
Malawi	15.4	5.9	5.0	365	870	7.8
Mauritius	1.3	11.3	4.0	8,755	14,330	3.7
Seychelles	0.9	1.1	4.0	11,711	25,140	3.5
Swaziland	1.2	3.9	0.6	3,725	5,930	6.5
Zambia	13.5	23.4	6.9	1,425	1,490	8.0
Zimbabwe	12.8	6.4	4.4	757		
Total	134.2	76.7				
Average			4.05	3,429.2	6,131.2	6.6

Source 1: http://www.afdb.org: 2010
Source 2: http://www.africaneconomicoutlook.org: 2010
Source 3: http://data.worldbank.org: 2010.

Anecdotal data further indicate that there are increasing contacts between EAC, COMESA, and SADC that will result into one of the largest economic unions in the world. The changes will increase trade between the three regions; potentially resulting into the largest market in Africa as President Kagame of Rwanda intimated in an interview in The EastAfrican July 5, 2005. He asserted:

...Further stressing and highlighting the African commitment to regional integration, as well as support of efforts to build larger markets of consumers by merging the East African Community (EAC) with the Common Market for Eastern and Southern Africa (COMESA) and the Southern Africa Development Community (SADC) that will represent a total population of over 570 million people 'with an average Purchasing Power Parity per capita of $ 6000'

Kenya and Egypt are the economic powerhouses in COMESA, although Mauritius, Seychelles, Botswana, and Swaziland have the higher income per capita and purchasing power parities per capita in the region. Kenya and Egypt have larger population numbers hence potentially bigger markets with rising individual incomes. Their other macroeconomic factors—plus Kenya having a business hub advantage—are some of the highest in the region and in Africa. Therefore, COMESA is an ideal region to do business in Africa by investing in it, but players must move in early before the channels are clogged and in order to put the necessary strategies in place to gain first-mover and incumbent advantages.

6.1.2.1. First-Mover and Incumbent Advantages

A first-mover and incumbent advantages are a firm's ability to be better off than its competitors as a result of being first to enter and being established in a market or being first in introducing a new and technologically superior product in a market segment. There are durable first-mover advantages, which improve a firm's market share, revenues, and profitability over a long period and short-lived advantages that confer benefits for a short time (Lanzolla et al., 2005).

Although no advantage lasts forever, firms that succeed in building durable first-mover and incumbent advantages tend to dominate their product categories in a market for a very long time from market infancy until well into its maturity. Coca cola is said to be a good example of companies that are able to build long-term first-mover advantages that end up being strong and unassailable incumbent advantages in many markets and countries it enters for the first time (Suarez et al., 2005).

The first-mover advantages include having the first pick of partners, suppliers, sites, marketing channels, and other competitive resources. First-movers are also able to establish their products and brands quickly and cheaply – well before marketing channels become cluttered and clogged with competing messages. Therefore, they are able to build an early base of customers who would find it inconvenient or costly to switch to the offerings of the later entrants. Although first-mover position would lead to mistakes, its practitioners point out that it gives them time to learn, make corrections, and adjustments in the new market (Williamson, 1997).

Late-comers may make fewer errors, but when they err; they will lack the time to recover (Williamson, 1997). Williamson further asserts thus: "When you come into the market early, you are not always right, but you have time to correct any mistakes you make on the way. If you are a latecomer, you have to hit a hole in one. There is no any time for detours and mistakes; unless you get it right the first time, which is always unlikely, you will never catch up. Obviously, first-mover and incumbency give not only a sustainable competitive advantage but, if well managed, will also give a solid and effective barrier to entry of new competitors" (Williamson, 1997).

For example, in the 1990's, South African Breweries tried—strongly and with a lot of fanfare and force displaying its global power without fear—to enter the East African beer market and failed because of the advantages of an incumbent—the East African Breweries—who had first-mover and incumbency advantages built over many years. The South African Breweries came in strong and built a large factory near Nairobi, Kenya. However, the company was not able to promote its brand—despite being global and resource rich—sufficiently enough to capture a reasonable market share and the distribution channels and the partnerships it needed to succeed were almost entirely owned by the East African Breweries.

The company wound up and left East Africa after three years leaving behind huge investments that are oftentimes being used by the East African Breweries. Therefore, first-mover and incumbency positions are sources of not only a sustainable competitive advantage, but also barriers to entry of latecomers. First-movers and incumbent companies can also build an entry barrier by differentiating, in the minds of customers, their products or services from the new entrant competitors' products or services as a result of first-mover and incumbency advantages it already possesses.

6.1.3. SADC

6.1.3.1. History and Present Status

The origins of SADC are fascinating following its unfriendly foundational triggers: the White South African apartheid policies. The concept of regional economic co-operation in Southern Africa first emerged in May 1979, among the frontline states, as a need to create a strong regional trading organization to counter apartheid South Africa. In April 1980, a declaration was adopted, by the frontline states that led to the formation of the Southern African Development Co-ordination Conference (SADCC). SADCC became the Southern African Development Community (SADC) in 1992.The original and key member states of SADC are Angola, Botswana, and Democratic Republic of the Congo, Malawi, Mozambique, Madagascar, Mauritius, Namibia, South Africa, Tanzania, Zambia, and Zimbabwe (See Figure 4).

Figure 4. SADC countries

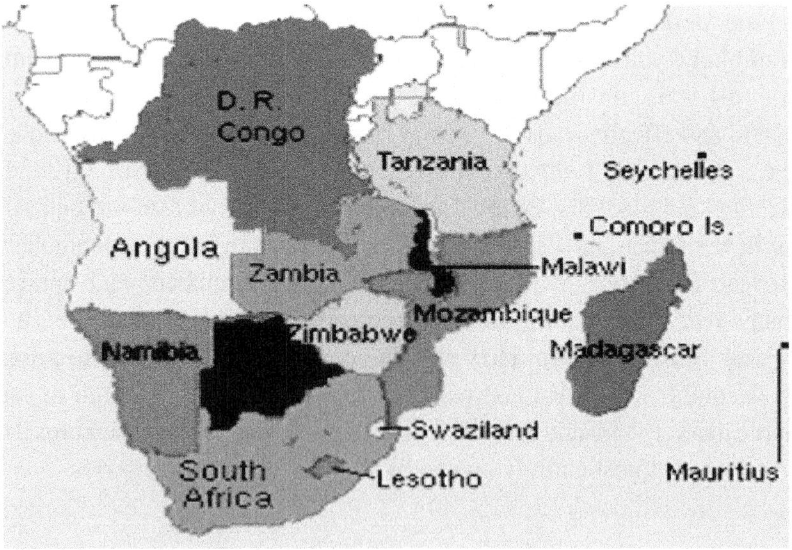

6.1.3.2. Objectives of SADC

According to the SADC protocol, the initial objectives of SADC were: to achieve economic development, alleviate poverty, minimize dependence on apartheid South Africa, enhance the standard and quality of life of the peoples of Southern Africa, and support the socially disadvantaged through regional integration and trade. These objectives were to be achieved through increased regional integration and trade, built on democratic principles and equitable and sustainable development. Initially, the SADC countries adopted a framework of co-operation based on the following assumptions:

- Deeper economic co-operation and integration, on the basis of balance, equity, and mutual benefit, providing for enhanced investment and trade, and increased freedom of movement of factors of production, and goods and services across national borders of member countries;
- Common economic, political, social values and systems, enhancing enterprise and competitiveness, democracy and good governance, respect for the rule of law and the guarantee of human rights, popular participation, and the alleviation of poverty; and
- Regional solidarity, peace and security, in order for the people of the region to live and work together in peace and harmony to improve their living standards.

In order to addressing national priorities through regional action, the SADC countries adopted an innovative idea of allocating countries sectoral responsibilities. Therefore, most member states have been allocated the responsibility and accountability for coordinating one or more economic sectors.

This allocation of responsibility involves proposing sector policies, strategies and priorities, performance standards, processing projects for inclusion in the sectoral programs, monitoring and evaluating progress, reporting to the Council of Ministers the progress of the sector, and making recommendations for improvement. In some cases, however, SADC has not lived up to its principles, particularly the principles of democracy and good governance, in that some of the worst dictators and ineffective leaders in Africa are in this region. President Mugabe of Zimbabwe is a good and living example.

6.1.3.3. Current Economic Overview in the SADC Free Trade Area

In 2007, the combined Gross Domestic Product (GDP) for the Southern African Development Community was US$488.2 billion with a per capita income of US$3020 and Purchasing Power Parity of US$5917, one of the highest in Africa. Individual national economies are structurally diverse and at varying stages of development.

South Africa, the region's most developed economy - an economic powerhouse in the region - has a population of 50.5 m and a GDP of $259.5 billion, a per capita GDP of US$8,070 and PPP of US$10,710, which is more than half the combined GDP of the other Southern African countries. Therefore, South Africa is considered an economic leader, not only in the Southern African region, but the whole of Africa in fact.

South Africa has an excellent infrastructure, a good business climate, and well-established and competitive companies that operate, not only in the region, but also in the whole of Africa. The South African Breweries (SAB), for example, is a global company listed in the London Stock Exchange. The country successfully staged FIFA World Cup in 2010, which has enhanced its image in the world and its economic powerhouse status in the region.

Botswana is also one of the countries performing well economically and politically within SADC. It has the highest regional per capita income of $8533 and PPP of $14,550 and bolstered by its diamond mining and ranching industries, coupled with a sound political and governance environments, Botswana continues to experience steady economic growth and being attractive to foreign direct investments.

Challenges of the cold war and post-cold war disarmament and economic reconstruction and continuing internal strives have adversely affected economic performance in Angola, Congo DR, and Zimbabwe. The Zimbabwean economy has experienced a sharp deterioration in the 1990's and 2000's, with real GDP contracting by about 30 percent during that period and inflation reaching 600 percent in 2003, before dropping to 124 percent in 2005.

The problem in Zimbabwe is what has been common in many African countries; that is, the African "big man" and hero worship mentality that makes leaders—President Mugabe and his cronies—prefer serving their exaggerated personal egos to the good of their nations and people. This unfortunate attitude has destroyed formerly robust, prosperous, and flourishing economies in Africa.

However, Zimbabwe has now a unit government in place, which, hopefully, will revive the shattered economy and put the country on the road to recovery and growth. On the other hand, the economies of resources-rich DRC and Angola have also begun to experience GDP growth as peace agreements in both countries take hold. With large and heavy Chinese investments—mainly in infrastructure—that are currently going on in these countries, their economic development chances will be considerably enhanced.

SADC is now a free trade area, since September 2008. Furthermore, SADC is a free trade area, with countries that are well endowed with natural resources that have a good business climate, and a well-developed infrastructure. Both South Africa and Botswana are stable and progressive democracies and have a large potential for accelerated economic growth now and in the future. The anticipated merger of SADC and COMESA will create one of the most vibrant, growing, and powerful economic regions and trading blocs in Africa if not in the world in the future (See Table 5).

6.1.4. The Economic Community of West African States (ECOWAS)

West Africa, other than Nigeria, is characterized by small and medium-sized economies necessitating regional integration to enlarge their markets. The Economic Community of West African States (ECOWAS) is a regional grouping of the fifteen West African countries, founded on May 28, 1975 with the signing of the Treaty of Lagos. The mission of the trading area is to promote economic integration and trade in western Africa and hence economic development of the region. The grouping overlaps with the Francophone West African Economic and Monetary Union (WAEMU) described below. ECOWAS is a largest African trade region after COMESA and SADC, in terms of the number of countries, population, and regional GDP and GDP per capita.

The community was founded to achieve collective self-sufficiency for the member states by means of economic and monetary union creating a single large

Table 5. Key macroeconomic factors for the SADC countries

Country	Population (Millions)	GDP USD (Billions)	GDP Growth Rate (%)	GDP per Capita USD	PPP per Capita USD	Inflation Rate (%)
Angola	19.6	103.9	8.2	5,318	5,230	10.0
Botswana	2.0	15.0	4.4	8,533	14,550	6.2
Lesotho	2.2	1.9	4.0	1,106	2,050	6.7
Mozambique	23.9	14.3	7.5	535	970	7.2
Namibia	2.3	12.9	4.4	5,293	6,560	6.6
South Africa	50.5	378.1	2.8	8,070	10,710	6.2
Seychelles	0.9	1.1	4.0	11,711	25,140	3.5
Tanzania	46.2	25.6	6.8	532	1,500	12.7
COMESA countries in SADC	110.7	54.8	4.1	6,603	8,710	5.9
Total	258.3	607.6				
Average			5.1	5,300	8,380	7.2

Source 1: http://www.afdb.org: 2010.

Source 2: http://www.africaneconomicoutlook.org: 2010.

Source 3: http://data.worldbank.org: 2010.

trading bloc. The ECOWAS Secretariat and the ECOWAS Bank for Investment and Development—based in Ghana—are its two main institutions that implement regional policies (See Figure 5).

The region's integration level is where it has already achieved free movement of persons, goods, and services. The region is currently working towards a monetary union. Almost half of the countries of the region including Liberia, Ivory Coast, Togo, Sierra Leone, Guinea- Bissau, Guinea, and Nigeria - have, however, experienced conflicts and socio-political instability, in recent times, that hindered the countries from participating fully in the economic activities of the region. The African Development Bank is assisting the region with the harmonization programs in order to bring the WAEMU and ECOWAS and the Western African Monetary Zone—Liberia, Gambia, Guinea, Sierra Leone, Nigeria, and Ghana—under one monetary area to enhance regional trading and investment (Afdb report 2008). The region has a regional bank – ECO Bank - with over 783 branches worldwide. The bank should help in trade and investment harmonization in the region (See Table 6).

As shown in the table above, the total population of the fifteen countries is more than 308 million. Nigeria, the largest country in Africa, is the economic powerhouse in the ECOWAS region. It accounts for over 52% of the region's total population, with a GDP of US$ 241.5 which is over 65 percent of the regional total GDP with a GDP per capita of US$1502 and PPP per capita of US$ 2,290.

Figure 5. ECOWAS countries

Table 6. Key macroeconomic factors in the ECOWAS region

Country	Population (Millions)	GDP USD (Billions)	GDP Growth Rate (%)	GDP per Capita USD	PPP per Capita USD	Inflation Rate (%)
Cape Verde	0.5	2.2	5.1	3,798	3,980	3.3
Gambia	1.8	1.2	5.6	506	1,750	4.8
Ghana	25.0	39.2	8.3	1,570	1,810	8.2
Guinea	10.2	5.9	5.1	498	1,020	16.7
Liberia	4.1	1.7	8.8	374	540	5.6
Nigeria	162.5	241.5	6.9	1,502	2,290	10.1
Sierra Leon	6.0	2.2	6.2	374	840	11.7
Total WAEMU region	98.8	74.3	5.7	5,976	10,610	3.5
Total	308.9	368.2				
Average			6.5	1,824	2,855	8.0

Source 1: http://www.afdb.org: 2010.
Source 2: http://www.africaneconomicoutlook.org: 2010
Source 3: http://data.worldbank.org: 2010.

Nigeria is also one of the leading oil producers in Africa. In fact, Nigeria is the second largest oil producing country in Africa after Libya (Bernstein and Rasco, 2007). The region's total GDP is currently US$308.9 billion with a regional GDP per capita of US$ 1,824, PPP per capita of US$ 2,855, and an annual inflation rate of 8.0 percent.

6.1.5. The West African Monetary Zone

The West African Monetary Zone is a group of five countries in ECOWAS that plan to introduce a common currency, the Eco, by the year 2015. The five countries are Gambia, Ghana, Guinea, Nigeria, and Sierra Leone. Liberia—also a member of ECOWAS—has expressed an interest in joining the group. Nigeria dominates the group and should help to make this monetary union project a success.

The WAMZ was formed in 2000 to try to establish a strong stable currency to rival the CFA Franc. The eventual goal is for the CFA Franc and Eco to merge giving ECOWAS a single currency. The West African Monetary Institute based in Ghana is preparing the launch of the new currency. The institute is intended to be the forerunner of a regional central bank to manage the currency. However, several of the WAMZ's countries suffer from weak currencies and chronic budget deficits.

These deficits are plugged by their central banks printing more and more notes of decreasing value of their currencies. These fiscal difficulties are making it difficult to move to a regional single currency and eventually the WAMZ central bank (Afdb Report, 2008).

6.1.6. Regional Integration in the African Francophone Countries

Francophone countries are those Africa countries that were either French colonies or countries that speak French in Africa. These countries are in the CFA Franc monetary union. Therefore, they use the CFA France as their currency. The CFA Franc is regulated by the French Treasury and pegged to the Euro. The countries have a common central bank, the Central Bank of West African States (BCEAO) located in Dakar, Senegal, for the western African countries, and the Central Bank of Central African States (BEAC) located in Yaoundé, Cameroon, for central African countries. Both central banks issue and regulate the same currency for their regions.

To ensure convertibility - particularly to the Euro - of the CFA Franc, the Banque de France guarantees the value of money issued by the BCEAO and BEAC, in exchange for maintenance of reserve deposits at the French Central Bank and strict controls on the creation of new money. Accordingly, the CFA Franc is widely regarded as a "hard currency" and companies can quote prices in CFA Franc globally and throughout the two regions.

As shown in the table below and since 1995, owing to the stability of the currency, inflation rates have been in the single digits for all of the CFA Franc Zone countries. Furthermore, there are no restrictions on the repatriation of profits from investments in the two regions. There is also a relatively free movement of capital and labor in the two regions.

6.1.7. The West African Economic and Monetary Union

The West African Economic and Monetary Union (WAEMU) is one of the CFA Zone regional organization grouping eight states, in West Africa. The regional grouping was established in 1994, to promote economic integration and trade among member countries. As mentioned above, the countries share a common language and currency; French and the Franc. The countries also share a regional stock exchange based in Abidjan, Ivory Coast.

Therefore, the economic union level of the regional integration process and a common monetary unit, the Franc, characterize WAEMU. The member countries are Benin, Burkina Faso, Ivory Coast, Guinea-Bissau, Mali, Niger, Senegal, and Togo. Specifically, WAEMU objectives are:

- Greater economic competitiveness, through open and competitive markets, along with the rationalization and harmonization of the legal framework and investments rules;
- The convergence of macroeconomic policies and indicators;
- The creation of a common market for increased trade and free movement of factors of production particularly capital and labor; and
- The coordination of sectoral policies and the harmonization of monetary and fiscal policies to accelerate economic development in the region (See Table 7).

In terms of its achievements, WAEMU member have implemented macroeconomic convergence criteria and effective surveillance mechanism; have adopted a customs union and common external tariff; have harmonized indirect taxation regulations; and have initiated regional, structural and sectoral policies and enhanced free trade among partners, which currently stands at $ 8 billion annually, increasing at 12 percent per annum (AFDB, 2008).

As shown in the table above, the region has a total population of 98.8 million people. The total GDP for the region is $ 74.3 billion with an average per capita income of about $ 747 and purchasing power parity per capita of $ 1,326. The region's inflation rate is one of the lowest in Africa at an average of 3.5 percent. The

Table 7. Key macroeconomic factors per country and regional averages in WAEMU

Country	Population (Millions)	GDP USD (Billions)	GDP Growth Rate (%)	GDP per Capita USD	PPP per Capita USD	Inflation Rate (%)
Benin	9.1	7.5	4.2	802	1,620	5.4
B Faso	17.0	10.1	5.3	600	1,300	3.9
Guinea Bissau	1.6	.9	4.6	629	1,240	3.4
Ivory Coast	20.2	22.4	8.6	1,195	1,710	3.6
Mali	15.8	10.7	3.5	669	1,040	3.8
Niger	16.1	6.5	11.2	374	720	2.9
Senegal	12.8	12.9	4.2	1,119	1,940	2.6
Togo	6.2	3.3	4.2	588	1,040	2.6
Total	98.8	74.3				
Average			5.7	747	1,326	3.5

Source 1: http://www.afdb.org: 2010.
Source 2: http://www.africaneconomicoutlook.org: 2010.
Source 3: http://data.worldbank: 2010.

region is indeed ideal for business in agriculture and agro-business and development of manufacturing industries from extractive industries of cotton, groundnuts, oil, and bauxite.

A September 2002 IMF survey cited the WAEMU as "the furthest along the path toward regional integration and trade" of all the regional groupings in Africa. The region has developed a suitable and ease of doing business climate, including free movement of capital and labor—although there is social and political instability in some of the member countries—that supports indigenous entrepreneurs and ensures an inflow of long time direct foreign investments to the region. The region's direct foreign investments are currently 3 percent of the world total foreign direct investment flows (World Investment Report, 2008).

Furthermore, ECOWAS and WAEMU have developed a common program of action on trade liberalization and macroeconomic policy convergence. ECOWAS and WAEMU have also agreed on common rules of origin to enhance trade, and ECOWAS has agreed to adopt WAEMU's customs declaration rules and compensation mechanisms (ECOWAS Annual Report 2008). Consequently, WAEMU may eventually have an important influence in the increased integration and trade in Africa, particularly in the ECOWAS region.

6.1.8. Economic Community of Central African States

The Economic Community of Central African States (ECCAS) is also a francophone organization. It is a regional economic community for the Central African states for the promotion of regional economic co-operation in Central Africa. It uses a single currency too, the Central African French Franc, particularly by the five former French colonies—Gabon, Congo Brazzaville, Cameroon, Central African Republic, and Chad—with a central bank in Yaunde, Cameroon that issues the currency. The currency is also pegged to the Euro through the French Treasury, which also ensures its stability and convertibility to other currencies.

The importance of ECCAS is due to the comprehensiveness of its target membership and its ultimate goal of establishing a Central African Common Market, focusing on four key priority areas, namely:

- To develop capacities to maintain peace, security and stability – as essential prerequisites for economic and social development in the region;
- To develop physical, economic, and monetary integration;
- To develop a culture of human integration;
- To establish an autonomous financing mechanism for ECCAS;
- To promote trade, the institutions of a genuine common market, and greater solidarity among peoples and towards under-privileged countries and regions.

Common institutions that have already been planned include a common parliament and common court of justice and the region's legal and financial systems have been standardized. And because of its centrality, in Africa, scholars have designated ECCAS as a major pillar of the African Economic Community, despite of its social and political instability in the past. This is one of the African regions that have experienced most political turbulences, civil wars, and most unstable governments in the past and even today in Central African Republic. These turbulences have been particularly severe in Chad, Central African Republic, DRC, Rwanda, and Burundi (See Table 8).

Cameroon is the economic powerhouse in this region despite its poor governance and being one of the poorest and most corrupt countries in Africa. But Gabon and Equatorial-Guinea have the highest per capita GDP and PPP per capita in the region. DRC is potentially the biggest market with 68 million people, followed by Cameroon with 20 million people, and Angola almost 20 million people, but with low per capita income and very poor business climate.

Table 8. Key macroeconomic factors per country and regional averages for ECCAS

Country	Population (Millions)	GDP USD (Billions)	GDP Growth Rate (%)	GDP per Capita USD	PPP per Capita USD	Inflation Rate (%)
Cameroon	20	26.4	4.4	1,260	2,330	2.7
C Brazzaville	3.7	8.7	5.7	3.485	3,240	4.9
Chad	11.5	12.0	7.0	823	1,360	2.6
CAR	4.5	2.0	4.2	489	810	2.8
DRC	67.8	15.2	5.1	231	340	15.1
Gabon	1.5	17.0	4.4	11,114	13,740	3.1
Angola	19.6	103.9	8.2	5,318	5,230	10.0
Burundi	8.6	2.3	4.8	271	610	9.7
Rwanda	10.9	6.1	7.6	583	1270	6.0
Sao Tome & Principe	0.2	.2	4.4	1,473	2,080	6.5
Equatorial Guinea	0.7	19.0	4.0	27,748	25,620	7.1
Total	149	212.8				
Average			5.4	4,800	5,148	6.4

Source 1: http://www.afdb.org: 2010.

Source 2: http://www.africaneconomicoutlook.org: 2010.

Source 3: http://data.worldbank.org: 2010.

Cameroon is perceived, in the Transparency International annual reports, as one of the most corrupt countries in Africa and the DR Congo and Angola have gone through long periods of civil war and instability. Gabon, Angola, and Cameroon are oil rich countries in the region that gives them an investment advantage. It is important to note that Burundi and Rwanda are in the East African Community and COMESA and Congo DR and Angola are in COMESA and SADC too.

Both WAEMU and ECCAS have common agreements meant to promote integration more effectively and hence increase the flow of trade in the two regions:

- The UEMOA (Union Economique et Monetaire Ouest Africain). Under this treaty, the WAEMU member countries have undertaken to coordinate their economic, financial, and structural policies;
- The CEMAC (Communauté Economique et Monétaire de l'Afrique Centrale). The long-term goals of CEMAC are to promote a convergence of macroeconomic policies, stabilize the common currency, create a single market, and harmonize sectoral policies and development in the Central African region;
- The agreement known as OHADA (Organisation pour l'HArmonization du Droits des Affaires en Afrique) which harmonizes a broad range of legal systems that previously covered a wide disparity in business law, codes, rules, regulations, and local conventions affecting businesses.

The OHADA agreement creates a number of uniform acts and sets up necessary organizations to implement the acts. These acts cover commercial law, law of commercial companies and economic interest groups, organization of securities, bankruptcy proceedings, and discharge of liabilities, law of debt collection, accounting, property rights, and arbitration of disputes. These are important laws and structures that will ensure a viable and sustainable business climate and increased integration in the region.

6.1.9. Association of WAEMU and ECCAS with France

One will always wonder and question the wisdom of the two Francophone regions having strong ties to France, with their currency, monetary, and fiscal policies being determined and controlled by the French Treasury. France is still having a strong hold in these countries as it did during the colonial times, using them as sources of cheap raw materials and markets for French manufactured and high value products. This association has made it difficult for these countries to more fully integrate with other ECOWAS countries making a bigger economic region.

France has something like a standing army in these countries and the regions to suppress, it is anecdotally said, any movements that might be viewed, even remotely, to be against French interests in any of these countries. Many observers in Africa think that the French army is the cause of instability in Ivory Coast, for example, since it cannot allow the Ivorian government army to have access to the northern half of the country since a northern attempt to succeed after the 1999 elections. In fact, the French army was instrumental in the removal of Mr. Gbabo and installation of Mr. Quattara as the president of Ivory Coast during the 2010 disputed presidential elections.

All the same, how healthy these relationships are, to the francophone countries involved and their people, is difficult to tell. In any case, these countries are the least stable, socially and politically, in Africa and are some of the poorest countries not only in Africa, but in the world despite being rich in natural resources that include land and large deposits of underground water. A recent report in the New Times by Nicolas Kristof described Togo and Niger as some of the least happy countries in the world today.

These countries should ally themselves more deeply to Africa, particularly in their respective African regions—ECOWAS and COMESA—to get out of the debilitating French relationship that is definitely detrimental to them. They should also get their political act together and deal with perennial insecurity and instability in these countries, two conditions that are a poverty trap in a country experiencing them. Otherwise, these countries will always be poor and a laughing stalk of the world because of their chronic poverty and hunger. Allying themselves more deeply with ECOWAS and COMESA will increase trade in the regions. This will lead to enhanced and more diversified economic development necessary to deal with pervasive poverty and chronic hunger in these mineral rich countries that France and its companies have exploited over the years.

6.1.9. The Maghreb Economic Union in North Africa

The Maghreb—a place of the sunset in Arabic—is an economic union and trade region in Northern Africa. It is also regarded as a Pan-Arab trade agreement that aims at economic and political unity in North Africa. According to scholars, the region is strategic and its strategic relevance—particularly to Europe—is based on the fact that, collectively, the region boasts large deposits of phosphate, oil, and gas, and it is a transit center to southern Europe from Africa. The shortest point from the Maghreb countries to Southern Europe—from Morocco to Spain—is just 8 miles across the Straits of Gibraltar.

The idea for an economic union of the Maghreb states began with the independence of Tunisia and Morocco from France in 1956. The actual union was not established until 1989; aiming at guaranteeing cooperation with similar regional institutions in order to promote regional trade and economic development to take part in the enrichment of the international dialogue to reinforce the independence of the member states and to safeguard their natural assets (See Figure 6).

The region is currently an attractive business area to the European Union. According to BusinessWeek (May 2009), led by Morocco and Tunisia, and because of their low labor costs, the region, of about 189 million people, is attracting direct foreign investments—more than $30 billion over the past five years—to build everything from auto and aerospace factories to five-star resorts and hotels, and call centers for multinational corporations.

Euler Hermes (2009), a consultancy that analyzes investment risk, now rates the region safer and better than Hungary, Romania, and Bulgaria, in terms of business risk and ease of doing business. The region is reforming and perfecting institutions and creating a favorable business climate to attract more and increasing foreign direct investments (BW May 2009).

The table below indicates the key macroeconomic factors that show the economic health of the region. The key factors are the total population, GDP and its growth rate, the GDP per capita, the Purchasing power parity (PPP) per capita for the region and annual inflation rate. The PPP is high and the annual inflation rate is low making the region an attractive investment area (See Table 9).

Carol Matlack and Stanley Reed (BW May 2009) assert that the Maghreb's appeal to Europe is even for more obvious reasons. It's in the Continent's backyard:

Figure 6. Arab Maghreb Union (UMA)

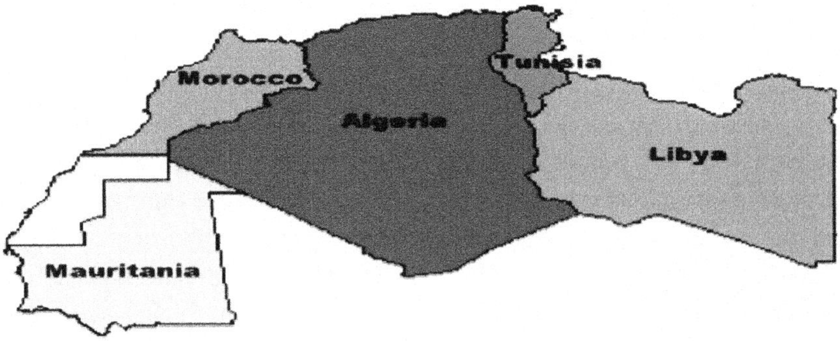

Table 9. Macroeconomic factors per country within the Maghreb Union

Country	Population (Millions)	GDP USD (Billions)	GDP Growth Rate (%)	GDP per Capita USD	PPP per Capita USD	Annual Inflation Rate (%)
Algeria	36	187.4	3.1	5,244	8,310	4.3
Libya	6.4	41.1	20.1	13,982	26,000	6.0
Mauritania	3.5	5.4	4.7	1,151	2,400	6.0
Morocco	32.3	105.6	4.5	3,054	4,880	1.6
Tunisia	10.6	47.1	2.5	4,297	9,030	4.7
Total	88.8	386.6				
Average			7.0	5,546	10,124	4.5

Source 1: http://www.afdb.org: 2010.
Source 2: http://www.africaneconomicoutlook.org: 2010.
Source 3: http://data.worldbank.org: 2010.

Tangier, in Morocco, as mentioned earlier, lies just eight miles from Spain across the Strait of Gibraltar. The region's governments have been relatively stable, albeit autocratic—however, they have gone through radical changes in recent days through the Arab Spring revolution—and they were business-friendly. It is also cheap to do business in the area, with factory wages averaging from $195 to $325 a month. Compare that with the average of $671 monthly paid in Eastern Europe and $350 paid in China. Hopefully the same business-friendly conditions will prevail after the Arab Spring has come and settled down.

Another attraction for multinationals in this region is skilled labor, due to high literacy levels. The schooling in countries like Morocco and Tunisia are some of the highest in the world. For example, the World Economic Forum ranks the quality of math and science education in Tunisia 7th in the world (the U.S. is 48th). Morocco has even opened an American-style university in the Atlas Mountains, where all courses are taught in English and students are expected to spend at least one semester abroad enhancing their ability to work globally and for the multinationals that wish to invest in Morocco in particular and in the Maghreb Economic Union generally.

However, trade among the Maghreb members is still very low. In the 2007 Regional Trade Report (RTR), the Secretary General of the Union asserted that Maghreb nations currently export more goods to the European Union – mainly raw materials - than to other countries in the region. This is "in spite of the efforts made on the level of the Arab Maghreb Union bilateral relations. Trade amongst Maghreb neighbors constitutes just a mere 3% of the total foreign trade of the countries in the region, except for Tunisian-Libyan exchanges, where figures show considerable growth of trade" (RTR, 2007).

Therefore, there is an urgent need to create a favorable climate—political and institutional—to increase trade in the region to enhance its economic development. As stated earlier, research data indicate that countries in the same region that trade more with each other grow faster and global trade has grown fastest regionally in the last fifty years and greatly contributed to advancement of the countries involved in the trade (Ghemawat, 2005). The European Union and NAFTA are cases in point.

Furthermore, the region needs to trade more with other African regions to increase intra-African trade. Currently, there is not much contact, in terms of trade, between the region and Sub-Saharan Africa. In fact, the region has had no any significant contact with the African Economic Community since its inception in 1991, in Nigeria, as the Logos declaration, although some countries, in the region, are seeking to be integrated individually with the other African regional trading blocs. Libya, for example, is a member of the Common Market of Eastern and Southern Africa (COMESA). Their fully joining the other African regions will make Africa an enviable and powerful economic region, effectively competing well - by exploiting its abundant opportunities - with other large and powerful emerging markets such as India, Brazil, and China.

In conclusion, African regional integration and trade remains one of the most crucial pillars around which African global trade marginalization can be addressed. Therefore, regionalization and greater integration of Africa are some of the key strategies that will help to propel the content into faster economic development to deal with poverty and hunger in the continent.

With increased economic development and improved socio-political environments, the continent is increasingly creating business opportunities, as a last frontier, which local entrepreneurs and multinational corporations must take advantage of to create increasing value for their stakeholders. And we now turn to the description of the African business opportunities and the strategies needed to exploit these opportunities.

REFERENCES

AFDB. (2008). *African economic development: The bank's annual report*. Tunis, Tunisia: AFDB.

AFDB. (n.d.). Retrieved from http.//www.afdb.com

Annan, K. (1999). *Peace and development: One struggle two fronts*. Retrieved from http://www.un.org/News/Press/docs/1999/19991019.sgsm7187.doc.html

AUC. (2012). *The commission strategic plan, 2009 – 2012*. Addis Ababa, Ethiopia: AU Commission.

Balfour, F. (2009, June 8). The surprising strength of South East Asia. *Business Week*.

Deng, F. M., & Zartman, W. I. (2002). *A strategic vision for Africa: The Kampala movement*. Washington, DC: The Brookings Institution.

EE. (1999). *American history*. Encarta Encyclopedia.

Frankel, J., & Rose, A. (2000). *An estimate of the effects of currency unions on growth*. Unpublished.

Ghemawat, P. (2005, December). Regional strategies for global leadership. *Harvard Business Review*. PMID:16334585.

Han, J. C. Y., Wild, J. J., & Wild, K. L. (2008). *International business* (4th ed.). Upper Saddle River, NJ: Pearson.

Juma, C. (2011). *The new harvest: Agricultural innovation in Africa*. Oxford, UK: Oxford University Press.

Kituyi, M. (2012, January 28). A free trade road map for Africa, but who will keep their promise?. *Daily Nation*.

Lynch, R. (2000). *Corporate strategy*. London: Pitman Publishing.

Mahajan, V. (2009). *Africa rising: How 900 million African consumers offer more than you think*. Amazon Kindle.

Marcelo, G. (2012, February 10). CobWeb of obstacles that make Africa unable to trade with itself. *Daily Nation*.

Mbaku, J. M. (1995). Emerging trade blocks and the fortune of African participation in the world economy. *Journal of Economic Integration, 10*(2). doi:10.11130/jei.1995.10.2.141.

Mbaku, J. M. (1998). Improving African participation in the global economy: The role of economic freedoms. *Business and the Contemporary, 10*(2).

Mbaku, J. M. (2004). *Institutions and development in Africa*. Africa World Press.

Moyo, D. (2008). *A small price to pay: Financing Africa's infrastructure bill. Global Economics Paper No: 174*. New York: Goldman Sachs.

Moyo, D. (2009). *Dead aid: Why aid is not working and how there is a better way for Africa*. New York: Farrar, Straus, and Giroux.

Porter, M. (1990). *Competitive advantage of nations model*. Retrieved from www.valuebasedmanagement.com

Porter, M. E. (1990). *The competitive advantage of nations*. New York: Free Press.

Porter, M. E. (1998, November-December). Clusters and the new economics of competition. *Harvard Business Review*. PMID:10187248.

Rozakis, L. (2007). *Schauni's quick guide to writing great research papers* (2nd ed.). New York: The McGraw-Hill Companies Inc..

Sachs, J. (2005). *End of poverty: The economic possibilities for our times*. New York: Penguin Books.

Suarez, F., & Lanzolla, G. (2005, April). Half-truths of first-mover advantage. *Harvard Business Review*. Editor. (2009, May 11). An interview with the Liberian President. *Time*.

UNCTAD. (2003). *International trade report*. New York: United Nations Trade and Development Report.

Wild, J. J., Wild, K. L., & Han, J. C. Y. (2008). *International business* (4th ed.). Upper Saddle River, NJ: Pearson.

Williamson, P. J. (1997, September-October). Asia's new competitive game. *Harvard Business Review*.

World Bank. (n.d.). Retrieved from http://data.worldbank.org

Chapter 6
Doing Business in Africa and African Business Opportunities

ABSTRACT

This is a key chapter in this book. It is central to the book's message and explains fully the concept "doing business in Africa." The chapter further classifies African business opportunities into enabling and specific opportunities. Specific opportunities are precise areas of Foreign Direct investments. The enabling opportunities are resources and institutions that make investing and doing business in Africa possible and easier. These resources and institutions include USA, European, Chinese, Brazilian, and Indian strategies to promote investment and "doing business in Africa." These strategies further include linkages and several USA, European, Indian, Brazilian, and Chinese institutions focusing on promoting African trade and business. Moreover, the various perspectives of Foreign Direct Investment in Africa are elucidated and African countries are classified according to their economic development and performance levels.

DOI: 10.4018/978-1-4666-4570-7.ch006

1. DOING BUSINESS IN AFRICA

Africa is the world's second-largest continent by landmass and contains more than 15 percent of the world's population. Sub-Saharan Africa is unique in that it has the largest number of countries per square area of any developing region. A large portion of Sub-Saharan Africa's population lives in landlocked countries compared to other regions; for example, Sub-Saharan Africa is 40% landlocked versus 23% for Eastern Europe (AER, 2010). The region is also unique for its low population density, which accentuates internal transport and communication costs. Sub-Saharan Africa remains one of the world's poorest regions but is growing fast at an average of 5.5 percent per annum in the last decade (ERA, 2010).

In a region where the basic needs of much of the population remain unmet, investment opportunities in the consumer sectors are limited for now. The consumption potential in the longer term, however, could be substantial as the region has favorable demographic trends – 70 percent of the population is under 30 years old and 40 percent is younger than 15 years old with increasingly improved educational standards. Economic growth and incomes per capita are accelerating. African Development Bank expects African GDP growth of 7.5 percent in the coming decade. A middle class is also developing fast (Benoni, 2010; AER, 2010).

As mentioned in chapter four, one of the more interesting opportunities in Africa currently resides in what the International Finance Corporation (IFC) and several academics have termed the 'Base of the Pyramid' (BOP). This represents those at the bottom of the consumer pyramids in many countries, who are poor by any western poverty line, but by their sheer numbers still constitute a significant purchasing power (Prahalad, 2005).

In Sub-Saharan Africa, the IFC currently estimates the BOP market at $429 billion, representing the region's dominant consumer market segment, with 71% of aggregate purchasing power. Even in South Africa, the region's largest and most modern economy, the BOP constitutes 75% of the economy. Other countries in the region offering even larger BOP market opportunities are Ethiopia $84 billion and Nigeria $74 billion (Moyo, 2009; AER, 2010; Prahalad, 2010; Juma, 2011).

Moreover, to many outsiders, Africa has long been a volatile and an unstable business environment with economies overly dependent on low value natural resources (Saltmarch, 2010). As a consequence, doing business in Africa has always been perceived as a difficult and a complex initiative and undertaking. Other reasons being the numerous difficulties and processes, both real and perceived, associated with conducting business in Africa. The numerous limitations and processes, combined with a fragile investment climate, include poor property rights, economic poverty, corruption, social and political instability, inadequate infrastructure, difficulties in identifying and choosing business partners, and, in a majority of cases, small and unviable national markets. However, the size of markets are currently changing or enlarging with increasingly advancing regional integration and trade (Mbaku, 1998; Annan, 1999; Deng, et al., 2002).

With regards to the complexities of doing business in Africa, the 2005 World Bank's world annual "Doing Business" Report revealed that, on average, Africa was the most difficult place to do business in the world when it comes to red tape, corruption, social and political instability; all those increase cost of doing business; and the perceived risks of doing business in Africa. The bureaucracy is meant to make the process of doing business in Africa slow and complicated in order to corruptly induce the investor to pay rent to private individuals and government officials.

The said World Bank 2005 report, further examines regulatory obstacles and ranks business performance using metrics such as ease of starting and closing a business, hiring and firing workers, certainty of enforcing contracts, getting partners, getting credit, and protecting investors. In the previous two years—2003 and 2004—sub-Saharan Africa had also been found to have reformed less than any other region of the world.

Yet, in recent times, a growing number of companies now talk of Africa as a land of opportunity and that Africa has always been ready for business (Mahajan, 2009). After all, not every African country is socially and politically unstable and with red tape. And, in any case, social and political instability and red tape are not really African problems per se, they are global problems. Countries like South Africa, Ghana, and Tanzania are good investment decisions; much better than many Asian countries that regularly experience sectarian and religious violence and are even victims of terrorist attacks targeting foreigners and foreign investments.

Still, a clutch of companies are already working in sectors like breweries, clean energy, aviation, engineering, defense, agriculture, tourism, and mining hoping to benefit from positive growth forecasts for Africa (Saltmonch, 2010). "If there was any more of Africa, we'd be investing in it," asserts Graham Mackay, the Chief Executive Officer of SABMiller (Mahajan, 2009). The brewing giant, formerly based in South Africa, but now headquartered in London, currently has interests in 29 African countries and increasingly intensifying business into other countries (Mahajan, 2009). Its positive attitude towards Africa will definitely enable the company to rip great benefits before competition intensifies. Its first-mover and incumbency will not only be a barrier to entry by others, in its industry, but it will also be a source of a first-mover and incumbency advantages that will give the company a sustainable competitive advantage in the African countries it has operations.

Again, with recently fewer conflicts, more democratic elections, institutional reforms, and economic growth rates that have gradually begun to compete with those of other strong developing and emerging regions like China, India, and Brazil, Africa is proving itself to be a continent of positive change (Deng et al., 2002). For the first time—in 2008—since "Doing Business" by the World Bank started tracking doing business institutional reforms, an African economy, Rwanda, among other African countries, led the world in reforms.

The report states that Rwanda has steadily reformed its commercial laws and institutions since 2001. In the past few years, it introduced a new company law that simplifies business start-ups and strengthened minority shareholder protections and general property rights. Entrepreneurs can now start a business with two procedures and in three days in Rwanda. Rwanda has also enacted new laws in order to improve regulations to ease access to credit. Other reforms removed bottlenecks at the property registry and the revenue authority, reducing the time required to register property by 255 days.

Overall, Rwanda introduced reforms in 7 out of the 10 categories covered in the report. The categories were: Starting a business, Dealing with licenses, Hiring and firing workers, Registering property, Getting credit, Protecting investors, Paying taxes, Trading across borders, Enforcing contracts, and Closing a business. In this regard, Rwanda rose from 143rd the previous year (2007) to 67th place in 2008 in the ease of doing business rankings making it as attractive to invest in as any country in any region of the world. Several other African countries are also carrying out similarly desired reforms; like Kenya has just—on August 4, 2010—overwhelmingly approved a new constitutional dispensation that improves the climate of doing business including enhanced individual and property rights.

Furthermore, since the late 1990s, developing countries have generally been the fastest growing markets in the world, for most products and services. Companies have lowered their costs by setting up manufacturing facilities and service centers in these areas where skilled labor and trained managers are relatively inexpensive (Khanna et al., 2005).

In this regard, Africa represents such a set of emerging markets with great potential and business opportunities enhanced by increased economic and regional integration (Mbaku, 1998). Regional integration in Africa is critical and it is enlarging previously small national markets into larger and competitive markets comparable in size to the currently attractive markets such as China, Brazil, and India, the emerging markets that are phenomenally growing.

Still, the countries of Africa are increasingly becoming mature and reforming democracies. With improved governance and enhanced reforms, African countries continue to foster a stable, predictable, and conducive business climate, with improving business environment rankings for many countries in each African region (EIU, 2009). Moyo (2009) has suggested several other reasons that are important and increase Africa's present attractiveness in business opportunities. The reasons include:

- Environmental resources such as oil, copper, gold, lumber, cocoa, diamonds, incomparable tourist attractions, and appropriate soils and land terrains for growing quality tea, coffee, and other food crops like corn, rice and wheat for local consumption and export;
- On the back of the market-based policies, instituted in the late 1980s and 1990s, African countries have benefited from a positive dividend. This has left Africa's macro-economic fundamentals on the up such as growth is rising, inflation is going down, and there is more transparent, prudent, and stable monetary and fiscal policies being pursued by African governments; and
- Despite the negative news headlines, particularly in the western press, there have been some noteworthy improvements in the social indicators in many African countries. In Kenya, for example, HIV prevalence rates have fallen from 15 percent in 2001 to 6 percent in 2006 and to 4 percent 2008 (UNAID 2008 Report). A commentator on the BBC also asserted recently "Sub-Saharan Africa continues to bear the brunt of the Aids pandemic but, many countries like Kenya and Uganda, stand out as some of the countries that appear to be turning the tide on HIV/AIDS. The proportion of the population infected with HIV/AIDS has fallen from 14% in 1997 to around 3% now. That is good news, but there are huge challenges that still lie ahead to ensure those gains are maintained and sustained for a long time to completely reverse the situation"
- There have also been some notable strides in the political landscape across the continent; more than just on paper. For example, of forty-eight sub-Saharan countries, over 50 percent hold regular democratic elections that can be deemed free and fair. The occurrence of democratic elections and decline in levels of perceived corruption in a number of countries, for example, Angola, Ghana, Senegal, Tanzania, and yes even Nigeria, point to a vastly improved investment and business climate;
- Fast developing financial market institutions such as growing and transparent stock exchanges—with increasing foreign participations in the stock markets, in many African countries. Accordingly, today, sixteen Africa countries boast well-functioning and transparent stock markets with market capitalization in 2008 (excluding South Africa) of around US$200 billion (around a quarter of Africa's total GDP). In three of the last five years, African stock exchanges have ranked among the best places to invest, with listed stock returns averaging 40 percent, with increased/growth in liquidity, measured as turn over, in the stock exchanges, of 50 percent in 2005 to 2006 alone.

The regional integration in Africa is also creating, not only bigger markets, but forcing small national markets to reform faster because of peer pressure, making it easier and more attractive to do business all over Africa. According to the Abuja Declaration of 2001revisted in Addis Ababa in 2011, the intention of the African leaders is to make Africa one large free trade area by the year 2017; creating business opportunities and competitive markets for outsourcing back office services and manufacturing operations comparable to India and China today (Mukhisa, 2012).

China and India are the world's foremost and largest emerging markets, at the moment, growing at phenomenal rates of 8-10 percent and the two countries are expected to have a middle class of 2 billion to 3 billion people, earning $ 5000 a year, in the next decade (Prahalad et al., 2010). But a regionally integrated and united Africa, with her great endowment of abundant environmental and human resources, should provide an excellent, unrivalled, alternative emerging market to the world.

In any case, and according to the World Bank World Economic Report 2008, 12 African countries—with 240 million people—have a higher per capita income than China and 20 African countries—with 400 million people—have a higher per capita income than India making them equally attractive markets. Therefore, all things considered, Africa is the last frontier for global business development to create increasing value for global corporations and local entrepreneurs.

Given its many sources of potential growth, Africa presents what can be termed the final frontier for investors looking at developing markets. Its bountiful natural and human resources present a host of opportunities (Bernstein, 2007). "Africa is the current economic battleground and the last frontier," Mr. Ichikowitz, a South African investor, said recently in Paris, where he was attending an investors' conference. "The Chinese and the Indians are coming in with huge amounts of cheap capital and a very open approach enhancing Africa's role in the world economy."

In The EastAfrican of July 5, 2010, President Paul Kagame of Rwanda further enhanced the notion of describing Africa as a last business frontier when discussing African business opportunities to investors in London recently. He asserted that "in recent years, Africa has progressed in many areas, particularly in economic growth, pointing out that those who still hold incorrect perceptions of Africa are missing great opportunities in the rising Africa. Africa has worked relentlessly to overcome the barriers to investment, it has reformed institutions and business regulations, and it has welcomed investment in key sectors such as telecommunications, energy, and banking. He further stressed and highlighted Africa's commitment to regional integration, as well as support of efforts to build larger markets of consumers by merging the East African Community with the Common Market for Eastern and Southern Africa (COMESA) and the Southern Africa Development Community (SADC) representing a total population of over 570 million with an average Purchasing Power Parity per capita of $ 6000".

"Moreover, the advantages of investing in Africa include the fact that the continent has experienced exponential growth particularly in infrastructure and energy, and holds attractive prospects in ICT, agro-business, mining, real estate, and construction. Also pointing out that these opportunities should be viewed in the light of "...the growing market potential of the African population, which by the end of this year will see Africa join India and China in surpassing one billion people".

Speaking on the importance of private equity in shaping the future of the African continent and in pursuit of African business opportunities, he asserted that as private investors looking for innovative investment opportunities and healthy returns, they represented ideal partners for Africa's pursuit of "a continent that is prosperous, economically and politically interconnected, internationally respected continent, that is in charge of its own destiny." China is aggressively expanding into Africa benefitting from these business development opportunities in the continent. However, before delving into Chinese investments in Africa, exploiting the African business opportunities and the definition of the African investment market, let us first look at the concepts of global foreign direct investments.

1.1. Global Foreign Direct Investments

According to the Organization for Economic Cooperation and Development (OECD) (2013), Direct Foreign Investment (FDI) is going into business that may include production in a country by a company in another country, either by buying a company in the target country or by expanding operations of an existing business in that country. Direct Foreign Investment is in contrast to portfolio investment which is a passive investment in the securities of another country such as stocks and bonds. Broadly, direct foreign investment includes mergers and acquisitions, joint ventures, strategic alliances, building new facilities, reinvesting profits earned from overseas operations, and intercompany loans.

According to the UN Conference on Trade and Development (UNCTAD), global inflows of Direct Foreign Investment (FDI) in 2010 totaled $1.12 trillion, slightly more than the $1.11 trillion recorded during 2009. More than $100 billion of FDI poured into China that year making it the world's second-largest recipient of such investment after the USA that received over $ 186 billion in FDI.

Over the past two decades, Direct Foreign Investment (FDI)—although only 5% of the global FDI flows—has become a vital source of economic development for the African continent. With an increase from approximately US$ 9 billion in 2000 to US$ 18 billion in 2004 and US$ 88 billion in 2008, FDI has become a major source of finance for Africa's development. But FDIs also address other issues such as human capital development, infrastructure, technology transfers, and enterprise development, and are likely to increase FDI spillover effects and contribute to economic growth and diversification.

Although the natural resources sector is traditionally a major recipient of FDI flows to Africa, high-value activities in services and manufacturing have recently attracted important investments. In addition, the global food crisis has stimulated foreign investors' interest in Africa's arable land. In the past, the agricultural sector has faced scant investment leading to low productivity, and a rapid increase in global and domestic demand of food, in recent years, is encouraging greater technological investment in agriculture improving productivity in this key sector of African economies. At this crucial juncture, the continent is now presenting itself as a new frontier for FDI.

This is particularly striking when considering that ODA flows to Africa reached US$ 44 billion in 2008, only half of FDI inflows. As mentioned above, foreign investors can provide many benefits to African economies: in addition to bringing more capital, tax revenues, exports and export diversification, foreign investors can also inject new technologies and corporate know-how into the local economy through fostering close linkages with local suppliers and other business partners.

For FDI to contribute fully to economic and social progress in Africa, host-country governments need to create a policy environment that enables them to maximize development returns on investment. Governments should thus develop a set of policies that promote direct foreign investments into their countries (UNCTAD, 2009).

1.2. American Companies Doing the Catching-Up from Chinese Government and Companies in Investment in Africa

Shambaugh (2013) describes China thus: "China is the most important rising power today. In two decades, China has moved from the periphery to the center of the international system. Every day and everywhere, China features prominently in global attention. Wherever one turns, China is in the news – gobbling up resources, soaking up investment, expanding its overseas footprint, asserting itself in its Asian neighborhood *and in African resources exploitation and building infrastructure,* being the sought-after suitor in global investments and governance diplomacy, sailing its navy into new waters, broadening its global media exposure and cultural presence, and managing a mega-economy that is an engine of global growth. China's global impact is increasingly felt on every continent, in most international institutions, and on many global issues. By many measures, China is now clearly the world's second leading power, after the United States, and its aggregate economy is due to surpass that of the United States sometime around 2025" *if not earlier.*

Furthermore, Hagerty and Connors (2011), two American business commentators and writers, assert that U.S.A companies are racing to catch-up China in investments in Africa. During a series of trips to Africa in 2010, for example, Tim

Solso, a Cummins Inc., Chief Executive Officer, had a calming realization: China was beating him and other Americans, even European corporations, at their own game in Africa *with hands down.*

Western European companies, many of which had lingering business interests in Africa from colonial days, also took their eye off the ball. Western Europe's share of overall trade—the sum of imports and exports—with sub-Saharan Africa dropped to 30% in 2009 from 52% in 1990, according to McKinsey. The share of China and other Asian countries in Africa trade more than doubled to 30% from 14% in the same period and increasing steadily, while North America's share slipped to 13% from 16% during the same period.

So the chief executive of Cummins Inc., a maker of truck and machinery engines, vowed to catch up, which is easier said than done. However, he plans to quadruple the company's sales in Africa to about $1 billion within five years, investing $15 million annually to train staff and build sales offices from Johannesburg to Casablanca. The company recently installed, in South Africa, an executive to oversee Africa operations, previously supervised from Europe and Indiana.

James Hagerty further discussed the push by many other U.S. companies, including General Electric and Caterpillar, vying for a stronger foothold in Africa. Cummins has ramped up sales of generators to clients particularly in Nigeria. Cummins joins a growing number of U.S. companies vying for a stronger foothold on the continent. Caterpillar Inc., the giant maker of construction equipment, is selling more trucks to Mozambique and Zambia. Harley-Davidson Inc. is opening dealerships in Botswana and Mauritius. General Electric Co. has its first aircraft-leasing office in Ghana for Central and West African airlines and has opened a hub office for all Africa, in Nairobi, Kenya. Google Inc., Archer Daniels Midland Co. and Wal-Mart Stores Inc. are among the dozens of other U.S. companies moving in or expanding into Africa to compete with the Chinese and others in the African markets.

Until now, "Africa has been just a rounding error for us," says Brady Southwick, Cummins's new head of Africa operations. U.S. companies' game of catch-up shows the perils of waking up late to the next big frontier market, Africa and the importance and effectiveness of the incumbency advantages China and India have to the disadvantage of the USA and the rest of the developed world. The continent's economy is forecast to grow to $2.6 trillion in 2020 from $1.6 trillion in 2008, fueled by booms in mining, agriculture and development of ports, roads and other infrastructure, and an educated young population providing cheap labor and middle class status according to McKinsey Global Institute. The middle class is growing, and total household spending now exceeds that of India.

Getting in early to the African market allows companies to build up strong brands and sales channels that can reap big profits in the long-run. That's what China has done in Africa over the past two decades. It has aggressively promoted trade and investment, courting countries by offering aid in exchange for favorable trade terms. China's government has provided funds to build a telecommunications network in Ethiopia, the Merowe Dam in Sudan, and railways in Libya and Nigeria. And a railway line, oil pipeline, and a highway, together, estimated to cost $ 24 billion, linking Kenya, Ethiopia, and South Sudan to Lamu—a port in Kenya—among many other projects in Africa. China has a true incumbent advantage in Africa not only against the American corporations but companies from other regions of the world. Often times, *first-mover and incumbent advantages* create barriers to entry for late comers into a market (Williamson, 1997).

1.3. The Definition of the African Investment Market and its Risks

Various countries of the world have their definitions and interpretations of private investments—or Foreign Direct Investment—and markets for these investments in Africa. These definitions and interpretations have influenced the choices they make in these investments and how the final success is determined by these choices (Hansen, 2012).

Anecdotal data indicates that Chinese investments in the world, including those in Africa, are led by the Chinese government and therefore decisions to invest outside China and in Africa are arrived at faster than investors from other countries do. USA investors, for example, usually use a rational model where everyone involved in the decision to invest has to be virtually convinced before the decision to invest is made after almost endless to and fro discussions. Therefore, the rational decision model may take forever to arrive at the actual investment decision hence the one major possible reason why investors from the USA and other countries are doing a catch-up of China in their foreign direct investments in Africa today.

U.S. private investment in Africa, like any business investment, is undertaken when an investor decides that the expected returns outweigh the known and unknown risks as perceived by those looking at the investment. Since Africa presents an enormous upside for returns, it must be deduced from the current paucity of U.S. private investments in Africa—particularly outside the extractive industries—that the risks are perceived by U.S. investors to be even larger than Africa's profit potential. Many scholars and the contributors to the materials for this statement seem united in their view that Africa is riskier to foreign investments than other regions of the world are significantly overblown.

Assuming that U.S. Government policy is to increase U.S. private investment in Africa, the task of U.S. agencies must be to reduce those specific investment risks which the market cannot itself overcome. In other words, the U.S. Government's task must be to correct market failures. This may seem like a commonplace observation, but it is actually fraught with complications in the light of existing U.S. Government policy. To begin with, the "market" for U.S. investment in Africa is very poorly understood, most especially by the U.S. "aid" agencies which dominate U.S. public and private involvement with the continent.

A "market" is simply a set of conditions that allow inputs to be introduced, related activity to occur, and outputs to be removed. In a simple trading market, for example, money and goods are introduced and then removed, with the only "related activity" being their exchange between the parties. Even for such a simple process, however, a large number of conditions must be in place.

At a bare minimum, there must be a forum in which both parties can reliably verify that the money and goods are actually on the table and removable. This in turn requires an identified and secure space, a legal system setting and enforcing the rules of engagement and for the exchange, ways to move the money and goods to and from the exchange, and so forth.

When direct investment rather than mere trading is undertaken, the number of relevant conditions increases exponentially. To start with, the inputs are seldom the same as the outputs. One may send materials to build a factory, and produce shoes as outputs. Even the money introduced and removed must often run through a conversion process. As for the "related activity," this is a whirlwind of interactions, purchases, sales, contracts, licenses, and labor. The sets of conditions applicable to these individual actions may overlap in part, or they may be unique. For an investor to determine whether a project is feasible, the investor must try to determine what conditions are required for each action, whether they are present, and whether they can be navigated to finish the desired project. This is what is simplistically referred to as the "return versus risk" calculation.

In the case of Africa, the "market" for U.S. direct investment has hardly been explored, so that its contours and conditions remain largely opaque and thus frightening for most U.S. business planners. For example, such a presumably simple matter as the purchase of a plot of land for a factory in Ghana can lead to unforeseen headaches as the U.S. investor runs into the complexities of a tribal land law that is both unknown and unimagined in U.S. corporate offices. Such pitfalls are called "unknown" risks, which are added to "known" risks such as those of expropriation, restrictions on profit-repatriation, and currency inconvertibility. But most of African currencies are convertible to international currencies like the Yen, dollar, and the Euro.

For most would-be U.S. investors and their funders, the risk-profile formed by these various, often inchoate risks points to a chance of large to total loss. This in turn raises the cost of project capital sky-high, if it is even available in the first place. Consequently, U.S. investors cannot achieve the financial "escape velocity" needed to reach Africa and its high-growth markets to invest.

To correct this fundamental "market failure" for U.S. private investment in Africa – the inability of business planners to develop risk-profiles that will attract affordable financing—"unknown" risks must be reduced to "known" risks, and these "known" risks must be then minimized by mitigation and offsets to allow a net-positive outlook for profits in American investment in Africa. The American government and its agencies can help a great deal in robustness and dynamism of this process; otherwise the American investors will always be doing a catch-up from the Chinese in the African investment market with its profitable potential (Hansen, 2012).

2. ENABLING BUSINESS OPPORTUNITIES IN AFRICA

In discussing the emerging business opportunities in Africa, one can easily categorize them into enabling and specific business opportunities. Enabling business opportunities are background and business climate conditions in the African economies and /or factors related to the African economies that support and promote business and investments in Africa. Specific opportunities, on the other hand, are areas of specific investment by corporations and entrepreneurs to create increasing value for their stakeholders.

Considering the risk profile of each African country or region, as might be expressed by the business environment and climate model, discussed above, the African continent and its allies offer many business-enabling opportunities, for exploitation by global companies and by domestic entrepreneurs. There is no region in the world with such a diverse array of enabling opportunities as Africa. The African business enabling opportunities include:

2.1. Macroeconomic Factors

According to Bernstein et al. (2007), the African economy is expanding at rates that exceed global growth rate and it is expected to do so for the next decade. African economic growth has been strong and should remain strong in the future because largely of commodity prices stimulated by Indian and Chinese high demand of these commodities for their expanding industrial complexes. International organizations including the IMF, World Bank, the Economist, and OECD, have also published solid economic growth forecasts for the continent, suggesting that the economy will grow at over 6 percent annually in the next decade. The African Development Bank predicts that African GPD will grow at 7.5 percent from 2010 to the feasible future. Therefore, as per capita incomes continue to rise and income distribution improves, a large consumer class—hence a large market for products and services—is emerging in Africa.

Furthermore, Africa's projected macroeconomic performance factors, indicated below; suggest that there exists a large market emerging for products and services in Africa. Therefore, these indicators, covering the period 2010 to 2014, provide the most concrete and first enabling opportunity of doing business in Africa. Taking a current average of the purchasing power parity of approximately $2000 per year, you have an estimated market size of over $ 2 trillion per year, a large market indeed, nearing the current Chinese market of approximately $ 2.5 trillion (EIU, 2009; AFDB, 2010).

Still, other than Zimbabwe, Sudan, and Somalia, general inflation, in Africa, is expected to be in the single digit—5 to 7 percent—in the next five years (EIU, 2009). Therefore, Africa will be, by all means, a low cost region to do business in by outsourcing manufacturing, research and development, and basic back office services. Low cost will not only make Africa able to diversify its productivity capacity, but it will also make Africa competitive. African products and services will effectively compete in the global markets as Asian markets are doing today. It is important to note that the competiveness of China, India, and other Asian emerging markets is lower-cost advantage, which Africa, with the right mix of economic and business policies and improved investments in education, infrastructure, and healthcare, should surpass, in the very near future (See Table 1).

2.2. Regional Integration

Regional integration and the creation of regional trading blocs and free trade areas, customs unions, and common markets, with similar trade and investment laws, are not only critical as they provide tremendous new opportunities for business in Africa, but they also create and provide bigger markets for goods and services.

The free trade areas, custom unions, and common markets, now accelerating in Africa, make entry into any part of Africa, to do business, much easier and less costly. They simplify legal and administrative structures to do business in the con-

Table 1. Macroeconomic performance factors for Africa 2010 - 2014

Year	2010	2011	2012	2013	2014
Real GDP Growth (%)	7.5	7.5	7.5	8.2	8.3
Population (m)	1,048.1	1,069.1	1,090.4	1,112.2	1,134.4
GDP (US $ b)	882	948	1020	1110	1200
GDP Per Head (US $)	837	948	1,010	1,100	1,200

Source: The Economist Intelligence Unit (2009) and African Development Bank (2010)

tinent and improve the business environment and climate generally. They increase inter-African trade that creates opportunities for employment and wealth creation, which, with improved income distribution, will increase consumers hence larger markets for products and services.

However, researchers (Rasco, et al., 2007) estimate that the high net worth individuals in Africa will rise by 6.1 percent and surpass the $ 1.2 trillion level wealth ownership through 2011, suggesting further wealth consolidation and concentration in a few hands in Africa making larger market creation difficult. For the continent to continue to develop, increased wealth distribution is critical and must be achieved, both in the short and long run, for Africa to be an attractive business market in the world.

2.3. Endowment of Abundant Natural Resources

Africa is filled with a lot of potential and risk, and in the next decade, both should provide investors with opportunities and poise the continent to enter an unprecedented stage of economic development while exploiting its abundant resources (Rasco et al., 2007). Africa is one of the world's leading producers of oil, gas, and diamonds, gold, cocoa, copper, uranium, has expansive arable land and exotic and unique wildlife sanctuaries and friendly people. African people are the friendliest people in the world and courtesy is natural to them (Diamond, 1998).

In discussing the value of natural resources, Kenya, Rwanda, and Ethiopia, in East Africa, for example, produce the best coffee—Arabica and Robusta coffee—in the world, from their unique land resources. Ivory Coast and Ghana are leaders in the production of cocoa in the world. Kenya, Tanzania, South Africa, and Botswana have the most beautiful and incomparable wildlife sanctuaries in the world. With improved democracy, governance and a transparent, accountable, and business supporting leadership, it should be easier and cheaper for international companies to exploit these abundant natural resources to create great value for their stakeholders. Starbuck Corporation is doing that in Rwanda, Ethiopia, and Kenya by obtaining high quality coffee for its many coffee shops around the world (Porter et al., 2011).

Scholars (Rasco and Bernstein, 2007) have further argued that Africa should be able to produce enough food to meet world needs in the near future. Africa is one of the largest continents in the world with an estimated 24 million square kilometers—almost one-quarter of the world's landmass—which is largely arable land. There are vast amounts of underutilized arable land in Africa that could be put to use relieving what has become one of the key constraints on global food production—the lack of arable land. This could present an even greater opportunity for many African nations, as the need to produce and export food may become a more pressing and urgent in the future, using irrigation technologies that exploit underground water.

Scientists say that the notoriously dry continent of Africa is sitting on a vast reservoir of groundwater. They argue that the total volume of water in aquifers underground is 100 times the amount found on the surface. The British geological team has recent produced the most detailed map yet of the scale and potential of this hidden water resource in Africa. The report states that this water will easily and cheaply be available for irrigation schemes in Africa (McGrath, 2012).

The world continues to struggle with constraints on food production and a lack of arable land. Africa, with its abundant land, could become a major food exporter, especially to countries like China and India that are struggling to feed their people and should become major food importers in the coming decades. As the Malawian President—the late Bingua wa Mutharika—asserted, in this regard, in an African Union Heads of State and Government meeting in February 2010:

We all know that Africa is endowed with vast fertile soils, favorable climate, vast water basins, and perennial rivers that could be utilized for irrigation farming and lead to the Green Revolution, and mitigate the adverse effects of climate change. We can therefore grow enough food to feed everybody in Africa and have plenty for export (Juma, 2011).

Africa has tremendous potential in agricultural business too. As proof of the need to develop agricultural resources in Africa, the World Bank recently announced a $500 million project for the development of the Niger Basin Water System and surrounding ecosystems. The project will take place over the next 12 years and will develop the Niger Basin for Nigeria, Benin, Mali, Guinea, Burkina Faso, Cameroon, Chad, and Ivory Coast. The project is designed to achieve sustainable water resources and improve water resources productivity including for irrigation, household consumption, and electricity generation (Bernstein, 2007).

African governments have also agreed to add to this potential in African agriculture. Hence, African governments have recently agreed to increase public investment in agriculture by a minimum of 10 percent of their national budgets and raise agricultural productivity by at least 6 percent in the next five years. Definitely, Africa can enhance this agricultural productivity through increased and efficient irrigation schemes (AU Commission 2009 – 2012 Strategic Plan).

2.4. African Population

Population growth rates and a younger demographic profile are favorable for Africa. According to the UN, population growth in Africa, through 2015, is expected to rise fastest in the world at 2.2%. The population of most African countries continues to be youthful, with children and youth aged 30 and under constituting over 70 percent of the continent's total population. High population rates and strong rural-urban migration have also led to high urbanization rates in Africa (ERA, 2010).

The share of the working population is set to accelerate over the next decade compared to a declining trend for the rest of the world. African youth—those under the age of 15—is expected to be 42 percent of its total population during this period. This presents some interesting business possibilities for Africa because it will provide the nations of Africa with young workers who will want to learn, train for skills, innovate, earn, and spend their earnings and of course most likely save some for investment. The challenges for the African leaders and governments will be to provide appropriate education, healthcare, and an appropriate business infrastructure so that they can become innovative and productive workers and big consumers in the new African global economy thus creating large markets for products and services (Wang, 2008).

Moreover, with currently fifteen percent of the world's population residing on the continent of Africa, the African continent's resources include a well-educated and rapidly urbanizing population that is a good source of qualified, quality, and low cost labor. Tanzania, for example, is one of the most urbanized countries in Africa, with over 40 percent of its population living in urban areas (EIU, 2009) which, theoretically, makes Tanzanian workers highly mobile from area to area in search of business and employment opportunities in the recently established East African Common Market (Juma, 2011).

Again, in a majority of African countries, literacy levels are high, with an increasing number of people having college education, albeit slowly. These are key indicators of availability of qualified and quality talent that is cost effective. Furthermore, the use of IT is becoming commonplace in Africa today. It is also important to note that the African people are, as mentioned above, the friendliest and most welcoming people in the world (Diamond, 1998). It is, therefore, more encouraging, sagacious, and wholesome to do business with the African people than with people from any other cultures in the world.

3. LEGAL FRAMEWORK AND INSTITUTIONAL SUPPORT WHEN DOING BUSINESS BETWEEN THE USA AND AFRICA

There are several supportive resources, legal frameworks, and institutions when doing business between the USA and Africa, for example. They have considerably contributed to the development and increased trade and business between the USA and Africa in the last three-decade. Some of the legal frameworks and institutions are:

3.1. The African Growth Opportunity Act (AGOA)

The African Growth and Opportunity Act (AGOA) is a United States Trade Act that significantly enhances U.S. market access for currently 41 African countries, mostly for textile exports. The Act originally covered the 8-year period from October 2000 to September 2008, but amendments in July 2004 further extended AGOA to 2015. The Act gives the African countries an opportunity to export textiles to the American market free of import controls. Its main objective is to help Africa develop through trade and investments rather than through aid and debt.

The Act has given rise to the development of a multiplicity of Export Processing Zones in many African countries. In these zones, foreign and local investors are shielded from bureaucratic and costly government procedures and therefore can quickly produce products destined for export to the USA at tax-free arrangements, extending up to 20 years. This arrangement also enables companies to enjoy tax-free privileges on their profits during that period. The arrangements are beneficial to participating African countries to the extent that they give rise to investments that have created jobs; creating over 300,000 jobs since AGOA inception in 2000 (Kristof, 2012).

The zones are open, for investment, to all interested investors from anywhere in the world, including local entrepreneurs, provided their products are destined for export and that their input is forty percent local. It is expected that products from these zones should be competitively priced, in global markets, particularly in USA market, due to their anticipated low production costs.

Furthermore, in these zones, foreign investors can partner with the local entrepreneurs to exploit the opportunities offered by the AGOA Act. South Africa, for example, is assembling BMW 3-series sedans cars, in Rosslyn City, for the USA market under the AGOA Act arrangements (Aquila no, 2005). The exports to the USA under AGOA have grown steadily during the last decade reaching over $81 billion in 2008 giving rise to over $64 billion trade surplus in favor of Africa (US Department of Commerce Report, 2009). A similar legal arrangement with the European Union would help Africa to grow further in creating jobs and wealth in the continent.

Still related to AGOA, in creating enabling business opportunities in Africa, is the strategy for Africa announced by President Obama recently. According to Kituyi (2012), the strategy entails several key elements that will promote business opportunities for American corporations and entrepreneurs in Africa on one hand and African entrepreneurs in the huge and large and profitable American market on the other hand. Among other things, Kituyi (2012), has described the strategy thus:

The core US interest in the African region is stated as ensuring the security of the US, her citizens, and allies; promoting states that are partners of the US in global matters, expanding US trade and investment opportunities, preventing conflict and fighting poverty. The strategy identifies four key objectives to focus on to achieve its goals: Strengthen democratic institutions, spur economic growth and development, advance peace and security, and promote business opportunities for American corporations and entrepreneurs in Africa and for African businesses and entrepreneurs in the American market through AGOA for example.

3.2. The United States Commercial Service

When doing business in Africa, American and African businesses can turn to the U.S. government for assistance. The U.S. Commercial Service is the trade promotion unit of the International Trade Administration. U.S. Commercial Service trade specialists in 107 U.S. cities and in more than 80 countries, work with American companies to help them get started in exporting or increase their sales to existing and new global markets. For example, the United States Commercial Service has an office in Dakar, Senegal meant to promote American businesses in Africa. The office covers eighteen Central and West African countries including Nigeria. Additionally, most embassies, consulates, and U.S. Government offices, overseas, have commercial sections that can provide market research, counseling services, and assistance in making contacts with U.S. and African businesses. The commercial sections are equipped with valuable resources to help businesses learn more about the market and to help locate potential customers, distributors, partners, and agents. Furthermore, there is a latest tool created by the U.S. Commercial Service meant to help businesses find buyers and sellers of their products analyze and qualify new markets, and close trade deals with other countries (USA Department of Commerce 2009 Annual Report).

3.3. The Export-Import Bank (EX-IM Bank)

Another tool available to American exporters and importers is the Export-Import Bank of the United States; an independent agency of the federal government. The Ex-IM Bank has one mission: *helping the private sector to create and maintain jobs by helping finance exports*. In over 60 years of operation, the Ex-IM Bank has used loan guarantees and insurance programs to support over US$ 300 billion in exports of U.S. goods and services.

The Ex-IM Bank is committed to making credit available for sellers of U.S. merchandise to qualified buyers in Africa, and recently it created a separate division that focuses on the development of increased lending in Africa to purchase American capital items such as airplanes and IT equipment. Lately, the bank has a $120 million credit facility covering short and long term lending with Angolan banks to enable private companies to have expedited access to American goods and services by Angolan importers. It also has a facility with 14 Nigerian banks covering long-term loan and insurance guarantees in support of American exports to Nigeria (2009 EX-IM Bank Report).

3.4. The Overseas Private Investment Corporation (OPIC)

The OPIC corporation offers U.S. investors political risk insurance against certain adverse action by foreign governments and against political violence. OPIC's political risk insurance also protects firms against expropriation and inconvertibility of foreign currencies to U.S. dollars that affect the repatriation of profits and other payments. In addition, OPIC offers long-term financing, directly or through guarantees, for commercially viable overseas projects that support U.S. foreign policy objectives. Therefore, African and American businesses can benefit from OPIC operations and various investment opportunities it creates and supports in Africa.

3.5. The African Diaspora Marketplace Initiative (ADM)

In 2010, the USA government, through USAID and in collaboration with Ecobank and Western Union Foundation, started an African Diaspora business initiative—The African Diaspora Marketplace (ADM)—meant to support the African Diaspora in the USA to start and run businesses in Africa applying the education and experience gained in the USA. The process is meant to export American technology and start businesses in Africa to enhance African economic development to create jobs in Africa in order to deal with poverty in the continent (Kamau, 2012).

A successful applicant, in this initiative, will receive $50,000 as a startup capital and an additional $25,000 – $50,000 in technical assistance to support the development of the business. This is a key business opportunity for the African Diaspora in the USA and for USA entrepreneurs to partner with Diaspora entrepreneurs to do business in Africa.

It is anticipated that ADM is an initiative that will encourage economic growth and employment in Africa by supporting US-based Diaspora entrepreneurs with ideas for start-ups and establish businesses in Africa. The first African Diaspora Marketplace (ADM) was held in 2010 and focused on grants towards agribusiness, renewable energy, and information and communications technology. The countries that qualify for consideration for the ADM grants include Kenya, Uganda, Tanzania, Rwanda, Ethiopia, Angola, Benin, Botswana, Cote D'Ivoire, Democratic Republic of Congo, Ghana, and South Africa.

4. AFRICAN CURRENCIES, BANKING SYSTEM, LEGAL FRAMEWORKS, AND STOCK EXCHANGE MARKETS

African currencies are an enabling opportunity in doing business in Africa. They may be low in value and in purchasing power but many of them are freely convertible into the dollar and other major currencies such the Euro, the Yen, the Yuan, and the Sterling Pound. Currency risk in Africa has also declined considerably due to the efficient and effective management of current accounts and exchange rates by the African governments. The currency exchange rates are usually flexibly market determined and generally stable (Rasco et al., 2009).

Additionally, in the last decade or so, the African countries have developed increasingly advancing Stock Exchange Markets for raising capital, in which shares are freely traded. According to financial market observers, in the African region, stock market capitalization of listed companies is soaring substantially reaching $ 200 billion in 2007 over a quarter of African GDP (Moyo 2009). The continued growth of local markets for financial services should be a key opportunity for growth in the business community. Another source of capital may be private equity, as many African companies have not yet attracted global attention. As the world of private equity continues to search for new markets for investors, Africa could provide a solid opportunity.

Furthermore, each of the seven African regions, discussed above, has a regional stock exchange that is comprised of the stock exchanges from each of the member countries, of the region, as members. These regional stock exchanges are currently making efforts to amalgamate into one African stock exchange in the near future (Wang et al., 2008). There is increasing foreign participations in these exchanges. For example, 20 percent - recently allowed to rise to 40 percent - of daily trading in the Nairobi Stock Exchange is foreign participation (Nairobi Stock Exchange Annual Report, 2010).

There is also a well-established banking system and a legal framework that enhances the effectiveness of managing the Stock Exchange Markets. There are global banks such as Barclays Bank and Standard Bank operating in many – particularly English speaking - African countries. A regional bank like Eco Bank of ECOWAS has over 783 branches globally many of them in Africa. Local banks, like Kenya Commercial Bank of Kenya, are growing and spreading in their regions enabling business and financial transactions in the region and allover Africa.

5. COST OF DOING BUSINESS IN AFRICA

Costs of doing business in Africa are relatively lower than in many other emerging markets. In Africa, labor is cheap averaging US$350 a month and large quantities of raw materials are available at significantly low cost (Moyo 2009). With regional integration gradually advancing, resulting in standardized trade and investment procedures, entry into large portions of Africa will be at considerably low business start up costs. Furthermore, and relative to South East Asia, doing business in African would be cheaper—in terms of communication and transportation—to the USA and Europe because Africa is much nearer to the USA and Europe than South East Asia is to the two regions.

However, poor infrastructure has made doing business in Africa slow and expensive making it unattractive investment destination. Also due to low productivity and therefore lack of global competitiveness, African firms are not able to compete on the integrated world market. But, African governments, through the African Union and Regional Economic Communities (RECs), are seriously addressing these issues through increased integrated country and regional infrastructure development schemes (AU Commission 2009 – 2012 Strategic Plan).

6. NATIONAL LITERACY LEVELS AND IT LITERACY

Due to high literacy levels, information and communication technologies are fast advancing in Africa. Computer literacy is rapidly increasing, particularly in the urban areas. Therefore, the telecommunication industry is growing rapidly as Africans consumers demand more, and better, communication services. Internet use is becoming widespread and the use of the mobile phone has expanded, considerably, in the last five years, but the industry still has tremendous upside potential (Rasco et al., 2007). It is estimated that one in every a thousand Africans has a mobile phone today, with a lot of potential for expansion. Landline phones are also expanding rapidly and it is estimated that there will be a telephone for every 10,000 people in the year 2015 (Mbaku 2004). As the population and per capita income continue to rise, the telecommunication industry appears poised to grow quite rapidly in the coming decade in Africa.

According to scholars and researchers (Bernstein et al., 2007; Moyo 2009; Wang et al., 2008), the effort to connect Africa technologically to the rest of the world by reducing IT related costs is seriously under way, and U.S. software giant Microsoft plans to be a big part of it. The company, through its Emerging Segments Marketing Division, is putting several plans into action in Africa including:

- Microsoft, the government of Burkina Faso, the African Development Bank, and the UN Economic Commission for Africa hosted a forum for "Best practices for IT" in Africa. The forum came out with a list of recommendations called The Ouagadougou Declaration, which called for African governments to develop e-governance strategies;
- Microsoft is offering its Microsoft Innovation suite software package, which includes all of its key software, for only $3.00;
- The UN and Microsoft have announced a partnership to set up PC refurbishment centers in Africa. Microsoft estimates that by 2010 there will be about 1 billion decommissioned computers in Africa. They believe that many of those used computers could be made available to allow small businesses across Africa to attain computer access at a much lower cost;
- The refurbishment effort would help in achieving Microsoft's goal of having 1 billion more computer users across the globe by 2015, many of them in Africa.

7. WORLD TRADE ORGANIZATION (WTO) MEMBERSHIP

Being members of WTO by African countries is essential not only to promote trade and investments among African countries, but also trade and investments with the rest of the world (ERA, 2010). All African countries are members of the WTO. The WTO membership is a source of negotiated trade and investment rules and regulations that are uniform worldwide. These rules protect investors and make investment across the world, including Africa, safer, easier, more reliable, and predictable. WTO also deals with trade disputes between countries. The WTO rules further enhance trade among African countries, regions, and with the rest of the world (ERA, 2010).

Within the WTO framework, African countries are negotiating and entering into trade agreements referred as the Economic Partnership Agreements (EPA) with the European Union (ERA, 2010). These agreements are meant to expand trade between Africa and the European Union countries. The African regional integration schemes are built into these negotiations and agreements that ensue. And the agreements are expected to boost business and trade, particularly for agricultural products, between Africa and the European Union creating business opportunities for corporations and entrepreneurs (ERA, 2010).

8. REFORMS AND EASE OF DOING BUSINESS RANKINGS

The institutional environment in Africa—the rule of law, freedom of the press, independent judiciary, and general business environment—remain low and weak according to the well-known institutional rankings such the World Economic Forum's Global Competitiveness Index and the World Bank's Doing Business Rankings. But these reports mask the considerable changes and improvements and rapidly increasing pace of reforms that has taken place in Africa during the last decade (ERA, 2010).

The economic freedom or business climate environment rankings for African countries are improving over the years. Countries like South Africa, Zambia, Botswana, Mauritius, Kenya, Ghana, Namibia, Rwanda, and Uganda are having an average ranking of 6.5, in 2007. The highest ranked country, in the world, is Hong Kong, with a ranking of 8.8 (Singapore 8.6, USA 8.5, and UK 8.4) (EIU, 2009). High ranking implies a higher quality business environment and the greater reliance on markets in the allocation of economic resources rather than by the state. Low ranking, on the other hand, indicates countries in which resource allocation systems have been politicized and the government is the dominant institution in decision making in the economy. The indicators analyzed in the business environment and economic freedom ranking model include political elements, macroeconomic factors, market opportunities, policy towards private enterprise and competition, policy towards foreign investment, foreign trade and exchange controls, taxes and tax rates, capital markets, labor markets, the infrastructure, and of course, governance (EIU, 2009).

Africa is rapidly reforming in all these elements (EIU, 2009). Two African countries, for example, Kenya and Ghana, ranked among the top 10 reformers globally in 2007. Over the 2006/2007 fiscal period, Ghana eased access to credit, reduced bottlenecks in property registration, cut time to import and introduced arbitration in commercial courts. Over the same period, Kenya eliminated 110 business licenses, reduced waiting period for land valuations, and expanded the private credit bureau database to include retailers and utilities. Furthermore, there have been greater improvements in other performance indicators such as governance, accountability, perception of corruption, and political stability in countries like Botswana, Mauritius, Rwanda, Ethiopia, and Ghana than in industrialized countries such as Greece and Italy (Wang et al., 2008). It is possible low rankings of African countries by these global institutions are done—like the mostly failed IMF/World Bank 1980's and 1990's structural adjustment programs—without an appropriate African input and therefore they do not really and accurately reflect the true African situation.

The economic reforms many African countries have undertaken in the last two decades have fiscal discipline that has generated smaller public and private deficits, more prudent use of resources, lower inflation, and higher international reserves, all of which make Africa less vulnerable to cyclical downturns. Less vulnerability to downturns will ensure sustainable African economic development that will create jobs and wealth thus creating markets for products and services (Moyo, 2009).

9. MULTILATERAL AND BILATERAL DEBT WRITE OFFS AND CREDIT RATINGS OF AFRICAN ECONOMIES

African debt has almost been halved—from a peak of $ 200 billion with $ 88 billion written off in recent times—in the last decade as a result of comprehensive debt relief from persistent campaigns by civil society under the banner of make poverty history and the enhanced Heavy Indebted Poor Countries (HIPC) and Multilateral Debt Relief (MDRI) initiatives (Wang et al., 2008).

Still, a lot of Africa debt is outstanding and therefore, American and European corporations—and even Indian and Chinese companies that are increasingly doing business in Africa—can create and increase business opportunities in Africa by campaigning to influence the G8 countries, the World Bank, the IMF, and other bilateral and multilateral lenders, to write off the remaining African debts owed—to these countries and institutions—by African countries. And insist that the savings from the debt write offs are strictly invested in education, infrastructure, healthcare, agriculture, institutional reforms, and protection of the environment in the African countries obtaining the debt relief. Investments in these six critical national development sectors, in the African countries, will not only stimulate businesses and create jobs, hence wealth and purchasing power, but their development will also make it a lot easier and cheaper to do business in Africa.

Moreover, low debt ratios have improved African countries' credit ratings—by the international credit rating agencies such as Standard and Poor Agency—that will accelerate capital flows to Africa. Increased capital flow to Africa will enhance economic development to further improve business opportunities (Wang et al., 2008). Positive credit ratings have also allowed some countries to tap international capital markets for urgently needed funds for development.

Ghana, for example, issued a $ 750 million international bond in September 2007, which was four times oversubscribed. Gabon followed suit in December 2007 with a $ 1 billion bond under similar terms. Two Nigerian banks, GT Bank and Diamond Bank, as well as the Kenyan mobile operator Safaricom, have all been able to tap international equity markets over the last two years (Wang et al., 2008). All these economic occurrences are important testimonies to Africa's economic and market reforms prowess opening business opportunities.

10. LINKS TO CHINA AND INDIA

Despite the historical, geographical, political, social, educational, and cultural differences between China and Africa, there are still many lessons from China's technological transformation that can inspire Africa's efforts to turn around its low growth rates and thus increase its pace of development. Therefore, a major source of Africa's more encouraging growth and development prospects—that is creating enabling business opportunities—is the new, large, and more diversified availability of development funding from China and India. Africa's traditional dependence on the West—particularly the Organization for Economic Cooperation and Development (OECD) countries—for investments and aid funds—is declining, while investments and funding from other emerging markets, particularly China and India, is accelerating (Moyo, 2009).

Over the years, "China's relations *and trade* with Africa have blossomed. Trade went up from less than $ 5 billion in 1995 to $ 127 billion in 2010. The growth in trade is largely the result of Africa's abundant oil and mineral reserves. Oil comprises 80 percent of African exports to China (Angola accounts for 37 percent of China oil imports alone). It is followed by timber, diamonds, copper, and iron ore. In return, China exports machinery and equipment, appliances, apparel, and footwear to Africa" (Shambaugh, 2013). The trade balances are said to be currently in favor of China, but China and African countries are developing trade strategies to have the trade in favor of Africa.

China and its parastatals, including its national banks, are proving to be some of the most important sources of public and private sector investments and infrastructure finance for Africa. In return, China has gained access to Africa's huge resource deposits to meet its tremendous growth needs as it gallops to greater economic prosperity surpassing Japan in the process, in 2010, as the second largest economy in the world after the USA (Barboza, 2010).

According to Barboza (2010), after three decades of spectacular growth, China passed Japan in the second quarter of 2010 to become the world's second-largest economy behind the United States of America. However, the recognition came in early August in 2010, when the government of Japan said that Japan's economy was valued at about $ 5.12 trillion or $ 1.28 trillion in the second quarter of 2010 alone, slightly below China's $ 5.32 trillion, or $ 1.33 trillion in the second quarter of 2010 too.

Experts say unseating Japan—and in recent years passing Germany, France, and Great Britain—underscores China's growing clout and bolsters forecasts that China will pass the United States as the world's biggest economy as early as 2030 if not sooner with the Chinese economy growing at a staggering 10.5 percent per annum, while the USA economy growing at an anemic 2 percent per annum. The milestone, though anticipated for some time, is the most striking evidence yet that China's ascendance is for real and that the rest of the world will have to reckon with a new economic superpower that is seriously engaged in other emerging markets like those of Africa. Africa should be to learn from the Chinese accelerated growth rate.

America's gross domestic product was about $14 trillion in 2009 while that of China was about $ 4.7 trillion. If one extrapolates the two growth rates, China's economy will definitely pass the USA economy much earlier than 2030. "This has enormous significance," said Nicholas R. Lardy, an economist at the Peterson Institute for International Economics. "It reconfirms what's been happening for the better part of a decade: China has been eclipsing Japan economically. For everyone in China's region and Africa, they're now the biggest trading partners rather than the U.S. or Japan" (Barboza, 2010).

For Japan, whose economy has been stagnating for more than a decade, the figures reflect a decline in economic and political power. Japan has had the world's second-largest economy status for much of the last four decades, according to the World Bank. And during the 1980s, there was even talk about Japan's economy someday overtaking that of the United States (Brboza, 2010).

But and while Japan's economy is mature and its population aging, China is in the throes of urbanization and is far from developed, analysts say, meaning it has a much lower standard of living, as well as a lot more room to grow with a strong sense of adventure, vigor, and rigor, while the USA and Japanese economies are tired and needs a great deal of creative and innovative ideas to reinvigorate them to their bygone dynamism and prowess (Barboza, 2010). Just five years ago, China's gross domestic product was about $2.3 trillion, about half of Japan's. There is strong evidence that similar spectacular results would be achieved by Africa as it works closely with China in education, trade, investments, and infrastructure development.

For example, China has bid for oil blocks in Nigeria and Angola in return for financing railways and roads. The most ambitious project to date, however, has been an agreement with the Democratic Republic of Congo (DRC) to finance $ 9.3 billion—later reduced to $ 6 billion—worth of infrastructure projects including roads, railways, dams, water and sanitation, electricity, and airports in return for rights to five copper and cobalt mines in DRC southern mineral belt, which contains some of the world's richest ore deposits (Wang, et al., 2008). And the latest investment yet will be the largest ever. That is the $ 24 billion investment for a rail line, a road, and an oil pipeline from Juba, South Sudan, to Lamu in Kenya's north coast with a branch to Addis Ababa Ethiopia from central Kenya. The project will include a 165 square kilometers water dam that will provide water for irrigation, drinking, and generating electricity (Kang'aru and Mureithi, 2013). Certainly, all these investments will improve the opportunities of doing business in Africa but the opportunities must be well and effectively managed by the Africans for the sole benefit of the African people.

India has also been using its Export-Import Bank to support the development of power projects in Nigeria and Sudan, where it is developing natural resources interests. Indian infrastructure support in Africa averaged $ 500 million per year in 2003-2007. Other emerging markets like Brazil are making tremendous support to African development through their contribution to African infrastructure, agriculture, education, and IT development that is enhancing doing business in Africa (Wang et al., 2008).

However, African countries must be wary of China and India in their insatiable need and quest for resources. Relying on China and India can easily turn Africa into a mercantilist region and state for the provision of cheap raw materials and markets for high priced manufactured products and services produced in China and India. Such a relationship would turn Africa into its colonial and postcolonial status and will continue to contribute to Africa's current state of pervasive and chronic poverty and hunger.

Africa should negotiate better prices for their resources and to use their increasing revenue from these resources to appropriately diversify their economies. They should use these resources to improve both quantity and quality of education, innovation and technology, healthcare, and to be able to competitively manufacture value added products for global markets. It is also very important that the African countries use some of these revenues to improve their agricultural practices, technology, and systems as a means of increasing food production.

Surplus food can be used to not only sustainably deal with chronic hunger in Africa, but also as export to China and India that are expected—as discussed earlier - to need large quantities of food imports in the next decade or so to feed their aging populations. Scholars (Prahalad, et al., 2010) estimate that China and India will have between 2 billion and 3 billion middle class consumers, with a $ 5000 per capita income, in the next decade that will need large quantities of food and other perquisites of life. The two countries will, therefore, provide a large market for African food exports and hence business opportunities in the agricultural industry.

11. AFRICA-ASIA TRADE

According to the African Economic Report (2010), African trade has remained highly volatile and pro-cyclical and continues to be largely determined by global economic developments. The continent's merchandise trade remains undiversified, both in portfolio mix and destination. Unprocessed agricultural products, mineral mining, and raw fuel products constitute at least 80 percent of exports. Most of these exports go to Europe and North America even though there has been a discernible shift towards Asia, especially China and India. This trade portfolio and destination concentration exacerbated the vulnerability of Africa to the western countries' economic and financial crises with dire consequences on the African economies.

Moving forward, it is clear that Africa needs to build on the continuing shift in its trade structure towards Asia so that its strategic interests are protected and generate resources for economic development to create an enabling environment for business opportunities. Specifically, the growing trade with China, India, and other Asian countries should be different in terms of composition from that which the region has had with the advanced countries of Europe and the USA. This will happen if deliberate efforts are made to ensure that it is not just a shift of the same exports from the traditional markets to the new markets.

Instead, African trade with the phenomenally rising economies of Asia should be tangibly different by composition, with increasing share of manufactured goods and services. This has implications for the flow of investments from Asia to Africa, which must go beyond the extractive sectors to establishing joint ventures that add value to the raw commodities within Africa. This will ensure that Africa-Asia trade and investment help to create decent jobs in the value-adding sectors and hence deal with the pervasive problems of poverty and hunger in Africa and, additionally, increase opportunities of doing business in Africa.

12. SPECIFIC BUSINESS OPPORTUNITIES AND INVESTMENTS IN AFRICA

Enabling opportunities create an environment and supportive and conducive conditions that make doing successful business in Africa possible and easier. Specific opportunities are the real elements of the environment that can be developed, through Foreign Direct Investments, to create value for stakeholders and the nations of Africa. Africa is filled with specific opportunities and a diverse resource base that can provide sufficient stimuli for economic and business development so that the region should continue to thrive for many years to come (Mahajan, 2009).

However, the specific business opportunities in Africa require critical thought and strategies to find and exploit them. These opportunities are open to all those interested in doing business in Africa. Indeed, there is a growing and increasing convergence of product and service needs in all Africa (Mahajan, 2009), albeit cultural differences may present differences in specific products and services that may be offered and required in each nation or region of Africa. Definitely, there are differences within nations too because of social and cultural differences including religion, language, ecosystems, infrastructure, and technology in use.

Some African regions have certain competitive advantages that others do not have. The analysis below assume prior research and attempts to present a general picture of what Africa requires and can be produced competitively at the moment and areas it has a competitive advantage over the other regions of the world (Mahajan, 2009). Therefore, the following specific business opportunities are suggested for the various African regions and countries covering several and different industries. They have been classified into ten key industrial or market groupings:

12.1. Key Business Opportunities in the Healthcare Sector in Africa

Despite the complexities of the problems and challenges of healthcare in Africa, healthcare in Africa presents many business opportunities for astute local and global entrepreneurs and corporations. These opportunities exist in:

- Pharmaceuticals to manufacture and supply drugs required for treatment of HIV/AIDS, malaria, Tuberculosis, and other diseases;
- Manufacture and distribution of treated mosquito nets;
- Manufacturing and distribution of immunization kits;
- Incorporation of healthcare insurance companies to offer insurance services to the rising African middle class. It is estimated that there are 300 million potential middle class populations in Africa today and increasing at 2.5 percent annually.
- Building new hospitals and well equipped healthcare delivery services including diagnostic and research services;
- Incorporation of financial service institutions to finance healthcare development in Africa;
- Build and equip healthcare training institutions to train paramedics including nurses, medical technicians, and social workers, some to be employed in the West;
- Create, equip, and operate counseling centers, dialysis facilities, and ambulance services.

12.2. Key Opportunities in Information Technology and Communications

- Information Technology in terms of small business process packages, including accounting, selling, and production packages for all regions of Africa;
- Internet development including service centers and networking in all cities and towns in Africa;
- Manufacturing of mobile phones: Africa has the fasted growing market and rate of mobile phones in the world today. There is a growing demand for quality and low priced mobile phones in all regions of Africa. Initially, it may be necessary to export these phones to the various regions with plans to manufacture them in the most cost effective region as the demand for them becomes stronger. You can site factories in the regional economic powerhouses discussed in chapter five above.

12.3. Key Opportunities in Agriculture, Livestock, and Agro-Businesses

African food needs are massive. Add to this an increasing demand of food globally, particularly by India and China, and then you have a huge business opportunity in agriculture in Africa. Africa has abundant arable land and labor which, with sound policies and technology, could be translated into greatly increased production, incomes, and food security. This has not materialized because of lack of consistent policies, appropriate technology application, and effective implementation of strategies arising from the neglect of the sector.

Specifically, Africa has 733 million hectares of arable land, which is 27.4 percent of the world's land mass, compared with 570 million hectares for Latin America, and 628 million hectares for Asia. Only 17% of African arable land is cultivated, 3.8% of African's surface and ground water is harnessed, while irrigation covers only 7% of cropland (3.6% in Sub-Saharan Africa). A recent British geological survey established that Africa has the largest amount of underground water in the world including in the Saharan region. "Scientists say that the notoriously dry continent of Africa is sitting on a vast reservoir of groundwater. They argue that the total volume of water in aquifers underground is 100 times the amount found on the surface. This team has produced the most detailed map yet of the scale and potential of this hidden African resource" (McGrath, 2012). This large quantity of water can be tapped to greatly increase irrigated agriculture in Africa. Clearly, there is considerable scope for both horizontal and vertical expansion in African agriculture (AER, 2010; Juma, 2011).

Furthermore, agriculture is considered central to African economies—it generates 34% of the Gross Domestic Product (GDP) and 60% of employment—but it is treated like other sectors, each with their own distinctive institutions and with little regard for their relationship with the rest of the economy. This view is reinforced by traditional approaches, which argue that economic transition occurs in stages that involve the transfer of capital from agricultural sector to the individual sectors. Both the sector and stage approaches conceal important linkages between agriculture and other sectors of the economy. A more realistic view is to treat economies and their various sectors as systems of innovations that reinforce each other (AER, 2010; Juma, 2011). Specific business opportunities in African agriculture include:

- Tea processing for export from the East African/COMESA regions in partnership with local processors. Kenya and Malawi are well known for producing quality tea in the world that is often needed to blended with teas from other regions of the world to improve the tea quality overall;
- Coffee processing and exporting from the East African region (Kenya, Rwanda, and Ethiopia) in partnership with local grinders, processors, and entrepreneurs. Kenya produces Robusta coffee, Rwanda and Ethiopia produce Arabica coffee and their coffee are often blended to produce higher quality coffee;
- Growing food crop-stables such as corn, wheat, and rice. The demand for these crops will considerably increase in the coming decades. One can also grow African green vegetables for export too to areas or countries of large African Diaspora;
- Exportation of fruits such as bananas, oranges, and cashew nuts from West Africa;
- Palm oil and Cocoa processing for export in Nigeria, Ivory Coast, and Ghana. Ivory Coast and Ghana are two leading producers of cocoa in the world;
- Food franchises in the major cities of Africa. This strategy may require growing raw materials to obtain the high quality food standards required to have a sustainable competitive advantage. It is often said that McDonald Corporation is pursuing this strategy in Russia, where it is growing potatoes and producing beef for its restaurants to ensure high quality products. The same can be done with beef in Kenya, South Africa, and Botswana and export beef to all Africa even the world;
- Growing of indigenous foods such as yam and cassava in West Africa and sweet potatoes and arrowroots in East Africa and exporting them to the USA and European cities where there are large numbers of African Diasporas. It is important to note too that Africa's arable land is reducing at an alarming rate due to population increases, therefore, the urgent need for growing indig-

enous foods that require relatively smaller land sizes in order to grow enough food to feed the rising population numbers and hence effectively deal with chronic food shortages and hunger in the continent;

- Cattle ranching for production of beef for export in Botswana and Kenya. There are large tracks of semi-arid land in these countries that companies can lease for ranching operations to produce beef for export particularly to the Middle-East markets and increasingly to China and the USA;
- Fertilizer manufacturing and or export. Almost all African countries currently import their fertilizer. It is estimated that Africa needs 6 million tons of additional fertilizers annually to meet its food production needs. A firm interested in this business can initially export to the continent and then begin manufacturing, in a suitably selected region or in one of the regional economic powerhouses, either as a joint venture with local entrepreneurs or government, or a greenhouse operation. Fertilizer is a strategic agricultural input in all African countries; therefore, African governments will welcome and support this business with possible tax shields. Furthermore, Africa is ripe for a green revolution like that that occurred in India and Mexico over three decades go to feed its increasing population that today suffers from chronic food shortages. Every African country almost experiences food shortages, annually, and therefore, hunger in Africa, is a big business opportunity far into the future;
- Irrigation systems. Develop and implement different irrigation systems in different semi-arid regions of Africa so as to improve and increase cultivation of various crops such as corn, wheat as well as fruits such as pineapples and oranges and of course livestock development. For example, almost 50 percent of land in Kenya is semi-arid. The irrigation systems and arrangements will assist in dealing with chronic food shortages and hunger in Africa and growing food for export particularly to India and China that are anticipated to need food imports in coming decades (Prahalad, 2010). Tapping ground water will enhance the irrigation systems and arrangements in Kenya and in many other countries including the Saharan countries;
- Develop man-made fishponds, from existing rivers and fresh water lakes, to grow and export fish filet to America and Europe. Many African countries have all Season Rivers which can be diverted to make fish ponds. Additionally, the water can be used for irrigation to enhance food production to deal with African hunger. It is important to note that the Eastern African lakes—Victoria, Tanganyika, and Nyasa—are fresh water lakes and the lakes produce excellent tilapia that is popular in the world particularly with Africans in the Diaspora;

- Producing and packaging horticultural produce for export to Europe, the Americas, India, and China. It is anecdotally said that as Indians and Chinese become wealthier; their admiration and appreciation of roses is increasing more intensely.

12.3.1. Renting of Land in Africa

There is an increasingly worrying phenomenon occurring in Africa today concerning African land. Anecdotal data and press reports indicate that Africa is selling or leasing its arable land to global hedge funds from Europe and to other countries. These institutions and countries buy or lease the land to cultivate and to grow food crops for the countries involved and for bio-fuel. The leases are for long periods. A case in point is that of Tanzania. It has been recently reported that Tanzania has leased several million hectares of its arable land to the government of Bangladesh for 99 years to grow rice. Other information sources further indicate that the Tanzanian peasants have been removed from their ancestral land to make room for the leases without compensation.

Furthermore, the government of Bangladesh has brought, to Tanzania, its people, mostly women, as employees to grow the rice. The government of Tanzania will take 40 percent and Bangladesh will take 60 percent of the resulting crop. It is not clear whether the government of Bangladesh will pay – and how much - for the leased land and the crop they will take. More so, these arrangements appear to have created employment for the people of Bangladesh and not Tanzanians, perpetuating the exploitation of Africans by foreigners as it has happened over the years.

There is nothing wrong in Africans leasing land to other people or countries. However, and if African nations enter into land sale or lease agreements with hedge funds and other governments to grow food crops and for fuel; one would expect and hope that this strategy is part of a greater national scheme and strategy to eradicate poverty and chronic hunger in Africa and to grow food for export to generate resources for national development. Such moves could also be viewed as part of a global attempt at creating business opportunities in Africa. But Africans must be in full control in creating and managing such arrangements. The arrangements should also be debated and appropriately approved by their respective parliaments before agreements are eventually entered into to safeguard national resources and minimize corruption in such agreements.

In addition, the leasers of African land should bring in the technology, train and employ the African labor and management to use such technology and to manage such farms. The African governments should be wary of anybody who wants to do and manage such arrangements for them. The African governments should decide how the resulting crop is shared and crop given away should be paid for in full at market prices.

Africa has bled, been used, and plundered by others long enough and therefore, modern African leaders and policy makers should be careful to ensure that the African resources are used purely and solely for the enrichment of the African people. Africa should not continue enriching others as it has done over the centuries and time immemorial at the expense of its people. African nations must also not be misled to pursue destructive policies—decided outside Africa by non-Africans—as it did during the structural adjustment programs of the 1980s and 1990s that left Africans poorer than they were at the start of those programs (Moyo, 2009).

Still, one is left wondering how Africa will ever recover or be compensated from the damage done to Africa by such externally formulated and misguided programs that have impoverished its people over the years. Between 1970 and 1998, for example, when the World Bank and IMF structural adjustment programs were at their peak, poverty in African rose from 11 percent to a staggering 66 percent! That is roughly 600 million out of 1 billion Africans trapped in a quagmire of poverty – a truly large and shocking figure indeed (Moyo, 2009).

When discussing the need for the USA to sell food to China and Saudi Arabia, Clinton (2011) has also noted that in the past few years, China, Saudi Arabia, and other countries with lots of money and limited capacity to feed themselves have bought or leased land in Africa and Asia to produce food, with minimal *positive* results for them and for the countries with the land. Foreign owners are far more likely than domestic ones to disrupt traditional farmers and over utilize land and water, thinking that they can always go somewhere else when the land plays out or when there is no more water for irrigation.

Clinton (2011) further asserts that a far better course is to build the capacity of developing countries, including those of Africa, to grow enough food, *with sustainable agricultural practices*, to feed themselves, and increase the incomes of their farmers. Some of the farmers will also become exporters to China, *India,* Saudi Arabia, and other countries with food deficiency, but they will grow food in a way that enhances land fertility, their self-sufficiency, and their prosperity in the long-run.

12.4. Key Opportunities in Manufacturing

- Furniture manufacturing in Western, and Central Africa where there is a lot of timber from the expansive rain forests in these regions. Ghana and Cameroon are leading timber producers for export in Africa. More timber can be produced in Congo DRC and Congo Brazzaville, including in the smaller states in the region;
- Biotechnology development to manufacture drugs, particularly for malaria, including nets for malaria prevention, diagnostic equipment and vaccination

kits for children and adults, HIV retrievals, and tuberculosis medicines basing manufacturing in the regional economic powerhouses discussed in chapter five above;

- Textile manufacturing in the Export Processing Zones ensuring having a sustainable cost advantage over China and India and exporting the same to the US under the AGOA arrangements and to Europe under EPA arrangements;
- Cement exports/manufacturing. Anecdotal data indicates that many African countries are planning to use cement for road construction and therefore large quantities of cement will be required to meet this demand for cement now and in the future.

12.5. Key Opportunities in Tourism, Wildlife, and Entertainment

In commenting on a recent tourism business forum in Nairobi, Kenya, Straziuso (2012) states that new high rise hotels is the face of Africa today. Nairobi, for example, has seen the construction of several upscale properties in recent years, as developers eye an increase in business travel to a continent with rising business prospects.

International hotel developers are planning nearly 40,000 new rooms across Africa in the coming years to cater for increased business travel to Africa. Travel and tourism in Africa generate about $ 164 billion a year, 9 percent of the continent's total GDP and tourism generates almost 19 million jobs in Africa, 7.1 percent of all employment in the continent. And this business is expected to grow in the coming years. Other specific opportunities in this growing area include:

- Africa has a definite competitive advantage in wildlife that is exotic and a lot of them—likely lions—are mostly found in the African savanna;
- Business opportunities are in wildlife management including building of lodges/camping sites, tour/safari operations, and filming operations to promote wildlife attractions in Kenya/Tanzania and South Africa/Botswana and northern Ghana and Nigeria and central African countries;
- Entertainment in terms of cinemas and video libraries in major cities and towns in Africa.

12.6. Key Opportunities in Oil, Gas, and Mineral Mining

- Oil and gas exploration and adding value to oil and gas by building oil refineries. It is estimated that there are each 4 billion barrels/cubic meters of untapped oil and gas deposits in the coast of Tanzania alone. Nigeria and Angola are the largest oil producers in Sub-Saharan Africa. All Maghreb countries and South Sudan are large oil producers too. There is oil in Cameroon, Mauritania, Ghana, Gabon, and many other smaller African countries including lately Uganda and Kenya;

- Mining operations and adding value to precious metals—such as gold, diamonds, copper, and gemstones—in Angola, South Africa, Zambia, Namibia, Tanzania, Mauritania, Mali, DRC, and Botswana to mention but the major producers.

12.7. Key Opportunities in Electricity Generation and Distribution

- Electricity generation, related equipment, and technology are in high demand in Africa. Many African countries depend on hydroelectric generation of electricity that depends mostly on rainwater; the rain that is generally unreliable in most parts of Africa. Therefore, many Africa countries are electric power deficient with regular power cuts that seriously impacts on the cost of electricity further impacting the cost of products and services. To generate more and sustainable electric power, including development of renewal sources of energy, is going to be a growing business opportunity in Africa for a long time to come.

More significantly, Africa is endowed with huge renewal and non-renewable energy resources that are under-utilized. These resources are unevenly distributed. Yet, there is minimal interstate energy trade which would have created economies of scale to attract investment. Geothermal resources are available in abundance in Africa; and yet the continent exploits less than 1 percent of its estimated geothermal potential. Furthermore, the continent receives abundant solar radiation and has coal and wind energy resources. These energy resources can be harnessed to meet the continent's energy needs into the foreseeable future. Developing and harnessing these abundant resources is a great business opportunity in Africa (AU Commission 2009 – 2012 Strategic Plan).

12.8. Key Opportunities in Education and Training

American, Chinese, and European universities can do business in Africa: Africa is exciting and vibrant with educational opportunities for western and Asian universities. The demand for education, in Africa, particularly continuous or executive education, is high and strong. The African universities cannot cope with what is described, in

Kenya, as module II or parallel programs. These programs accommodate working students, who attend classes in the evenings and weekends. For example, if you go to the University of Nairobi these days, 5pm to 9pm, Monday to Friday and the whole day Saturdays and even Sundays; the place is bustling with activities with students, of all ages attending classes. The programs are in so much demand that many Kenyan universities, particularly the so called public universities—government owned universities—are buying high rise office blocks, in Nairobi centre city, to gain a competitive advantage and, of course, to accommodate the rising number of students (Daily Nation October 13, 2009).The programs cover many of the university courses including business administration, accounting and finance, science and medicine. The students pay their fees and/or get financial support from their employers. There is also a government funded agency—Higher Education Loan Board (HELB)—that extends educational loans to interested and qualified students:

- American, European, and Chinese universities, particularly the most popular ones—the Ivy League schools and State Universities—could open campuses in the major African cities like Nairobi, Lagos, Accra, Johannesburg, Cape Town, and Cairo;
- Alternatively, the foreign universities can go into joint ventures with the local universities.

12.9. Key Opportunities in Banking, Investment, Financial, and Other Services

Opportunities in financial and investment services are increasing in bounds and rips in Africa as the continent develops and becomes part of the global economy. Governments need huge financial resources for infrastructure development. These opportunities include:

- Mutual and Hedge funds investments, particularly in the stock markets;
- Private equity and sovereignty wealth funds investments;
- Provision of insurance and reinsurance services;
- Investments and financial instruments including sovereign and private bonds;
- Advertising services;
- Credit rating services;
- Leasing and hire purchase services; medical and healthcare services.

12.10. Key Opportunities in Water Provisions and Water Management

- Africans are poorly and unsustainably supplied with water despite permanent rivers and streams scattered all over the continent. The Africans are water hungry, as it were, everywhere and all the time;
- Water management has never been done professionally well in Africa since independence. Therefore, provision of sustainable water to large cities and urban centers of Africa and even in the African rural areas—for human and animal consumption—is a massive challenge and business opportunity for many years to come.

Furthermore, and according to UNCTAD (2008 Report), there is great business potential for trade in primary commodities, including meat, tropical beverages, cotton, diamonds, and non-ferrous metals, in the Southern African region. It further asserts that a few resource-intensive basic products, such as cotton, yarn, cement, and some types of woven fabrics, could also be extensively traded in.

Opportunities also exist for intra-regional trade in food items, such as maize/corn, sweet potatoes, cassava and cassava products, and fish, as well as live animals and bovine meat in the Western African region. In the Eastern African and Southern African regions, there is a scope for increasing inter-regional trade in water, electricity, tourism, services, and creative industries such as filming, music, dance, and handicrafts.

13. AFRICAN COUNTRIES CLASSIFIED IN TERMS OF THEIR ECONOMIC PERFORMANCE, EASE OF DOING BUSINESS, AND BUSINESS OPPORTUNITIES

In 2010, South Africa hosted the World Cup of football and the message that it is Africa's time reverberated across the world like the cacophony of a million vuvuzelas—South African traditional trumpets—announcing that Africa's moment had come. Economists, consultants, and company executives all suggested that the African economy, which had languished during the last two decades of the 20th century, because of the failure of the poorly designed and implemented IMF/World Bank structural adjustment programs of the 1980's and 1990's, was finally stirring up (Chironga et al., 2011).

The challenges of doing business in Africa and how to overcome them are discussed, in details, in chapters nine and ten below. However and according to UN data, today Africa offers a higher return on investment than any other emerging markets.

For several reasons: Competition is still less intense and a few foreign companies have a major presence in Africa, and a strong pent-up consumer demand. Therefore, companies that desire strong revenue and profit growth can longer ignore Africa.

Over the past decade, Africa's real GDP grew by 4.7%, on average – twice the pace of its growth in the 1980s and 1990s. By 2009, Africa's collectively GDP of $ 1.6 trillion was roughly equal to that of Brazil and Russia. Africa is among the fastest-expanding economic regions in the world today. In fact, Africa and Asia, excluding Japan, were the only continents that grew during the 2007/2008 economic and financial meltdown. Although Africa's growth rate slowed to 2% in 2009, it bounced back to nearly 5% in 2010, and 5.2% in 2011 (Wamelen et al., 2011).

Wamelen et al., 2011, further assert that despite the challenges—poor infrastructure, poverty, low education levels, famine, poor and corrupt leaders, and poor business climate—Africa faces, it has great potential in business opportunities, particularly for consumer companies. Africans spent $860 billion in 2008 – 35% more than $635 billion that Indians spent, and slightly more than $821 billion of consumer expenditures in Russia. If Africa maintains its current growth trajectory, consumers will buy $1.4 trillion worth of goods and services in 2020, which will be a little less than India's projected $1.7 trillion but more than Russia's $960 billion.

Other sources of Africa's potential for accelerated economic development and development of business opportunities include:

- Increased regional integration and trade to increase Africa markets and generate economies of scale that will reduce cost of production to increase the competitiveness of African products and services in the domestic and global markets;
- Expected increase in commodity price and diversification of the African economies to increase value adding to African products, services, and factors of production including labor;
- Increasing, in African, political stability and safety as a result of improved governance and increasing democratization that will attract increased foreign direct investment into the continent;
- The African governments are adopting market friendly policies. Many African governments are adopting "smart" regulations like in many South East Asian countries in order to make it easier and cheaper for companies to enter and do business in Africa;
- African economies are becoming healthier as governments shrink budget deficits, trim foreign debt, and bring inflation down. Since 2000, African countries have cut combined foreign debt from 82% of GDP to 59% and rcduced budget deficits from 4.6% of GDP to 1.8% percent, which sent inflation rates tumbling from 22% to 8%.

Scholar (Lund et al., 2011), have, further, drawn data on African economies from a variety of sources and organizations such as the World Bank, IMF, Organization for Economic Cooperation and Development (OECD),and the Economist Intelligence Unit to be able to categorize African countries into economic performance, ease of doing business, and business opportunities groups. Economists usually group countries by income level and/or geography; however, business consultants and practicing managers use economic diversification and level of exports to categorize countries into business opportunities.

As economies develop, agriculture and natural resources account for a smaller and smaller share of GDP, while the share of high value manufacturing and services grows. That boosts per capita income, with a 15% increase in manufacturing and services as a share of GDP usually resulting in the doubling of per capita income. Exports are the means by which emerging economies earn hard currency to pay for imports of capital goods, services, and technology. In most African countries, imports of goods, services, and technology account for half of the investment in Africa, making exports a critical enabler of economic growth. The following are the broad categories of the African economies using the above categorization criteria, namely economic diversification, ease of doing business, and export earnings and per consultants' and managers' categorization of economies:

Diversified Economies: These economies include Egypt, Morocco, South Africa, Botswana, Tunisia, Mauritius, Namibia, among others. These economies have relatively high per capita incomes and stable GDP growth than most of the other economies despite the political risks—the Arab Spring—that have come to the fore particularly in North Africa in recent months. They have reformed consistently over the years. Services in these countries such as banking, insurance, tourism, telecommunication, and retailing, account for more than 70% of GDP growth in these countries over the past two decades.

These countries are also the largest African consumer markets. 90% of the households in these economies have increasing discretionary income. That makes them ideal places for consumer-dependent businesses to anchor their operations. They are relatively easy countries to do business. Wal-Mart, a large USA retailer, for example, recently struck a $2.4 billion deal to pick up a 51% stake in one of South Africa's largest retailers, Massmart, which has retail stores in 13 other African countries.

The problem with these diversified African economies is that they have higher labor cost than China, India, and Asia generally and therefore struggle to compete even in low-value manufacturing industries in global markets. They urgently need to expand exports to achieve economies of scale, considerably improve productivity, educational standards, healthcare, and governance, more reform to improve the business climate, and build a solid infrastructure as the lifeline of their economies to reduce cost of operation in these economies in order to be competitive in the domestic and global markets. Increased participation, by these countries, in regional integration and trade initiatives in their regions will considerably enhance their market reach and enable them achieve higher economies of scale to considerably improve their competiveness in domestic and global markets.

The Oil Exporting Economies: Africa's oil and gas or commodity exporters have the continent's highest per capita—although poorly distributed—but they are also the least diversified African economies mainly of the resource curse disused earlier. The oil and gas countries include Libya, Nigeria, Angola, Sudan (South Sudan), Equatorial Guinea, Algeria, Congo PR, and Gabon; they are the largest oil and gas producers in Africa. They are growing rapidly and because of their income levels—although poorly distributed—they are attractive markets for high-end goods and services.

The greatest challenges of oil or commodity exporters generally has been persistent political instability and the inability to resist the temptation to over invest in oil and gas or commodity exploitation, which makes the countries vulnerable to oil and/or commodity prices decline, rather than create a diversified economy. These countries also need to urgently improve their education, infrastructure, governance, and diversification of their economies to improve their economic sophistication, produce high value but competitive products and services for the domestic and global markets to enhance their growth rates rather than simply rely on exports of pure raw commodities. They should increase their participation in regional integration and trade in their respective regions to increase market reach for their products and services to enhance their efforts to diversify their economies.

The Transition Economies: The African transition economies include Ghana, Kenya, Uganda, Tanzania, Senegal, Mozambique, Cameroon, Rwanda, Zambia, and Madagascar. These countries have lower per capita income than the first two categories but they are growing rapidly. Tanzania and Rwanda, for example, are expected to grow at almost 7% and 8% respectively, on average, in the next two years (Karambu, 2012).

Though the agricultural and the resource sectors of these countries, together account for as much as 35% of GDP and two-thirds of exports, the countries are increasingly exporting manufactured goods and service to other African countries that result from increasing regional integration and trade in Africa in recent years. The penetration of banking, telecommunication, and modern retailing services is much lower in many of these countries than it is in the diversified economies, but that offers attractive business opportunities in these economies.

Several transition economies are likely to increase their commodity exports in the coming years which will enhance their growth rates. In Ghana and Uganda, for example, recent oil discoveries will boost tax revenue, making it easier for them to diversify their economies. These countries should also invest more in education; infrastructure, both in-country and inter-regional infrastructure; agriculture; governance; participate more in regional integration in their regions; and in "smart" regulations to enable them attract foreign direct investment to diversify their economies. A diversified economy—increased manufacturing and services and their exports—adds more value to the economy and creates better paying jobs hence enhancing wealth creation and a market opportunity for products and services.

The Pre-Transition Economies: These economies are absolutely poor; with annual GDP per capita of just $330 on average despite that some of them are rich in raw materials and plenty of arable land. These countries include Congo DR, Ethiopia, Mali, Sierra Leone, Niger, Central African Republic, Burkina Faso, Burundi, among others. These countries have grown at 7%, on average, since 2000. However, their growth has been erratic in the past. These countries also differ greatly, but all of them lack basics, such as stable governments, strong public institutions, viable infrastructure, and sustainable agricultural development.

These countries need to invest heavily in education; infrastructure, agriculture, governance, and institutional reform in order to attract some form of foreign direct invest to exploit their abundant natural resources. They should also participate more in regional integration initiatives in their regions in order to enlarge their market reach to enable them diversify their limited economies. All these investments will offer great business opportunities to local and global entrepreneurs and corporations particularly in those countries that are part of high-level regional integration schemes such as Burundi that is in the already achieved East African Common Market – requiring free flow of goods, services, labor, and capital among member countries. The countries comprise of Kenya, Uganda, Tanzania, Rwanda, and Burundi, with a total regional population of 139.9 million people (Kituyi, 2012).

As discussed above, trade and business opportunities in Africa are rife and new ones continue to increasingly emerge. And the chances for their exploitation are improving daily through economic and institutional reforms by the African countries. For any company seeking to enter into the potentially hazardous yet certainly profitable African environment and market, well thought out market screening and entry strategies must be creatively developed and deployed to enter and do business in Africa. The following chapter will delve deeper into market screening stages and market entry strategies that can be employed to enter into the African market and will provide ways of gathering quality information to analyze and evaluate these difficult and yet necessary processes of market screening, selection, and entry strategies.

Table 2. Key economic indicators of African countries

Development Level/Country	GNI per Capita (USA $	Population (Million)
Diversified Economies – 8 countries		
Botswana	6,790.0	2.0
Egypt	2,440.0	82.5
Ivory Coast	1,160.0	20.2
Mauritius	1,030.0	3.5
Morocco	2,900.0	32.3
Namibia	4,500.0	2.3
South Africa	6,090.0	50.5
Tunisia	4,060.0	10.4
Oil Exporting Economies – 10 countries		
Equatorial Guinea	14,540.0	0.7
Libya	12,320.0	6.4
Nigeria	1,180.0	162.4
Angola	3,940.0	19.6
Gabon	7,740.0	1.5
Congo Rep.	2,150.0	4.1
Algeria	4,750.0	35.9
Mauritania	1,030.0	3.5
Sudan/S. Sudan	1,270.0	43.2
Chad	620.0	11.5
Transition Economies – 10 countries		
Cameroon	1,180.0	20.0
Cape Verde	3,270.0	0.6
Ghana	1,230.0	25.0
Kenya	790.0	41.6
Madagascar	430.0	21.3
Mozambique	440.0	22.9
Rwanda	520.0	10.9
Tanzania	530.0	46.0
Uganda	500.0	33.8
Zambia	1,070.0	13.2

continued on following page

Table 2. Continued

Development Level/Country	GNI per Capita (USA $	Population (Million)
Pre-Transition Economies -25 countries		
Benin	780.0	9.1
Burkina Faso	650.0	16.9
Burundi	170.0	8.6
CAR	470.0	4.5
Comoros	750.0	0.8
Congo DR	180.0	67.7
Djibouti	1,270.0	0.9
Eritrea	340.0	5.4
Ethiopia	390.0	84.7
Gambia	450.0	1.8
Guinea	400.0	10.2
Guinea-Bissau	590.0	1.5
Lesotho	1,040.0	2.2
Liberia	200.0	4.1
Malawi	330.0	15.4
Mali	600.0	15.8
Niger	350.0	16.0
Sao Tome and Principe	1,200.0	0.2
Seychelles	9,760.0	0.9
Sierra Leone	340.0	10.0
Somalia	n/a	9.5
Swaziland	2,630.0	1.2
Togo	490.0	6.8
Zimbabwe	460.0	12.6

Sources: Chironga et al., 2011 and www.bbc.com on March 16, 2012.

Notes: GNI: Gross National Income - GDP covers domestic production transactions only - includes international transactions that include Diaspora remittances. The highest GNI per capita in Africa is that of Equatorial Guinea of $14,540.0 and the lowest is that of Burundi at $ 170.0. Somalia is a failed state; therefore it is not possible to measure its national income or product. The richest country in the world, Norway, has a GNI per capita of more than $ 56,000. The USA GNI per capita is over $ 46,000.

Africa's accelerated growth after 2000 is due to the end of the debilitating IMF and World Bank structural adjustment programs of the 1980's and 1990's – plus persistently poor African leadership - that impoverished Africa and left Africa worse off economically and poorer than it was in the 1970's. And that is how Africa fell behind the Asian Tigers (Singapore, Hong Kong, Taiwan, and South Korea) and the Asian Club (Malaysia, Thailand, and Indonesia) many of them that gained independence at the same time as many African countries and were at the same level economically in the early 1960 (Moyo, 2009).

13.1. Mapping Out the Categorization of African Economies

Africa's growth accelerated after 2000—at end of the debilitating structural adjustments programs, see note below—and continued even during the 2008/09 global recession. It is more robust and vibrant today growing at more than 5.2% on average. However, Africa's 54 nations are at different stages of developing as their varying levels of exports, economic diversification and sophistication reveal. The economies fall into four categories, described above, in terms of growth and business opportunities: diversified economies, oil exporting economies, transition economies, and pre-transition economies (Chironga, et al., 2011). Moreover, they are expanding their small and unviable markets through increasing regional integration and trade as discussed in chapter five above. The African countries' actual key economic indicators are categorized and shown in Table 2.

REFERENCES

AFDB. (2010). *African development bank economic report, 2010*. Tunis, Tunisia: AFDB.

Annan, K. (1999). *Peace and development: One struggle two fronts*. Retrieved from http://www.un.org/News/Press/docs/1999/19991019.sgsm7187.doc.html

AU. (2012). *African union strategic plan 2009-2012*. Addis Ababa, Ethiopia: AU.

Barboza, D. (2010, August 15). China passes Japan as the second-largest economy in the world. *New York Times*.

Benoni, C. (2010, December 14). I foresee 7.5 percent growth rates in Africa in 2010: African development bank (AFDB) president, Donald Kaberuka. *The East Afrrican*.

Bernstein, R., & Rasco, J. (2007, July 23). Africa, the final frontier. *Merrill Lynch Report*.

Chironga, M., Leke, A., & van Wamelen, A. (2011). *Checking the next growth market: Africa*. Boston: Harvard Business School Publishing in partnership with the Economist Intelligence Unit of the Economist Magazine.

Clinton, W. J. (2011). *Back to work: Why we need smart government for a strong economy*. New York: Alfred A. Knopf.

Deng, F. M., & Zartman, W. I. (2002). *A strategic vision for Africa: The Kampala movement*. Washington, DC: The Brookings Institution.

Diamond, J. (1998). *Guns, germs, and steel: The fates of human societies*. New York: W. W. Norton and Company.

ERA. (2009). *Economic report on Africa*. Addis Ababa, Ethiopia: AU Commission.

ERA. (2010). *Economic report on Africa*. Addis Ababa, Ethiopia: AU Commission.

EX-IM Bank. (2009). *World investments by EX-IM bank report*. Washington, DC: The Export and Import Bank of America.

Frederick, B. (2009, June 8). The surprising strength of South East Asia. *Business Week*.

Hansen, P. C. (2013, January 1). *Compendium*. Working Group on American Investment in Africa.

Juma, C. (2011). *The new harvest: Agricultural innovation in Africa*. Oxford, UK: Oxford University Press.

Kagame, P. (2009, May 30). Regional integration, an interview. *Daily Nation*.

Kamau, S. (2012, February 11). African diaspora to boost investment in Africa. *The East African*.

Karambu, I. (2012a, January 23). Kenya's growth rate to fall behind other East African states in the next two years: Quoting Mr. Wolfgang Fengler of the World Bank. *Daily Nation*.

Karambu, I. (2012b, February 8). Trade barriers costing Africa billions of dollars, says World Bank. *Daily Nation*.

Khanna, T., Palepu, G. K., & Sinha, J. (2005, June). Strategies that fit emerging markets. *Harvard Business Review*. PMID:15938439.

Khanna, T., & Pelepu, G. K. (2005, May). Strategies for emerging markets. *Harvard Business Review*. PMID:15938439.

Kituyi, M. (2012a, January 28). A free trade road map for Africa, but who will keep their promise?. *Daily Nation*.

Kituyi, M. (2012b, June 30). Obama's strategy for Africa and the continent's reality. *Daily Nation*.

Kristof, N. D. (2012, June 30). Africa on the rise. *New York Times*.

Mahajan, V. (2009). *Africa rising: How 900 million African consumers offer more than you think*. Amazon Kindle.

Mbaku, J. M. (1998). Improving African participation in the global economy: The role of economic freedoms. *Business and the Contemporary, 10*(2).

Mbaku, J. M. (1998a). Emerging trade blocks and the fortune of African participation in the world economy. *Journal of Economic Integration, 10*(2).

Mbaku, J. M. (2004). *Institutions and development in Africa*. Africa World Press.

McGrath, M. (2012, April 20). 'Huge' water resource exists under Africa. *BBC World Service*.

Moyo, D. (2008). *A small price to pay: Financing Africa's infrastructure bill. Global Economics Paper No: 174*. New York: Goldman Sachs.

Moyo, D. (2009). *Dead aid: Why aid is not working and how there is a better way for Africa*. New York: Farrar, Straus, and Giroux.

NSE. (2010). *Nairobi stock exchange annual report*. Nairobi, Kenya: NSE.

OECD. (2008). Definition. In *The OECD Benchmark Definition of Foreign Direct Investment* (4th ed.). Paris: OECD.

Prahalad, C. K. (2005). *The fortune at the bottom of the pyramid (BOP): Eradicating poverty through profits: Enabling dignity and choice through markets*. Philadelphia: Wharton School Publishing.

Prahalad, C. K., & Meshelkar, R. A. (2010, July-August). Innovation's holy grail. *Harvard Business Review*. PMID:20648874.

Pralahad, C. K., & Hamel, G. (1989, July-August). Strategic intent. *Harvard Business Review*.

Rasco, J., & Bernstein, R. (2007, July 23). Africa, the final frontier. *Merrill Lynch Report*.

Saltmarch, M. (2010, August 2). South Africa tries to scale the industrial ladder. *New York Times*.

Shambaugh, D. (2013). *China goes global: The partial power*. Oxford, UK: Oxford University Press.

Straziuso, J. (2012, October 7). Africa sees hotels rise with its economic gains. *The Philadelphia Inquirer*. Country Forecast. (2009, November). Sub-Saharan Africa regional overview. *The Economist Intelligence Unit*.

UNAIDS. (2008). *UNAIDS annual health report, 2008*. Geneva, Switzerland: UNAIDS.

UNCTAD. (2003). *The African growth opportunity act (AGOA): A preliminary assessment report prepared for the United Nations Conference on Trade and Development*. New York: UNCTAD.

UNCTAD. (2008). *United Nations conference on trade and development annual report, 2008*. New York: UNCTAD.

UNCTAD. (2009). *UNCTAD world investment report*. New York: UNCTAD.

United Nations Economic Commission on Africa (UNECA) and African Union Commission. (AUC). (2010). *Economic report on Africa (ERA) 2010*. New York: UNECA/AUC.

USA Department of Commercial. (2009). *Annual 2009 report*. Washington, DC: US Government.

Wachira, K., & Mureithi, F. (2013, June 3). Coming soon, Kenya's greatest and largest water dam. *Daily Nation*.

Wang, J. Y. (2007). What drives China's growing role in Africa. *IMF working paper 07/211*. Washington, DC: IMF.

Wang, M., Garner, J. F., & Silver, V. (2008). *GEMs equity strategy: Sub-Saharan Africa: Improved fundamentals priced near term*. New York: Morgan Stanley.

Williamson, P. J. (1997, September-October). Asia's new competitive game. *Harvard Business Review*.

World Bank. (2005). *Doing business in 2005: Removing obstacles to growth*. Washington, DC: The World.

Chapter 7
A Strategic Model for Entering African Markets

ABSTRACT

This chapter looks at managerial mind-set and cultural orientations as major dimensions to be considered in global business. Furthermore, the chapter elucidates sites and market entry evaluation criterion, including identification and discussion of foreign markets' entry modes and synergies created by various modes. It further analyzes the global and African markets' specific entry strategies to do business in Africa. It also examines appropriate timing in market entry including risks and challenges in entering foreign markets—particularly African markets—to do business.

1. INTRODUCTION

Firms often try to achieve their goals to increase their market share, revenues, profits, and cash flows by entering into foreign markets or by introducing new products in foreign markets where they are already present. Operating in foreign markets and sites, such as those of Africa, is different from operating in a particular company's domestic market. Foreign markets present special challenges and opportunities.

Despite the benefits of the proximities—geographic, economic, political, and administrative proximities—that might exist between domestic and foreign markets, there will always be differences in culture, legal systems, social and political norms, language and language accents, tastes, distribution channels complexities, and the general business atmosphere and even resources like labor's characteristics

DOI: 10.4018/978-1-4666-4570-7.ch007

and behavior (Wild et al., 2008). A company that tries to apply strategies, products, and services from their home markets to new markets without seriously considering adoption will most likely fail in those markets at some point in the future (Lymbersky, 2008).

Therefore, there will always be a need to thoroughly screen and evaluate potential foreign markets and sites, including those of Africa, before entry to ensure that the firm will be able to succeed by developing and achieving a sustainable competitive advantage in the new market. To enter a foreign market, the firm must evaluate the market potential, the costs of entry and operation, and the benefits as well as the associated risks. Scholars (Wild et al., 2008; Lymbersky, 2008) have developed a series of techniques and strategies for foreign markets and sites screening and evaluation before entry. But, before we discuss these techniques, it is important that we analyze the various company orientations influencing the choosing such strategies and factors that will influence the decision-making process in selecting, entering, and successfully operating in foreign markets.

2. BASIC COMPANY ORIENTATIONS IN CHOOSING AN ENTRY STRATEGY

The selection of possible markets to enter does not only depend on external factors. It also depends on the internal factors and the cultural orientation of the company itself. This orientation has significant influence on a company's international operations such as recruitment and deployment of employees and managers and strategy formulation and implementation. Scholars (Wild et al., 2008; Lymbersky, 2008) have suggested four types of management approaches and/or cultural orientations that can influence firms when entering foreign markets. They include the following major classifications:

2.1. Ethnocentric Orientation

The ethnocentricity orientation is found in old fashioned companies and leadership that are homeland bound. Other scholars (Nancy Alder and Allison Gunderson, 2007) describe and look at the phenomenon of ethnocentricity from a parochialism perspective. Parochialism, in this respect, means viewing the world solely through one's own eyes and perspective. A person with a parochial perspective neither recognizes other people's different ways of living and working nor appreciates that such differences can offer significant *business* opportunities or creates serious consequences.

People in all cultures are, to a certain extent, parochial. Journalists, politicians, and managers alike, for example, have frequently decried America's parochialism. Americans speak fewer foreign languages, demonstrate less interest in other cultures, and are more naïve in global business situations than most of their trading partners. As described in chapter 6 above, American managers are slow in recognizing business opportunities in Africa, for example, and they are doing the catching up behind Chinese in Africa.

Therefore, managers of ethnocentric oriented or parochial companies believe that their home strategy and values will be acceptable and work everywhere in the world. Therefore, individuals of home country manage operations in foreign markets. The mindset of these managers is that their way is the only right way to do business. They focus heavily on the home market and their international operations only exist to improve their competitiveness and supply resources to the home market. Subsidiaries outside the home country are centrally managed from the home office and the organization is inflexible and does not leave much room for local adjustments. Hence, local managers have little influence in the operations of the organization. The advantages of this organizational orientation include:

- Tight control of operations from homeland;
- Useful for companies that produce products associated with certain countries such as French Champagne and Italian wine;
- It recreates style of home operation in foreign markets;
- Ensures shared core values throughout the organization and globally;
- Produces loyal and trusted managers.

This management approach has several disadvantages, however, which include:

- It is costly to the organization because of relocation of managers from home market to foreign markets;
- Foreign managers have no actual contact with local reality;
- It creates foreign image of the organization in foreign markets;
- Poor understanding of local customers, employees, and other environmental factors;
- Highly inflexible when dealing with local environmental changes that need adoption of new strategic initiatives and therefore can lead to unintended negative effects and failure in global markets as it happened with many of Japanese firms in the last two decades;
- May reduce the firm's ability to compete in foreign markets because product and service creation, manufacturing, distribution, and delivery may be dominated by foreign ideas and characteristics that local people might resent.

Ethnocentric orientation—the Toyota, Toshiba, Takeda, etc., "Way" at home and in foreign affiliates—has been associated to both the source of great and tremendous success of Japanese companies in the global markets in the 1970s and 1980s and their steady decline in recent decades; leading to the overall low growth and, at times, decline of the Japanese national economy in the last two decades (Black et al., 2010). In 1995, for example, Japanese companies accounted for 141of the companies and 35.2% of the revenues of Fortune's then brand-new Global 500 list; the revenue generated from an amazing 95% of goods sold by Japanese companies around the world were made in Japan. By 2000, however, their share of revenue had fallen to 20.8%, and by 2009, it had shrunk to 11.2%, with only 68 Japanese companies making the list (Black et al., 2010).

During the same period, USA firms—that are often thought to be less ethnocentric—portion of Global 500 companies' revenues—which was 28.4% in 1995—grew slightly, to 30.5%. Firms from the European Union and Switzerland—which are thought to be much less ethnocentric—meanwhile, increased their portion of revenue from 31% to 36%.

However, much of Japanese loss has been a gain for firms from emerging markets whose portion of revenue rose from 0.9% to 10.4% (Black et al., 2010). The Japanese firms' "Way" is characterized by a substantial asset base and techniques that allow for the achievement of economies of scale and driving costs down while maintaining a high quality of products that Japanese demand, an isolated domestic market, an uncontentious and homogeneous labor force, and all of the same cultural orientation and undiversified team at the top.

Scholars (Wild et al., 2008; Lymbersky, 2008; Black et al., 2010) have suggested several strategies to deal with ethnocentricity so that companies are easily adaptable to new culture, and ever-changing business and competitive environments in global markets. And in order to have management and leadership teams that are more open-minded about strategy and business models and have experience dealing with diverse workforces and customers.

These strategies include: firstly, early "expatriation" of managers, which is a deliberate effort to send managers out into the world on overseas assignments in order for them to learn and experience other cultures, talent, customers, and opportunities outside their home markets. PepsiCo, Unilever, and Colgate-Palmolive corporations extensively use this strategy to increase the global experience of their young managers.

Secondly, because organizational power will always reside in the company's world headquarters, companies "inpatriate" employees, which is to bring foreign executives to their headquarters to enrich their knowledge, experience, and trust with headquarter management. Nestle is one multinational company that recognizes and applies this strategy effectively.

Though the countryside surrounding the company's headquarters in Vevey is very Swiss, the office environment feels like the United Nations. Nestle brings in people from around the world, from the most junior to the most senior, to ensure that top executives get to know the company's best talent. The inpatriated individuals also build long-lasting relationships, which they can leverage wherever they end up (Black et al., 2010).

Lastly, diversified education and training programs is a critical strategy for global competitive success. Therefore, successful global competitors have a series of global management and leadership development programs. They use a variety of development and delivery programs to achieve this, including:

- In-company training, covering employees from the company;
- Inter-company training which involves bringing together managers from various companies, including competitors' employees, into appropriately designed training programs; and
- Institutional training such as use of appropriate university departments and consultants to develop high-level customer-designed and multimodal programs targeting high-potential middle-level managers.

Sadly, these sorts of intense global management development and training programs are not common in Japanese firms, and when they are conducted they are oftentimes filled only with Japanese employees and thus the decline of Japanese companies in the global markets in recent years (Black et al., 2010).

2.2. Polycentric Orientation

This management approach assumes that managers in other countries or markets are as good as local managers sometimes even better, which localizes operations and gives autonomy to local managers. The management of this orientation is also well aware of the differences in consumer tastes and preferences in other markets. Therefore, they adapt their products and sometimes even try to build local image of the company. The company pursuing this orientation needs to take care that the local companies do not develop the desire to be independent of the home company. The advantages of this management approach include:

- Gives autonomy to local managers hence motivates them;
- Puts local managers, who are intimately familiar with the environment, in charge of company operations;
- Saves relocation costs;
- Makes the company attractive to local customers improving sales and profitability;

The disadvantages of this management style include:

- Loss of control of foreign operations;
- If there is poor sharing and uncoordinated use of resources, there will be loss of organizational synergy.

2.3. Geocentric Orientation

These kinds of organizations provide their products or services to the world market and they recruit managers globally. Their global subsidiaries are all part of a globally operating network and they serve cross-cultural target groups. Strategy is usually centrally formulated but locally implemented with any desirable adjustments made to meet local environmental needs and differences. Its advantages include:

- Best managers employed and deployed globally;
- Products and services sold globally with needed local adjustments;
- It develops global managers who seek global opportunities;
- Provides high synergic effects particularly in sharing of globally trained managerial resources.

The disadvantages of this approach include:

- Expensive to coordinate;
- Loss of home values to the global organization.

2.4. Regiocentric Orientation

This is an approach of grouping countries regionally when entering new markets. Regiocentric oriented companies often group different countries together that show similar characteristics. These characteristics can be the language, similarity in customer behavior, and similarities in administrative procedures.

In Europe, for example, a company can group Austria, Switzerland, and German together because of language and in Africa a company can group Kenya, Uganda, and Tanzania together because of language and similarities in administrative procedures and Egypt, Tunisia, Libya, Morocco, and Algeria together because of similarities in language and religion. The advantage of this strategy is that the company is able to enter a large market at once achieving economies of scale and scope and saving cost.

2.5. What It Takes for Companies to Successfully Go Global

Shambaugh (2013) has enumerated and explained conditions and criteria necessary to successfully go global by multinational corporations and asserts that although there is no single model for success in global markets, there are a number of commonalties of factors needed for multinationals corporations to compete successfully in today's globalized and highly competitive world. Obviously, a company must be able to operate and deploy resources on a truly global basis and not just regionally, including sales and distribution channels, production facilities, supply chains, logistic networks, Research and Development centers, and employees. In particular, it must have a genuinely multinational management staff that possesses a global mind-set and is capable of operating in multiple cultures and languages. It should also possess globally recognizable brands and invest substantially in advertising to maintain and grow brand presence.

An effective global multinational corporation must have the ability to leave behind management practices and paradigms that are successful at home and adopt new practices and paradigms that work abroad. It should have well-defined human resources programs for recruitment, promotion, rotation, retention, continuous training, and clear performance indicators. It must have well-thought-through strategic plans for geographical expansion and foreign market penetration. It must have a clear understanding of its comparative advantages, strengths, and weaknesses, and find strategic market niches.

A successful multinational corporation should know and obey the regulatory and legal environments of foreign countries, support national goals, be transparent, adopt "best practices," maintain strict accounting procedures, and institute genuine corporate governance and oversight. Successful multinationals are aware of the difficulties of mergers and acquisitions and prefer strategic alliances and partnerships that may be a better mode to leverage comparative advantages and thus expand a global footprint. They must also understand external-internal linkages of foreign multinational corporations; that is, many potential corporate partners abroad also seek to grow their business inside other countries.

3. SITE AND FOREIGN MARKETS EVALUATION CRITERION

First and foremost, before a foreign market or site to sell and or to produce is selected, in Africa, or anywhere else in the world, for that matter, the market and site should be thoroughly screened and evaluated, keeping search and screening costs as low as possible.

Wild et al. (2008), assert that two important issues concern managers during the market and site screening process. First, they want to keep search costs as low as possible. Second, they want to examine every potential market and every possible location. To accomplish the two goals, they suggest that managers should follow a four-step criterion of the screening and evaluation processes namely:

- Identification of the basic market appeal which entails assessing market demand for the product and service and viability of the production facility, in terms of determination of where to site the production facilities, assessing the availability of key resources such as skilled labor, distribution channels, and financial resources and their cost;
- Assessment of the nation or regional business environment involving the analysis and assessment of cultural factors, that will affect the salability of the product; political, social, and legal factors; image of the country in terms of ease of doing business rankings; and macroeconomic economic factors such as GDP per capita at market prices and at Purchasing Power Parity level and per capita, inflation level, interest rates, currency exchange rates, and the total infrastructure including roads, railroads, telecommunications, electric power, sewage and water supply;
- Measurement of the market potential in terms of total sales and future demand of the product and or service;
- Eventual evaluation and selection of the market or site which involve visiting the market and site, competitor analysis and evaluation, and finally commitment of the company resources in terms of company finances, technology, and talent to entering the market.

The data for African market and site evaluation will usually be difficult to obtain in many countries of Africa. However, several ways of obtaining information exist that will involve use of government agencies, university research facilities, for secondary data, and employment of private consultants to gather, analyze, and evaluate primary data. But the firm should always ensure, regardless of the source of the information, that the information it obtains is relevant to its special and specific needs of its decision-making and that the information provides sufficient evidence to improve the quality of the decisions made.

Many analysts use analytic tools that include Country Portfolio Analysis (CPA) as a start of market analysis and measurements (Ghemawat 2005). The Country Portfolio Analysis includes focusing on the country's GDP and Purchasing Power Parity, levels of consumer wealth and their propensity to consume, and levels of inflation. The CPA tool emphasizes sales before looking at costs and risks of doing business in a particular country.

Most of the costs and risks result from barriers created by distance. By distance is not only meant geographic separation, although that is important. Distance has also cultural, administrative, and economic dimensions that can make foreign markets considerably more or less attractive. When the screening process is successful and a decision has been made to enter a foreign market, a comprehensive marketing plan should be developed before entry to guide the marketing of the product and or service in the new market.

4. MARKETING PLAN

A market entry strategy is the planned method of delivering goods or services to a new target market and successfully and effectively distributing them in the new market. When these arrangements involve importing or exporting products or services, the arrangements refer to establishing and managing contracts in a foreign country from the home market. In developing eventual market entry strategies, a firm first creates a marketing plan for its product or service in the new market based on the 4Ps (8Ps) of the marketing mix namely the product, place, promotion, and price (people, process, PR, and physical facilities).

Therefore, the market plan is an integrated program which involves the kind of products and or services to market in global markets, where to market them, when to market them, how to market them, the promotional strategies to attract and retain customers, and the prices to charge in the new markets, as opposed to the domestic market. Usually, a scheming pricing strategy is used at the introduction stages of the product/service and the real market price is established as the product or service goes through its life cycle in the new market and its attractiveness and demand in the new market is determined (Lymbersky 2008).

Other important considerations of the market plan, at this stage and of course in the future as the product gains increased entry and in order to enhance the sustainable competitive position of the firm in the new market are good public relations to promote the brand image of the product; the process, its efficiency and efficacy to deliver the products to consumers; the quality of the people who produce and deliver the product and provide services to consumers; and the physical facilities such as transportation equipment, warehouses, and distribution centers—including whole selling and retailing facilities—that eventually avail products and services directly to the consumers (Wild et al., 2008; Lymbersky 2008). Eventually, a budget is prepared to control all these operations.

5. MARKET ENTRY OPTIONS

Companies seek entry to new markets to sell and/or manufacture their products. A market entry option is the institutional arrangements by which a firm gets its products, technologies, human skills, and talent to a new market. Therefore, when an organization has made a decision—through its market screening, evaluation efforts, and a marketing plan—to enter a foreign or new market, there are a variety of options open to it. These options vary with timing, cost, risk, the product characteristics, and the degree of control, which can be exercised over these operations. The specific option chosen depends on the firm's resources, the market experience of the firm in the market, and the potential size of the market. Scholars have postulated three broad categories of global markets entry strategies each with several elements of alternative entry strategies (Han et al., 2008). These strategies include:

- Exporting, importing, and countertrade that are, arguably, the lowest level of entry and with limited control of the whole entry process;
- Contractual entry strategies that include management contracts, licensing, franchising, and turnkey projects. A turnkey project is a process whereby a firm builds a project from start to end and hands it over to the financing company or nation;
- Investment entry strategies, the most complex and riskiest, and they include wholly owned subsidiaries; joint ventures, with local entrepreneurs; mergers and acquisitions; and strategic alliances.

Each of these strategies has its advantages and disadvantages. The simplest form of entry strategy of course, is exporting/importing and countertrade, using either a direct or indirect method such as an agent and distributors and/or export/import management companies. Countertrade is a system of international trade in which countries exchange goods or services, rather than pay for imports with currency or receive cash for exports. More complex forms of entry modes, as discussed above, include truly global operations, with a high degree of control and increasingly riskier operations that may involve joint ventures, merging and acquiring existing businesses, strategic alliances, and green-field manufacturing in export processing zones or any other designated places in the new market.

Having decided on the form of an entry strategy, decisions have to be made on the specific channels to use to reach the final consumer or user, which may include distributors, wholesalers, and retailers. Many agricultural products of a raw or commodity nature use agents, distributors or involve Government agencies, whereas processed materials, whilst not excluding these modes, rely more heavily on more sophisticated forms of access such as having company sales force, distribution centers, and promotional programs (Lymbersky 2008).

6. TIMING IN GLOBAL AND REGIONAL MARKET ENTRY

What countries to enter and when depends mainly on the financial resources of a company, the product lifecycle, and the product itself and its characteristics. Therefore, after selecting a possible market or a group of markets to enter, it is important to choose the right timing. Finding the right timing is called cross-cultural timing strategy (Lymbersky 2008). Due to rapidly changing market conditions, due to globalization, technological development, political changes, and competitive threats, finding the right time to enter a market can be a difficult but important decision to make. A cross-cultural timing strategy answers the question whether a company should enter different markets simultaneously or successively.

According to Lymbersky (2008), the different timing strategies available to management of a firm include:

- Waterfall strategy;
- Wave strategy;
- Sprinkler strategy.

He asserts that the waterfall strategy is a popular version of the systems development life cycle model for software engineering. Often considered the classic approach to the systems development life cycle, the waterfall model describes a development method that is linear and sequential. The Waterfall development has distinct goals for each phase of development that must be achieved before the next phase begins. Imagine a waterfall on the cliff of a steep mountain. Once the water has flowed over the edge of the cliff and has begun its journey down the side of the mountain, it cannot turn back. It is essentially the same concept with waterfall development in the timing of market entry strategies.

Once a phase of development is completed, the development proceeds to the next phase and there is no turning back. That is true too when the strategy is applied to market entry in global markets. The firm enters the new markets in a sequence, one after the other, until it has entered and is performing in all the markets it wanted to enter in the first place, of course with experiential adjustments in each market.

Christopher Lymbersky first described the wave strategy in his seminal book "Market Entry Strategies: Texts, Cases, and Readings in Market entry Management" in 2008. A company that wants to expand its business to other countries in a wave fashion can employ this strategy. The wave strategy focuses on cultural differences and classifies countries into market groups that show similar characteristics to the home market of the company and those that show differences between the home market and the foreign market and then enter the markets accordingly in groups first those similar to the home market and secondly those that are dissimilar to the home market until entry to all markets is achieved. In this respect, the wave strategy is a mix of the sprinkler strategy and waterfall strategy.

The sprinkler strategy is where all suitable markets or countries, and in accordance to their market-groupings, get entered at the same time. And the waterfall strategy, as described above, is where one market gets entered at a time and several in a row. These strategies are, however, very theoretical. In the real world, we often find a mixed timing to enter foreign markets. Usually markets that get grouped into the first wave are markets that are similar to the home market with little variations and are entered using the waterfall and or sprinkler strategy.

Based on the thoughts of Hofstede and Hall (1997), countries that show similar cultural characteristics such as Germany, Austria, and Switzerland, in Europe, and Kenya, Uganda, and Tanzania, Rwanda and Burundi in Eastern Africa would be grouped together and entered together and then strategies to enter neighboring countries such as Ethiopia, Sudan, Congo DRC, and Mozambique are developed and implemented later in the next wave, sprinkling and water falling. In each grouping, a suitable country should be chosen as a hub such as the economic powerhouse in a region. In the African circumstances, economic powerhouses include Nigeria, in western Africa, Kenya in East and Central Africa, South Africa in Southern Africa, and Egypt in northern Africa.

The same process could be followed in the French Western African countries which include Senegal, Ivory Coast, Mali, etc. and French Central African countries grouping together such countries as Cameroon, Gabon, Congo Brazzaville; and Maghreb nations that groups together countries such as Morocco, Algeria, Mauritania, Libya, Tunisia, and Egypt even if strictly Egypt is not a member of the Maghreb Economic Union, as discussed in chapter five above, it is well linked to all the Maghreb countries in terms of language, educational systems, political and economic systems, and infrastructure, that key element in economic development. Lymbersky (2008) has suggested benefits and disadvantages of each timing strategy. The benefits of the Waterfall Strategy include:

- The company can learn from their mistakes;
- The risk of failing in more than one country at the same time is eliminated because products will only be offered to the next market once the prior entry has been a success;
- The waterfall strategy leads to an extension of the product life cycle, the product starts a new life in each market;
- Scarce resources do not need to be supplied and applied to all countries at once.

Disadvantages of the Waterfall strategy include:

- A competitor can use the time a product takes to enter the next market and enter the market earlier gaining ground in the market;
- Competitors are able to prepare and build up entry barriers if they assume that the company will enter their market as well;
- Good or bad experiences can be misinterpreted which could lead to wrong conclusions about other markets.

Advantages of the Wave strategy include:

- The risk of failure is minimized by entering similar markets first;
- Economics of scale can be explored step by step;
- Entries get financed out of existing cash-flows generated from markets entered first;
- The learning effects are the highest.

Disadvantages of the Wave strategy are:

- Capital resources to finance the first wave need to originate from the home market;
- Failure or success in the first wave may be misleading as the situation of the next market.

The benefits of the Sprinkler strategy include:

- The early market entry in all suitable markets at the same time contributes to higher market entry barriers for competitors that want to follow;
- Since cash-flows can be generated in more than one market at the same time, the amortization time for fixed costs such as research and development might be quicker;
- The entry risk is shared among all markets.

Disadvantages of the Sprinkler strategy:

- Very capital-intense;
- Mistakes get made in all market at the same time. Therefore, careful research and planning is very important for the success of the whole company and the strategy;
- Major false decisions based on poor evidence might ruin the whole company.

It will always be difficult to recommend a single timing strategy for all entry situations. This is because market conditions in different countries are different and may prefer one timing strategy as opposed the other timing strategy. However, thorough research and documentation of the findings of market conditions will always suggest and dictate the best entry timing strategy for each market or market segments a company wants to enter.

7. FACTORS TO CONSIDER IN MARKET ENTRY

Unlike domestic markets, foreign markets are complex and demanding—in financial resources, human energy, and skills—to enter and operate successfully. There are several key factors to consider when planning to enter and successfully operate in foreign markets. Many companies successfully enter and operate in a niche market without ever expanding into new whole markets. Some businesses achieve increased sales, brand awareness, and business stability by entering and operating in a whole new market (Lymbersky, 2008).

Developing a market entry strategy involves a thorough analysis and the understanding of potential competitors and possible customers. Some of the relevant factors that are important in deciding the viability of entry into and successful operation in a particular market include analyzing the country or region's environmental factors; the image of the country, in terms of its security and stability, and ease of doing business ranking; the firm's core competency; trade barriers; localized consumer knowledge; price localization; competition; distribution channels; and export subsidies to local firms (Lymbersky 2008). It is also important to consider the synergies to be created by any strategic alliances and or acquisition that the company might enter into (Dyer et al., 2008).

Dyer et al. (2008) conclude that when pursuing collaboration as a growth or entry strategy, managers must carefully analyze and determine several key factors before deciding whether to acquire or to ally with a company. Once they have determined what kind of resources they plan to combine, the type of synergies they are hoping to create, and the market and competitive factors they face, managers can use this framework to choose the strategic options best suited to their situation. Managers should weigh each factor depending on its importance to their industry. In all cases, the collaboration competencies a company already posses should be considered in making the final alliance and or acquisition decision.

7.1. Types of Synergies and How They Are Created

Scholars state that the overarching purpose of alliances and acquisitions is to create synergies in operations of two organizations or firms that are allying or involved in an acquisition arrangement. Synergy is the effect achieved of increased value created—in terms of increased market share, sales, revenue, cost minimization, competitiveness, and profits—in the joint and in the leveraging use of the resources of two firms or organizations. Therefore, synergy is the greater result achieved when two firms work together than the sum of the value created by the two firms working separately. The amount of synergies achieved will depend on the optimum and skillful combination of the two firms and the efficient use of their combined resources.

Singh et al. (2004) assert that companies create different kinds of synergies by combining and customizing their resources differently. Those resources combinations or interdependencies require different levels of coordination between firms and result in different forms of combination to create different amount or kind of synergies. Organizations or firms potentially create the following types of synergies when allaying or acquiring:

First, companies create modular synergies when they manage resources independently and pool only the results for greater profits – the synergies are modular because modularly independent results produce them. An example is an airline and a hotel allying and combining resources to manage passengers in their operations. Non-equity alliances are usually best suited to generate modular synergies.

Secondly, firms drive sequential synergies when one company completes its tasks and passes on the results to a partner to do its part or complete the process of product or service production. In this case, the resources of the two firms are sequentially interdependent. An equity-based alliance may work better in this case. A good example is a biotech firm developing a drug, which it passes on to a pharmaceutical company to manufacture, market, and sell the drug.

Thirdly, companies generate reciprocal synergies by working closely together and executing tasks through an iterative knowledge-sharing process. Not only do firms have to combine resources, but also they have to tool and customize them a great deal to make them reciprocally interdependent. An acquisition is a better strategy to pursue to achieve these synergies rather than pursuing an alliance in this case.

7.2. Synergies Achieved at Strategy Formulation and Implementation Levels

When discussing strategy formulation and implementation, Kim et al. (2009) have identified other synergies that occur when companies align, well, their value propositions. In developing what they call a reconstructionist strategic initiative to exploit opportunities in the external environment—simultaneously using a differentiation and a cost leadership competitive styles—firms create three propositions namely a value proposition, a profit proposition, and a people (employee) proposition and when these propositions are well aligned in the strategy they produce reinforcing or leveraging synergies.

Reinforcing and or leveraging synergies can also occur in a situation where highly and eagerly motivated and conscientious employees are working together to achieve goals as a team. Therefore, a team oriented organization, with well-trained and motivated employees working in well-structured teams, create reinforcing and leveraging synergies and the organization prospers, more so in turbulent times.

8. RISKS IN MARKET ENTRY

Africa is filled with potential and real risk and this risk is perceived differently by different people intending or are already doing business in Africa. The psychometric model—that uses the Likert Scale to measure the degree of feelings people have about situations they are in—and the cultural theory are the two models most commonly used to understand risk perception in business situations like those pertaining in Africa (Hostfede and Hall, 1997).

The psychometric model has been utilized in many risk perception studies and is entrenched in psychological research. It focuses on the measurement of particular attributes of risk sources. The cultural theory, on the other hand, seeks to understand risk perception and risk-related behavior based on the lifestyles of those being exposed to the risk (Cutter, 1993; Slovic et al., 1980). A general finding of these studies is that experts and lay people differ in their perceptions of the enormity of risk inherent in activities they are involved in. That is true about risk perception of the African business environment by business executives and entrepreneurs that are doing or wish to do business in Africa.

8.1. Risk Perception

Risk perception is the term frequently used to refer to and describe the understanding people have—in their holding environments—before making judgment when asked to evaluate hazardous activities and technologies (Slovik, 1987). A holding environment consists of any relationship in which one party has the power to hold the attention of another party to facilitate adaptive work, in this case risk perception and dealing with it (Heifetz, 1994). Although the risk perception field has attracted a lot of attention from a wide range of disciplines, however, the concept of risk remains quite ambiguous in the empirical literature (Slovik, 1987).

One interpretation for inconsistent findings in the empirical literature is the poorly defined concept of risk itself (Sjoberg, 1991). The concept of risk is commonly applied in varying situations; it is defined differently in diverse situations and contexts. Kate and Kasperson (1983) define risk as the probability of experiencing harm in the future actions taken by an individual or group of individuals.

To identify a behavior, as a risk—the uncertainty of consequences in placing a bet—is not the same as the risk of losing small versus large amount of money. This differentiation is usually discussed in the literature as the probability of an event occurring as well as the magnitude of the consequences of the event. There are five stages in conducting a risk assessment in the process of perceiving it (Cutter, 1993):

- Determination that a particular hazard is linked to a specific effect of outcomes or loss;
- Examination of the management of exposure and how that is linked to the adverse outcomes or loss. This stage is frequently referred to as the dose or response assessment;
- Actual assessment of the danger of the exposure to the hazard or financial loss;
- Risk characterization, which is the description of the nature and magnitude of the risk;
- Develop a consistent and sustainable methodology that will advance the area of risk perception

8.2 Definition and Management of Risk

Definitions of risk in business are dicey and involve a high degree of subjectivity. To most people, the word risk connotes the possibility of a bad and negative variation of the expected outcome, perhaps earning a negative return on an investment, or worse, losing the entire sum of money invested (Smart, et al., 2007). However, in foreign market entry, a risk is a probability that the reality of business expectations—such as demand for a product, currency exchange rate stability, and inflationary trends—may vary, sometimes considerably from the plans or expectations, because of global or specific changes in a new market's environmental factors—government policy, war, terrorism, and political leadership—from those expected at the market entry planning time. The degree of variation will, of course, depend on the accuracy and completeness of the information used when planning. And indeed, the qualities of the planning itself and of course the efficiency and effectiveness with which the plans are implemented, both of which imply the quality of planning and implementing personnel.

Furthermore, scholars (Bremmer, 2005; Smart et al., 2007) have defined and analyzed business risk in terms of the events and trends in the context of countries. These environmental changes include political, financial, economic, and social changes in the context of countries. Thus, risk is a set of environmental events or trends, in a country, that will negatively affect a firm's ability—in market share, in costs, in revenues, and eventually in profitability—to create value for stakeholders.

Bremmer (2005) asserts that there are both economic and political risks in a country. Economic risks include stagnation or dropping of a country's GDP growth, increase in inflation, and reduction in the balance of payments. Political risk is the impact of politics on markets of countries, which are influenced by the passage of laws, the foibles of leaders, the promotion and tolerance of corrupt practices, and the rise of popular movements; in short, all the factors that might politically destabilize a country. The interest in risk management, particularly political, financial, and economic risks has grown in recent times because of the following developments:

Firstly, international markets are more inter-connected than ever before. A shock in one part of the world spreads fast throughout the rest of the world. The 1997 Asian financial crisis and 2008 Western markets financial meltdown are good examples. A bank failure in New York, like Lehman Brothers in September 2008, has a domino effect worldwide.

Secondly, the off shoring trend is growing. Businesses shift operations to countries where labor is cheap, but labor is cheap for a reason. In countries where off-shoring is done—like India, the oldest off shoring countries in the world, and lately in Kenya—the living conditions for the working and middle classes can be harsh and therefore there is a greater threat of unrest than in developed countries with their large, relatively prosperous middle class. Off shoring presents other risks such as infringements on intellectual properties of developed countries by some emerging market economies.

Thirdly, the world is increasingly depending on energy from states troubled by considerable political risk such as Saudi Arabia, Iran, Nigeria, Russia, Angola, and Venezuela as good examples of such troubled and risky countries in the world today. As global supply struggles to keep pace with rising demand, political instability in these oil-producing states can quickly produce shock waves all over the world that can trigger oil price increases in a moment that can negatively impact on the cost of operation of companies worldwide (Bremmer 2005).

It is difficult to imagine a business that cannot be affected by at least one or all these developments. And corporation's exposure to volatility will only grow as supply chains become more complex and global and as developing and volatile economies increasingly participate in international trade.

Hanisz and Zelner (2010) have identified and analyzed what they describe as policy risk. Policy risk is caused by political and policy decisions by current or new politicians. Policy risk, therefore, is the risk arising from the fact that a government can, in a discriminatory manner, change the laws, regulations, or contracts governing investments—or will fail to enforce them—in a way that reduces the investor's financial returns.

They further assert that when a firm with a value generating technological or management capability invests abroad, its shareholders and the host country's citizens stand to benefit. But, no matter how good the apparent fit between what foreign companies and what host countries need, success is far from assured. Elections and other political events, economic crises, and changing social attitudes can disrupt the best-laid plans in both emerging and advanced economies. The interplay of these forces—and the implications for the political choices that multinational firms make—will become especially prominent as national governments chart an uncertain course toward stabilization following the global financial meltdown of 2008.

They also state that international firms best able to anticipate and manage these related policy risks and opportunities would have the strongest competitive advantage. As with the management of any risk or an uncertainty, political mastery becomes a source of a competitive advantage in addition to a means of avoiding losses. Companies must learn how they can frame and shape political debate in countries where they operate to minimize business risks. And they must learn on how to apply political pressure, either individually or as part of a coalition. Ways of applying political pressure or shaping the debate in a country to minimize policy risks include:

- Presenting ventures as fair, equitable, and economic growth enhancing partners is a simpler and powerful means of securing political support than providing a cost-benefit analysis;
- Investing in goodwill by supporting solutions to local problems;
- Network of relationships in a society influence policy outcomes, especially in countries with weak legal systems. To turn these networks to their advantage, international investors must identify and engage local politicians' power bases. This is to ensure that locals have a stake in the firm's success by:
    - Use of local suppliers;
    - Employ and train locals;
    - Support public projects, such as education, agriculture, infrastructure, healthcare, and Research and Development;
    - Support local government's economic policy;
    - Where necessary, carefully use home government for influence

Slywotzk et al. (2005) have also identified what they describe as strategic risk. Strategic risk is an array of external events and trends that can devastate a company's growth trajectory and thus destroying shareholders' value. These events and trends are generally financial, hazardous, and operational. Specifically, they include events that can squeeze industry margins causing technological shifts, erode brand equity, change the competitive climate and landscape, cause project failure, and cause market stagnation.

Generally, risks must be managed by systematically identifying, assessing, and responding to them appropriately. Therefore, companies must devise appropriate strategies to manage risk such as constantly having their eyes on the horizon and developing capabilities that will allow them to anticipate and respond to the upcoming changes and disruptions in emerging markets. And they should also remain open to opportunities for cooperation between the private and public sectors in those markets. Such cooperation can improve the economic environment and thus mitigate the risks of doing business in developing countries and other emerging markets (Garten 1997). Other risk mitigating strategies include:

- Insurance, options, and futures;
- Creative innovations in products, costs, and demand;
- Brand renewal and extensions;
- Collaboration with suppliers.

Furthermore, and according to Breemer and others (2005), strategic risk management should allow managers to move from a defensive posture to an offensive posture. People typically focus on the perils of risk, and the managerial response is to seek ways to minimize exposure to it. But the pursuit of growth requires companies to take risk and to place bets on specific products, channels, customer segments, and new business models. Strategic business management, besides limiting the downside of risk, should help managers to improve the odds of success behind those bets by forcing them to think more systematically about the future and helping them to identify opportunities for growth in their industries and market segments.

8.3. Current Issues in Risk Management

The 2008 financial meltdown, leading to serious global economic slowdown - and even shrinkages in many countries including the United States - has compelled scholars to look into risk management with fresh insights and in the context of current global business events. Stulz (2009) has identified and described ways companies mismanage risk particularly in the financial markets institutions emphasizing the impact of these factors in the 2008 financial meltdown.

Quoting the *Financial Times of London,* he asserts: "it is obvious there has been a massive failure of risk management, over the years, across most of the financial markets particularly in Wall Street." He names six basic ways in which risk management does fail, nearly all of them exemplified in the 2008 financial crisis. Therefore, conventional risk management fails because of:

- **Relying on Historical Information:** Particularly financial and accounting information – data that is not reliable and complete in a rapidly changing business environment;
- **Inappropriate Measurements:** Measurements that are narrowed and based on incomplete data;
- **Failure to Communicate:** Risk management systems will provide little protection if risk managers do not communicate effectively to all concerned in their organizations;
- **Overlooking Knowable Risks:** Risk managers simply overlook many types of risks and sometimes even unintentionally create some of them;
- **Overlooking Concealed Risks:** Organizations have a tendency to expand unreported risks particularly when people think short-term and are pursuing personal goals instead of those of the whole organization;
- **Rapidity of Changes in the Business Environment:** Not managing risk in real time because of the rapidity and volatility in the rates of change taking place in the business environment that are difficult to predict with existing financial models and therefore hedge against them.

Eventually, effective risk monitoring and management boils down to the basics of getting the right information, from the right sources, of the right amount, at the right time, to the right people, such that those people can make the most informed judgments possible. There should be appropriate organizational hierarchies to avoid information filtering when information is sent up the management chain, leading to delays or distortions in sharing important information with senior management.

More so, organizations should develop a set of ethical standards and a risk culture—in their firms—that accepts and understands the limitations of the sophisticated risk management models—and hence calling for intuitive thinking—and with that the firm should increase the value of risk management. Finally, it is important to note that risk management is a complex and dynamic process, therefore, risk managers should be responsible for making sure that the risks their firms takes are the risks their firms want to take. As a result, they must constantly monitor, hedge, insure against, and mitigate the firms' known risks all the time (Stulz, 2009).

The risk of an investment may simply be too great to justify entry into certain markets. But, in many cases investors who explicitly recognize the dynamism of the environment they are facing and implement appropriate strategies to address it will find the risks quite manageable (Henisz et al., 2010).In market entry risk analysis, monitoring, and management, some companies prefer to develop their own market entry plans; others outsource the process to specialized companies in the local environment to minimize risks assuming that these agencies exist in sufficient numbers and of the right quality for the company to choose from. The knowledge of the local or target market by those specialized companies can mitigate a lot of business risks for a firm entering a new market (Zelner, 2010).

9. STRATEGIES FOR ENTRY AND COMPETITIVENESS IN AFRICA

To find the balance among global efficiencies, worldwide learning, multinational flexibility, and achieving competitive advantage in international strategic orientation and management, companies typically adopt one of the following entry and competitive strategies in global markets (Lymbersky 2008):

9.1. Home Replication Strategy

This is a strategy whereby a company attempts to transfer their main competitive style and competitive advantages from its home market to the foreign market. The strategy aims at replicating the home market competitive advantages that the company has in the foreign market it wants to enter. The home replication strategy is often adopted when the needs for flexibility and global integration are very low. Its main advantage is cost savings. Its main disadvantage is that it does not consider local circumstances. The competitors can take advantage of this to enter and take market share.

9.2. Multidomestic Strategy

A company that operates relatively free subsidiaries in various foreign markets in which it has business is utilizing a multidomestic strategy. The subsidiaries have the freedom to focus on the appropriate value proposition to customers in the market they operate in. The local companies have power and authority to hire employees locally, to customize marketing campaigns, products, services, and other operational techniques. The multidomestic strategy is very effective when cultural differences among markets are big. Its disadvantages include:

- It requires a lot of adaption of conditions in each market;
- It generates very low economies of scale;
- It achieves low global efficiencies; and
- It is costly to coordinate operations in various markets.

9.3. Global Strategy

According to Lysermby (2008), the global strategy is almost the opposite of the multinational or multidomestic strategy. The global strategy, however, sees the world as one market with a fundamentally homogeneous customer tastes worldwide. Its goals include the production of standardized products and services to achieve a very high level of economies of scale. One headquarter usually directs the production and marketing of the products and services for the world market. Powers and decision-making are centralized. It focuses on standardized marketing campaigns and goods as well as a standardized distribution system.

Sony uses a global strategy. It designs and produces TV sets, stereos, and gaming consoles for the global market, but adapts cheap parts like power supplies and fuses to the local markets. For companies that follow the global strategy, it is often easy to have their products produced in low cost countries, such as China, where the production costs are low and then distributed worldwide.

In every respect, the global strategy is similar to the home replication strategy in that it operates alike in every country it enters. The difference is that a firm using the home replication strategy believes—ethnocentrically—that its way of doing business in the home market is the best and should work in all its markets worldwide. Meanwhile, a company that uses the global strategy, however, develops one strategy for the whole world, but makes appropriate adjustments where applicable.

9.4. Transnational Strategy

The transnational strategy tries to combine the benefits and advantages of the global strategy with the benefits and advantages of a multidomestic strategy. A company that uses the transnational strategy attempts to achieve the benefits of the economies of scale but it does not centralized all its power and decision making in one headquarter. It creates special units in order to balance between the three goals of efficiency, worldwide learning, and flexibility.

This means that some critical functions like research and development and product production processes can be centralized in certain parts of the world. Other operations like marketing and human resources are decentralized in order to be able to adapt these operations to local environment and culture. One problem with this strategy is coordination of the various subsidiaries in different countries and markets and the cost associated with it.

10. SPECIFIC MARKET ENTRY AND COMPETITIVE STRATEGIES TO DO BUSINESS IN AFRICA

As discussed in chapter eight below, a firm's strategy is simply a game plan, or a road map, or blueprint as to how it will enter and compete in the market place. It is a statement of what value proposition a firm intends to offer that will cause customers to prefer it to the competition. The value proposition maybe based on a price which results from low cost operation and superior efficiency. It may also result from offerings of superior innovation, technological leadership, and superior customer service, which will lead to the adoption of a differentiation competitive strategy (Porter 1996; Thomson 2005). Differentiation in the sense that the way the firm packages and delivers the product will be different from the way the competitors will do it. All these approaches are true in domestic and global markets.

A good strategy successfully differentiates a firm from its competitors and it is difficult to imitate and it gives the firm a sustainable competitive advantage. A bad strategy is easily copied, or basically makes the firm's value proposition worse (Pfeiffer 1998); making the firm to lose a competitive advantage. In this regard, a good competitive strategy combined with a first-mover advantage will not only give a firm a sustainable competitive advantage, but will enable a firm to create barriers to entry of new entrants.

To enter Africa, establish and run a successful business, a firm has to devise and deploy company specific entry and competitive strategies. The firm should understand the challenges of doing business in Africa, and then decide on its intent and the ambition to do business in Africa. Simply put, the company must have a *vision and mission* to succeed in Africa.

Therefore, the type of business, the complexity of its processes, the company's business model, the kind of products and services involved, will dictate the firm's entry and competitive strategies in Africa. Strategically, it is advisable to enter Africa regionally because of large regional market sizes that are being built through regional integration in Africa and in consideration of the following elements of distance as postulated by Ghemawat (2005):

- Cultural proximity, which is similarities in cultural values, language, consumption propensities, and social fabric. Trade between countries who share a language, for example, will be three times greater than countries without a common language. All African regions share at least one language, English or French or an indigenous language like Swahili in East and Central Africa and Arabic in North Africa.

- Geographic proximity, which is sharing borders and distance in areas of doing business that, will affect transportation costs and distribution networks. Trade between countries that share a border is over 300 times more than trade with distant countries;
- Economic proximity, which will involve considering the wealth of the people of the regional countries and infrastructure similarities, monetary and fiscal policy alignments, currency convertibility, similarity in tariff regime, and investment licensing rules. Trade between countries that share economic factors is over 600 percent more than trade with distance countries in the economic proximity dimension.
- Administrative and political proximity: Historical and political association shared by countries greatly affects trade between them because of similarities in legal systems, political behavior, and social networks. Colony-colonizer relationship, for example increases trade by 900 percent and that is why Britain, France, and Portugal have kept close to their former colonies in Africa at the expense of these countries in that they still treat them as sources of raw materials and markets for manufactured products from them.

In consideration of these four elements of distance, Ghemawat (2005) has proposed several regional entry strategies that will also impact on competitive strategies. These strategies include:

The Home Base Strategy: This strategy involves direct exports to national or country markets with sales agents and or distributors. This strategy achieves economies of concentration as opposed to economies of diversion. Its disadvantage is lack of room to grow and failing to hedge risks adequately because the firm does not have a presence in the new country.

The Portfolio Strategy: This involves acquiring or setting up an operation outside the home region, in the region of new business that reports directly to the home base. It can be through a firm's own newly developed facility—organic growth—or an acquisition. It is usually the first strategy adopted by companies seeking or desiring to establish a presence in new outside markets that they can serve from home. A good example is Toyota's investment in the United States - in the United Motor Manufacturing Industry, a joint venture with General Motors - in California in the early 1980s that was followed by several others organic plants in later years that eventually made Toyota a very successful company in the USA auto industry (Ghemawat 2005);

The Hub Strategy: This involves building regional bases or hubs that provide a variety of shared resources and services to national operations that are stand-alone units. This is a multi-national version of the home-based portfolio strategy and its advantage is that costs are shared among the countries of the region. It is popular with companies that want to add value at the regional level. The challenge of this strategy is how to standardize to achieve economies of scale at the same time ensure customization to cater for national differences without risking losing the competitive edge gained through scale and scope economies.

The Platform Strategy: This is having an arrangement whereby the regions are run from one regional point, in the entire strategy system, requiring standardization to achieve economies of scale and scope by having overhead costs spread to all the regions. This is a profitable strategy. However, it is difficult to cater for regional and cultural differences without losing the economies of scale and scope and a competitive edge through the rise of niche competitors.

Mandate Strategy: This strategy is geared towards achieving economies of specialization as well as economies of scale and scope. This strategy involves producing and supplying from particular regions, which are specialized in performing particular roles and producing products/services for the whole organization and for all other regions. The challenges with this strategy are that particular regions can hijack the entire or the overall strategy, difficulties in handling regional variations and inflexibility may creep into the overall strategy and hence inevitable change initiatives, to meet changes in the competitive business environment, may be difficult to introduce. It increases resistance to change because of regional managers defending their turfs when headquarters or other regions suggest necessary change initiatives. Based on Ghemawat (2005) model, the following strategies are recommended in making business debut into Africa:

Open Hubs: A firm wanting to enter Africa or already in Africa can reconfigure itself to have four Hubs, that are appropriately combined with the platform strategy; one hub in East Africa, situated in Kenya; the second one in Southern Africa, situated in South Africa; the third one in West Africa, based in Ghana, the fourth one based in Senegal to cover French West and Central Africa, and the fifth one in Morocco to cover the Maghreb countries. The five countries are chosen on the basis of their centrality, in their regions; they have well developed infrastructure; have high business environment rankings, their currencies are relatively convertible to other regional currencies, to the dollar, and to other major currencies; and the majority speak English and French and have high literacy levels.

General Motors is currently using Kenya as a hub for assembling various models of vehicles, particularly pickups and trucks, for the other regions of Africa. GE also has an office for the whole Africa in Nairobi, Kenya. Microsoft, Dell, Toyota, and HP Corporations are using South Africa as a hub for the whole of SADC and COMESA regions and even for the American and European markets. Renault-Nissan also assembles cars and trucks in Tunisia for the Maghreb Economic Region.

Sales Offices: Initially open sales offices, in various countries, using local agents and distributors to introduce the products or services to the market with promotional and sales support from the hubs. Barclays Bank PLC and HP are doing this from South Africa for the most of Africa.

Manufacturing Centers: Where costs, operational and structural conditions allow, it is advisable to start manufacturing in the hubs and market the products and or services in the whole of Africa. The South African Breweries is pursuing these arrangements by producing in South Africa, and marketing its various products all over Africa and in some cases, it does marketing jointly with the local breweries, as it is the case with the East African Breweries, in East Africa

Joint Ventures: Enter into joint venture arrangements with existing businesses or develop new businesses with the local entrepreneurs. In every African country; at least in East and Southern Africa and Ghana and Nigeria, in West Africa, there is a strong and growing entrepreneurial class that foreign investors can jointly work with to develop new business ventures and/or acquire existing businesses. These arrangements can still be done from the hubs.

Franchising: The franchiser/franchisee relations can also be developed. The South African companies are using this approach, particular in the fast food industry, to do business in East and West Africa today.

Internet Sales: Selling through the Internet is a viable and effective entry strategy. It is interesting to note that the second hand car market is highly developed in Africa and a lot of the ordering of the cars, from say Japan, Dubai, and Britain and paying for them, is done on line. Any product can be sold through the Internet these days and anywhere in Africa, but the goods must be moved to the final consumer and therefore the four dimensions of distance must be considered, namely cultural distance, geographic distance, the administrative and political distance and the economic distance, before making the final decision of using the Internet.

11. WORKING WITH THE AFRICAN GOVERNMENTS

When entering African markets, it is important that the firm tries to leverage the host African governments' development goals—as much as possible—as part of a company's entry and competitive strategy. African governments, like any other developing and emerging market governments, typically see themselves in a long-term race to accelerate their economic development in the face of competition from highly developed countries on one hand and from other developing and emerging markets, with lower labor costs, such as India, China, and Brazil, on the other hand. Although they recognize the benefits of taking advantage of Adam Smith's invisible hand of the market to drive growth, they are far from convinced of the advantages of opening up their markets fully to unfettered competition that is not supportive of their visions and development plans (Williamson 1997).

Frequently, the proverbial hand needs very visible guidance (Williamson 1997). As a result of this mentality, it is possible that African governments would like to award monopoly rights, concessions, and protection to companies whose investment commitments are carefully aligned to their national goals such as investing in agriculture and agro-businesses, in the rural areas, to stem up the large inflow of people seeking jobs in the urban areas and at the same time contributing to eradicating rural poverty. The message is clear: making the host government your silent partner is an important part of the successful and sustainable entry and competitive strategies. Garten (1997) further asserts that companies that establish deep local roots and show, by dint of example rather than empty rhetoric, that their strategies are aligned with the long-term goals of the host country, stand the best chance of prospering in developing and emerging markets particularly those of Africa. At the same time, such companies help keep up-coming countries on the track of economic and political progress that are indeed essential for future and sustainable business success for the supporting companies. Therefore, to really succeed in entering African markets, companies must follow a structured and systematic market screening process that incorporates technologically high quality information gathering and processing. They should choose the most appropriate mode of entry that matches their overall international strategy and the chosen strategy must align well with the firm's business model, corporate-level strategy, competitive style, and organizational structure. The organizational structure should support and enhance the competitive style chosen in each market. Several competitive styles are discussed in the following chapter. Overall, therefore, in successfully entering African markets, firms must adopt business models that also respond to specific countries' economic and social needs and eventually make the officials of a country feel that they have a stake at the success of the firm.

REFERENCES

Adler, N. J., & Gundersen, A. (2007). *International dimensions of organizational behavior* (5th ed.). Thomson Southwestern.

Andrews, K. (1980). *The concept of corporate strategy* (2nd ed.). Dow-Jones Irwin.

Barney, B. J. (1986). Organizational culture: Can it be a source of sustained competitive advantage? *Academy of Management Review*, *11*(3).

Barney, B. J. (1991). Firm resources and sustained competitive advantage. *Journal of Management, 17*(1). doi:10.1177/014920639101700108.

Barney, B. J. (1997). *Gaining and sustaining competitive advantage*. Reading, MA: Addison-Wesley Publishing Company, Inc..

Barney, J. H. (2002). *Gaining and sustaining competitive advantage* (2nd ed.). Upper Saddle River, NJ: Pearson International Education.

Bharadwaj, S. G., Varadarajan, P. R., & John, F. (1993). Sustainable competitive advantage in service industries: A conceptual model and research propositions. *Journal of Marketing*, 57.

Black, J. S., & Morrison, J. A. (2010, September). A cautionary tale for emerging market giants: How ethnocentric leadership in corporate Japan knocked its companies off the world stage. *Harvard Business Review*.

Breemer, I. (2005, June). Managing risk in an unstable world. *Harvard Business Review*.

Bungay, S. (2011, January-February). How to make the most of your company's strategy: The art of translating top management's aspirations into concrete action on the ground. *Harvard Business Review*.

Bwisa, M. H., & Nafukho, F. M. (2012). *Learning entrepreneurship through indigenous knowledge*. Nsemia Publishing Company.

Campbell, A., & Alexander, M. (1997, November-December). What is wrong with strategy? *Harvard Business Review*. PMID:10174797.

Chandler, A. D. (1962). *Strategy and structure: Chapters in the history of the American industrial enterprise*. Cambridge, MA: Massachusetts Institute of Technology Press.

Cullen, J. B., & Parboteeah, P. K. (2008). *Multinational management: A strategic approach* (4th ed.). Thompson Southwestern.

Dyer, J. H., Prashant, K., & Harbir, S. (2004, July-August). When to ally and when to acquire. *Harvard Business Review*. PMID:15241957.

Garter, J. (1997, September-October). Troubles ahead in emerging markets. *Harvard Business Review*.

Ghemawat, P. (2001, September). Distance still matters: Hard realities of global expansion. *Harvard Business Review*. PMID:11550630.

Ghemawat, P. (2005, December). Regional strategies for global leadership. *Harvard Business Review*. PMID:16334585.

Ghemawat, P. (2010, March). Finding your strategy in the new landscape. *Harvard Business Review*.

Gitman, L. J., & McDaniel, C. (2005). *Future of business* (5th ed.). Thomson South-Western.

Harry, K., & Alexander, M. (2009, December). When you shouldn't go global. *Harvard Business Review*.

Khanna, T., Palepu, G. K., & Sinha, J. (2005, June). Strategies that fit emerging markets. *Harvard Business Review*. PMID:15938439.

Khanna, T., & Pelepu, G. K. (2005, May). Strategies for emerging markets. *Harvard Business Review*. PMID:15938439.

Kim, C. W., & Mauborgne, R. (2004, October). Blue ocean strategy. *Harvard Business Review*. PMID:15559577.

Lymbersky, C. (2008). *Market entry strategies: Texts, cases, and readings in market entry management*. Laboratory Press.

Parboteeah, P. K. (2008). *Multinational management: A strategic approach* (4th ed.). Thompson Southwestern.

Shambaugh, D. (2013). *China goes global: The partial power*. Oxford, UK: Oxford University Press.

Smart, S. B., Megginson, W. L., & Gitman, L. J. (2007). *Corporate finance* (2nd ed.). Thomson Western.

Stulz, M. R. (2009, March). Ways companies mismanage risk. *Harvard Business Review*.

Wild, J. J., Wild, K. L., & Han, J. C. Y. (2008). *International business* (4th ed.). Upper Saddle River, NJ: Pearson.

Williamson, P. J. (1997, September-October). Asia's new competitive game. *Harvard Business Review*.

Zelner, B. A., & Henisz, W. J. (2010, April). The hidden risks in emerging markets. *Harvard Business Review*.

Chapter 8
A Model for Doing Business in Africa:
Principles of Strategic Management and Corporate-Level and Competitive Strategies

ABSTRACT

The chapter focuses on developing a business and competitive model to create and successfully manage a business in Africa. This includes strategic positioning of a firm in a market, corporate-level and competitive strategies that firms need to develop in order to successfully create a sustainable competitive advantage in the industries, and market segments they will compete in. Strategy and strategic management are defined and described fully. The perspectives and paradigms of formulation, implementation, and evaluation of a strategic intent are fully explored and covered here including determining the sources of a sustainable competitive advantage for a firm in an industry through the creation of a variety of competitive advantages.

1. INTRODUCTION TO STRATEGY AND STRATEGIC MANAGEMENT INSIGHTS

Effective strategic management enables a company to grow and to compete successfully in its industry and market segments. It is able to develop a sustainable competitive advantage in these markets. Therefore, strategic management is a com-

DOI: 10.4018/978-1-4666-4570-7.ch008

prehensive and fundamental framework for achieving the firm's fundamental goals (Porter, 1996; Lymbersky, 2008).The concept of strategy has been borrowed from the military and adapted for use in business. Strategy is a term that comes from the Greek word *strategia*, meaning "generalship in the military" (Mintzberg, 1987).

In the military parlance, therefore, strategy often refers to maneuvering troops into position before the enemy is actually engaged. In this sense, strategy refers to the effective preparation and deployment, in advance, of troops in war. Once the enemy has been engaged, then attention shifts to tactics of implementation of the war strategy. Here, the effective employment and use of troops and equipment is central and critical to war success. Substitute "business" for war and "resources" for troops and the transfer of the concept of strategy to the business world begins to take form (Hart 1967).

Notwithstanding, various scholars have defined strategy in a number of different ways. Strategy is management's action plan for running the business and conducting operations. It is a process of selecting and performing unique activities to create unique value for a unique set of customers (Mintzberg 1994; Porter 1996; Thompson 2008). Crafting a strategy represents a managerial commitment to pursue a particular set of actions, decisions, and moves taken to attract and retain customers, and grow the business. The strategy aims at competing successfully to improve the company's market share and eventually financial performance. Managers always try to create a strategy that gives their firm a sustainable competitive advantage and hence develop barriers to entry by competitors in their market segment (Thompson 2006; Porter 1985).

Other scholars have described strategic management as the art, science, and craft of formulating, implementing, and evaluating cross-functional ideas and decisions that will enable an organization to achieve its long-term goals and objectives of satisfying customers and ensuring successful financial performance. It is a creative and analytical process of specifying the organization's vision, mission, goals, and objectives; developing policies and plans, often in terms of projects and programs, which are designed to achieve these objectives and then allocating resources accordingly to implement the projects and programs (Chandler, 1962; Andrews, 1980; Mintzberg, 1994).

Strategic management is at the highest level of management. Strategies are typically initiated, planned, and guided by the Chief Executive Officer, approved by the Board of directors, and then implemented by employees under the supervision of the management team. However, when designing a strategy, the senior management must engage, explain the strategy, seek ideas, and clarify expectations to all employees to have employee ownership of the strategy. Thus, reduce resistance to changes required in the successful implementation of the strategy. Otherwise, if the employees are not engaged, involved, explained, and expectations are not made clear to them, you will experience resistance and opposition to initiatives to implement the strategy from all parts of the organization (Mauborgne, et al., 2005).

It is important to remember that organizations are open systems. They often obtain resources from the external environment, which they convert into products and services by adding value through their transformation process. They in turn deposit the products and services into the external environment for the customers and consumers. Therefore, organizations should always ensure that there is a match between their internal conditions and the external environment. An organization achieves this match through an effective strategy. Without this match there will be a strategic problem for the organization that can only be corrected by developing an effective strategy that matches the organization's internal conditions with its external conditions (Hart, 1967; Mintzberg, 1987, 1988).

Therefore, an effective strategic management program provides an overall direction to the enterprise and closely relates the business to its environment. It creates a strategic alignment between the organization and its environment hence achieves a desired strategic consistency that is necessary for effective organizational performance and survival in the long run. There is strategic consistency when the actions of an organization are consistent with the expectations of management, and these in turn are in agreement with the market and the general context. When there is no agreement and consistency between the strategy and its business environment then you have what scholars describe as a strategic problem in the organization. That is, what the firm produces is not what exactly what the market wants. There is a disconnection between the company and its customers and other stakeholders (Porter, 1980, 1985).

As a plan for achieving increased return for invested resources, a strategy must be well defined and coordinated and aligned with changes in the external environment. A well-defined and aligned strategy coordinates divisions and departments, engages all organizational members to reach company-wide goals and objectives efficiently and effectively. A clear and appropriate strategy focuses on the activities performed best to achieve a sustainable competitive advantage in the industry. The foundation and building blocks of a sustainable competitive advantage are: superior performance, superior quality of products and services, superior customer responsiveness, and sustained superior innovation.

All these attributes of a sustainable competitive advantage mostly emanate from the core competencies of the firm. Firms built their core competencies – special abilities and skills over time - from the knowledge, implicit and explicit talents, skills, and experiences of their employees (Prahalad et al., 1990). Prahalad et al. (1990), cites Honda Motor Corporation as an example of a successful company that has built core competencies in its engine technology over time.

2. STRATEGY FORMULATION

Many of the concerns facing managers when formulating a strategy are the same for both domestic and international companies and even for not-for profit organizations. The three types of organizations must determine what products and services to produce, where to produce them, and where and how to market them competitively to achieve financial success for for-profit organizations and service delivery for non-profit institutions. Therefore, in strategy formulation, the organization will set fundamental goals and work out strategic plans that will lead to reaching these goals efficiently and effectively (Chandler, 1962).

Strategy formulation process goes through two key processes: strategic thinking and strategic planning. The strategy process uses both strategic thinking and strategic planning to develop an effective strategy, particularly in developing its corporate and competitive strategies. Strategic thinking is a creative, novel, divergent, and convergent process carried out by organizational members in order to develop a strategy. On the other hand, strategic planning is an analytical, aligning, converging, and resource allocating process in order to implement a strategic intent. Strategic planning includes budgeting in order to allocate adequate resources to specific goals, objectives, and programs and of course it eventually leads to the measuring the effectiveness of the strategy.

Therefore, strategy formulation is preceded by an imaginative and creative analysis of capabilities and strengths to identify what a company does better than the competition. The assessment of the competitive environment—including the analysis of the five industry forces as per Porter's industry model—is part of the analysis using a SWOT analysis technique. A SWOT (Strengths, Weaknesses, Opportunities, and Threats) analysis is the tool managers use to do capability and environmental assessment and consequently design an appropriate strategy there-from.

Usually, strategy formulation permits managers to step back from their day-to-day activities and get a fresh perspective on the current and future direction of their company and its industry. In that regard, the managers bring their collective insights and perspectives to bear on the strategic direction they create (Thompson, 2006).

Campbell and Alexander (1997) have suggested three groups, in visionary organizations, whose strategic insights and perspectives impact on the strategy formulation and implementation process in organizations; on how to create more value for the stakeholders than the competitors do. Therefore, most insights and perspectives that are important to formulation and implementation of the strategy reside in the minds of the operating and other managers in the three groups, meaning that strategy formulation and strategy implementation should be treated together.

Therefore, strategists—in organizations—fall into three camps when discussing insights and perspectives to design a strategy: those who focus on operating issues, those whose focus in gazing into the future, and those who focus on behavior, culture, and learning. Some strategists are members of more than one camp, although they often exhibit a strong bias towards one of the three approaches.

First, there is the group that focuses on operating issues and proclaims the value of such processes as reengineering, time-based competition, benchmarking, total quality management, empowerment, delegation of responsibilities, and quality circles. And there are many other tools for managing and evaluating the effectiveness of today's operations, and for finding better ways of doing things in the future. Although they rarely lead to great strategies, they have been found to lead to solid, workable strategies that come out of insights and perspectives gained from solving operating problems. Toyota's remarkable success, in the auto industry, for example, came about from the consistent application of many of these tools in its company operations usually referred to as the "Toyota Way" in management and academic circles.

Secondly, there are the performance improvement processes and ideas endorsed by the future-gazing camp that defines the factors critical to future success of the organization. Those processes and ideas involve choosing which critical factors to focus on when designing the strategy based on appropriate organizational capabilities. Competitive-strategy analysis in the Michael Porter Mold (1980, 1985) is one way of defining the critical factors for success. Scenario building and analysis, a long-term planning tool commonly used by Shell, is another way of getting at the same outcome. The strategic intent analysis developed by Gary Hamel and C. K. Prahalad (1996) is yet another approach that gets similar results.

Thirdly, the behavior-and -culture camp, which comprises two groups of proponents. First, there are the data-free-planning enthusiasts. This group believes that a clear vision developed through ideas such as those of Hamel and Prahalad's strategic intent is the key to successfully discovering strategic insights and perspectives that in turn enhance the vision of the organization and consequently its strategic design. Secondly, there is the behavior-and- culture camp that focuses on organizational learning as per Chris Argyris's double loop learning principles. The learning eliminates defensive routines that make managers more receptive to new insights and ideas. Peter Senge also provides ideas on organizational learning that make development of insight more likely. He asserts that systems thinking are some of the most effective ways to increase learning and develop more insights in an organization that impact on its strategy formulation.

Consequently, the foundations of a global organization are its vision, mission, and long-term goals and objectives developed from various managers' insights and perspectives. Therefore, before an organization embarks on its strategic journey, it must define these elements. The Objectives, for example, make the vision and mission operational while providing clear and measurable targets and granular metrics with accompanying deadlines.

The vision, mission, goals, and objectives generate strategic alternatives and the strategies should help determine the structural character of the organization. Strategy determines structure and the linkages between an organization's functional and operating units. Structure should be adaptable and flexible enough to meet changing strategic needs and environmental circumstances of the organization (Chandler 1962; Mintzberg 1994).

2.1. Description of Company Vision, Mission, Goals, and Objectives

2.1.1. Vision Statement

Every good strategy starts with a good vision of where you ultimately want the firm to go (Friedman et al., 2011). Therefore, strategy formulation starts with the definition of the vision of the firm. Designing a strategic orientation that succeeds needs a clear vision. Companies that enjoy enduring success have a strong vision that guides them and that remains fixed while their business strategies and practices endlessly adapt to an ever-changing world. The dynamic of preserving the core while stimulating progress is the reason that companies such as Hewlett-Packard, 3M, Johnson and Johnson, Procter and Gamble, Sony, Siemens, and Toyota became elite institutions able to renew themselves and achieve superior long-term performance (Collins and Porras, 1996).

A vision is a written statement of what the company wants to be now and in the future. It is an image of the future the company seeks to create. It is how the organizational members want it to look like to its key stakeholders. The key stakeholders are shareholders, employees, customers, and suppliers of materials and services. The needs and expectation of all stakeholders need thorough analysis. The vision does not change during the life of the organization. A well-conceived vision must embody two major components: core ideology and envisioned future (Collins and Porras 1996).

2.1.1.1. Core Ideology

According to Collins and Porras (1996), the core ideology defines the enduring character of the organization. It is a consistent identity that transcends products, market life cycles, technological breakthroughs, management fads, and individual leaders. Core ideology provides the glue that holds an organization together as it grows, decentralizes, diversifies, expands globally, and develops work-place diversity. The core ideology consists of two parts:

- Core values;
- Core purpose.

According to Alder et al. (2007), a value is that which is explicitly or implicitly desirable to an individual or group. Values influence the selection and choices people make from available modes, means, and ends of action. Values can be both consciously and unconsciously held. Values therefore reflect relatively general beliefs that either define what is right or wrong or specify general preferences.

Research has shown that personal and corporate values affect corporate strategy. Managerial values affect all forms of organizational behavior: including selection and reward systems, superior /subordinate relationships, group behavior, communication and alignment in the organization, leadership, conflict management styles, and approaches to negotiating.

Hence organizational core values are a small set, not more than five and not less than three, of timeless guiding principles and tenets that direct the company's operations to meet its stakeholders' varied needs. Scholars state that a statement of more than five principles will be general, clouded, platitude, rhetoric, and lacks focus. The purpose of core values is to inspire organizational members and differentiate a company from the competition. For example, HP's inspiring core values, developed by the company founder, W. Hewlett and D. Packard, at the start of their company, are the following four powerful values and they include:

- Deep respect for the individual;
- A dedication to affordable quality and reliability of products and services;
- A commitment to community responsibility;
- A company exists to make technical and technological contributions for the advancement and welfare of humanity.

The core purpose is an organization's reason for existence or being. An effective purpose reflects people's idealistic motivations for doing the company's work. It does not just describe the organization's output or target customers: it captures the soul of the organization. A purpose is like a guiding star in the horizon, forever pursued but never reached. The examples of purpose statements by visionary and enduring companies include:

- **3M:** To solve unsolved problems innovatively and creatively;
- **Cargill:** To improve living standards around the world by reducing hunger;
- **Sony:** To experience the joy of advancing and applying technology for the benefit of the public;
- **Wal-Mart:** To give ordinary folks the chance to buy the same things as rich people do;
- **Walt Disney:** To make people happy.

2.1.1.2. Envisioned Future

The second primary component of the vision framework is an envisioned future. That is big, hairy, audacious, long-term goals and a description how they will be achieved. Some of envisioned futures of international companies are:

- Become a $ 125 billion company by the year 2000 through an effective supply chain management strategy (Wal-Mart, 1990);
- Become the company most known for changing the world-wide poor-quality image of Japanese products by producing products of unparalleled quality (Sony, 1950s);
- Become the dominant player in commercial aircraft and bring the world into the jet age through research and development (Boeing, 1950);
- We will destroy Yamaha! By creating an effective core competence by building an architecture of superior products in the company (Honda, 1970);
- Become the Harvard of the West through improvement of what the university offers based on a strong research portfolio (Stanford University, 1940s).

Eventually, the vision is developed by combining the elements of the core ideology and envisioned future and by vividly describing the result of the combination. The vision must be described passionately, emotionally, enthusiastically, and convincingly to catch the attention of all stakeholders. The basic dynamic of visionary companies is to preserve the core and stimulate progress and the vision becomes the context of operations. The vision statement should incorporate customers, the product, stockholders, technology in use, and employees. For example Citibank's vision statement can be summarized thus: "*To become the most powerful, the most serviceable, and the most far-reaching world financial institution that has been, through highly motivated employees, and creation of high value for stockholders*" (Collins et al., 1996). Here also is Wells Fargo's—an international financial services company—very ambitious vision statement: "*We want to satisfy all our customers' financial needs, help them succeed financially, be the premier provider of finan-*

cial services in every one of our markets, and be known as one of America's great companies and employer of first choice." The core ideology and its element and an envisioned future are implied in the fabric of these vision statements.

2.1.2. Mission Statement

A mission statement is a written statement of why a company exists and what it plans to accomplish and how it plans to accomplish it to reach its vision e.g., *Supply the highest level of service in our market segment by provision of quality products to meet ever changing customers needs through innovation by highly motivated employees in order to exceed stockholders' expectations.* The mission makes the vision operational. It gives meaning to the vision. The vision is an end state and the mission is the journey to that end state (Collins and Porras 1996). The vision is a beacon or star in the horizon and a mission is a framework to enable you reach the beacon or star far away in the horizon.

Sony's mission statement is representative of statements by many visionary companies. It runs thus: "We will create products that become pervasive around the world through individual ability and creativity and a well-known and customer admired brand…We will signify innovation and quality that rival the most innovative company anywhere in the world…Made in Japan by Sony will mean something fine with the highest degree of customer satisfaction level…" (Collins et al., 1996). The characteristics of an effective mission statement include:

- Mission statements often describe how a company's operations affect *stakeholders* – how all parties, ranging from suppliers and employees to stockholders, consumers, and communities, are affected by a company's activities;
- The mission statement of an international business depends on the type of business, the stakeholders, and the most important aspect of the business for goal achievement. Companies must be sensitive to the needs of stakeholders in different nations and communities;
- Stockholders' needs for products and financial returns must be balanced against the public interest in countries where production is located and where products are sold.

2.1.3. Goals and Objectives

When designing a strategy, managers must also define goals and objectives at the various levels of the organization in order to make the mission operational and achievable. High-level goals are stated in general terms at the corporate level of a business, "to be number one global company in each industry in which we compete or leave." Objectives are mostly defined at the business unit level. Business-unit objectives are more specific, "to mass produce a zero-pollution emissions automobile by 2010." Department-level objectives often carry numerical performance targets, "to increase market share by 5 percent in each of the next 3 years." Therefore, goals are general and objectives are very SMART (Bwisa et al., 2012):

- **S**pecific;
- **M**easurable;
- **A**ttainable;
- **R**ealistic;
- **T**imed.

2.1.4. An African Country's Vision Statement

An African country can have a national vision statement to guide its national development initiatives running thus:

To be a launching pad where innovators and entrepreneurs from the region and the globe want to locate their operations because its work force is well-educated and highly productive; its infrastructure and Internet bandwidth are advanced and excellent; its openness to talent from the region is second to none; its funding for basic research is generous ; its rule of law, patent protection, and investment climate are business friendly and "smart"; its tax code is superior and compares well with the best tax code in the world; the country is open to regional and global collaboration and cooperation; and finally the country's products and services are competitive and are first choice in the regional and global markets (Friedman et al., 2011).

This vision statement has all the information and elements the country needs to develop its mission statement and national goals and objectives. These statements, goals, and objectives can guide the nation in its allocation of national resources to ensure rapid and successful economic development to deal with poverty and hunger both of which are prevalent in Africa today.

2.2. Identifying Core Competency and Value-Creating Activities

Once the vision, mission, goals, and objectives have been variously defined, a firm has to determine whether it has the capability and resources to achieve or to eventually reach the vision and do better than the competitors. It must therefore analyze its core competencies, and the value chain activities that create value for customers better than the competitors do. The value chain represents all the activities the firm performs to create value for customers better than the competitor, from product design, acquisition of raw materials, conversion of raw materials into products, the technology in use, marketing of the products, selling the products, and eventually providing effective after sale service.

2.2.1. Unique Abilities of Companies

Core competency is a special and unique ability that enables a firm to provide a product and or a service that competitors find extremely difficult or impossible to equal or match. It refers to multiple skills coordinated to form a single technological outcome. For example, like making engines in Honda that spawns a variety of core products (Prahalad et al., 1996).

Skills are learned through on-the-job training and personal experience, whereas core competencies are skills developed and built over a long period and are difficult to teach and therefore difficult to copy by competitors. Core competency represents accumulated and learned experience over the years. Their development involves many levels of people and functions. Unlike physical assets, which do deteriorate with use and over time, competencies are enhanced as they are applied and shared.

Therefore, the real sources of competitive advantage in organizations are to be found in management ability to consolidate corporate-wide technologies and production skills into competencies that empower individual businesses to adapt quickly to changing opportunities. Core competencies, as a collective learning experience in the organization, lead to the development of skills that are distinctive to the organization. Core competencies result from communication, engaging, involving, and a deep commitment to working a cross organizational boundaries. They cannot be developed in isolation in an organization or in one business unit; they grow and get nurtured company-wide over the years.

Therefore, before managers formulate effective strategies, they should thoroughly analyze their companies, their industry, and the national business environment(s). They should also examine industries and countries being targeted for potential future entry. In-depth analysis helps managers discover core competency and abilities needed and the activities that create customer value and where necessary appropriately create the architecture needed to build the new competencies.

In a lot of cases, managers use a SWOT (Strengths, Weaknesses, Threats, and Opportunities) framework as a tool for doing organization analysis. A SWOT Analysis summarizes the key issues from the business environment and the strategic capabilities of an organization that are most likely to impact on the strategy development. The aim of SWOT Analysis is to identify the degree to which the strengths and weaknesses of the organization are relevant to and capable of dealing with the changes taking place in the business environment in order to counter threats and to exploit opportunities in the environment to create increasing value for stakeholders.

2.2.2. Value Chain Analysis

Similarly, an analysis of organizational value chain activities is necessary before crafting a strategy. This is the description and evaluation of value creating activities of the firm in order to determine the most effective way to combine and fit them together to create sustainable value for customers. It involves a process of dividing a company's activities into primary and support activities and identifying how to use them more creatively to create unique values for customers better than the competitors to built a lower cost, or best-cost, and or a differentiation competitive strategies to achieve a competitive advantage over the competition.

In the Michael Porter Framework (Porter, 1980, 1985), Primary activities are those that directly create a unique value for customers and they include inbound and outbound logistics, manufacturing, marketing and sales, and customer service. Support activities are those that support and enhance value creation and they include firm administrative infrastructure, human resource management, accounting, technology development, and procurement. Core competencies enhance the effective and efficient application and management of the value chain activities.

Each primary and support activity is a source of strength or weakness for a company in creating unique values for customers that differentiate the firm from competitors hence giving the firm a sustainable competitive advantage. Value chain activities of a firm can be increased and improved, over time, in order to improve the firm's value proposition, to maintain industry leadership in meeting changing customer needs.

2.3. Consideration of the National and International Business Environments

Business opportunities and threats—for and against a firm—are found outside the firm in its external—immediate and global—environments. The firm will acquire resources from the external environment, which it will convert into products and service and deposit the products and service back into the market in the external environment. Therefore, the firm must understand the external environment well, in terms of suppliers of resources and customers for the products and services. Otherwise, there will be a dysfunctional relationship between the internal conditions and external environment and the firm will suffer financially.

The firm must also understand the threats it faces in the external environment, including competitors, to be able to hone appropriate strategies to deal with these external threats. Some of the issues the management of a firm will, therefore, focus on in analyzing the domestic and global external environments include but not limited to:

- National differences in language, religious beliefs, customs, traditions, climate, and geography complicate strategy formulation;
- Manufacturing processes must sometimes be adapted to the supply of local workers, local customs, traditions, and practices;
- Differences in political and legal systems complicate international strategies;
- Different national economic systems complicate strategy formulation too;
- The level of technological advancement in a country will affect where the products will be produced, packaged, and how they will be distributed to end users;
- The way resources are used will affect the price of the product and or service.

2.4. Formulating International Strategies

Strengths and capabilities of international companies and environmental forces play a role in international strategy formulation. Depending on the results of its capability and environmental analysis, there are two international approaches available to a company in developing and formulating an international strategy and effective positioning of the company (Han et al., 2008):

- **Multinational Strategy which is characterized by:**
    - Adapting products and marketing strategies in each national market to suit local preferences;
    - Benefit of the strategy: monitor buyer preferences in each local market and respond quickly and effectively to new and emerging buyer preferences;
    - Drawback of the strategy: it cannot exploit scale economies in product development, manufacturing, and marketing;
    - Not suited to industries in which price competitiveness is a key to success because it does not exploit economies of scale and scope to lower operating costs company-wide and hence low prices in the market.
- **Global Strategy which is characterized by:**
    - It offers the same products using the same marketing strategies in all markets;

- Companies take advantage of scale and location economies by producing entire inventories or components in a few optimal locations. They perform product research and development in one or a few locations and design promotional campaigns and advertising strategies at headquarters;
- Benefit of the strategy: cost savings from standardized products and marketing; lessons learned in a market are shared. Suitable in markets where price is a source of competitive success;
- Yet a global strategy may cause a company to overlook differences in buyer preferences due to taste differences;
- It does not allow modification except for paint color or small add-on features;
- Competitors can step in and satisfy unmet local needs creating a niche market and possibly destroying a company's competitive advantage.

2.4.1. Corporate-Level Strategies

Each company defines the domain of business that it wants to engage in by answering these questions. What direction should a company take? What businesses to enter and leave? Simply stated, these questions express the essence of corporate-level strategy. Fundamentally, the answers to these questions will set the direction for the company, the strategies developed to get it there, and success in reaching its stated fundamental goals and objectives (Henderson and Zakon, 1983).

Hence, a corporate-level strategy is the pattern of decisions by corporate level executives that determine and reveal its objectives, purposes, or goals, produces the principal policies and plans for achieving those goals, and defines the range of businesses the company is to pursue, the businesses it wishes to exit, the kind of economic and human organization it is or intends to be, and the nature of the economic and non-economic contribution it intends to make to its stakeholders (Chandler 1962; Andrews 1980; Mintzberg 1991).

Therefore, diversified companies must formulate a corporate-level strategy by identifying the markets and industries in which they wish to enter and leave. And carrying out any and necessary diversification to achieve the desired and optimum balance and number of businesses the company needs. There are several types of diversification strategies including concentric—diversifying within the industry—diversification; conglomerate—diversification to other industries—diversification; vertical—diversifying to retail—diversification; backward—towards the acquision of raw materials or inputs—diversification; and horizontal—acquiring existing businesses—diversification either concentrically or as a conglomerate.

Therefore, the diversification strategy aims at creating a portfolio of strategic businesses units the company has and wants to have representing the various industries it wants to successfully compete in and to minimize risk in its business portfolio. There are several frameworks used to analyze the various strategic business units in the company's portfolio in order to determine what new businesses to acquire, enter, expand, maintain, and what businesses to exit or harvest and when.

2.4.2. Models Organizations Use to Formulate Corporate-Level Strategies

A model is a set of integrated ideas and techniques on how to solve organizational problems (Guillen, 1994). The most popular models for corporate strategy analysis include the BCG Growth-Share model developed by the Boston Consulting Group and the GE Industry Attractiveness and Competitive Strength model developed by McKenzie. The BCG model is a four quadrants matrix in which business units are placed according to their growth rate and market share. Conceptually, exploration of the characteristics of the growth-share matrix provides a shortcut to understanding a company's existing position, options, and alternatives available to develop a portfolio of businesses that have valuable synergic effect to each other and can minimize organizational risks (Henderson, 1983).

In the BCG model, the businesses are euphemistically and metaphorically described as the Stars—high growth and high market share businesses, consuming a lot cash to grow further to eventually mature and become cash cows; Question marks—high growth and low market share businesses, needing a lot of cash injections too to develop them to stars and eventually cash cows; Cash cows—low growth rate but high market share businesses, in mature industry and source of cash to invest in stars and in question marks; and Dogs are both low growth and low market share business, needing down-sizing or exit strategy. The categorization of businesses in this manner will help company executives to decide on which businesses they wish to retain and develop and which businesses they can exit, all with an appropriate growth and exit strategies.

The GE model does the same analysis and achieves the same result but the analysis focuses on the industry attractiveness and the competitive strength of the business in the industry, using a nine quadrants matrix. One can achieve the same results by using Porter (1980) five industry forces discussed in details below because of its frequent usage in strategy analysis.

Eventually, overall objectives for different business units are developed and the role of each unit, in the portfolio, in reaching those objectives is determined. The overall goal is to create strong synergies among the business units, create increasing value, and minimize risks to the firm. The corporate-level and portfolio strategy may entail adopting one or all of the following strategic positions:

2.4.1.1. Growth Strategy

- A growth strategy is designed to increase the scale or scope of a corporation's operations. Scale refers to the size of a corporation's activities; scope refers to the kinds of activities it performs and geographic spread of the business;
- Organic growth relies on internally generated growth through imaginative creativity and innovation;
- Other methods of growth are mergers and acquisitions, joint ventures, and strategic alliances, franchising, licensing, and management agreements. Partners in pursuing these strategies include competitors, suppliers, and buyers; firms join competitors to reduce competition, expand product lines, or expand geographically.

2.4.1.2. Retrenchment Strategy

A retrenchment strategy aims at the following activities:

- Reduces the scale or scope of a corporation's businesses. Corporations cut back the scale of operations when economic conditions worsen or competition increases by closing factories with unused capacity and laying-off employees;
- Corporations reduce the scope of activities by selling unprofitable business units or those that are not growing and not making enough money to support themselves and use the money to meet needs of growing units.

2.4.1.3. Stability Strategy

- Guards against change and used to avoid either growth or retrenchment;
- Corporations have met objectives, are satisfied with accomplishments, and see no opportunities or threats, an unlikely situation in competitive markets today, with ever changing and volatile business environment.

2.4.1.3. Combination Strategy

- Mixes growth, retrenchment, and stability strategies across a corporation's business units;
- Most common strategy because rarely do international corporations follow identical strategies in each business unit and they are likely to have a combination of units as depicted by the BCG Model.

2.4.2. Competitive Strategy

2.4.2.1. Principles of Competitive Strategy

Scholars and management practitioners have always grappled with the issues of competitive success of firms in their markets in order for these firms to be sustainably profitable. The discussions have become more urgent and intense in recent years as globalization has increased. The corporations are, not only competing in wider market arenas, but are also competing with corporations from all nations in the world. They are also facing a volatile at worst and best continuously and radically changing business environment.

The business world is characterized by volatility, change, and increasingly demanding customers with vigilant competitors. The history of business is littered with remains of companies whose competitive advantages, once robust, simply withered away over time because of their inability to effectively respond to changes in their business environment (Stalk et al., 2004). Therefore, competition will be more present and will always remain an important factor of the market reality in the ever changing business environment. Increasing competitive forces make it investable and more challenging than ever before for firms to develop appropriate and sustainable competitive strategies.

Competitive strategy is often referred to as a business-level strategy (Thompson 2006). It is similar, in conception and in many other aspects, to corporate-level strategy. Corporate-level strategy focuses in developing the direction and growth of the corporation and the role of its strategic business units to assist the corporation to achieve its vision and mission. Also, as the strategic business units of the corporations, they pursue growth and other corporate-level strategies at the same time, but their major focus is the competitive success of the corporation. Therefore, business units advance competitive strategies that make them successful in their industries and market segments.

A firm's competitive strategy is simply a game plan as to how it will enter, attract, and retain customers in a chosen market. It is a statement of what long-term value proposition a firm intends to offer that will cause customers to always prefer it to the competition. The value proposition maybe based on price, resulting from low cost operation; superior innovation; technological leadership; superior customer service, resulting in a differentiation strategy; and superior efficiency, resulting into increased productivity leading to lower cost per unity produced and hence low and competitive unit price enhancing its lower cost strategy - or some combination of these differencing factors; all based on the firm's core competencies that it has built over time.

In explaining what they call a structurist view of competitive strategy formulation as opposed to what they refer to as the reconstuctionist approach, Kim et al, (2009), assert that executives often develop a corporate and competitive strategies by nearly always beginning with analyzing the industry or environmental conditions in which they operate. They often assess their internal strengths and weaknesses and the strengths and weaknesses of the players that they are up against. With these industry and competitive analyses in mind, they set out to curve a distinctive strategic position where they can outperform their rivals by building a sustainable competitive advantage.

To obtain such an advantage, a company generally chooses either to differentiate itself from the competition for a premium price or to pursue lower costs strategy. The organization then aligns its value chain accordingly, creating manufacturing, marketing, and human resource operational strategies in the process. On the basis of these strategies, financial targets are set and budget allocations are made and necessary organizational changes are made in order to be able to implement the strategy.

A good competitive strategy successfully differentiates a firm from its competitors and it is difficult to imitate and gives the firm a sustainable competitive advantage. A bad strategy is easily copied, or basically makes the firm's value proposition worse (Pfeiffer 1998); making it difficult for the firm to be competitively successful in the long-run. An effective competitive strategy creates a position in the industry, determines unique activities to achieve the positioning, trades-off the activities, and creates a fit of the activities that locks out imitators by creating a chain of activities that is as strong as its strongest link (Porter 1996). Therefore, a firm's competitive strategy consists of moves, actions, or unique activities carried out to:

- Analyze value chain activities in order to configure them appropriately to create unique and sustainable value for customers;
- Develop unique products and/or services for a target market giving a unique value offering to a unique set of customers;
- Attract and retain customers in the market by meeting their value expectations, that is current and emerging expectations;
- Withstand competitive pressures from competitors;
- Strengthen the firm's market position through continuous imaginative value creation and innovation.

The objectives of a competitive strategy include:

- Developing a sustainable competitive advantage. A sustainable competitive advantage is achieved when a firm is more profitable and financially more successful than the competition for 5-10 years (Porter 1996);

- Cultivating clientele of loyal customers;
- Knocking the socks off rivals, ethically, and honorably;
- Consistently innovating to meet changing customer needs with new products and services. And to create barriers to market entry by potential competitors;
- Develop and enhance the firm's core competencies as a source of sustainable competitive advantage.

2.4.2.2. Strategic Analysis and the Industry Forces

According to Porter (1980), the basic unit of analysis for understanding competition is the industry. He asserts that an industry is a group of competitors producing products or services that compete directly with each other. A strategically distinct industry encompasses products or services where the sources of competitive advantage are similar. Therefore, firms develop competitive strategies based on what has come to be popularly known as Porter's five-industry forces analysis model.

Porter's five forces analysis is a framework for the industry structure analysis and business and competitive strategy developed by Michael E. Porter in 1980. It uses concepts developed in industrial economics to derive five forces which determine the competitive intensity and therefore attractiveness of an industry. Attractiveness in this context refers to the overall industry profitability. An unattractive industry is one where the combination of these forces acts to drive down overall profitability. A very unattractive industry would be one approaching pure competition. These five industry forces that shape industry competition and thus its profitability are: the Threat of New Entrants to the industry, Rivalry among Existing Competitors in the industry, Threat of Substitute Products or Services, Bargaining Power of Suppliers, and Bargaining Power of Buyers.

Porter referred to these forces as the microenvironment to the firm, to contrast it with the more general macro environment. The forces consist of those factors close to a company that affect its ability to serve its customers and make a profit. A change in any of the five forces normally requires a company to re-assess the marketplace. The overall industry attractiveness does not necessarily mean that every firm in the industry will return the same profitability. Firms are able to apply their core competences, and their effective business models to achieve a profit above the industry average. A clear example of this is in the airline industry. As an industry, profitability in the airline industry is low and yet individual companies, such as Southwest Airlines, by applying unique business models, have been able to consistently make a return in excess of the industry average (Porter, 2008).

According to Porter, the five forces model should be used at the industry level; it is not designed to be used at the industry group or industry sector level. An industry is defined at a lower, more basic level: a market in which similar or closely related products and/or services are sold to buyers. Firms that compete in a single industry should develop, at a minimum, one of the five forces analyses for its industry. Porter makes it clear that for diversified companies, the first fundamental issue, in corporate strategy, is the selection of industries – that is lines of businesses - in which the company should compete; and each line of business should develop its own, industry-specific, five forces analysis in order to develop an appropriate competitive position in that industry. This industry analysis should include a thorough competitor analysis.

Competitor analysis, in marketing and strategic management, is an assessment of the strengths and weaknesses of current and potential competitors. This analysis provides both an offensive and defensive strategic context through which to identify opportunities and threats in the industry. Competitor profiling coalesces all of the relevant sources of competitor analysis into one framework in the support of efficient and effective strategy formulation, implementation, monitoring, and adjustment.

Given that competitor analysis is an essential component of corporate and competitive strategies, it is argued by scholars (Thomson, 2006) that most firms do not really conduct this type of analysis systematically enough. Instead, many enterprises operate on informal impressions, conjectures, and intuitions basis gained through the tidbits of information about competitors every manager continually receives. As a result, traditional environmental scanning places many firms at risk of dangerous competitive blind spots due to a lack of robust competitor analysis (Porter, 1985). An effective competitor analysis uses SWOT (Strengths, Weaknesses, Opportunities, and Threats) analysis as a tool for determining the strengths and weaknesses of the firm to face the competitors and the opportunities and threats the firm will encounter in the external environment as it faces the competition before choosing a competitive strategy.

Furthermore, in pursuing an advantage over its rivals, a firm can choose from several competitive moves that can be incorporated into a chosen competitive strategy including:

- Changing prices, raising or lowering prices to gain a temporary advantage;
- Improving product differentiation, improving features, implementing innovations in the manufacturing process and in the product itself;
- Creatively using channels of distribution, using vertical integration or using a distribution channel that is novel to the industry;
- Exploiting relationships with suppliers to enhance the supply chain strategy;
- Improving cost efficiencies and consequently prices through consistent cost innovations using techniques such as quality cycles, virtual teams, total quality management, and reengineering processes;

- Do organizational analysis and evaluation using the 7S model (strategy, structure, systems, super ordinate values, skills, staff, and styles) to discover where necessary changes and improvements need to be made to improve organizational efficiency and effectiveness in order to successfully manage competitive rigors in the market.

2.4.2.3. Strategic Positioning of a Firm

After a successful industry forces analysis and in a competitive business environment, it is always important for individual firms to set themselves apart from the rest by having products or services that are more competitive in the global and domestic markets. This differentiation will enable them to acquire a greater market share than the competitors. And eventually be more profitable than the average performer in their industry.

The only way by which firms can set themslves apart is by achieving a sustainable competitive advantage. A sustainable competitive advantage is achieved by operating at the lower cost, by commanding a premium price through a better offering, or by doing both (Porter, 2001). Cost and price advantages can be achieved in two ways. One is operational efficiency and effectiveness. That is doing the same things the competitors do but doing them better.

Operational efficiency and effectiveness advantages can take myriad forms, including better technologies, superior inputs, better trained employees, or a more effective organization structure. However, over time, these advantages can be imitated by competitors because of their generic nature and their sources being available to all participants in the industry (Porter, 2001).

The other way—and a more viable and sutainable way—to achieve a sustainable competitive advantage is through an effective strategic positioning of the firm; doing things differently from competitors and in a way that delivers a unique value to customers. This can mean offering a different set of features, a different array of services, or different logistical and delivery arrangements.

To establish and maintain a distinctive and diffentiated strategic position, Porter (2001) has suggested that a firm needs to follow six fundamental principles leading to both a defferentiated product or service and a lower cost competitive strategies. The six positioning principles are:

First, the firm must start with the *right goal and objective*: superior long-term return on investment—annual profits as a percentatage of capital employed—is the most ideal and a superior goal and objective for commercial organizations. Only by grounding strategy in sustained profitability will real economic value be generated. Economic value is created when customers are willing to pay a price for a product or service that exceeds the cost of producing it. When goals and objective are defined in terms of volume or market share leadership, with profits assumed to follow, poor strategies often result. The same is true when strategies are set to respond to the perceived desires of investors.

Second, a company's strategy must enable it to deliver a unique *value proposition to customers*, or a set of benefits, different from those that competitors offer. Strategy, then, is neither a quest for the universally best way of competing nor an effort to be all things to every customer. It defines a way of competing that delivers a unique value in a particular set of uses or for a particular set of customers.

Third, strategy needs to be reflected in a *distinctive value chain* performed distinctively. To establish a sustainable competitive advantage, a company must perform different activities than rivals or perform similar activities in different ways. A company must configure the way it conducts its supply chain strategy, manufacturing, logistics, service delivery, marketing, human resource management, and so on differently from rivals and tailored to its unique value proposition. If a company focuses on benchmarking and adopting best practices, it will end up performing most of its activities similarly to competitors, making it hard to gain a sustainable competitive advantage. Benchmarking and reengineering can only be used to enable you to figure out where you need to focus your innovations to be different.

Fourth, robust strategies involve *trade-offs*. A company must abandon or forego some product features, services, or activities in order to be unique at others. Such trade-offs, in the product and in the value chain, are what make a company truly distinctive. When improvements in the product or in the value chain do not require trade-offs, they often become generic and new best practices that are imitated because competitors can do so with no sacrifice to their existing ways of competing. Trying to be all things to all customers almost guarantees that a company will lack any sustainable competitive advantage.

Fifth, strategy defines how all the elements of what a company does *fit* together. A strategy involves making choices throughout the value chain that are interdependent; all a company's activities must be mutually reinforcing. A company's product design, for example, should reinforce its approach to the manufacturing process, and both should leverage the way it conducts after-sales service. Fit not only increases competitive advantage but also makes a strategy harder to imitate. Rivals can copy one activity or product feature fairly easily, but will have much more difficulty duplicating a whole system of competing. Without fit, discrete improvements in supply chain, manufacturing, marketing, or distribution are quickly matched. Fit is best achieved by developing a firm's core competencies over time. You develop core competencies—special skills and abilities—through employees training, experience, and organizational alignment.

Finally, successful strategy involves *continuity* of direction. A company must define a distinctive value proposition that it will stand for, even if that means forgoing certain opportunities. Without continuity of direction (vision), it is difficult for companies to develop unique skills, core competencies, and assets or build strong reputations with customers. Frequent corporate "reinvention", then, is usually a sign of poor strategic thinking and planning and a route to mediocrity. Continuous improvement is a necessity, but it must always be guided by a strategic direction and a continuous purpose.

2.4.2.4. The Generic Competitive Strategies

Porter (1980, 1985), and other scholars (Thompson, 2006), have identified and described five generic competitive strategies that can give a firm a sustainable competitive advantage, in its industry. These strategies include:

- **Lower-Cost Leadership:** This is striving to be the overall low-cost provider of products and/or services in the industry. It is achieved through productivity improvement, economies of scale, and learning curve effects;
- **Broad Defferentiation:** This is striving to build customer loyalty by differentiating one's products/service offerings and utilities from rivals' products/services through appropriate packaging, dilivery efficiencies, branding, and the way the products and services are presented to customers;
- **Best-Cost Provider:** This is striving to give customers more value for their money by combining an emphasis on cost with an emphasis on upscale differentaition. Consequeently, you provide high quality products/services at lower cost than the competitors in a strategic group. Toyota provides lower priced Lexus cars than the competitors in a luxury line segment or group of cars like the BMW and Volvo;
- **Focus Strategy based on Low Cost:** This is concentrating on a narrow buyer segment, out- performing rivals on low cost offerings;
- **Focus Strategy based on Differentiation:** This is offering niche members a product or service that is unique to them and customized to their needs through packaging, branding, delivery, and availability.

Notwithstanding and according to Porter (1980), underlying the concept of generic strategies is that competitive advantage is at the heart of any strategy, and that achieving competitive advantage requires a firm to make choices. If a firm is to gain an advantage, it must choose the type of competitive advantage it seeks to attain and a scope within which it can be attained and pursued accordingly.

He goes on to say that the worst strategic error is to be stuck in the middle, or to try simultaneously to pursue all the generic strategies at the same time because of the inherent contradictions of the strategies. However, other scholars have established that these generic strategies can be applied concurently and proposed other competive strategic options such as the Delta model and the Blue Ocean approach, both outlined below, to achieve concurent application of the generic competitive strategies.

2.4.2.5. The Delta Model: Adaptive Management for a Changing World

Hax and Wilde II (1999) have asserted that existing management frameworks do not describe all the ways that companies are competing successfully today. They state that when queried, senior executives concurred that conventional theories and business practices do not provide the necessary guidance and support for decision making in a world of change, complexity, and uncertainty. The authors' research on more than 100 companies is the basis of their Delta model which (1) defines strategic positions that reflect fundamentally new sources of profitability, (2) aligns these strategic options with a firm's activities and provides congruency between strategic direction and execution, and (3) introduces adaptive processes capable of continually responding to an uncertain environment.

They describe three strategic options having three distinct economic perspectives namely best product, customer solutions, and system lock-in. These strategic options provide a mechanism for defining the vision of a business. Outstanding real-life business successes achieved through strikingly different strategies and drawn from fundamentally different sources of profitability illustrate the nature of these strategic positions.

The Delta model links strategy with execution by selecting a distinctive strategic position and then integrating it with a company's collective processes. The authors identify three fundamental processes that are always present and are the repository of key strategic tasks: operational effectiveness, customer targeting, and innovation.

Strategy must adapt continuously, and implementation must respond to market changes and to greater understanding of the market that becomes apparent only during implementation. A firm's actions must be aligned with its strategic position, and the results must give feedback for adapting the strategy. The authors outline common responsive mechanisms for obtaining feedback from the adaptive processes and suggest metrics that are essential to adaptation. To anticipate the future, it is necessary to track performance against the adaptive processes, which are the initiatives enabling the strategy. The Delta model provides a rich overall framework that integrates a firm's options and activities without running the risk of oversimplifying the context in which it makes decisions.

2.4.2.6. The Blue Ocean Strategic Option

The other way in which it is suggested that a lower cost leadership and differentiation can be applied concurrent to achieve a competitive advantage is the Blue Ocean Strategic framework proposed by Kim and Mauborgne (2005): The Blue

Ocean Strategic framework—as opposed to Red Ocean or traditional strategy—is the process by which managers use strategic moves as a basis of analysis to create a business strategy that creates uncontested market space and makes the competition irrelevant by creating a new demand for the product through the rationalization of product/service utilities and price. A strategic move is the set of managerial actions and decisions involved in making a major market-creating business offering of an existing product or service. The strategic move creates a new market space and new demand for the product or service through value innovation that entails product cost and utility improvements.

The strategic moves discussed in Blue Ocean Strategy are moves that have delivered products and services that open and capture new market space, with a significant leap in demand of an existing product. The cornerstone of Blue Ocean Strategy is value innovation as opposed to value creation and value innovation is achieved through lowering of costs and product/service differentiation.

Value creation is improvement on the existing product utilities and value innovation is creating new benefits and utilities into the product, and lowering its cost at the same time, that makes the customer better off or draws new customers to the product. Therefore, value innovation involves concurrent application of low cost and differentiation approaches to competition. It said, by proponents of blue ocean strategy, that blue ocean strategic moves can create brand equity that lasts for decades. The analytical tools and frameworks for developing a Blue Ocean Strategy by Kim et al. (2005) include:

- The Strategy canvas or map, which indicates the benefit offerings on the horizontal axis and their level of offering on the vertical axis;
- The value curve, which traces the benefit offerings on the canvas or map to clearly demonstrate the level of benefits, offered across the board. The divergence of the curve from the competitors' curves indicates the achievement of a blue ocean strategic orientation;
- The four actions framework, which describes how to create the product, benefits offerings through additions, eliminations, reductions, and enhancements of the product benefits.

There are seven steps or principles in formulating a blue ocean strategy, namely:

- Reconstruct market boundaries across alternative industries, across strategic groups, across buyer groups, across complementary products and service offerings, across the functional-emotional orientation of an industry, and even across time;
- Focus on the big picture not the numbers to be able to draw the strategic map;

- Reach beyond existing demand by creating new product utilities to increase demand by existing customers and to attract new customers;
- Get the strategic sequence right through introduction of new product utilities, determining the price to attract increased customer demand and new customers, have target-cost through cost innovations, and adopt the new product;
- Ensure that you effectively deal with organizational hurdles in actualizing the blue ocean strategy. The hurdles will originate from employees, business partners, customers, and the general public;
- Overcome organizational hurdles through tipping point leadership that focuses on the effective use of the disproportionate influence factors in the organization. The actual organizational hurdles include: cognitive hurdles, resource hurdles, motivational hurdles, and political hurdles;
- Build execution into the strategy through the three E fair processes of engagement, explanation, and expectation clarity.

The sustainability of the blue ocean strategy is ensured though continuous value innovation. The continuous value innovation is often achieved through cost reduction on one-hand and product and service utilities improvement and rationalization on the other hand.

3. THE VARIETIES OF COMPETITIVE ADVANTAGE

A competitive advantage is something a firm can do that rivals cannot match (Greenwald, et al., 2005). It is a set of unique features of a company and its product and service that are perceived by the target market as significant and superior to those of the competition. It is a factor or factors that cause customers to patronize a firm and not the competition (Gitman, et al., 2005). A competitive advantage either generates higher demand or leads to lower cost of the product or service. Demand competitive advantages give firms a unique access to customers. Also known as customer captivity, this type of advantage generally arises from customers' habits, searching costs, or switching costs that are considered in customers' buying decisions in order to continue staying with the firm.

Cost or supply advantages, by contrast, almost always come down to a superior technology. That is a technology that competitors cannot duplicate because it is protected by a patent. The other competitive advantage is a much larger scale of operation accompanied by declining marginal costs that competitors cannot match too as a result of an innovation and expansion of the market.

These three factors—customer captivity, proprietary technology, and economies of scale—generate most competitive advantages in organizations in various industries. The other sources of advantage, such as government support or protection and superior access to information tend to support these three key advantages.

Strategic positioning of a firm, various competitive strategies, and the varieties of competitive advantage reinforce each other and always form a strong foundation of a firm's sustainable competitive advantage in its industry. The management of a firm needs to create a vibrant environment where these elements of competitive strategy are strengthened as it seeks to achieve a sustainable competitive advantage in its industry or market over the years.

3.1. Sustainable Competitive Advantage

The aim of true strategy is to master a market environment by clearly understanding and anticipating the actions of other economic agents, especially competitors and conquering them sustainably. However, true competitive advantages are harder to find and maintain than people realize, so they must always be searched and looked for hard in customer captivity, proprietary technology, and economies of scale, which create most competitive advantage in organizations in various industries (Greenwald and Kahn, 2005).

Essentially, the development of sustainable competitive advantage lies at the core of strategy development. For a firm to have a sustainable competitive advantage, it has to have business strategies that improve the competitive position of its products and services in the market place. This improvement is achieved by always securing and retaining the three competitive advantages—customer captivity, proprietary technology, and cost—discussed above for a long time; for at least five years.

Therefore, a sustainable competitive advantage involves every aspect on the way the organization competes in the marketplace. Its real benefit comes from advantages that competitors cannot easily imitate. Hence, to be sustainable, a competitive advantage needs to be more deeply embedded in the organization i.e. in its intangible resources such as skills, experiences, culture, and investment over time. It involves seeking and achieving something unique and different from competitors most of the time (Hill and Jones, 2001).

A sustainable competitive advantage is usually created or achieved over time. It is based on stability and continuity in relationships between different parts of an organization and external business networks. External business networks consist of multiple relationships, with each participating firm gaining the resources needed to build core competencies to obtain a sustainable competitive advantage. Porter (1985) discusses the formation of "coalitions" that allow the sharing of activities in order to support a firm's competitive advantage. However, Porter emphasis is on the "value chain" approach which focuses on activities within a single firm—that have external relationships—and how a firm can carry them out well, efficiently and effectively to create a sustainable competitive advantage.

3.2. Sources of Sustainable Competitive Advantage

The foundation of a sustainable competitive advantage has been described, by scholars, as superior quality, superior customer responsiveness, superior efficiency, and superior innovation of products and services and their costs (Thompson, 2006). Therefore, sources of sustainable competitive advantage must be factors in the company that enhance and extend these four elements sustainably to ensure that the firm has all or one of the three advantages discussed above—customer captivity, proprietary technology, and lower cost through economies of scale—at all times.

According to Barney (1991), a firm is said to have a sustained competitive advantage when it is implementing a value-creating strategy not simultaneously being implemented by any current or potential competitors and when those other firms are unable to duplicate the benefits of this strategy. He asserts that understanding sources of sustainable competitive advantage has become a major area of research in strategic management in recent times (Porter, 1985; Rumelt, 1984).

Recognizing the importance of an effective strategy to firms—creating tomorrow's competitive advantage faster than competitors copy the ones possessed today—Day and Wensley (1988) focused on the elements involved in competitive advantage. Specifically, they identified two categorical sources of sustainable competitive advantage namely: superior skills, which are the distinctive capabilities of personnel that set them apart from the personnel of competing firms, and superior resources, which are the more tangible requirements for advantage that enable a firm to exercise its capabilities to build core competencies.

In the present business environment of employment volatility and uncertainties, one might question whether personnel could truly be considered a source of a sustainable competitive feature of a firm. But if these personnel truly understand customers' needs and are able to foster intimate business relationships with them, develop and deliver quality products and services, they must be able to retain employment with the firm, then, of course, they most certainly qualify as a source of sustainable competitive advantage (Srivastava et al., 1998).

Prahalad and Hamel (1990) suggest that firms combine their resources and skills into core competencies, loosely defined as that which a firm does distinctively well in relation to competitors like Honda does with engines. Therefore, firms may succeed in establishing a sustainable competitive advantage by combining skills and resources, including leveraging them, in unique and enduring ways. By combining resources in this manner, firms can focus on collectively learning how to coordinate all employees' efforts in order to facilitate growth of specific core competencies that result in building a sustainable competitive advantage.

Bharadwaj et al. (1993) discuss the specific combinations of skills and resources that are unique to service industries. For example, they propose that the greater the complexity and co-specialization of assets needed to market a service, the greater the importance of innovation as a source of sustainable competitive advantage will become. They also propose that brand equity becomes an important source of sustainable competitive advantage in service industries as the level of service offered becomes more intangible and when consumers have a great need to overcome perceptions of risk.

Building on the assumptions that strategic resources are heterogeneously distributed across firms and that those differences are stable over time, Barney (1991) examined the link between firm resources and sustainable competitive advantage. He posits that there are four empirical indicators of the potential of firm resources to generate sustainable competitive advantage: value, rareness, imitability, and substitutability. He argues that firm resources can only be a source of sustainable competitive advantage when they are valuable, rare, inability to be imitated and inability to be substituted.

Resources are valuable when they enable the firm to conceive of and implement strategies that improve its efficiency and effectiveness. These valuable resources must be rare that is not owned and controlled by a large number of competing firms for them to be a source of sustainable competitive advantage. Furthermore, competing firms must face a cost disadvantage in imitating or copying these resources and that there must be no strategically equivalent valuable resources that are themselves either not rare or imitable. Similarly, Hunt and Morgan (1995) propose that potential resources can be most useful when categorized as financial, physical, legal, human, organizational, informational, and relational and sustainably fully enhanced in those categories.

Wernerfelt's (1984) explains the resource-based view of achieving sustainable competitive advantage. This view holds that continuously developing existing and creating new resources and capabilities in response to changing market conditions can achieve sustainable competitive advantage. Among these resources include capabilities, networks, economy, brands, and knowledge that represent the most important value-creating assets. The firm's opportunity to sustain the competitive advantage is determined by both the distinctive capabilities and the reproducible capabilities and their unique combination the firm creates to achieve synergy to produce competitive products and services at competitive prices by efficient and effective use of these resources.

The distinctive capabilities are those characteristics of the firm which cannot be replicated by competitors, or can only be replicated with great difficulty. Distinctive capabilities can be of many kinds: patents, exclusive licenses, strong brands, effective leadership, teamwork, and tacit knowledge. On the other hand, reproducible capabilities are those that can be bought or created by the competition and thus, by themselves cannot be a source of sustainable competitive advantage. Most of the technological systems, unless patented to the firm, fall in this category.

In order to sustain the competitive advantage, a firm should keep learning and upgrading on how to do things better, and keep spreading that knowledge throughout its organization. Learning provides the catalyst and the intellectual resource to create sustainable competitive advantage. The desire and the ability of an organization to continuously learn and upgrade from any source and to rapidly convert learning into action provide the ultimate competitive advantage. Thus, firms must continuously leverage the power of knowledge. Tacit or implicit knowledge can be used as a source of sustainable competitive advantage because it is difficult to copy (Day and Wensley, 1988).

They argue that all knowledge is not the same and that there is explicit knowledge that can easily be written down. Such knowledge as patents, procedures, formulations or engineering designs is referred as explicit. The explicit knowledge can create competitive advantage, but its self-life is increasingly brief, as it can be replicated easily by other organizations. Tacit or implicit knowledge on the other hand is far less tangible and is deeply embedded into an organization's operating practices. This is what is more often referred to as the organizational culture. Because tacit knowledge is much harder to detail, copy, or distribute, it can be a source of competitive advantage that is quite difficult for competition to replicate.

Radical innovations by firms usually give them long-term corporate success. Although most corporate investments mainly revolve around improvements to existing products and processes, it is new game-changing breakthroughs that launch a company into new markets, enable rapid growth, and create high return in investment. Such radical innovations too come out as sources of sustainable competitive advantage.

People are the main sources of competitive advantage. Equally, they can be the main source of competitive disadvantage. Competitors can copy technologies, products, and structures. No one, however, can match a firm's highly charged, motivated people who care and are loyal to the company. People are the firm's most important asset, but most often underutilized. They are the firm's repositories of knowledge and skill base that makes the firm competitive. Well trained and highly motivated people are critical to the development and execution of strategies, especially in today's faster-paced, more perplexing world, where top management can no longer assure the firm's competitiveness.

Prahalad et al. (1990) argue that corporate culture plays a key role in creating sustainable competitive advantage. The strength of an organization's culture is one of the most fundamental competitive advantages. A firm must, however, build and preserve an innovation-adept culture, a culture of commitment, a culture of discipline, one where employees passionately pursue the organization's cause and mission. Only then can a firm be better positioned for success, particularly in building a sustainable competitive advantage.

Barney (1986) underscores the fact that in order for a firm's culture to provide sustained competitive advantages, and thus by implication, be a source of sustainable superior financial performance, three conditions must be met. First, the culture must be valuable; it must enable a firm to do things and behave in ways that lead to high sales, low costs, high margins, or in other ways add financial value to the firm. Because superior financial performance is an economic concept, culture, to generate such performance, must have positive economic consequences. Second, the culture must be rare; it must have attributes and characteristics that are not common to the cultures of a large number of other firms. Finally, such a culture must be imperfectly imitable; firms without these cultures cannot engage in activities that will change their cultures to include the required characteristics, and if they try to imitate these cultures, they will be at some disadvantage in terms of reputation and experience compared to the firm they are trying to imitate.

The level and quality of service offered by a firm to its customers in many cases become a key focus to value generation and the subsequent sustainable competitive advantage. Srivastava et al. (1998) identify two forms of assets that contribute to this end. First, it is the relational market-based assets, which are those that reflect bonds between a firm and its customers and/or channel members. This bond allows for the firm to produce highly customized products required by the customer. Secondly, the intellectual market-based asset which is that detailed knowledge that firm employees possess concerning their customers' needs, tastes, and preferences. These market-based assets are rare, unique, valuable, and difficult to imitate, thus providing an excellent potential sources of sustainable competitive advantage for a firm.

Porter (1995) looks at the activities of a firm's value chain as the basic units of competitive advantage. He argues that competitive advantage is based on the fact that advantage can arise from many sources and shows how all advantages can be connected to specific activities and the way that activities relate to each other. It entails discovering the underlying causes of advantage in an activity, i.e. why firms achieve lower cost and how activities create tangible buyer value.

Firms seeking to develop sustainable competitive advantages from their activities must be organized and managed on a framework based on strategy, structure, systems, style, skills, staff, and shared values, the 7s framework. To improve, companies have to pay attention to all the seven factors. All these are interrelated, such that a change in one has a ripple effect on all the others. Hence, it is impossible to make progress on one without making progress on all. An attempt to combine all these factors requires effective leadership and strong focused management style. It requires an employee-centered leadership.

An employee-centered leadership can be another source of sustainable competitive advantage and it is, actually, the necessary and most important condition for long-term competitiveness. In particular, in the knowledge-economy, what is proving to be most effective is the emerging style of value-based leadership, both as motivation for constant innovation up and down at all organizational levels and as a source of unity and power of intellect, will, passion, eagerness, enthusiasm, persistence, rigor, and vision that creates synergies that propel successful companies in their quest for and achievement of sustainable competitive advantage.

Effective leadership focused on building sustainable competitive advantage seeks to continuously improve on the firm's value adding systems. Such a firm becomes a continuous improvement firm. A continuous improvement firm is a firm that is continuously improving on customer value due to improvements in productivity initiated by the members of the general workforce. The key success factors in this endogenous, incremental, and continuous technological and operational change is the organization and management of the firm in such a way that all members are motivated to promote change and they are supported in their efforts to do so.

What is remarkable about the continuous improvement firm is its ability to operate simultaneously in all innovative arenas: new product, new technology, new systems, new organizational forms, new motivational styles, and new customer relationship management. These innovations promote entrepreneurial behavior in the organization with its attendant benefits of improving organizational performance through appropriate competitive styles. Toyota Motor Corporation and Honda Company are good examples of continuous improvement companies. These two Japanese companies have been able to produce high quality and most fuel efficient cars in the world through their continuous improvements philosophies.

Finally, firms should own their competitive advantages and manage change effectively to ensure their ability to maintain sustainable competitive advantage. Market leading firms have identified factors that give them competitive advantage in their unique context. Such firms have figured out the importance of owning their competitive advantage in order to get fast to the market and sustain the speed in a manner that competition cannot match.

Barney (1997) observes that sustainable competitive advantage does not last forever even though it is founded on valuable, rare, and costly-to-imitate resources and capability. He argues that if the threats and opportunities that face a firm in its competitive environment remain relatively stable, then a firm with valuable, rare, and costly-to-imitate resources and if it is organized correctly will be able to continue to exploit them to gain a sustainable competitive advantage. Also if the types of threats and opportunities in the environment evolve in predictable ways, a firm with these kinds of resources and capabilities will often be able to exploit and modify them to maintain a sustainable competitive advantage. However, if a firm's threats and opportunities change in a rapid and unpredictable manner, the firm will often be unable to maintain a sustained competitive advantage unless it manages those changes successfully.

Barney (1997) maintains that the resource-based capability of the firm can help managers choose strategies to gain sustained competitive advantage only as long as the rules of the game in an industry remain relatively fixed. But after sudden and unpredictable changes in the threats and opportunities, what were weaknesses may become strengths and vice versa. He states that the competitive advantages of firms in this context are not competed away through imitation. Rather, they are replaced through the sudden and unpredictable changes in the threats and opportunities profile that face a firm.

Thus and although sustained competitive advantage will not last forever, they are not competed away through imitation but can be displaced through revolutionary environmental changes. In this regard, firms must act proactively toward the changes in their business environment in order to develop strategies to enable them to exploit new opportunities and counteract the threats that are poised by changes in the external business environment. McGahan (2004) has proposed four change trajectories—the alteration of reality—that managers must contend with as they struggle to sustain their competitive advantage in their various industries:

- **Radical Change:** Is characterized by:
    - A threat to a company's core activities – the activities that have historically generated profits for the firm. They are threatened when they become obsolete and less relevant to suppliers and customers because of new alternatives;
    - A threat to the company's core assets – the resources, knowledge, and brand capital that have historically made the organization unique – the threat occurs if they fail to generate value as they once did.
- **Progressive Change:** Is characterized by the following factors:
    - It is the most common change trajectory with over 43% companies changing progressively;
    - The core activities and core assets are neither threatened nor irrelevant;
    - Basic assets, activities, and underlying technologies remain stable;
    - Smart companies develop insights to improve core assets and core activities to generate increasing value for stakeholders.

- **Innovative Change:** Characterized by nuances not easily noticed and by it:
    - Core assets are under threat but core activities remain stable;
    - Companies continuously try to find ways to restore their core assets while protecting ongoing customer and supplier relationships;
- **Intermediating Change:** Is characterized by nuances not easily notices and by it:
    - Core activities are threatened with obsolescence, customers and supplier relationships are stretched and fragile;
    - Core assets retain their capacity to create value;
    - The challenge under intermediating change is to find ways to preserve knowledge, brand capital, and other valuable assets while fundamentally changing relationships with customers and suppliers – the core activities that create value using core assts.

Figure 1 indicates the achievement of competitive advantage over time, its size, and how it changes or erodes overtime. The issues and focus of management of a firm is to maintain the competitive advantage at the benefit period by effectively managing inevitable changes, strategic assets, and core activities to maximize customer value at this level and in order to slow the product moving to the erosion period. Some of the strategies needed to enhance customer value at the erosion level are to add new features and utilities to the product, reinvigoration of its packaging, and improvement of brand equity through creative innovation (Khan et al., 2005).

Figure 1. The building and eroding of competitive advantage

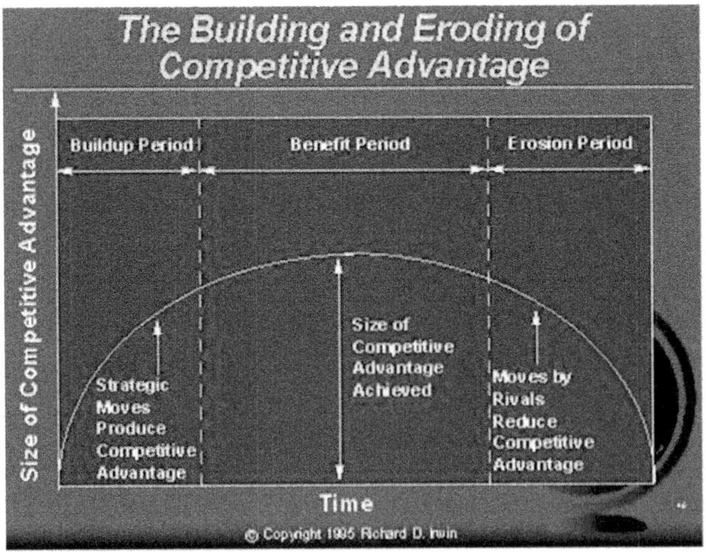

4. COMPETITION IN STRATEGIC GROUPS

A strategic group is a concept used in strategic management that groups companies within an industry that have similar business models and similar combinations of corporate and competitive strategies (Barney 2002; Miyamoto 2008). Strategy is the direction and scope of an organization over the long term, which achieves advantages for the organization while business model refers to an integrated set of ideas and techniques on how the firm will generate revenues and make money.

Hunt (1972) coined the term strategic group while conducting an analysis of the appliances industry after he discovered a higher degree of competitive rivalry than suggested by industry concentration ratios. He attributed this to the existence of subgroups within the industry that competed along different dimensions making tacit collusion more difficult. These asymmetrical strategic groups caused the industry to have more rapid innovation, lower prices, higher quality products and services, and lower profitability than traditional economic models would predict.

4.1. Strategic Group Analysis

Strategic group analysis provides insights into different competitors' approaches to the marketplace and the resulting implications for organizational and industrial performance. Strategic group analysis aims to identify organizations with similar strategic characteristics, following similar strategies or competing on similar bases (Karel et al., 1993; Hodgkinson, 1997). Such groups can usually be identified using two or perhaps three sets of characteristics as the bases of competition, such as:

- Extent of product or service diversity;
- Extent of geographic coverage; and number of market segments served;
- Distribution channels used;
- Extent of branding and marketing effort;
- Product or service quality and pricing policy.

Strategic group analysis is useful in several ways:

- Helps identify who the most direct competitors are and on what basis they compete;
- Raises the question of how likely or possible it is for another organization to move from one strategic group to another;
- Strategic group mapping might also be used to identify opportunities and can also help identify strategic problems;
- It can provide information to design and implement product promotion strategies.

In the USA, for example, press media and television advertising is intense in each strategic group to promote the product or service offerings in the various strategic groups. The companies often use a variety of caricatures—to depict their products and product benefits—to deal with customer apathy and cynicism in promotional messages. Apathy, attention deficiency, and cynicism appear to be high and commonplace among consumers. It is difficult to attract and catch customer attention that is also under attack from many other media that continuously demand the customer attention. That is in addition to the demands of extensive social media. Other writers have argued that it is difficult to communicate with American because 70 percent of Americans are functionally illiterate although technically almost 100 percent literacy rate (Friedman et al., 2012).

4.2. Identification of Strategic Groups

Porter (1980) defines a strategic group as a set of firms in an industry that follow the same or similar strategy. The similarity of their strategy is along the strategic dimensions of resource allocation, strategy execution, product and service offerings, and customer selection viewpoints. For example, the restaurant industry can be divided into several strategic groups, including fast food and fine dining, that competes on variables such as food preparation time, pricing, presentation, and ambience in the restaurant. The auto industry strategic grouping is based on car body shape and engine size and competition is often based on variables such as style, frills, color, fuel usage, and price (Karel et al., 1993).

Strategic group theory assumes (See Figure 2) that all firms in an industry face the same competitive environment and that differences in organizational capabilities account for differences in strategic behavior, including competitive style and scope (Porter 1980). Scope, in strategy, refers to the strategic decisions delineating the firm's participation in the marketplace. The selection of the market segments in which to compete and the types of products and services offered in these market segments are scope decisions (Porter 1985).

The number of groups within an industry and their composition depends on the dimensions—such as strategic resources, execution of the strategy, and customer view—used to define the strategic groups. Strategic management scholars and practitioners often make use of a two dimensional grid to position firms (See Figure 2) along an industry's two most important dimensions in order to distinguish direct rivals, those with similar strategies or business models, from indirect rivals. IN the diagram above, companies in groups A, B, and C share some aspect of competition such as product similarities in style and frills.

Michael Porter (1985) developed the concept of strategic group further and applied it within his overall system of strategic analysis. He explained strategic groups in terms of what he called mobility barriers. These are similar to the entry barriers

Figure 2. Strategic group mapping and intergroup rivalry (source: Porter, 1980)

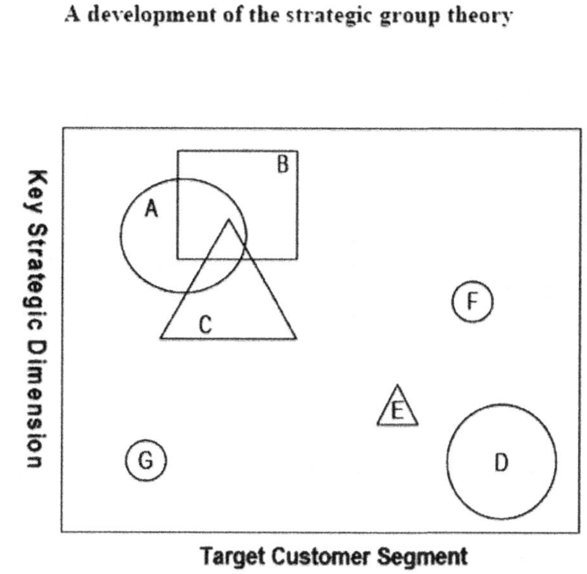

that exist in industries, except mobility barriers apply to groups within an industry. Because of these mobility barriers, a company can only get drawn into one strategic group or another. Strategic groups are not to be confused with Porter's generic strategies—cost leadership, differentiation, and focus, see Table 1,which are internal strategies and do not reflect the diversity of strategic styles within an industry.

Table 1 links industry forces with competitive strategy indicating how they impact each other. Of course, industry forces being environmental and in the market help in the determination of competitive strategies that are internal but help the firm to succeed in the market. The two have a symbiotic, dynamic, and synergic relationship. In this regard, competitive success is sustained by the firm in developing a variety of competitive advantages. These competitive advantages include:

- Customer captivity where by a firm offers customer benefits that are unique and difficult to copy by the competition and makes it costly for customers to change or transfer to the competition, because of searching and switching costs;
- Proprietary technology that improves productivity, product quality, and cost of production hence making product more competitive in the market through either product differentiation and/or lower cost leadership;
- Economies of scale that reduce product cost overall and make the firm competitive in the market through a lower cost leadership strategy.

Table 1. Generic strategies and industry forces relationships

Industry FFFForce	Generic Strategies		
	Cost Leadership	**Differentiation**	**Focus**
Entry Barriers	Ability to cut price in retaliation deters potential entrants.	Customer loyalty can discourage potential entrants.	Focusing develops core competencies that can act as an entry barrier.
Buyer Power	Ability to offer lower price to powerful buyers.	Large buyers have less power to negotiate because of few close alternatives.	Large buyers have less power to negotiate because of few alternatives.
Supplier Power	Better insulated from powerful suppliers.	Better able to pass on supplier price increases to customers.	Suppliers have power because of low volumes, but a differentiation-focused firm is better able to pass on supplier price increases.
Threat of Substitutes	Can use low price to defend against substitutes.	Customers become attached to differentiating attributes, reducing threat of substitutes.	Specialized products and core competency protect against substitutes.
Rivalry	Better able to compete on price.	Brand loyalty to keep customers from rivals.	Rivals cannot meet differentiation-focused customer needs.

Source: M. Porter (1980, 1985)

5. CORPORATE-LEVEL AND COMPETITIVE STRATEGIES IN THE AFRICAN CONTEXT

The principles of corporate-level strategy formulation are universal. They are applicable in Africa as they are elsewhere in the world. However, industry analysis, in Africa, as a basis for formulating a competitive strategy, presents special challenges. In addition to Port's (1980) five industry forces, African scholars have anecdotally suggested two additional forces that impact competitive strategy formulation in Africa. These forces need to be incorporated into the industry analysis model. The two additional forces are relationships, among employees and with suppliers and customers, in a company, on one hand, and government policy and behavior of government officials on the other hand.

Like many relational societies in the world, family is the basic unit of society in Africa and a lot of business relationships impacting on business emanate from the family. Being honorable and adhering to the norms of the group are critical behaviors for business in Africa. Enhancing one's status, protecting the group, and maintaining harmony—as in the family—are critical and primary goals of individuals in business.

Furthermore, professional and social networks are fundamental structures in doing business in Africa. They make relationships the cornerstone of any business activity. Relationships are a teeming and a daily affair in Africa. The Africans, like the Chinese with Guanxi, are highly relational people, which can affect confidence and trust with business partners, recruitment and deployment of labor, promotions, and rewarding of employees, and cost of labor, and even product differentiation. They profoundly influence individual outcomes in business.

Guanxi is a powerful and pervasive system of personal relationship in China that can divide the loyalties of employees. Again, relationships and personal connections come first in Chinese culture. Guanxi relationships are defined by a strict ethic of reciprocity that must be maintained over time. It affects daily business contacts, interactions, and decisions in a big way (Schuster and Copeland, 2006; Vanhonacker, 2004).

In the African context and in the personal ecosystem, relationships can affect awarding of contracts to suppliers and in dealing with customers. Many African managers employ on the basis of race, tribe, friendship, and a complex network of relationships. They award contracts on the basis of those they know well and they can trust. Trust grows and intensifies over a multiplicity of personal contacts such as having a drink and meal together. And more so in attending family functions such as weddings, birthdays, and funerals. Of course, Africans consider education, skills, experience, conscientiousness, eagerness, enthusiastic interest in the job, and ability to perform and deliver. But, employees overwhelmingly work together and with customers on a personal basis, including personal relationship and trust. In Africa it is said that the more the trust among individuals, the higher the degree of success of business exchanges.

And these relational complexities can greatly impact—positively or negatively—on the competitiveness of the firm and its success in the market place depending how they are managed. Therefore, the attitude and behavior of employees, at work, in the African context are largely influenced by relational factors. They also affect and influence the way customers react to promotions to buy the company's products and services, particularly in niche markets and business processes.

In Kenya, traditionally and initially, concessions are low and increase in size over time as relationships and trust grow and intensify. In South Africa, concessions are made begrudgingly at the end, only after everything else has failed to work. In Nigeria, agreements are reached slowly through compromises as relationships and trust increase in intensity (Schuster et al., 2006).

Oftentimes, these relational arrangements have been negative and have made companies uncompetitive in Africa if they are taken too far. Kenya is strewn with many cases of this nature – costly relationships. A good example is a flour milling company in Kenya, named "Ngano"—not its real name—that had been financially very successful in the 1970s and 1980s but suffered financially due to the overzealous application of these relational employment practices. Because of group think, brought about by company employees coming virtually from one community and village, the company could not change to meet radical changes taking place in the Kenyan business environment in the late 1980s and early 1990s instigated by the IMF and World Bank structural adjustment programs and increasing globalization. The company almost went out of business, but survived with a whisker. However, by the end of the 1990s its competitiveness had irreparably been damaged. The company lost market share and leadership in its industry.

African governments' actions and interferences in company operations should be built into industry analysis too. Governments in many parts of Africa impose taxes arbitrarily; are corrupt; influence appointment of executives, even in private corporations; and are slow to change regulations to improve the business climate. Government actions can affect company competitiveness by making it costly to operate as it affects the competitive pricing of products and services in the market. A poorly developed infrastructure, because of rampant corruption, for example, makes it difficult and costly for the firm to promote and deliver products and services to customers at competitive prices.

Therefore, companies need savvy managers to navigate the African business environment when formulating their competitive strategies. In this regard, a competitive style in Africa should be lower costs leadership. This is because African incomes are low today - although increasing - markets are fragile, and many people mostly choose products and services based on their prices in the market; a lot of it is also to do with their income levels. Africans' Purchasing Power Parity averages $ 2000 (Chiranga et al., 2011).

In the African context, the price of products and services – cost leadership strategy - maybe the key to success. As such, the strategies to achieve a sustainable competitive advantage in Africa may include: effective utilization of abundant and low cost and IT literate labor, intensive use of abundant environmental resources, correct hub selection, and appropriate outsourcing. In this respect and in summary, the following factors make Africa more attractive and competitive for business than many other developing and emerging markets:

- Friendly and hardworking people;
- Greater diversity;
- Increasing market sizes through advancing regional integration schemes;
- Abundant environmental resources;
- Low cost, quality, and IT literate labor;
- Increasing reforms to improve the business climate.

6. CHARACTERISTICS OF A GOOD AND EFFECTIVE STRATEGY

According to Kim et al. (2005), an effective strategy is characterized by three complementary qualities that include:

6.1. Focus

Every great strategy has focus, and a company's strategic profile—sources of competitive advantage—should clearly show it. The activities to formulate and implement the strategy should be and well aligned to achieve the strategic goals.

6.2. Divergence

Every Company's strategy should be uniquely divergent to meet its needs in the market. The strategy of a company should not be reactionary to competitive pressure. It should be a creative, novel, analytical, and well thought out process. When a company's strategy is formed reactively, as the company tries to keep up with the competition, it loses its uniqueness and therefore it will be difficult for the company to build a sustainable competitive advantage. A company's strategy should always stand apart from that of the competition.

6.3. A Compelling Tagline

A good strategy has a clear-cut and compelling tagline that attracts customers. A tagline is a shorthand description and summary statement of the strategy. A tagline is a memorable statement that expresses the offering of the firm. A tagline speaks to the customers. A good tagline must not only deliver a clear message but also advertise an offering truthfully, or else customers will lose trust and interest. In fact, a good way to test the effectiveness and strength of a strategy is to look at whether it contains a strong and authentic tagline. "The speed of a plane at the price of a car whenever you need it." That is the strategic tagline of Southwest Airlines; a very successful low cost American airline that initially operated in the Southwest of the USA, based at Houston, but today operates almost throughout the USA, using low fares as a strategic tool for strategic positioning in its market segment.

"Low prices everyday" was a strategic tagline of Wal-Mart previously. Wal-Mart is a leading retailer in the USA and in the whole world in fact. It has lately changed its tagline to "Save money. Live better." It changed its tagline maybe because many local and national retailers are using "low price" to describe their offerings too, making Wal-Mart lose its uniqueness and divergence. The new tagline captures their business philosophy better too, which is to make available to communities products and services at an affordable prices and with stores situated at convenient and accessible places. The stores have a very good ambience. The other large organization with an interesting strategic tagline is Home Depot Corporation, a home improvement retail company with stores across the USA. Its strategic tagline is "More saving, more doing that is the power of Home Depot."

On the other hand, when a company's strategy and market offerings lack focus, its cost structure will tend to be high and its business model will be complex in implementation and execution thus reducing the firm's competitiveness. When it lacks divergence, a company's strategy becomes "me-too" and not being able to stand apart from the competition in the market. It becomes easily imitated by the competitors. When it lacks a compelling tagline that speaks to buyers, it is likely to be internally driven or a classic example of innovation for innovation's sake with no great commercial potential and no natural take-off capability to attract customers (Kim, et al, 2005).

7. STRATEGY IMPLEMENTATION

Strategy implementation is about developing the necessary tactics to achieve the fundamental goals and objectives formulated in the strategy. Whether in Africa or anywhere in the world, successful strategy implementation goes through a process and clearly designated steps. Therefore, once a strategy has been successfully developed, with a profitable business model in mind, it must be carefully and fully implemented. Many challenges exist in implementing the strategy. These challenges are minimized when strategy execution is built into the strategy formulation; from the start to end of the strategic initiative.

When formulating a strategy execution process, it is important to remember that companies, like individuals, often have *a* tough time in translating thought into action. Strategy represents a significant shift from the status quo and it will generate fear and resistance (Kim 2005). A new strategy will, by necessity, demand changes in the organizational structure, culture of the organization, the management and leadership styles, policies, and systems in practice of the organization initiating the strategy.

Regarding the changes of a structure in response to a new strategy, scholars have always argued as to whether structure follows strategy and therefore structure should always change whenever there is a new strategic initiative by a firm. Some scholars like Henry Mintzberg (1994) suggest that strategy and structure move together and in addendum as a human left and right legs do. But there appears to be a general agreement, among strategy scholars, that structure—whether for global or domestic operations—always follows strategy in that structure should always change whenever there is a new strategic initiative by the corporation.

All the same, these changes, if not well handled, will generate a lot of resistance all over the company. This is because, when implementing a new strategy, it will spur problems in many areas that include resistance from the employees' mindset, difficulties in motivating the employee to implement the strategy, experiencing a perceived state of limited resources, and organizational politics; that is powerful vested interests that will resist the impending changes (Mauborgne, et al., 2005). Therefore, effective management of resistance will always be a key management responsibility in strategy implementation.

Scholars (Mauborgne et al., 2005; Campbell, 1997) have suggested several steps to follow to minimize resistance, ease, and accelerate the implementation of a new strategy. These steps include, but not limited to:

- Keeping strategy formulation and implementation as a joint process by drawing strategic insights from both operational and strategy managers;
- Communicate the strategy effectively to achieve complete alignment among employees;
- Engage and involve all employees in the formulation of the strategy to ensure its ownership by all employees at all levels;
- Explain fully, to all the stakeholders, all aspects of the strategy formulation, implementation, and obtain feedback;
- Continuously clarify management expectations to all employees of their responsibility in strategy formulation and implementation;
- Measure and evaluate the performance of the organization at regular intervals to determine the effectiveness of the strategy and give performance feedback to all employees;
- To ease and enhance measurements of strategic performance, use performance management models such as the Balanced Scorecard that give employees detailed granular measures that are easier to see and understand.

7.1. Strategic Briefing

The art of translating top management's aspirations into concrete action on the ground is always challenging. Scholars (Bungay, 2011) are always looking for ways to improve the process of strategy formulation and implementation both at corporate and business unit levels. Bungay has suggested an interesting process he describes as strategy briefing, a technique derived from the military. Through it, managers and their reports can move together from the uncertainty surrounding seemingly complex goals and performance measures to clarity about just what goals and objectives each person need to focus on and in what order of priority in order to achieve organizational success.

The briefing approach also helps managers set parameters for two variables that are the bedrock of high organizational performance: the extent to which people in the organization act in line with its leader's intentions, and how much freedom they have to take independent action. In essence, the briefing approach turns lofty strategic goals and objectives into a clear blue print for execution. The five steps Bungay suggests in implementing the strategic briefing process include:

- After an exhaustively thoughtful process, creative strategic thinking in a team environment, set a precise organizational intent and ensure it is well understood by all the team members. A clearly defined intent unifies a team's effort and focuses them to what needs to be done to achieve organizational objectives. Getting to the right statement is not easy, may require several tries, but a clearly defined statement of intent unifies the team's effort;
- Revise the statement of intent in the context of the company's situation in its market (s). Revisions of the statement are made, where applicable, and progress is made through an iterative process of formulation, critique, and readjustments;
- Determine measures or metrics, cost, time, quality, quantity, and market share, which best indicate whether you are achieving your goals and objectives;
- Define the tasks implied by your intent and that will help you achieve your intent over and in time;
- Define the boundaries, or constraints, that limit your team. A boundary puts limits on achieving possible alternative objectives, such as optimizing time versus cost and quality.

7.2. Stress-Testing the Strategy during Implementation

An economic downturn and volatility in the business environment can quickly expose the shortcomings of a firm's business strategy as it is being implemented. But can the firm identify the strategy's weak points in good times as well? And can the firm focus on those weak points that really matter and correct and strengthen them to keep the strategy on course? Strategy-stress test process will always help in this process and in answering these critical questions in stress-testing the strategy.

A stress test is an assessment of how a system—like the implementation of a strategic initiative—functions under severe or unexpected pressure or radical change. The stress test can help the firm determine the most important issues to address, whatever the economic climate or environmental conditions. By asking tough questions about the business—as part of the stress test—a firm can identify confusion, inefficiencies, and weaknesses in the strategy and its implementation and therefore take early corrective action. It can also generate a renewal of curiosity, a sense of adventure, passion, enthusiasm, and ambition to succeed in the organization.

Peter Drucker (1999) once said that "the most serious mistakes are not being made by firms as a result of wrong answers. The truly dangerous thing is asking the wrong questions." For many years, scholars (Simons 2010) have researched the drivers of successful strategy execution in a variety of companies and industries and identified seven strategy questions which all executives should ask and be able to answer in their firms during strategy implementation to identify the weakest parts of the strategy, inspiring decisions and timely appropriate action. Therefore, a firm whose executives master these questions is able to keep the fundamentals of its strategy execution on track, leading to its increased effectiveness.

The questions seem obvious, but the choices they represent can be tough, and their full implications are not always immediately clear. The first two questions compel you to set strict priorities. The next two assess the firm's ability to focus on those priorities by designating critical performance variables and constraints. Questions five and six investigate whether the firm is using techniques that will enhance creative tension, imagination, innovation, teamwork, and commitment. Question seven deals with the firm's ability to adapt its strategy to changing circumstances over time.

The seven questions are intended to be tools for stimulating rigorous and enthusiastic engagement in the organization. The ensuing discussions should involve everybody in the organization cascading down from the top of the organization to the lowest ranks. The discussions should focus on what is right and not whose is right. The questions include:

Who is your primary customer? A clear choice of a primary customer and an understanding when that choice changes are critical in business strategy. Therefore, choosing a primary customer is a make-or- break decision, because it determines how you allocate resources to customers. The idea is to allocate as much resources to customers—when creating their value proposition—as possible in order to meet and exceed their needs. Many companies resist choosing just one customer. Executives often attempt to avoid the adjective primary in describing their customers by stating that we have multiple customers. Scholars (Simons 2010) suggest that this is a sure way for underperformance.

Allocating resources to more than one customer, at the same time, will result in confusion and less-than-optimal service. However, the problem with maximizing resources for the firm's primary customer is that it will minimize resources available for everything else that does not create value for the primary customer. They should receive just enough resources to meet the needs of their constituents. Firms like McDonald's have consistently done well in creating value for their stakeholders—in terms of growth and profitability—by always focusing on their primary customers.

How do your core values prioritize shareholders, employees, and customers? Who is first in your strategy among the firm's key stakeholders: shareholders, employees, and customers as per the firm's core values? Companies that execute their strategy well have core values defined to reflect their relative importance of shareholders, employees, and customers. The core values—those statements that state what the company stands for and what is important—must indicate whose interests come first when difficult trade-offs must be made.

At some companies, customers come first. At others, it may be shareholders. And yet at others, it may be employees. There is no right or wrong choice. Each choice is based on a different theory of creating value by the respective firm. But choosing one and communicating it effectively is essential and critically important. For example, the choice of employees can make shareholders and customers contented. As Kelleher (2010) argues that if employees are treated well, they treat the customers well. If the customers are treated well, they will always come back, and shareholders will be happy because of the growth of their shareholding.

What critical performance variables are you tracking? Many managers complain that they are overwhelmed by how many things they are asked to keep track of in all-inclusive lists of performance measures. Companies keep many performance variables, in the mistaken belief that adding measures results in a more complete—and therefore better—scorecard.

Research data indicate that effective managers monitor only a small number of measures; those that could cause the strategy to fail if they are not done well and most effectively such as revenue growth and cost containment. Fewer critical measures ensure that management attention is on what really matters, that makes a difference and gives managers a chance to innovate and introduce new technologies to operations. Technology is the resource-liberating mechanism. It can make the once scarce now abundant and therefore technological innovation should be pursued hard in organizations (Diamandis and Kotler, 2012).

What strategic boundaries have you set? Every strategy carries a risk that an individual's actions will push the business off course. This risk intensifies when managers feel pressure to hit growth and profit targets. There are two ways to control such risk: You can tell people what to do or you can tell people what not to do. Telling people what to do helps assure that they will not make mistakes by engaging in unauthorized activities as they carry out their various responsibilities. This policy is the prudent approach where safety and quality are of paramount importance and concern like where you are operating or running a nuclear power plant or if you are overseeing a space launch. In such cases, you want employees to follow operating standard procedures to the letter.

However, if innovation and entrepreneurial thinking are important, you should follow a different approach. You should hire creative people and tell them what not to do. In other words, give them a long tether and the freedom to exercise their judgment and creativity, of course, within defined limits.

Setting clear boundaries also lets organizations avoid the waste and risk that inevitably accompany undisciplined growth. Violation or breaking the strategic boundaries should be accompanied with punishment and not reward and if this is done forcefully and consistently, it will enhance the message to that effect in the organization, reinforcing the importance of the prohibitions and the focus on things that matter to the firm's successful financial performance .

How are you generating creative tension inside the organization? The primary job of a firm's leadership is to make the forces of the outside market and competitive pressures felt inside the company. This can motivate employees to think and act like winning competitors, rousing them from their comfortable ruts and zones into innovators.

Simons (2010) has suggested several techniques that can generate creative tension and spur innovation in an organization. These techniques include:

- Assigning stretch and audacious goals and objectives: The most common way of motivating people to innovate is to set stretch and challenging goals and objectives for them and their deadlines;
- Ranking employees, teams, and business units according to performance: Many high-innovation and successful organizations rank and reward employees on the basis of demonstrated performance;
- Setting spans of accountability that are greater than normal spans of control: This is making employees responsible for across the board company goals like quality customer care and company growth;
- Allocating overhead costs across the board: Have managers be responsible for overhead costs. This process will help in achieving cost efficiencies overall in the organization;
- Creating cross-units or cross-businesses teams and where possible includes matrix accountability: This arrangement is likely to assist managers to work together to solve company problems, learn, and generate new and innovative ideas. New insights and perspectives are developed when people are forced out of their routines to work in teams. When they attend cross-unit meetings, employees, not only serve as emissaries for their units, but also return to their units with ideas and innovations from their colleagues.

As with each of these techniques, you need to balance the benefits and the costs. On one hand, you will generate creative tensions and innovative ideas as people present and negotiate multiple points of view. On the other hand, you will risk having the added bureaucracy slow down decision-making and project implementation necessitating balancing action in the application of these techniques.

How committed are your employees to helping each other? Although you want your employees to achieve their personal best, they must also work together towards shared goals by constantly engaging each other and sharing information and new ideas at all levels of the organization.

To create the high levels of alignment, engagement, and commitment that the firm requires among organizational members, leaders must build an organization that has the following attributes:

Pride in its purpose: When people have a vision and mission and are proud of them, they will assume responsibility for their success. The vision and mission may be expressed in an inspiring and motivating strategic tagline like "the world's most customer-centered company" or "Save Money live better" of Wal-Mart or "More saving, more doing that is the power of Home Depot."

Group Identification: Create an organization that employees view as elite. Belonging to an elite organization is, of course, a source of pride, one that carries with it a sense of discipline, urgency, and responsibility towards others in the group and a strong and deeply cultivated willingness to help each other to succeed as it generates feelings such as "we are in this together" and "if it fails we will all suffer the consequences".

What Strategic Uncertainties Keep You Awake at Night? At the root of every failed strategy is a set of assumptions about the future that eventually proved false. We assumed housing prices would never fall simultaneously across the country. We assumed asset diversification would eliminate risk. We assumed the migration to digital media would be slow and orderly. We assumed customers wouldn't accept fewer features in exchange for a lower price. One thing is certain in business management, the fact that today's strategy will not work tomorrow. At some point your products will become obsolete, your customers' tastes will change, or technology will render your business model uncompetitive or lead to the decay of your strategy and most of the time, strategies decay by being replicated, supplanted, exhausted, and eviscerated (Hamel et al., 2003).

Today's successes will be tomorrow's old news. The question is not if, but when. To adapt successfully, you must constantly monitor the uncertainties that could invalidate the assumptions underpinning your current strategy. Your entire organization must continually scan the competitive environment for changes and send intelligence up the line. And because everyone watches what the boss watches, if you want your employees to focus on specific issues, focus on those issues yourself. The most powerful way to signal what is important to you is to use your business control systems as interactive tools. Pay close—and visible—attention to the data they produce, and use them to generate questions that will activate the search for information throughout your business.

Depending on your business, the system you choose to use interactively could be a profit plan, a new business booking system, a balanced scorecard system, or a project management system. Any performance measurement system will do as long as it contains easy-to-understand information, requires face-to-face interaction among operating managers, focuses dialogues on strategic uncertainties, and generates new action plans. Once you have chosen a system, you must not only ask your employees to challenge deeply held assumptions, including your own, but also reward those who have the courage to tell you bad news.

7.3. Revision of the Strategy

General Powell (2012) in his seminal book: *It Worked for Me: In Life and Leadership,* asserts that strategic plans are neither successful nor unsuccessful until they are fully executed. And the successful execution of the plan is more important than the plan itself. Leaders and managers must be trained to expect the plan to need revision at the moment execution starts, and to always have a group of people in a back office thinking about what could go right or wrong with the plan and making contingency plans to deal with either possibility.

The organizational leaders must always be agile in thought and action. They must always be ready to revise a plan, or dump it altogether, if it is not working or if new opportunities and possibilities appear. Above all, the leaders must never be blinded by the perceived brilliance of their plans or their personal investment in them. The leaders must watch the execution from beginning to the end and do what it tells them to do to ensure effective execution of the plan.

8. MEASURING AND EVALUATING THE EFFECTIVENESS OF A STRATEGY

It is important that firms measure and evaluate the effectiveness of their strategic initiatives regularly. This is meant to measure the success of their strategy making process. Therefore, the strategy measurement and evaluation mechanisms should be built into the strategy at the onset of the strategy. These mechanisms should include the time intervals, within which the strategy should be measured and evaluated, the methodology to use to measure and evaluate the strategy, and the person to do the actual evaluation. In this regard, the process of measuring and evaluating the effectiveness of a strategic initiative consists of several activities:

- Review the basic factors on which the strategy was formulated in the first place and then check that there is no any change in any of those factors to necessitate changes in the strategic initiatives;
- Measure and compare the actual performance with budgeted performance;
- Determine the variances; negative or positive variances. Analyze the variances to determine their causes and decide how to deal with them;
- Take appropriate corrective action, where necessary, according to the strategy requirements.

8.1. Tools for Measuring and Evaluating Strategic Initiatives and their Success

There are many available management tools—of varying degree of sophistication—to use to measure and evaluate a strategy. These tools include the Balanced Scorecard framework. In recent years, use of the Balanced Scorecard to analyze and evaluate the strategic initiatives has greatly increased, among leading edge of performance measurement and evaluation oriented organizations (Kaplan and Morton, 2007).

According to Kaplan and Morton, the Balanced Scorecard is a set of measures that gives management a fast but comprehensive view of the business. It is the four perspectives—customer, operation, innovation and growth, and finance—framework that provides the metrics that can be used to develop and evaluate the effectiveness of strategic initiatives. The financial measures tell the results of the action already taken by the firm to create value for the stakeholders. They are complemented by operational measures on customer satisfaction, internal processes, and the organization's innovation and improvement activities. Some of these dimensions are operational measures that are the drivers of the future financial performance of the firm.

Think of the Balanced Scorecard as the dials and indicators in an airplane cockpit. For the complex task of navigating and flying a plane, pilots need detailed information about many aspects of the flight. They need information on fuel, airspeed, altitude, bearing, destination, and other indicators that summarize the current and predicted environment of the airplane. Reliance on one instrument can be fatal. Similarly, the complexity of managing an organization today requires that managers should be able to view performance and answer questions in several key areas at once. The Balanced Scorecard model helps to provide these measures (Kaplan et al., 2007).

Furthermore, the Balanced Scorecard is an increasingly popular methodology suited for deploying an organization's strategic direction, communicating its expectations to all employees, and measuring its progress towards agreed goals and objectives. The Balanced Scorecard methodology builds on key concepts of previous management ideas such as Total Quality Management, continuous improvement, benchmarking, empowerment, and measurement/feedback-based management (See Figure 3).

8.2. Pathways to Introducing the BSC System for Strategy Measurement and Evaluation

According to Kaplan and Morton (2007) and Mauborgne et al. (2005), the following are the suggested steps in introducing and maintaining an effective Balanced Scorecard in an organization:

- Make a commitment to the organizational vision, mission, objectives, and priorities at all levels of the organization, especially at the top level management who have the most complete knowledge and picture of the company's vision, mission, objectives, and priorities;
- Develop the corporate and competitive strategies of the organization;

Figure 3. The balanced scorecard model(source: Norton and Kaplan (2007))

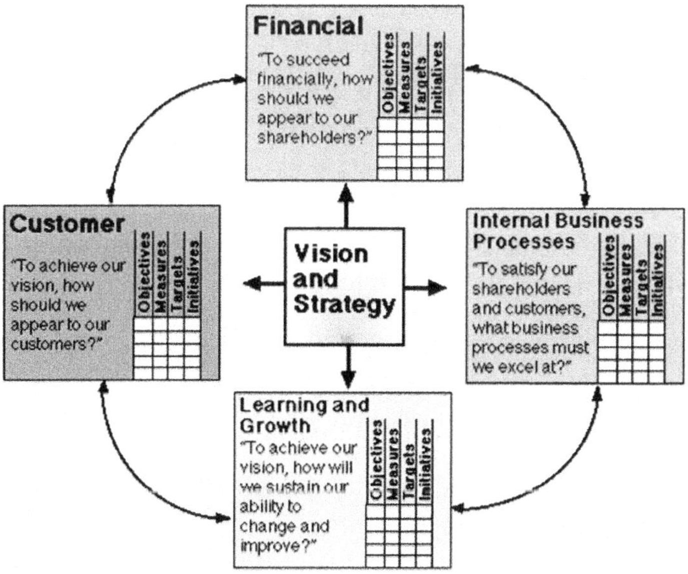

- Determine factors to be measured in each perspective in terms of time, quality, quantity, and cost and their specific objectives, targets, and measures for each goal;
- Establish clear milestones and review mechanisms to track progress, and ensure that internal recognition and rewards reinforce desired behaviors;
- Offer training in the BSC techniques to all employees to familiarize them with the BSC concepts and operation;
- Establish a reward and recognition system to foster high performance in the long-run;
- Break down organizational barriers to minimize resistance and increase the engagement of organizational members;
- Develop the Balance Scorecard at all levels of the organization;
- Review, measure, and evaluate performance of the strategy at predetermined intervals. And develop and evaluate strategies regularly using the four perspectives of the Balanced Scorecard

REFERENCES

Chironga, M., Leke, A., & van Wamelen, A. (2011). *Checking the next growth market: Africa*. Boston: Harvard Business School Publishing in partnership with the Economist Intelligence Unit of the Economist Magazine.

Collins, F. J., & Porras, I. J. (1996, September-October). Building your company's vision. *Harvard Business Review*.

Collins, J. (2001). *From good to great: Why some companies make the lip to greatness and others do not*. Brown Herron.

Collins, J. (2009a, May 25). How the mighty fall. *Bussiness Week*.

Collins, J. (2009b). *How the mighty fall*. New York: Harper Collins Publishers Inc..

Cullen, J. B., & Parboteeah, P. K. (2008). *Multinational management: A strategic approach* (4th ed.). Thomson Southwestern.

Cutter, S. (1993). *Living with risk*. New York: Routledge.

Day, G. S., & Wensley, R. (1988). Assessing advantage: A framework for diagnosing competitive superiority. *Journal of Marketing*, 52.

Diamandis, P. N., & Kotler, S. (2012). *Abundance: The future is better than you think*. New York: Free Press.

Drucker, P. F. (1994, September-October). The theory of the business. *Harvard Business Review.*

Drucker, P. F. (1999). *Management challenges for the 21st century.* New York: Harper Business: An Imprint of HarperCollins Publishers.

Dyer, J. H., Prashant, K., & Harbir, S. (2004, July-August). When to ally and when to acquire. *Harvard Business Review.* PMID:15241957.

Friedman, T. L. (2011, October 1). How did the robot end up with my job? *New York Times.*

Friedman, T. L. (2012, March 31). Why nations fail. *New York Times.*

Friedman, T. L., & Mandelbaum, M. (2011). *That used to be us: How America fell behind in the world it invented and how we can come back.* New York: Farrar, Straus, and Giroux.

Garter, J. (1997, September-October). Troubles ahead in emerging markets. *Harvard Business Review.*

Ghemawat, P. (2001, September). Distance still matters: Hard realities of global expansion. *Harvard Business Review.* PMID:11550630.

Ghemawat, P. (2005, December). Regional strategies for global leadership. *Harvard Business Review.* PMID:16334585.

Ghemawat, P. (2010, March). Finding your strategy in the new landscape. *Harvard Business Review.*

Gitman, L. J., & McDaniel, C. (2005). *Future of business* (5th ed.). Thomson South-Western.

Greenwald, B., & Khan, J. (2005, September). Strategy is local. *Harvard Business Review.* PMID:16171214.

Hamel, G. (2002). *Leading the revolution.* New York: Plume (Penguin Books).

Hamel, G., & Prahalad, C. K. (1989, May-June). Strategic intent. *Harvard Business Review.* PMID:10303477.

Hamel, G., & Prahalad, C. K. (1990, May-June). The core competence of the corporation. *Harvard Business Review.*

Hamel, G., & Prahalad, C. K. (1994). *Competing for the future.* Boston: Harvard Business School Press.

Hamel, G., & Välikangas, L. (2003, September). The quest for resilience. *Harvard Business Review*. PMID:12964393.

Han, J. C. Y., Wild, J. J., & Wild, K. L. (2008). *International business* (4th ed.). Upper Saddle River, NJ: Pearson.

Hart, B. H. L. (1967). *Strategy*. New York: Basic Books.

Hax, A. C., & Wilde, D. L. II. (1999, Winter). The delta model: Adaptive management for a changing world. *Sloan Management Review*.

Heifetz, R. (1994). *Leadership without easy answers*. Cambridge, MA: Harvard University Press.

Heifetz, R. A., & Laurie, D. (2001, December). The work of leadership. *Harvard Business Review*. PMID:10174450.

Henderson, B. (1983). The anatomy of competition. *Journal of Marketing*, 47.

Henderson, B. D., & Zakon, A. J. (1983). The concept of strategy and the growth-share matrix in corporate growth strategy. In Albert, K. J. (Ed.), *The Strategic Management Handbook*. New York: McGraw-Hill.

Henisz, W. J., & Zelner, B. A. (2010, April). The hidden risks in emerging markets. *Harvard Business Review*.

Hill, C. W., & Jones, G. R. (2001). *Strategic management theory* (5th ed.). New York: Houghton Mifflin Company.

Hoffman, P. N. (2000). An examination of the sustainable competitive advantage concept: Past, present, and future. *Academy of Marketing Science Review*, 4.

Hofstede, G., & Hall, E. T. (1980). *Culture: Consequences: International differences in work-related values*. Beverly Hills, CA: Sage.

Holiday, C. (2001, September). Sustainable growth, the DuPont way. *Harvard Business Review*.

Hunt, S. D., & Morgan, R. M. (1995). The comparative advantage: Theory of competition. *Journal of Marketing*, 59.

Kaplan, R. S., & Norton, D. (2005, July-August). The balanced scorecard: Measures that drive performance. *Harvard Business Review*. PMID:10119714.

Kaplan, S. R., & Grossman, S. A. (2010, October). The emerging capital market for nonprofits. *Harvard Business Review*.

Karel, C., & Ingemar, D. (1993). Rivalry, strategic groups, and firm profitability. *Strategic Management Journal*, 14.

Kasperson, J. X., & Kates, R. W. (1983). Comparative risk analysis of technological hazards: A review. *Proceedings of the National Academy of Sciences, 80*.

Keeler, D. (2010, November). Kenya: Rebirth of a nation. *Global Finance*.

Khanna, T., Palepu, G. K., & Sinha, J. (2005, June). Strategies that fit emerging markets. *Harvard Business Review*. PMID:15938439.

Khanna, T., & Pelepu, G. K. (2005, May). Strategies for emerging markets. *Harvard Business Review*. PMID:15938439.

Khanna, T., & Pelepu, K. (1997, September-October). Why focused strategies maybe wrong for emerging markets. *Harvard Business Review*.

Kim, W. C., & Mauborgne, R. (2005). *Blue ocean strategy: How to create uncontested market space and make the competition irrelevant*. Boston: Harvard Business School Press.

Kim, W. C., & Mauborgne, R. (2009, September). How strategy shapes structure. *Harvard Business Review*.

Lymbersky, C. (2008). *Market entry strategies: Texts, cases, and readings in market entry management*. Laboratory Press.

McGahan, A. M. (2004, October). How industries change. *Harvard Business Review*. PMID:15559578.

Mintzberg, H. (1973). *The nature of managerial work*. New York: Harper and Row.

Mintzberg, H. (1979). *The structuring of organizations*. Englewood Cliffs, NJ: Prentice Hall.

Mintzberg, H. (1987, July-August). Crafting strategy. *Harvard Business Review*. PMID:10280177.

Mintzberg, H. (1988, Summer). Crafting strategy. *The McKinsey Quarterly*.

Mintzberg, H. (1994). *The rise and fall of strategic planning*. New York: Basic Books.

Mintzberg, H., Ahlstrand, B., & Lampel, J. (1998). *Strategy safari: A guided tour through the wilds of strategic management*. New York: The Free Press.

Mintzberg, H., & Hames, A. W. (1985). Of strategy delivered and emergent strategy. *Strategic Management Journal*, *6*(3). doi:10.1002/smj.4250060306.

Mintzberg, H., & Quinn, J. B. (1988). *The strategy process*. Harlow, MA: Prentice-Hall.

Parboteeah, P. K. (2008). *Multinational management: A strategic approach* (4th ed.). Thompson South-Western.

Pearce, J., & Robinson, R. (1997). *Strategic management: Strategy formulation, implementation, and evaluation*. Upper Saddle River, NJ: Prentice Hall.

Porter, M. E. (1980). *Competitive strategy: Techniques for analyzing industries*. New York: Free Press.

Porter, M. E. (1985). *Competitive advantage: Creating and sustaining superior performance*. New York: The Free Press.

Porter, M. E. (1986). *Competitive strategy*. Boston: Harvard Business School Press.

Porter, M. E. (1990). *The competitive advantage of nations*. New York: Free Press.

Porter, M. E. (1996, November-December). What is strategy? *Harvard Business Review*.

Porter, M. E. (1998, November-December). Clusters and the new economics of competition. *Harvard Business Review*. PMID:10187248.

Porter, M. E. (2001, March). Strategy and the internet. *Harvard Business Review*. PMID:11246925.

Porter, M. E. (2007). *Global competitiveness: Implications for Kenya*. Nairobi, Kenya: Harvard Business School: Strathmore Business School.

Porter, M. E., & Kramer, M. R. (2011, January-February). Capitalism is under siege: Diminished trust in business is causing political leaders to set policies that sap economic growth: Business is caught in a vicious circle: The purpose of the corporation must be redefined around creating shared value. *Harvard Business Review*.

Porter, M. E., & Rivkin, J. W. (2012, March). The looming challenge to U.S. competitiveness. *Harvard Business Review*.

Powell, C. (2012). *It worked for me: In life and leadership*. New York: HarperCollins Publishers.

Prahalad, C. K., & Hamel, G. (2005, July-August). Strategic intent. *Harvard Business Review*.

Rumelt, R., & Lippman, S. (1982). Uncertain imitability. *Journal of Economics*, 13.

Schuster, C. P., & Copeland, M. J. (2006). *Global business practices: Adapting for success*. Thomson.

Singh, J. V., & Aaron, R. (2005, December). Getting off shoring right. *Harvard Business Review*.

Sjöberg, L. (1991). *Risk perception by experts and the public: Risk research report no. 4*. Stockholm, Sweden: Center for Risk Research.

Slovic, P. (1997). Perception of risk. *Science*. PMID:3563507.

Slywotzky, A. J., & Drzik, J. (2005, April). Countering the biggest risk of all. *Harvard Business Review*. PMID:15807041.

Srivastava, R., Shervani, T., & Fahey, L. (1998). Market-based assets and shareholder value: A framework for analysis. *Journal of Marketing*, 62.

Stalk, G. Jr, & Lachenauer, R. (2004, April). Hardball: Five strategies for trouncing the competitions. *Harvard Business Review*. PMID:15077367.

Thompson, A. (2006). *Crafting and executing strategy: The quest for competitive advantage: Concepts and cases*. AIPI Publishers.

Tregoe, B., & Zimmerman, J. (1980). *Top management strategy*. New York: Simon and Schuster.

Vanhonacker, W. R. (2004, April). When good Guanxi turns bad. *Harvard Business Review*.

Wernerfelt, B. (1984). A resource-based view of the firm. *Strategic Management Journal*, 5.

Williams, J. R. (1992, Spring). How sustainable is your competitive advantage? *California Management Review*. doi:10.2307/41167422.

Chapter 9
Challenges of Doing Business in Africa

ABSTRACT

This chapter enumerates and discusses fully the challenges of doing business in Africa. Other scholars (Ortiz, 2010) have described these challenges or environmental factors as a framework consisting of Social, Legal, Economic, Political, and Technological (SLEPT) conditions of a country for investment purposes. This framework, when combined with an appropriate granular measures model, proves useful to multinational companies, governments, individuals, and international organizations at the time to assist them in making strategic decisions and establishing investment priorities in Africa. Moreover, this chapter goes into the micro-level and looks at specific environmental factors that create challenges to the exploitation of African business opportunities. From that point of view, it reviews and explains concrete strategies to create business pathways in Africa.

1. INTRODUCTION

Challenges of doing business in Africa are a global reality but the African governments are reforming the influencing elements, in their business environments, in creating these challenges. Therefore, there are many institutional, economic, business, political, and social challenges that face Africa today. These challenges also include marginalization of Africa from the global economy, scarce development

DOI: 10.4018/978-1-4666-4570-7.ch009

finance, healthcare, poor infrastructure, climate change, poor leadership, and weak governance. Poor leadership and weak governance persist in virtually all African countries today.

The other specific and direct categories of the investment climate factors that present challenges in Africa, already discussed above, include: Starting a business, Dealing with licenses, Hiring and firing workers, Registering property, Getting credit, Protecting investors, Paying taxes, Trading across borders, Enforcing contracts, and Closing a business. But, many African countries continue to vigorously reform many of these elements today to create an attractive business climate.

Conflict and post-conflict reconstruction challenges prevail in many African countries, although in a lower scale today than before, hampering development efforts. Unemployment, chronic hunger, and endemic poverty stand out as major long-term development issues and problems for the continent to address. These problems persist despite the continent having large tracks of arable land and being well endowed with other environmental resources including a large amount of underground water (ERA 2010).

In most countries, these issues and challenges are interrelated and strongly interacting with each other. Poor leadership and weak governance, for example, breed conflict and make post-conflict recovery difficult. Unemployment and poverty—thus limited purchasing power as a business opportunity—become more entrenched where conflict, poor leadership, and weak governance persist (ERA 2010).

Furthermore, achieving economic growth and running a business in Africa has been some of the most daunting challenges in the last several decades. Since the 1980s, growth on the continent had been elusive, with economic stagnation and retardation becoming the defining characteristics for most African countries (Kempe, 1997). Concerted efforts by international development financiers, donors, and non-governmental organizations, including Multilateral Financial Institutions (MFIs), did not make significant headway in reviving African economies. This is despite the experimentation of several development models and paradigms, most of which emphasized structural reforms and were foreign designed and therefore alien to Africans (UNCTAD, 2003). These foreign designed programs increased poverty in Africa, particularly in the 1980s and 1990s. These were the decades of IMF and World Bank led structural adjustment programs that starkly failed to revive the African economies (Moyo, 2009).

The late 1990s, however, saw a significant shift in Africa's development paradigm. This led to increasing attention being given to Africa's participation in its own development planning. Increased ownership of its own development initiatives, strategies, capacity building of African professionals, knowledge management, and improved governance, among other development issues, became the hallmark of change in Africa (ERA, 2010).

At last, since the turn of the new millennium, Africa has generally started recording impressive economic growth—at fairly high growth rates—on a fairly consistent basis, especially over the last ten years, slightly interrupted by the 2008 world financial and economic meltdown (Kamara, et al., 2008). For example, the African Development Bank estimates that African GDP will, on average, grow at more than 7.5% in 2010 and beyond (Benoni 2010).

Despite Africa being able to see light at the end of the tunnel regarding the continent's economic development and in presenting business opportunities, there still continues to exist many challenges in ensuring sustainable growth and promotion of business in Africa. In the scheme and process of doing business in Africa, challenges should be surmountable. They are short-term impediments that are present in the African business environment—as discussed above—that can be overcome mostly by attitude, policy, and institutional reforms. And changes are inevitable if Africa hopes to prosper to improve the living standards of its growing population.

Other scholars (Ortiz, 2010) have described these environmental factors as a framework consisting of Social, Legal, Economic, Political, and Technological (SLEPT) conditions of a country for investment purposes. This framework, when combined with granular measures model, proves useful to multinational companies, governments, individuals, and international organizations at the time to assist them to make strategic decisions and establish investment priorities in Africa.

The ever-changing nature of the operating environment defines the scope and limitations of the SLEPT framework as a scanning management tool. However and here-in these environmental factors and the investment climate elements mentioned above have been more specifically dissected, described, and analyzed as business challenges of doing business in Africa. And their remedies have been suggested in chapter 10.

Therefore and despite a presence of exceptional and profitable business opportunities, doing business in Africa is not always going to be smooth and easy for entrepreneurs, corporations, and other organizations that need to do business in Africa. As mentioned above and discussed below, the challenges of doing business in Africa currently range from insecurity and instability to poor perceptions others have of Africa. It is important to note that the poor perceptions others have on Africa are always a reality to them that needs to be changed to reflect the actual and true reality of Africa in order to attract Foreign Direct Investments to Africa. Therefore, the specific and major challenges of doing business in Africa today include:

2. INSECURITY AND INSTABILITY

Security and stability are basic needs of the African people, in fact for all people of the world (Deng et al., 2002). Scholars and political analysts have described security and stability as all encompassing concepts and ideals that will enable African people to live in peace, harmony, and be able to develop. They create a situation of equal access to both the national resources and the ability to participate fully in the process of their governance (Deng et al., 2002).

Insecurity and instability is a situation—as it particularly and currently pertains in Somalia, Sudan, Guinea, Zimbabwe, Madagascar, Mali, Central African Republic (CAR), and the DR Congo—whereby there is lack of peace and national cohesion among the people of an African state and the state itself due to irresponsible and unaccountable governments that promote corruption and horizontal inequalities. And a governance condition that does not meet the social, political, cultural, economic, and human rights needs of its people (Deng et al., 2002). Insecurity and instability is a poverty trap for these countries.

Therefore, meeting the security and safety needs of African countries is an essential precondition for the development of any African state to deal with poverty. Businesses cannot thrive in an insecure and unstable environment. There are no predictability and certainty that are hallmarks of long-term business planning, investments, and commitment by firms. Security and stability are assured and underpinned by the rule of law; reduced ethnicity; popularly elected governments; transparent institutions; absence of corruption; absence of horizontal inequalities, through fair distribution of national resources and state power; and unequivocal respect for human rights.

It is important to note that Africa cannot sustain economic growth—at high rates and attract increased foreign direct investments and even indigenous entrepreneurs' investments—without a prolonged presence of security and stability in each African state and generally in Africa. Moreover and in recent years, insecurity and instability have increased considerably in Africa due to the emergency and rise of terrorists groups in several African countries including Nigeria, Kenya, and Mali. These terrorist groups need to be urgently contained to avoid a general deterioration of law and order that will ultimately undermine the important gains African countries are making in economic development to deal with high youth unemployment and poverty in the continent and in creating a business climate that encourages investment.

One important way of dealing with terror groups is information gathering so that action against them is taken before they strike. The other way is, of course, to train law enforcement officers and to equip them better and to deal with corruption in the police forces in order to avoid terror groups obtaining information on the state's strategies to deal with them before action against them is taken. The affected governments must always effectively be ahead of the groups.

In addressing a security conference—on security implications on business, economic growth, and general development—in Nairobi recently, Dr. Harrity Elletson, Chairman of the New Security Foundation, quoted in the Standard News Paper of September 14, 2012, by Jackson Okoth, asserted thus:

African states must deal with human rights issues, corruption, organized crime, and international terrorism among other security challenges to safeguard the rapid African economic gains over the last two decades. There is a fundamental link between security, business, and economic growth. Africa has become attractive to the rest of the world, but it must deal with security challenges that could undermine its prospects in economic development and in attracting direct foreign investments.

It is estimated that by 2050, two thirds of Africa's population will be of working age, a size that will be bigger than that of China or India. Recent discoveries of oil and natural gas deposits have also heightened Africa's importance to the global economy. The effects of globalization, increased privatization, and Information Communication Technology (ICT) revolution have created radically different environment where traditional security arrangements worldwide cannot control the situation anymore. In Kenya, for example, increased poverty, increasing or rising cost of living, tribal politics, impunity by politicians, and youth unemployment, are posing a security threat. Other causes of insecurity include higher energy costs, environment insecurity, organized crime, and the re-emergency of proscribed militia groups.

It is estimated that over 50 million people in Africa are living below the poverty line due to conflict in various parts of the continent, Twenty five years ago, Africa was the object of pity and guilt, a place to be shunned or avoided especially by business. Often, it was a focus of exploitation, rather than an opportunity for investment. Now things are different and continue to change. African economies are enjoying unprecedented economic growth creating increasing business opportunities. Whilst European and North American economies continue to battle recession, a fiscal crisis, and a debt burden, their African counterparts are seeing growth rates of six or seven percent. Estimates show that, over the next five years, the average African economy will grow faster than any of the Asian economies. Those strong growth rates, in Africa, will need strong security and safety in all African countries because of the contagion effects of insecurity.

3. LOW EDUCATION STANDARDS

Education is key and critical to sustainable economic development in any country. It is extremely important in creating and producing innovators and new entrepreneurs who create jobs and wealth that reduce poverty in the world and Africa in particular. Education produces skilled employees and thus can give a competitive advantage to a nation. African numbers in high education and research cohorts are dismally low and need considerable enhancement.

However, the international community has scored a major success in Africa by supporting the Millennium Development Goals (MDG) of universal primary education by 2015. Gross primary enrollment rates rose from 79 percent in 1999 to 92 percent in 2004. This rapid success at primary enrollment has, however, brought new concerns and challenges. Educational quality has not kept pace with quantity, at the primary level, and there have been no comparable improvement in numbers in secondary and tertiary enrollments (ERA, 2010).

Africa faces a growing skills gap compared with its international competitors particularly with Asian countries like China and India. While East Asian countries, for example, increased secondary enrollment rates by 21 percent points and tertiary enrollment rates by 12 percent points between 1990 and 2002, Africa in general raised its secondary rate by only 7 percent points and its tertiary enrolment rate by just 1 percent point. Real expenditure on tertiary education fell by about 28 percent between 1990 and 2002 and expenditure per pupil declined from $ 6,800 in 1989 to $ 1,200 in 2002. Staff-student rations in West African universities, for example, increased from 1:16 in 1990 to 1:32 in 2007 (World Bank, 2007a). Employer surveys also report that tertiary graduates are weak in problem solving, business understanding, computer use, and communication skills (World Bank, 2007a).

The lack of expanded access to and improved quality in post primary education has serious implications for the ability of Africa's economic diversification. Recent cross-country study—including a sample of African economies—indicates that there is a strong empirical link and correlation between export sophistication, manufacturing, and general development and the percentage of the labor force that has completed post primary schooling (World, 2007a). There is also a lot of empirical evidence to suggest that enterprises managed by university graduates in Africa have a higher propensity to export and thus creating quality jobs. More evidence exists too to the effect that among firms owned by indigenous entrepreneurs, those with university educated owners tend to show higher growth rates, better financial performance, and higher degree of sustainability (Wood and Jordan, 2002).

In discussing the problems of education, particularly unmet demand for increasingly important college and university education, in Africa, President Benjamin Mkapa—former president of Tanzania—recently asserted thus: "… On the other hand, pressure for increased enrolment in tertiary education continues unabated, especially as secondary school expansion creates an ever-increasing wellspring of young men and women looking for matriculation in the few tertiary education institutions Africa has. And, at 3.1 percent, Africa has the fastest growth of the tertiary education cohort population, compared to a global average of only 1.7 percent.

We cannot, unfortunately, ignore or wish away this escalating demand for expansion of enrolment in tertiary education. In 2007, for example, only 6 percent of the tertiary education cohort in sub-Saharan Africa was enrolled in tertiary education institutions. This should be seen against a global average of 26 percent. In North America and Western Europe, the rate was 71 percent that same year; in Central and Eastern Europe it was 62 percent; in Latin America and the Caribbean it was 34 percent; in Central Asia it was 31 percent; in East Asia and the Pacific it was 26 percent; in Arab States it was 23 percent; in South and West Asia it was 11 percent; and in sweet home sub-Saharan Africa it was only 6 percent! A huge improvement from where the colonialists left us, but still only 6 percent! Even South Africa, the best performer Africa has had a gross enrollment ratio of only 15.4 percent tertiary enrollment.

The other serious problem Africa faces is shortage of highly skilled manpower. So, where does Africa stand on this score? One indicator that can be used in measuring where Africa stands is the amount of new knowledge it creates in its universities. Since researchers do conceive and create new knowledge, their numbers can be a useful indicator of Africa's capacity to create a repertoire of competitive and skilled individuals who can lead Africa to economic fulfillment and being competitive in the global economy.

Estimates issued by the UNESCO Institute for Statistics show that between 2002 and 2007 Asia as a whole increased its share of world researchers from 35.7 percent to 41.4 percent, mostly at the expense of Europe and North America. In 2002, Africa had only 2.3 percent of the world researchers, and that share had not changed in 2007. For sub-Saharan Africa, if South Africa is excluded, Africa had only 0.6 percent of researchers in 2002 and still the same 0.6 percent in 2007. The phenomenal increase in Asia is to a large extent accounted for by China which had its share of world researchers increase from 14.0 percent in 2002 to 20.1 percent in 2007, putting it almost at par with the United States of America. Among them, the United States, China, European Union, and Japan have 70 percent of all researchers in the world............"

Africa cannot be competitive in the global economy with these dismal numbers of researchers and low enrollments in higher education generally! It must change and put more money in primary, secondary, tertiary, and university education, as India and China have done in recent years.

Africa should develop and fund research facilities, including centers of excellence. South Africa has, in recent years, backed new university research chairs and is trying to promote centers of excellence in the country, a situation that should be developed all over Africa for the continent to meet its critical manpower needs for economic development now and in the future (Saltmarch, 2010).

4. KNOWLEDGE AND INNOVATION

Related to the issues and problems of increasing educational quantity, quality, and research in Africa, is the challenges of acquiring knowledge and developing innovations and embedding them into operations to achieve sustainable economic development in Africa. With the increasing challenges of sustaining economic growth on the continent, the search for the foundations of growth sustainability in Africa is increasing, and the importance of knowledge, innovation, and technology are ever recognized and becoming important. In particular, there is the realization that Africa's growth needs should be centered around and driven by knowledge, in the context of growing knowledge-based economies on the continent (Kamara et al., 2008).

The recognition of knowledge as a critical element of economic growth is not new; the issue is long acknowledged as a factor behind the economic success of the developed world (OECD, 1996) and it is responsible for the current acceleration of economic development in India and China (Prahalad 2010). The dynamics embedded in knowledge-based economies have also been articulated by studies such as Romer and Gross (1994), with propositions that are now leading to new growth theories to explain the forces behind long-term economic growth based on knowledge and innovation.

In an environment where trends in knowledge development is taking a new twist, Africa now faces a big challenge as it tries to respond to the inevitable need to embrace science and technology as the basis for sustaining growth, and for competing in a global environment that is largely driven by knowledge and innovation. Thus, understanding the main elements of a knowledge-based economy, particularly the knowledge triangle—education, research, and industry—and how it can be harnessed for Africa to sustain growth remains critical (Kamara et al., 2008).

A knowledge-based economy refers to an economy in which the production, exchange, distribution, and use of knowledge is the main driver of economic growth, employment generation, and wealth creation (McKeon and Weir, 2001). In the OECD, for instance, it is estimated that more than 50 percent of the economy is knowledge based. For Africa, achieving even a half of that level in the near future is a major challenge that the continent should tackle with urgency in order to make knowledge and innovation a foundation of its development and hence create more business opportunities (Kamara et al., 2008).

5. AFRICAN POLITICAL LEADERSHIP AND WEAK GOVERNANCE

Kotler (2001) describes leadership as an action of mobilizing people towards a common cause or goal. For example, the African leadership can mobilize its people towards poverty and hunger eradication in the continent. It can also mobilize its people towards economic development and equitable distribution of the benefits of development. On the other hand, governance is ensuring that there are appropriate rules and regulations of conduct in human affairs and in particular in the legitimate use and application of common resources to achieve the common goal. It is exercising appropriately and legitimately earned power, authority, and control over nationals and their resources. Legitimacy is earned by being fairly elected in a fair election and in demonstrating high ability in solving human problems.

It is, today, a universally accepted fact that effective leadership and good governance are vital for economic development and poverty eradication in any African country (AU Strategy 2009-2012). Leadership and effective governance have always been Africa's Achilles' heel. Poor leadership and weak governance have seriously confronted all African countries since independence to today (ERA, 2010).

African leaders have always maintained the liberation resources and people mobilization stance—almost fifty years after independence of most of the African countries—instead of the development resources and people's commitment to development mobilization stance. A good example of this situation is South Africa where leaders talk and have a political posture and agenda today as if Apartheid is still rife in South Africa eighteen years since the end of apartheid, a program that the Patriarch, Nelson Mandela, dearly paid for. And yet, as they continue arguing, unemployment and poverty are increasing at an alarming rate in that country leading to increasing violence in cities and towns.

Generally, governance reforms in Africa are slow and often easily reversible. African leadership and governance have not transitioned from a struggle for independence leadership to an economic development and effective governance leadership. Progress in this domain needs to be consolidated and strengthened by up-scaling resources mobilization and application to move the leadership and governance agenda forward to focus on economic development to deal with pervasive poverty in Africa (AU Strategy 2009-2012). This mobilization together with Heiferzt's (1994) leadership strategies to manage adaptive changes in Africa, discussed below, will move African leadership and governance systems to a high pedestal level to effectively tackle African problems.

Former UK Prime Minister Tony Blair, who now runs an Africa Governance Initiative, in London, UK, recently said that the African continent is on the move; the changes needed are clear, obstacles are known but they are surmountable. However, the biggest obstacle to Africa's progress is its leadership and governance systems, particularly the leaders not getting things done after identifying the problem.

Mr. Blair further states that it is not about that the leaders do not know what to do; but doing it. For example, recent press reports in the French 24 TV Station—which confirms Premier Blair's assertion—indicate that African leaders meeting in Addis Ababa, Ethiopia, to celebrate the AU 50th anniversary, do not want to tackle crimes against humanity and they know very well that these crimes are rampant in the continent. They denounced the International Criminal Court (ICC)—calling it neocolonial—for trying African leaders against their crimes against humanity, particularly the recently elected Kenyan president Uhuru Kenyatta and his vice President William Ruto, who are both accused at ICC of having mastered minded the 2007/8 raping of women, killing of 1300 people, and displacement of 600,000 people after the disputed election that year.

However, it is important to note that, in the 34 of the African cases with the ICC, including the Kenyan case, the African authorities and governments invited the ICC to handle these cases. The reason by the African leaders being that the African leaders believed that their court and legal systems were incapable of handling such cases. African leaders are aware of the perennial murdering of innocent citizens and raping of women among other crimes against humanity in the Congo, Central African Republic, Niger, among others, but at the same time, they do not want the world to take action against the perpetrators of these heinous crimes against their people. It is highly ironical! They do not think of and even sympathize with the victims of these monstrous crimes.

In its proper sense, effective leadership and governance are crucial and fundamental in any nation. The hard part in Africa is not having the vision, but making it a reality. That needs a strong leadership and governance arrangements; important development elements lacking in most of Africa over the years (Butagira, 2012).

Mr. Blair challenged current African leaders to set clear and ambitious programs with accompanying effective leadership and governance systems to deliver on the plans, while urging that rich nations should adopt new ways of engaging with the African continent, particularly to improve its leadership and governance systems. The former premier underlined functional transportation and communication infrastructure, effective governments, intellectual knowledge combined with foreign direct investments, investment in education, agricultural technology, and expanded intra-Africa trade, through increased regional integration, as ingredients African leaders should undertake as necessary to spur the continent's growth to effectively deal with pervasive poverty and hunger in the continent (Butagira, 2012).

Moreover and according to anecdotal data and popular press, African leaders are insensitive to the needs of their people. They often do not follow their national constitutions to change political leadership as it has been seen in Kenya, Ivory Coast, Uganda, and Zimbabwe in recent years. Arbitrary leadership changes and abuses of the constitution create political instability and uncertainty, which in turn detract foreign direct investments into a country.

Unfortunately, the problems of poor leadership and weak governance in Africa are historical. For the majority of the African people and countries, the elites who took control of the neo-colonial states at independence turned governmental structures and systems into instruments of plunder for their own benefit. They imposed enormous costs on the general population, increased poverty, and marginalized the masses. Many African economies continue to be characterized by high levels of poverty, poorly developed physical infrastructure, and excessive external debt, political and bureaucratic corruption, political instability, destructive ethnic conflict, and other ills that remain significant restraints to economic development (Mbaku, 1998).

Many African leaders are still corrupt and despotic. And many still demonstrate the streaks of post independence poor leadership skills. Furthermore, much of the African leadership have no clear vision for Africa despite the fact that people of Africa have given them a mandate to lead in a lot of cases. The African leadership does not promote ethical business management and a good, supportive, and positive business climate, although this is changing in some countries like Rwanda and Ghana through concerted reforms (Deng et al., 2002).

Some of the African leaders are destroying the gains already made through the democratic changes of recent years by altering their national constitutions in order for them to stay in power beyond their constitutionally mandated terms. These changes have happened in Uganda and in Namibia a few years ago and recently in Niger. And there were failed attempts to do so in Nigeria, Malawi, and Zambia in recent years. Some leaders want to manipulate the electoral process in order to illegally and illegitimately gain and remain in power as seen in Kenya during the 2007 presidential elections and more recently in Ivory Coast in 2011. These manipulations have repeatedly led to unnecessary internal violence and chaos and retardation of economic development (www.bbc.com, 2011).

These arbitrary changes in the existing constitutional dispensations and manipulation of the electoral process do not augur well for business in African countries. They engender insecurity and instability in African countries and cast African nations as unpredictable and unstable. Predictability and certainty constitute essential factors, in business management, particularly in attracting foreigners to invest in a country and even long-term investments by local entrepreneurs (Deng et al., 2002).

In countries that are almost single-party political structures, like Tanzania, leadership is passed on to individuals of similar thought and character. Although the continuity of government, in these circumstances, gives a false sense of stability, predictability, and certainty, the one-party rule syndrome sets the stage for inefficient state administration and poor and unchallenged leadership. This is because single party mentality creates and promotes apathy, lethargy, groupthink, cynicism, and stifling conformity that destroys creativity and innovation in a country.

In addition, the country looses a national sense of adventure, ability to innovate, create, upgrade, and prosper. The country cannot develop technologies to transform the country particularly in agriculture and manufacturing to deal with poverty and hunger. The country is in fact potentially unstable and insecure. There is limited development, of the highly desired entrepreneurial class too. As it were, transformational leadership does not emerge to guide the development of all these critical national processes, as Ulimwengu asserts in the East African "… the Tanzanian chattering classes are clearly growing more and more restive as times passes, with too many people now saying out loud that the country is in a state of drift, that it lacks effective and transformational leadership" (Ulimwengu, 2009).

In fact, this type of leadership and governance situation promotes poverty and lack of excitement or passion to do anything useful in life. In a recent international report on human happiness, Tanzanians were described as the least happy people in the world as compared with Costa Ricans who were described as the happiest people in the world. In a scale of 1 to 10, one being the least happy and 10 being the most happy, Tanzanians were placed at 2.6 and Costa Ricans at 8.6 on the scale (Kristof, 2010).

Again, the cycle of similar leadership style and political behavior cannot spur aggressive, robust, vibrant, and dynamic national development and should slowly, but surely, die out in Africa. In this respect, scholars have offered suggestions to the effect that there should be a process of reconstructing and reconstituting the state, in Africa, to provide each African country with more competitive, accountable, transparent, and participatory governance structures. Multi-party politics and structures should be aggressively pursued and vigorously promoted in Africa to enhance political competition. This development will reinvigorate innovation in all spheres of the nation, particularly in entrepreneurship and business management. The assumption here is that political competition will be peaceful and sustainable to essentially ensure long-term security and stability of a country. The stability and security will continue to attract local and foreign investors to invest into Africa. And thus create jobs and wealth to deal with pervasive poverty and hunger in the continent (Deng et al., 2002).

The Nation Media Group, an East African group of newspapers, has attempted to measure the performance of African leadership over the years. The Group asserts that underutilization of Africa's immense economic opportunities, over which the Western world and the Eastern world desperately scramble, have become more evident due to poor African leadership. But the high number of democratic elections that took place in Africa, in recent times, suggests that there has been no despair in the quest for democracy and effective governance in Africa. However, the continent seems unable to successfully transfer power without violence and mass controversy only points a finger at the poor, and often crooked, leadership, which continues to plague the continent.

Nevertheless, there are a few gems. After a couple of years without a winner, the Mo Ibrahim Prize for good leadership and effective governance in Africa was finally called back into action—Cape Verde's former president, Pedro Pires, bagged the $5 million prize in 2012. Former presidents of Botswana and Mozambique received the first and second awards in 2007 and 2008, respectively.

In trying to explain why there was no winner of 2012 Ibrahim African governance prize, the Mo Ibrahim Foundation, in London, explained the terms and conditions of the prize thus:

The Ibrahim Prize for Achievement in African Leadership—the world's biggest individual prize—was not awarded this year as no suitable candidates were found, it was announced Monday. At a press conference in London, the Mo Ibrahim Foundation said it was not going to compromise on its standard of excellence in a leader.

The prize, set up by Sudanese-born billionaire, Mo Ibrahim, in 2006, carries a $5 million prize paid over 10 years and $200,000 annually for life from then on, with a further $200,000 per year available for 10 years for good causes backed by the winner. The award goes to a democratically elected African leader who has served their mandated term and left office in the last three years. "You make your bed; you have to lie on it. If we said we're going to have a prize for exceptional leadership, we have to stick to that. We are not going to compromise," Ibrahim said. The telecoms entrepreneur's foundation has awarded the annual prize only three times since it was established, plus two special awards given to South Africa's Nelson Mandela and former archbishop Desmond Tutu. Cape Verde's former president Pedro Verona Pires won the prize last year, 2011, while Botswana's ex-leader, Festus Mogae took the prize in 2007 and Mozambique's Joaquim Chissano in 2008.

With all the changes in government and revolutions, the 2011 index for measuring governance and grading African leaders was going to be a tricky one. To maintain the broadness of the index, the Nation Group continues to rely on a variety of measures to give a rounded evaluation of the leaders' performance.

They often use the Mo Ibrahim Index of African governance, the Democracy Index, the Freedom House's Press Freedom Index, the Transparency International's Corruption Index, and the United Nation's Human Development Index to develop a single index and grade for each leader. The final score on which the political leaders are finally judged is a weighted average score of all these indices.

In 2011, the leaders were graded using "A," as the best grade, and "F" as the worst grade. But there is a number of leaders like Mugabe of Zimbabwe who were difficult to grade and they were therefore given a "morgue" grade. In the final analysis, four presidents got an "A" grade—meaning that they promoted effective leadership and better governance in their countries. They included the presidents of Botswana, Cape Verde, Ghana, and Mauritius. The presidents of South Africa, Mali, and Namibia got a "B" grade each. The rest of the pack got a "C" and below meaning and demonstrating poor leadership and weak governance in Africa today and thus being one of the greatest challenges in African economic development and business management.

Moreover, Heifetz (1994, 2001) has proposed six principles that African leaders could apply to improve their leadership effectiveness. These principles will also help in the management of challenges in African governance and economic development to improve African prosperity. But, the principles must be appropriately applied by the African political and business leaders.

Adaptive work referred to in the principles consists of the learning required to address conflicts in the values people hold, or to diminish the gap between the values people stand for and the reality they face. Adaptive work requires a change in values, beliefs, or behavior in order to learn new ways needed to tackle, for example, economic development and social challenges. These principles include:

First, get on the balcony: Business and political leaders have to be able to view patterns of governing and management as if they were in the balcony. It does them no good to be swept up in the field of action. Leaders have to see the context for change or create one. Leadership must be able to identify struggles over values and power, recognize patterns of work avoidance, and watch for the many other functional and dysfunctional situations to change.

Without the capacity to move back and forth, to reflect on day to day, moment to moment, on the many ways in which an organization's or national habits can sabotage adaptive work, a leader easily and unwittingly becomes a prisoner of the system. The dynamics of adaptive work and change are far too complex to keep track of, let alone influence, if leaders stay in the fray or only in the field of play. Getting on the balcony is thus a prerequisite for following the other five principles.

Secondly, identify the adaptive challenges: When businesses cannot learn quickly in order to develop appropriate strategies to adapt to new challenges, they are likely to face their own form of extinction. An organization whose people clung to functional silos and valued pleasing their bosses more than pleasing customers and/or constituents could not become a great organization.

An organization dedicated to serving people, acting on trust, respecting the individual, and making teamwork happen across boundaries is likely to succeed in today's global and competitive business environment. And it is an organization in which the leadership is able to identify the symptoms of adaptive challenges at the appropriate time and take action to lead the organization to deal with the challenges. For the strategy to succeed, for example, the organization's leaders need to understand themselves, their people, and the potential source of conflict and resistance and thus develop timely strategies to deal with them.

Thirdly, regulate stress: Adaptive work—as a change process—generates stress and organizational members cannot learn new ways if they are overwhelmed by stress, but eliminating stress altogether removes the impetus for doing adaptive work. A leader must attempt three fundamental tasks to help maintain a productive level of tension in the organization. Adhering to these tasks will allow him or her to motivate people without disabling them:

- First, a leader must create a holding environment. This is creating relationships and conditions where diverse groups talk to one another about the challenges facing them, to frame and debate issues, and to clarify the assumptions behind competing perspectives and values;
- Second, a leader is responsible for direction, protection, orientation, managing conflict, and shaping norms. A leader provides direction by identifying the organization's adaptive challenge and framing the key questions and issues. A leader protects people by managing the rate of change. A leader orients people to new roles and responsibilities by training them, by clarifying business realities and key values. A leader helps expose conflict, viewing it as the engine of creativity and learning. Finally, a leader helps the organization maintain those norms that must endure and challenge those that need to change;
- Third, a leader must have presence and poise; regulating distress is perhaps a leader's most difficult job. Although leadership demands a deep understanding of the pain of change, it also requires the ability to hold steady and main-

tain the tension. The employees, colleagues, and customers will carefully observe verbal and nonverbal cues to a leader's ability to hold steady. He needs to communicate confidence that he and they can tackle the tasks ahead.

- Fourthly, maintain disciplined attention: Different people within the same organization bring different experiences, assumptions, values, beliefs, and habits to their work. This diversity is valuable because innovation and learning are products of differences. Yet, managers at all levels are often unwilling or unable to address their competing perspectives collectively. A leader must get all employees to confront tough trade-off in values, procedures, operating styles, and power. Scapegoating, denials, focusing only on today's technical issues, or attacking individuals rather than the perspectives they represent—all forms of work avoidance—are expected when an organization undertakes adaptive work. In this regard, disciplined attention to issues is the currency of effective leadership.
- Fifthly, give the work back to the people: Leaders must make everybody contribute to organizational endeavors. Everyone in the organization has special access to information that comes from his or her particular vantage point. Everyone may see different needs and opportunities. Getting people to assume greater responsibility is not easy. Not only are many lower-level employees comfortable being told what to do, but many managers are accustomed to treating subordinates like machinery that requires control. Letting people take the initiative in defining and solving problems means that management need to learn to support rather than control. Workers, for their part, need to learn to take responsibility. That is the essence of adaptive work and effective leadership.
- Sixthly, protect voices of leadership from below: Giving a voice to all people in the organization and community is the foundation of an organization that is willing to adapt and experiment, learn, and innovate, and hence be successfully competitive in the market. Therefore, leaders should give employees the tools to do the creative and analytical strategy work: analyze trends and discontinuities, understand core competencies, assess their competitive position, and map out potential opportunities and exploit them. That means, organizational leaders should encourage and support the emergence and development of leadership at all organizational levels and in the community. African leaders can use this model to manage their nations successfully.

6. POST-INDEPENDENCE MODEL OF GOVERNMENT

A government has two main duties: to maintain order and provide public goods such as roads, airports, energy, water and sanitation, education, agricultural research, basic healthcare, and basic telecommunication necessary for national development. It is also expected to create an appropriate business climate, ensure national safety and security, enforce business rules, create and impose property rights, and maintains the appropriate incentives system for entrepreneurs to create wealth needed to alleviate poverty and deprivation (Deng et al., 2002).

Scholars (Deng et al., 2002; Mbaku, 1998) have established that the post-independence African governments did not perform these functions well, particularly in supporting the emergence and development of the African entrepreneurial class. As a consequence, the development of indigenous capitalism, and emergence of domestic entrepreneurial class were impeded in most of the countries. Therefore, the African economies were unable to generate the wealth needed to confront endemic poverty. Instead of the governments functioning as agents of economic growth and development of the newly independent states, they were turned into instruments of plunder to benefit special interest groups and the political elites.

Mbaku (1998) asserts further that the post-independence African governments' activities in the economy have discouraged the development of viable economic infrastructures, stunted the development of indigenous capitalism, and the emergency of an African entrepreneurial class. They created a large urban sectors in each country that depended primarily on the surplus extracted from the poorly managed rural agricultural sector; and generally impeded economic growth and development. The development of institutional arrangements was not consensual. According to Mbaku (1998), an appropriate model of government is characterized by:

- Consensual and voluntary agreement of members with the participation of all individuals in the nation's development activities;
- Institutional arrangements designed by the people for their betterment and not imposed by external forces, be it foreign or local;
- Transparency, responsibility, and accountability in all governance structures;
- Nationals freely engage in exchange and contract with respect of property rights of individuals;
- Institutional arrangements reflect values, culture, aspirations, and expectations of the people;
- Establishing suitable structures and institutions for sustainable development.

7. POVERTY AND CLIMATE CHANGE

Arguably the two biggest challenges we face in this century—equally in Africa and the rest of the world—are to overcome poverty and to manage climate change. One cannot be achieved without the other. Investment in "climate smart" agriculture will be key to achieving both because quality investments in agriculture will help the poor—on average 70 percent of Africans live in rural areas—more than any other program, and because agriculture is key to both mitigation and adaptation to climate change.

It is the plants on the planet that absorb carbon dioxide, so it is between forests and the rest of the productive landscape to take carbon out of the atmosphere. The mitigation potential for improved climate smart agricultural practices is huge and needs to be tapped. It is a triple win: if done well, higher production and productivity leads to better incomes eliminating poverty and improving living standards, it improves community and environmental resilience, and it captures carbon dioxide (Voegle, 2011).

Africa is poor and on the margins of the world economy, albeit endowed with rich and abundant natural resources This is owing to lack of competitiveness and economic diversification and sophistication: 34 of the 49 of the world's least-developed countries are in Africa. Most countries in Africa are highly dependent on rain-fed agriculture and commodity exports. Agriculture is subject to periodic drought, and the prices of commodity exports can fluctuate substantially over short periods of time, making economic management to deal with poverty very difficult. Most economic and social indicators in Africa have deteriorated since the 1970s – although there was a spell of growth in the 1990s and 2000s supported by reforms and increased commodity prices (EIU, 2009).

For the typical resource-rich economy in Africa, natural resources are not sufficiently abundant to ignore what its structure will look like when the resource runs out. The relative price changes that occur in a resource exporting economy—symptoms of the "Dutch disease"—also place Africa's resource-rich countries at a disadvantage with respect to two major drivers of industrial change and economic growth necessary to reduce poverty, namely economic diversification and sophistication.

The Dutch disease is a phenomena by which there is the de-industrialization of a nation's economy that occurs when the discovery or increased exports of a natural resource raises the value of that nation's currency, making domestically manufactured goods less competitive with other nations, increasing imports, and decreasing exports. The term Dutch disease originated in Holland after the discovery of North Sea gas and the export of gas making it difficult for the country to diversify (Page, 2008).

Because the Dutch disease discourages the development of new tradable and exportable goods producing activities, it limits the scope for the diversification of the manufacturing sector and therefore stunts increases in the sophistication of manufacturing production and exports in the country. Both diversification and increasing sophistication in an economy have recently been linked to higher incomes and faster growth to reduce poverty (Page, 2008).

Scholars (Diamandis and Kotler, 2012), have described the Dutch Disease, which they describe as a resource curse, as a poverty trap among other poverty traps such as being a landlocked country and being stuck in a cycle of civil war and political instability. As exemplified by Nigeria, a resource curse (Dutch Disease) is an insidious poverty trap. The discovery of oil in Nigeria in the 1970s destroyed the country's flourishing peanut and cocoa industries. Poverty in Nigeria is pervasive ever since. More than 70 percent of Nigerians live on less than $2 dollars a day, a level of absolute poverty. Many of the Central and Western African countries—such as Congo DR, Central African Republic, Mali, Niger, Chad, and Guinea—are stuck in poverty because of being land locked and always in a state of civil war. A majority of them are former French colonies and protectorates!

Therefore, the most urgent and immediate problem for Africans to solve today is poverty. The issue is about how to create wealth. Africa needs to deal with rising, pervasive, and degrading poverty. Africans are much poorer compared to people from other parts of the world. Notwithstanding, poverty is not uniquely an African phenomenon, but a global problem. It affects every country in the world, and the difference lies in the levels and pervasiveness of poverty and therefore, poverty needs dedicated global efforts to combat it successfully. But poverty in Africa is massive and insidious; with fifty percent of African people living below the poverty line i.e. survives on less than $ 2 per day even in natural resources-rich countries (Moyo, 2009).

However, every African country, and with the support of the World Bank and the International Monetary Fund and the UN Millennium Development Goals strategies, has a poverty eradication strategy in place that if well managed, it is anticipated that Africa may reduce its poverty by fifty percent by the year 2015. The strategy is part of the Millennium Development Goals program—mentioned earlier in chapter two and above—that is being implemented by most African countries under the UN supervision (Opanga, 2010).

Juma (2011) asserts that the best solution to poverty and hunger alleviation in Africa is to provide the people with the means to earn income from available resources that they have and probably own. The majority of the African people lives in the rural areas and has large tracks of arable land. Therefore, the key solution to poverty in Africa should be more and quality investments in agriculture – in terms of technological innovation, effective food storage systems, infrastructure, entrepreneurial skills, and marketing - and an effective partnership between the private sector and the government of every country to create job opportunities for their citizens, particularly in agriculture and related agro-businesses. Other important and imperative measures—to boost agriculture—include small-scale irrigation schemes and development coupled with access to long-term financing, access to markets, and acquisition of commercial and skillful farming expertise by farmers.

Indeed, in Sub-Saharan Africa, agriculture directly contributes up to 34% of GDP and 64% of employment. Growth in agriculture is at least two to four times more effective in creating jobs and reducing poverty (Juma, 2011). Jobs create wealth! Furthermore, job creation has a domino and or multiplier effect in an economy: it creates wealth and increases the purchasing power of the people, which in turn creates demand for products and services usually produced by various industries and businesses creating more jobs down the line and the circle begins all over again. Therefore, most importantly and in the final analysis, poverty eradication—through employment creation—creates opportunities for business growth and hence its eradication should be a joint effort by African governments and private corporations in Africa.

8. INCOME INEQUALITIES

Despite the recent increase in economic growth in Africa, incomes in most of Africa are low and not evenly distributed, as discussed in chapter six above. Therefore, the income disparities in Africa are stark and much higher than seen in many parts of the world. Africa's distribution of income is among the worst in the world. Therefore, while a consumer class may arise in the continent, a large and sophisticated middle class will not emerge soon until governments commit themselves to better income distribution mechanisms (Mahajan, 2009).

For example, Nigeria is Africa's top oil producer and the 11th largest in the world. Despite solid oil revenues, which account for 80% of government revenues, more than 70% of the population lives in poverty of less than $2 a day (ERA 2010). Even a fairly developed economy like that of South Africa has a high income inequality measure of more than 33%, which is more than twice that of the US and more than three times that of the G-7 as per the UN's Human Development inequality measures (Bernstein, 2007).

The UN's Human Development Report measures income disparities using what it calls "inequality measures." According to the UN, this index shows "the ratio of the income or expenditure share of the richest group to that of the poorest." In this instance, it measures the top 10% income share less the poorest 10% income share to determine the index. These income inequality measures are much worse in many poorer African countries.

Improving the index through effective income distribution is critical to creating a viable middle class in African economies and hence larger markets for products and services. This process will create business opportunities in Africa. Therefore, proper income distribution and fairly sharing the benefits of economic growth, in Africa, must receive the urgent attention it deserves now and in the future to enhance African growth and development of market opportunities in the continent (Bernstein, 2007).

Furthermore, over the years, economist have struggled with answering the single most important question in their profession, the same one that compelled Adam Smith to write *The Wealth of Nations*: why are some countries rich while others are poor? Over the centuries, proposed answers have varied greatly. Smith declared that the difference between wealth and poverty resulted from the relative freedom of the markets; Thomas Malthus said poverty comes from overpopulation; and John Maynard Keynes claimed it was a byproduct of a lack of technocrats. Of course, everyone knows that politicians love listening to wonky bureaucrats! Jeffrey Sachs, one of the world's most famous economists and leader of the UN Millennium Development Goals, asserts that poor soil, lack of navigable rivers, and tropical diseases are, in part, to blame for poverty, particularly in Africa (Sachs, 2005). Others point to culture, geography, climate, colonization, and military mighty and the list goes on (Davidson, 2012).

But through a series of legendary—and somewhat controversial—academic papers published over the past decade, Daron Acemoglu and James Robinson (2012) have persuasively challenged many of the previous theories. If poverty were primarily the result of geography, say, or an unfortunate history, how can we account for the successes of countries like Botswana, Costa Rica, or Thailand?

Acemoglu and Robinson, quoted by Davidson (2012), argue that the growth of the wealth of a country is most closely correlated with the degree to which the average person shares in the overall growth of its economy; that is having equal benefits from the growth of the economy. It is an idea that was first raised by Adam Smith but was then largely ignored for centuries as economics became focused on theoretical models of ideal economies rather than the not-at-all-ideal problems of real nations.

Consider Acemoglu and Robinson's idea from the perspective of a poor farmer. In parts of modern sub-Saharan Africa, as was true in medieval Europe or the antebellum USA South, the people who work the fields lack any incentive to improve their yield because any surplus is taken by the wealthy elite. This mind-set changes only when farmers are given strong property rights, institutional and financial support, and are taught to discover that they can profit from extra production. In 1978, China began allowing its farmers to benefit from any surplus they produced. The decision, most economists agree, helped spark and stimulate the country's astounding and phenomenal growth over the last three decades (Davidson, 2012).

According to Acemoglu and Robinson's (2012) thesis, when a nation's institutions prevent the poor from profiting from their hard work, creativity, and innovation, no amount of disease eradication, technology transfer, education, and good economic advice or foreign aid or foreign direct investment seems to help. Davidson (2012) observed this phenomenon firsthand when he visited a group of Haitian mango farmers a few years ago. Each farmer had no more than one or two mango trees, even though their land lay along a river that could irrigate their fields and support hundreds of trees. So why didn't they install irrigation pipes? Were they ignorant, indifferent? In fact, they were quite savvy and lived in a region teeming with well-intended foreign-aid programs. But these farmers also knew that nobody in their village had clear title to the land they farmed. If they suddenly grew a few hundred mango trees, it was likely that a well-connected member of the elite would show up and claim their land and its spoils. What was the point to work hard and grow more mango trees? No incentive to do it until the land tenure rights were changed and the farmer's ownership of the land was enhanced.

Davidson (2012) encountered another side of Acemoglu and Robinson's thesis during what must have been one of history's great natural economic experiments: post-Saddam Hussein Baghdad, in Iraq. On April 9, 2003, the day the city was captured, one of the world's most tightly controlled economies suddenly became a free-for-all economy. Amid the chaos, many former state functionaries turned into entrepreneurs. Nearly every engineer from the ministry of housing, it seemed, had opened his own construction company. Satellite TVs, once illegal to all but very small elite, were sold on every major street. Under Hussein, only one company—widely rumored to be monitored by the intelligence service—offered Internet access, and it was incredibly bad and expensive. After it was gone, there were so many new Internet companies that had far more access options then than do today in Brooklyn, New York.

Yet the American authorities, who had not planned for this budding free market, all but destroyed it when they gave the bulk of new contracts to large companies from outside the country. Often, these outsiders subcontracted to Iraqi firms with close ties to the state's new political establishment. By the anniversary of the United States invasion, it was clear that economic success would again—as it was during Saddam Hussein's era—come from connections and corruption rather than talent, hard work, and Iraq entrepreneurs. Today, Transparency International ranks Iraq as one of the most corrupt nations on earth, a situation that is true and affects many African countries. An Iraqi friend once told Davidson that he had hoped Americans would teach the Iraqis how to be Americans. Instead, the Americans learned how to be Iraqi after the fall of Saddam Hussein (Davidson, 2012). In the final analysis, therefore, ownership of or having access to income generating resources, property rights, and successful entrepreneurs are three important ways a country can achieve and enhance income equality among its citizens.

9. RETENTION OF COLONIAL BUSINESS PARADIGMS AND PATTERNS OF TRADE

Although most African countries have been independent now for almost fifty years, they still maintain the business paradigms and trade patterns created, in these countries, during the colonial period. Today, and as they did during the colonial time, the African countries specialize in the production of primary commodities, such as oil and gas, agricultural products, and minerals. They add little value to these products to attract high prices in the market and create quality jobs. They export these products, at low prices, mainly to the former metropolitan countries and, of course, import manufactured and high value items from the metropolitan countries (ERA, 2010). They are increasingly doing the same arrangements with China and India today.

Mbaku (1995, 1998), in commenting on the trade relationships between African countries and their former colonizers, asserts thus "Trade relationships developed as a result of colonialism have been maintained with the former metropolitan countries. Quite often, these arrangements have been strengthened by tied aid and other development assistance programs. They have been designed and managed to keep African economies as sources of cheap raw materials and markets of high value imported manufactured products."

Other scholars have examined major systems of relations and preferences developed by the former colonizers—the Generalized System of Preferences and the African, Caribbean, and Pacific or well known as the Lome Convention for example—and concluded that these trade arrangements are based on poorly negotiated preferences. And have concluded that such preferences yield very little and limited gains and benefits to African countries.

They generally have or add very little economic value to the African countries. They offer only marginal benefits. In fact, these arrangements retard African development because they make African dependent on valueless arrangements for its development. Regional integration schemes and trade in Africa should considerably reduce African dependence on these useless arrangements of preferences and allow the African countries to begin to assert their political and economic independence in the world.

Therefore, reshaping a business orientation rooted in long colonial history is a major challenge in Africa. To completely change this one-sided process and redirect African businesses and trade, particularly to among themselves, is going to be a challenging process that needs considerable effort and determination from the African countries and their leaders. However, these changes, particularly those involving trade, will be easily and sustainably achieved through accelerated African regional integration to create regional trading blocs resulting in larger African markets (ERA, 2010).

But and in discussing regional integration in Africa, Dr. Mukhisa Kituyi (2012), a director in the Kenya Institute of Governance and a former Trade and Commerce Minister in the Kenya government, has clearly identified and analyzed a series of challenges faced by African countries in trying to achieve greater and more effective regional integration in Africa and how to deal with them, as the African leaders were meeting in Addis Ababa, Ethiopia, to initiate yet another continental free trade area agreement.

He asserts thus:

The heads of state meeting of the African Union in Addis Ababa this weekend is set to launch an initiative creating a Continental Free Trade Area (CFTA) by the year 2017.This effort reflects both a success and failure of past initiatives at integrating the economies of Africa to enlarge markets, to optimize on scale, rationalize infrastructure, and unbuckle the continent's productive forces.

Twenty years ago, Africa committed to The Lagos Plan of Action which envisaged a rapid consolidation of Regional Economic Communities (RECs) as building blocks to inter-lock into a continental customs union by 2019. As the dateline approaches, the goal appears elusive. While some regions like Eastern, West, and Southern Africa have made progress, elsewhere little has happened. Even where these RECs have grown, their negotiated rules and tariff structures have evolved in total disregard of what neighboring blocs are doing. As a result, what was conceived as building blocks for African integration have actually erected new barriers to trade between regions.

Still, the progress made in negotiating integration in the RECs has been a major learning process for the crafters of the new initiative. Simplifying and standardizing customs procedures and documentation, agreeing on rules of origin for tax-exempt goods and cutting down on red tape within regions, is the foundation upon which the quest for a trade regime for the whole continent is founded. It is a common truth that countries which trade best – and are richer - with the rest of the world first trade most with their neighbors. Intra-African trade, currently at about 12 per cent, remains way behind Europe, Asia, and the Americas, and leaves Africa the poorest continent.

The cost of trade logistics for land-locked African countries on average accounts for 40 per cent of the value of their products; by far the most costly in the world. A chill in the international environment has brought to the fore the urgency of concrete action on the continent to regionally integrate. The stalled Doha Round negotiations for a rules-based multilateral trading system have diminished the voice of Africa on global market access issues. The crisis in the euro zone has cast doubt on the medium-term access to Africa's most important traditional market. The arm-twisting and goal-shifting of Brussels in reviving the stalled Economic Partnership Agreement negotiations portends even worse for Africa's most important preferential market.

Yet even as the architects of the new CFTA effort get down to model the roadmap, celebrations will be very premature. Security concerns across the continent threaten the plan in its infancy. The protracted denouement of the Arab Spring Revolution has left uncertainty in The Arab Maghreb and shifted priorities in key countries of Egypt, Tunisia, and Libya. The dirty divorce between Khartoum and Juba is dramatically spinning into crisis mode with serious implications for both countries and their neighbors. Somalia continues to fester like an incurable wound on the east board with related escalation in the cost of containing piracy and terrorist activities. Beyond security challenges, Africa must learn to practice what it has signed up before looking to sign onto new undertakings.

The experience within existing RECs is not very encouraging. Many times old habits shroud implementation of new commitments. East Africa's recent experience bears this out. Seven years since the coming into force of the EAC Customs Union and nearly two years since launching the Common Market, the East African partners continue to play hide and seek with each other. A mountain of non-tariff barriers continues to suffocate cross-border trade. Uganda continues to seek extensions on a so-called list of sensitive products for which its input taxes are lower than for their neighbors. Last year (2011), Tanzania suspended maize "exports" to Kenya during a season of scarcity. This past month, government officers in Kenya have been complaining of Kenyan maize being "smuggled" into Uganda since the Kenyan Cereals Board announced it had run out of money to buy famers' produce. East African governments continue to attempt selective and solo subsidies either for fertilizer or grains at different times.

There is no model of a common market where customs duty on inputs is varied between member countries. You cannot be a common market while banning movement of cereals across borders. If you are a common market there is no longer export between countries. Goods and services are in free flow. The regime of subsidies by government must become a collective negotiated policy for all the countries in the REC.

If we fail the consistency test within a small and closely-knit effort like EAC, it casts major doubts on how much we will keep our word on abandoning trade restriction practices within a continental initiative. The leaders gathered in Addis should have the boldness to sign the commitment to a CFTA, but also understand and commit to the challenges of abandoning ancient habits. This is the only way Africa's integration will strengthen her hand in a mean and hostile global trading regime and to deal with pervasive poverty in the continent.

There are a lot of opportunities in regional integration and inter-Africa trade, as Karambu (2012) asserts, in quoting the World Bank, thus: "While uncertainty surrounds the global economy and stagnation is likely to continue in traditional markets in Europe and North America, enormous opportunities for cross border trade within Africa in food products, basic manufactures, and services remain unexploited."

It is also important to note that companies from the former colonial powers are the major companies doing business in Africa, creating stiff competition, particularly in the extractive and agricultural industries, not only to the local firms, but also to companies from other parts of the world that may wish to do business in African. Anecdotally, many Africans regard this situation as a continuation to exploit the African people. Examples of these metropolitan flag bearing and empire maintaining companies are Shell in Nigeria, Total in Gabon, and Unilever in Kenya and Malawi (EIU, 2009; AER, 2010).

10. AID AND DEBT DEPENDENCE IN DEVELOPMENT

According to Moyo (2009), the tale of bilateral and multilateral debt and aid to Africa began in earnest in the first three weeks of July 1944, after a meeting held at Mount Washington Hotel, in Bretton Woods, New Hampshire, USA, where the so-called Bretton Woods institutions—IMF and the World Bank—were born.

Against the backdrop of the Second World War, over 700 delegates from some forty-four countries resolved to establish a framework for a global development and financial and monetary management system at this meeting. The World Bank for Development and Reconstruction and The International Monetary Fund (IMF) to regulate the international monetary and financial system were born here and later strengthened to manage the world's economic development, monetary, and financial systems.

It was from this gathering that the dominant framework of aid-infused development model would emerge and continue up to today. Aid and debt dependency continues to be a major problem for the African countries. It has been argued that underdevelopment and poverty in Africa derives primarily from policy mistakes by well-meaning global policy makers and from the incompetence and ineptitude of the continent's public servants and politicians that failed to use foreign debt and aid profitably for the good of their countries and for their people. Instead, the African leaders, in particular, engaged in massive corruption on the resources generated by aid and debt.

Therefore, aid sent to Africa does not appear to have had a significant positive impact on poverty and deprivation. Moyo (2009) has further argued that aid has not functioned to help in improving social and economic conditions in Africa because of several reasons:

- First, donors, especially during the cold war, favored spending on military projects and forced domestic policy-makers to neglect important areas critical to growth and development such as investment in education, healthcare, infrastructure, energy, and agriculture;
- Secondly, sectors that are critical to and important to the development of the country rarely are allocated any resources and less than 6.5% of development aid or assistance received by developing countries over the years is allocated to these areas namely agriculture, education, healthcare, technology, and the environment, sectors that are essential to accelerated economic development in a country;
- Thirdly, the debt and aid resources were stolen and corruptly squandered by government officials to enrich themselves, their families, and friends without putting aid and debt to the productive sectors of the national economy;
- Fourthly, during the cold war, the policies of the developed countries favored African countries that were friendly with the former and as a result, Official Development Aid (ODA) was usually quite unpredictable and could not be depended on for making long-term development plans. In addition, many of the Western donors often attached conditions to aid that made effective use of the latter for development quite difficult;
- Lastly, in many instances, aid was driven by interest groups in the developed countries to sell their products, services, and technologies that were not suitable for African development because they were mostly obsolete and inappropriate technologies to the African environment. In fact, a lot of the aid money never reached the continent of Africa.

There is a sad story that vindicates Moyo's views on aid to Africa and it illustrates the tragedy and failure of aid to developing countries over the years as an instrument of economic development. The story is on the development aid to Afghanistan after its liberation from the Taliban in 2001. It is narrated by Acemoglu and Robinson (2012) in their seminal book on *Why Nations Fail: The Origins of Power, Prosperity, and Poverty*:

The story goes thus:

In December 2001, Afghanistan leaders and the international community met in Bonn, German, and came out with the Bonn Agreement that created a plan for the establishment of a democratic regime in Afghanistan. First, a grand nationwide assembly was set up which elected Hamid Karzai as the leader of the interim government. Things were looking up for Afghanistan. The international community thought all that Afghanistan needed now to get it on the road to democracy and economic development, was a large infusion of foreign aid. Representatives from the United Nations and several leading NGOs soon descended on the capital Kabul.

What ensued should not have been a surprise to anybody, especially given the failure of foreign aid to poor countries and failed states over the past five decades. Surprise or not, the ritual was repeated. Scores of aid workers and their entourages arrived in town with their own private jets, NGOs of all sorts poured in to pursue their agendas, and high level talks began between the government of Afghanistan and delegations from the international community. Billions of dollars were now coming to Afghanistan. But little of it was used to building infrastructure, schools, agriculture, healthcare facilities, or other public services essential for the development of inclusive institutions or even for restoring law and order in the country. While much of the infrastructure remained in tatters, the first tranche of the money was used to commission an airline to shuttle around UN and other international officials. The aid flows, rather than building infrastructure in Afghanistan, started by undermining the Afghan state they were supposed to build and strengthen.

Villagers in a remote district in the central valley of Afghanistan heard a radio announcement about a new multi-million dollar program to restore shelters to their area. After a long while, few wooden beams carried by the trucking cartel of an Ismail Khan, famous former warlord and member of the Afghan government, were delivered. But they were too big to be used for anything in the district, and villagers put them to the only possible use, firewood. So what happened to the millions of dollars promised to the villagers? Of the promised money, 20 percent of it was taken as UN head office costs in Geneva. The remainder was subcontracted to an

NGO, which took another 20 percent for its own head office costs in Brussels, and so on, for another three layers, including corrupt officials, with each party taking approximately 20 percent of what was remaining.

What happened in the central valley of Afghanistan is not an isolated incident. Many studies estimate that only about 10 percent of aid ever reaches its target. The Afghan experience with aid was in fact probably a qualified success compared to others. Throughout the last fifty years, hundreds of billions of dollars have been paid to governments around the world as development aid. Much of it has been wasted in overhead costs and corruption by dictators such Mobutu Sese Seko of Zaire, currently the Democratic Republic of the Congo (DRC).

Despite this unflattering track record of development aid, particularly to Africa, Latin America, and Asia, foreign aid is one of the most popular policies that Western governments, international organizations, such as the United Nations, and NGOs of different ilk recommend as a way of combating poverty around the world and in Africa. And of course, the cycle of the failure of foreign aid repeats itself over and over again without regret.

Still, African countries failed to use aid efficiently and effectively because they lacked competent laws and institutions to use received aid appropriately and effectively (Mbaku 2004). The lack of relevant laws and institutions led to the wrong and ineffective use of direct foreign investments too for the good, growth, and development of the African countries to reduce pervasive and chronic poverty in Africa. According to Mbaku (1998, 2004) proper laws and institutions should have been in place to serve the following purposes:

- Improve the use and functioning of foreign resources as instruments of local development;
- Prevent opportunism on the part of the domestic elites and foreign and indigenous entrepreneurs;
- Provide fair, effective, and predictable structures for individuals and groups to compete for benefits of foreign investments and particularly benefits of economic development in general;
- Provide a system of well-defined property rights, especially in environmental resources;
- Prevent foreign investors from exploiting the country, while providing them the opportunity to earn a fair return for their committed resources;

- Improve the ability of both domestic and foreign entrepreneurs to engage in employment and wealth creation;
- To enable domestic entrepreneurs to prosper and become market champions in domestic and global markets over time.

In recent years, however, there have been concerted efforts, particularly by international civil society organizations, aimed at writing off debt owned by developing countries – including those owed by African countries also discussed in chapter two as a strategy to assist these countries in economic development to eliminate pervasive poverty. But, many observers anecdotally argue that the assumption that debt cancellation alone can solve the poverty situation in Africa is not entirely correct. It is solving the world trade imbalances and removal of trade barriers and market exclusion—particularly by the European Union and the USA—that would solve the poverty situation in Africa through increased exports, particularly of those products originating from agriculture.

Notwithstanding, immediate and complete debt cancellation by multilateral and bilateral lenders will definitely help in accelerating poverty alleviation in Africa. This is especially if the money so cancelled or forgiven is invested in education, healthcare, infrastructure, agriculture, protection of the environment, legal and institutional reforms in order to create the capacity needed to grow and develop the continent of Africa sustainably (ERA 2010).

11. HEALTHCARE AND DISEASE PANDEMICS

The rudimentary health care systems in many Sub Saharan African nations present a critical challenge of doing business in the region. This is particularly in the light of the ongoing HIV/AIDS pandemic. HIV/AIDS adds to operating costs and lost man-hours in many organizations in African countries.

Today, HIV/AIDS is the single most important threat to human and economic development in the entire Third World, mostly in Africa. In fact, in many countries of the world, HI/AIDS is threatening to reverse nearly a half a century of improvements of the human condition. It is estimated that there are over twenty six million Africans infected by the HIV virus and the death rate is over two and half million people annually, with three million new infections reported yearly (UNAIDS Report, 2006).

Where poverty is prevalent and pervasive, so is infectious diseases like HIV/AIDS, malaria, and tuberculosis are prevalent (UNAID Report, 2008). However, it is important to note here that the prevalence of these infections, like poverty, is not an isolated African problem, it is a global problem; one that calls for concerted global efforts to resolve. For example a recent press report indicated that HIV infection rate is 19 percent in an estate about three miles from the White House in Washington!

Unfortunately, financial constraints have hampered the creation and expansion of adequate strategies to contain and reverse the trends of these diseases sustainably. Still, much research effort is routinely being directed toward the enhancement of preventative and treatment strategies in resource poor settings. And some countries, like Kenya, in Sub Saharan African governments have been able to reverse the HIV/AIDS infection and prevalence rates in the last decade (UNAID Report, 2008).

HIV/AIDS prevalence rates in Africa differ from region to region. The highest prevalence rates are in Southern Africa (17 percent in South Africa to 35 percent in Botswana) and the lowest rates are in Western and Northern Africa, ranging from one percent to five percent in these areas. In East Africa and the COMESA region in general, the prevalence rates are lower today than they were ten years ago raging from 4 percent in Kenya to 13 percent in Uganda (UNAIDS Report, 2006).

It is anticipated that HIV-1 transmission rates will be contained and completely reversed by the year 2015 (WHO Report, 2006). This is because the prevention and cure of HIV/AIDS and other infectious diseases like malaria and tuberculosis are part of the Millennium Development Goals action plans in many African countries meant to eradicate many of these diseases. The eradication of these diseases will release resources for development in other important sectors such as agriculture.

12. INSTITUTIONAL VOIDS AND CULTURAL MILIEU

Institutional void is a term used by Khanna (2005) to describe the absence of basic institutions in developing countries—including African countries—that make markets fail. He asserts that how well an economy helps buyers and sellers—in capital, labor, and product markets—to come together and transact business is important and depends entirely on adequate and well-functioning business laws and institutions.

Institutional voids cause failures in these markets. Ideally, therefore, every economy should provide a range of economic and political institutions in order to facilitate the functioning of markets. But, developing countries in general fall short of this in a number of ways including lack of adequate and quality institutions to provide reliable information, too much regulations, and inadequate, corrupt, and inefficient justice systems.

There is a limited sophistication of the entire institutional infrastructure in many African countries. This institutional failure includes political and social systems, openness in society and in the product, labor, and capital markets. The limited institutional sophistication has led to institutional voids in many areas of business, in

Africa, such as having few firms for searching, recruiting, and training employees; lack of reliable and superior intermediaries such as credit-rating, advertising, and investment analysis agencies, venture capital firms and angel investors, merchant banks, and quality audit firms; and the presence of inadequate, inefficient, and corrupt legal systems (EIU 2009).

Related to this is the question of cultural milieu. In Africa, personal contacts and friendship are critical and come before business relationships. Therefore, before entering into a business contract, in Africa, one has to develop friendship and personal relationship, which is usually slow and takes time to develop. This leads to costly delays of entering into contracts, leave alone realizing them. There is also too much dependence on strenuous and time-consuming regulations in the business environment that complicates the cultural milieu further in that one has to develop personal relationships with corrupt government officials to be able to go round these regulations (ERA, 2010).

13. INTER-AFRICAN INFRASTRUCTURE

Infrastructure is the lifeblood of any modern economy. And the story of America's rise to global economic leadership, for example, cannot be told without taking into account the vast and ambitious building projects that paved the way for growth and commerce. The workers, who bridged waterways, built a mighty railroad and an impressive interstate road network that spanned a continent, and constructed the nation's backbone from steel and concrete did much more to commerce than transform the American landscape. They provided the underpinnings for future generations' prosperity (Friedman et al., 2011).

Furthermore, President Obama of the USA reemphasizes and indicates the importance and criticality of infrastructure in job creation in modern times in the USA and in other countries for that matter. He states, in his 2011 Job Act, that job generating priorities are building the twenty-first century infrastructure among other priorities that include leading the world in green technologies, restoring the American manufacturing base, and doubling exports (Clinton, 2011).

The economic infrastructures of the majority of the African countries—roads, railroads, bridges, electricity, water, airports, sea ports, sewage disposal facilities, and telecommunications—are rudimentary at best and poorly developed; do not have the ability to serve as an anchor for productive economic activities; are incapable of meeting the needs of entrepreneurs; and generally do not have the capacity to serve effectively as instruments of development. Essentially, they do not represent a firm foundation of the rapid generation of wealth that is required if the continent is to pull itself out of its present malaise and poverty any time soon (Moyo, 2009; AER, 2010; Juma, 2011).

According to Juma (2011), infrastructure is defined here as the facilities, structures, associated equipment, services, and institutional arrangements that facilitate the movement of people, flow of economic goods, services, and ideas. Infrastructure represents the foundational base for applying technical knowledge in sustainable development and relies heavily on innovation, technology, and civil engineering.

The importance of providing enabling infrastructure to an economy cannot be overstated. Modern infrastructure facilities will also need to reflect the growing concern over climate change by doing detailed environmental impact assessment whenever and wherever new infrastructure is envisaged to be developed. Interestingly and unlike other regions of the world, Africa's poor infrastructure represents a unique business opportunity and a chance to adopt new approaches in the design and implementation of infrastructure facilities in the continent.

Infrastructure is key and critical in doing business anywhere in the world. Without good roads, a functioning rail system, an effective air transport system, and a speedy telephone and Internet systems—although cell phone and Internet services are growing rapidly and widely in Africa—there will be no meaningful business transactions in order, for example, to achieve an efficient and effective supply chain management. If there is no reliable water, an effective sanitation system, and electricity supply, businesses will not function continuously, efficiently and effectively and acquiring alternative sources of these resources add to operating costs that make the country less competitive and thus unable to effectively market products in the domestic and global markets.

Except for the Republic of South Africa, infrastructure is very poor in many African countries. The roads are in a deplorable state and congested, the rail system does not function well and is not reliable, and the telephone and air transport services are inadequate, within the countries and between the countries of Africa (Mbaku, 2004). Despite this appalling state of infrastructure in Africa, it is important to note that many African nations have realized the vital importance of the infrastructure in meaningful national development and are, with the assistance from China particularly, currently investing a lot of resources in infrastructure development but not enough to make an immediate impact (Wang 2008). A lot still needs to be done now and in the future.

There is therefore a great demand for resources to build new infrastructure and to rehabilitate existing infrastructure so that they can become positive contributors and bedrocks to wealth creation and to the eradication of poverty and to be structures that are critical for maintaining and sustaining a productive and viable economy. The UN Economic Commission for Africa (ERA, 2010) asserts that Africa should generally aim at achieving an investment ration/GDP of at least 35 percent to infrastructure, similar to the rates attained by East Asia countries that are growing phenomenally. Of particular importance, is focusing on the quality of investment in infrastructure and to increase infrastructure stock from 39 percent of that of other developing countries today by investing at least $31 billion annually for the foreseeable future, together with drastic improvements in the efficiencies of the existing infrastructure, in order to close the gap.

Without adequate infrastructure, African countries will not be able to harness the power of science and innovation to meet sustainable development objectives—such creating jobs and reducing poverty—and be competitive in international markets. Roads, for example, are critical for supporting rural development. It has been suggested too that increasing the stock of infrastructure by 1% in an emerging country context could add 1% to the level of GDP. But in some cases, the impact has been far greater: for example, the Mozal aluminum smelter investment in Mozambique not only doubled the country's exports and added 7% to GDP, but it also created many, new, and high value jobs. It also added new skills in the country (Juma, 2011)

14. CORRUPTION

A large literature exists to support the argument that corruption is one of the most important costs of doing business in Africa. Corruption is unofficial renting taking and bribe seeking from businesses mostly by corrupt government officials. Although corruption is a universal problem, appearing both in developed and developing countries, it is pervasive in most African economies. In fact, some scholars argue that it is the most important constraint to human development and progress in Africa (Hope et al., 2000). Despite massive injections of aid to Africa, corruption has hindered its effectiveness in development to lift the African peoples from debilitating poverty and under-development (Moyo, 2009).

Transparency International regularly gives the public corruption perception of over 150 countries around the world. Some African countries, particularly Nigeria, Kenya and Cameroon, are always perceived as some of the most corrupt countries in the world. In fact, Nigeria is usually perceived and described as the most corrupt country in Africa (TI Report, 2008).

Corruption is a tough issue to deal with in an African environment. It is almost culturally ingrained in the African mind and therefore it is persistent. But the regular assessment and country reports by Transparency International are helping African leaders to come to terms with corruption in the business and public affairs of their countries and its destructive effects are well known. Therefore, many African countries are coming up with institutional and legal frame-works to deal with the issue of corruption.

These changes require a shift in attitudes and beliefs from the general public, business and political leaders. Dealing with the debilitating effects of corruption on business is imperative if the bright future of Africa is to become a reality. Transparency International perception reports should be intensified and made at shorter regular intervals, say every six months. TI should get regular financial support, for its surveys, from the international community in order to carry out more intensive surveys with a wider reach and exposure to help Africa deal with corruption successfully.

The African governments must also make sure that their institutions and legal systems, to fight corruption, function efficiently and effectively to positively improve the perception of their countries as regards to corruption. Their success here will enable them to attract foreign investments that are necessary in creating wealth, in their countries, to eradicate poverty and deprivation.

Recent surveys, however, indicate that the corruption perceptions are changing positively as the African countries put in place institutional and legal frameworks to help them combat corruption hard and successfully. But the war is far from being won. More pressure and efforts are needed now and in the future to combat this debilitating monster in the African economies (Moyo, 2009; ERA, 2010; Juma, 2011).

15. LACK OF WELL-DEVELOPED AND LARGE INDIGENOUS CORPORATIONS IN AFRICA

Africa has not been able to create and develop many large and successful indigenous companies to leverage their governments in developing the continent. Large indigenous companies are a commonplace in other regions of the world such as Asia. Indigenous companies have a stake in the development and success of their countries and local communities (Khanna et al., 2005). Their local communities and countries are what the companies have to survive on and their launching pad to go global (Porter, 1990). And they are their fall back if things become difficult out there in the competitive and volatile global markets. Oftentimes, the indigenous companies can also act as economic stabilizers in turbulent times and generally promote national development in their regions.

Indigenous companies support job and wealth creation and can help in ensuring financial stability goals of their home countries. It is often and anecdotally said that the negative effects of the 1997 Asian financial crisis—and even the effects of the 2008/9 world economic meltdown—were considerably minimized in Asia by the presence and efforts of such large indigenous companies. In 1997, many of these companies continued earning foreign exchange during the crisis, which stabilized the local currencies faster than it could have happened without these foreign earnings by indigenous companies (Williamson, 1997).

Other than Japanese companies, Asia has other strong companies—some of which are now global—that started as family companies, with government support, such as the Chaebols of South Korea. Korean Chaebols are similar to the Japanese Keiretsu. Their differences are that Japanese Keiretsu is mostly inter-company owned. But, the Cheabols are mostly family owned. However, both have strong support from their governments particularly to go global and being competitive in global and domestic markets.

There are also the Business Houses of India, the Singapore Inc. of Singapore, and the National Champions of other Asian countries that include national companies from Malaysia, Thailand, and the Philippines (Williamson 1997; Khanna et al., 2005). The South Korean Chaebols include well-known companies like Samsung Electronics Company, KIA Motors, LG Electronics, and Hyundai Motor Corporation. The India Business Houses include Tata Group—which has recently designed and produced what is yet to be the smallest and cheapest car in the world—the Nano—and the Mahindra (Khanna et al., 2005).

Williamson (1997) asserts that in a world in which recourse to the law can be difficult and trust plays a pivotal role, the Asian companies prefer to rely on an interdependent network, often bolstered by crossing-shareholding and family or ethnic ties, than on impersonal markets. The companies do not only help with economic development in their regions, but they provide stiff competition to Multinational Corporations in the region and often force Multinational Corporations to develop business strategies that are supportive of the region's development. The indigenous companies, particularly the Korean Chaebols, also produce highly competitive products in the global markets.

As Williamson (1997) further states:

Many businesses venturing into Asia for the first time are surprised to find that their toughest competitors in the region are neither familiar Western rivals nor well-known Japanese companies, but they are the less well-known Asian companies based in other Asian countries. And Western businesses are changed by their Asian competitors' use of indigenous and unusually but highly effective set of strategies and tactics – unorthodox approaches that often turn textbook management thinking on its head.

The indigenous companies use these strategies and tactics to enter the market quickly and win market share and increase sales quickly. This competition is also helpful to the Asian governments and their nationals in accelerating development in their countries. Asian governments oftentimes support the indigenous companies in allocating to them the monopoly rights, preferential procurement awards, and financial support through credit arrangements.

He goes on to say "Asian governments commonly award monopoly rights, concessions, and protection to companies whose investment commitments are carefully aligned with national goals. Asian multinationals are keenly aware of the advantages of aligning their strategies with those of their host countries making multinationals to do the same" (Williamson, 1997).

As one CEO of a large indigenous Asian corporation says, "Western delegations keep coming here talking about free trade and opening up our markets as if this must be good for us. Frankly, we are not convinced. We have clear national goals to grow certain new strategic industries. Asian multinationals often have a better understanding of how to align their investments with those goals for the good of the region. And they have better capability to make and assemble products that are locally customized to meet local needs and augmenting local technologies" (Williamson, 1997).

African countries also need to support the development of indigenous corporations, not only to support and leverage the economic development of the African countries, but also to stabilize their financial markets in times of financial and economic crises. Indigenous companies could also attract foreign direct investments from multinationals - through strategic alliances, joint ventures, and franchises - because of the positive perceptions they create to multinationals as to the sustainability of the African markets. This appears to have happened in Asia, as to the safety and stability of the business environment in the region.

The success of indigenous African companies will create a sense of certainty, predictability, security, and safety of the business environment in which the indigenous corporations operate in their African countries. This can give assurances to foreign corporations that it is safe and profitable to invest and do business in Africa.

However, a few such big indigenous companies exist in Africa that can be models in the development of more indigenous companies in Africa. They include the South African Breweries and Beverages Company, whose headquarters are in London and registered in the London Stock Exchange. Currently, the company operates in 29 African countries. There are also several indigenous banks that operate regionally in Africa, even in countries where foreign banks based in Africa have never been like in the new nation of Southern Sudan - because of difficulties to operate profitably in these countries.

These banks include ECO Bank of ECOWAS, Kenya Commercial Bank of Kenya, Standard Bank of South Africa, Equity Bank of Kenya, and GT Bank and Diamond Bank both of Nigeria. Included in this group of pioneers, are African airlines such as the Kenya Airways, South African Airways, and Ethiopian Airways that connect Africa to the rest of the world.

These African companies and the flag carriers should be encouraged and supported to go more global too like the Asian giants have done so that they will be the African champions to support the development and globalization of Africa. The African airlines, in particular, can increase their global reach by focusing on the carriage to Africa and back of the African Diaspora—there are 40 million Africans in the Diaspora (Moyo, 2009)—in the various regions of the world including those in North America, Australia, and Europe.

For Africa to develop faster, particularly through the private sector, indigenous entrepreneurs and companies should not only be encouraged, but also supported with appropriate policies to make them grow to eventually go global as per Porter's (1990) competitive advantage of nations' model. The future of successfully doing business in African will largely depend on the global partnerships and success of the indigenous companies, as it is the case in Asia and other regions of the world.

16. NEGATIVE PERCEPTIONS OF THE AFRICAN IMAGE

Commenting on the persistence of poor African image in the world today, Mofadal (2010) asserts that it is a well known fact that Africa faces many challenges in its quest for a better life for its citizens as spelled out by the UN's Millennium Development Goals (MDGs). One of the biggest hurdles in Africa's road to development, albeit not recognized by many, is the continent's tarnished image that is a direct result of many factors; some are internal while others are external.

In spite of the various positive developments that have taken place in different parts of the continent in recent years, Africa's image is still that of a hopeless place. It is seen as a place that is riddled with disease, poverty, tribalism, poor governance, corruption, civil wars, and hunger. And increasingly it is a region known for persistent terrorist attacks of innocent people in countries like Nigeria and Kenya by Boko Aram and Ola-Shababu, respectively.

One of the biggest challenges in the quest for image change is that image is invisible. The bull of image cannot be grabbed from its horns. Image is imprinted in the unconsciousness of the person. This in turn affects one's decision whether he/she is a politician, businessman, journalist, activist, ordinary citizen, or an NGO official. A bad image makes the viewer see only one slice of the reality. He/she sees only the empty part of the cup. This is definitely true of the African image in the world today (Mofadal, 2010).

Rightly or wrongly, this negative image of Africa has also been maintained by the world media, opinion leaders, particularly those in the West, and church leaders from outside Africa. They see and treat Africa as a basket case, a charity case, a war torn continent with disease plagued countries, and a hunger ravaged continent. In fact, countries with low hunger indexes, in the Global Hunger Index by the World Food Program, are in Africa.

However, the 2009 global hunger index report—a survey published by the International Food Policy Research Unit of the World Food Program—reveals that the Congo DR has seen the steepest rise in hunger in the world since the 1990's followed by Burundi, the Comoros, Zimbabwe, Liberia, the Gambia, Sierra Leone, Somalia, and Swaziland in that order. The only other country, in the world, that is in this demeaning list is the isolated North Korea (WFP Report 2009).

The western media depicts Africa as an insecure, unpredictable, and dangerous place to live and do business. In a recent article in the New York Times, for example, the writer created an excessively inaccurate and exaggerated impression that Nairobi, Kenya, is a very dangerous city to children and western women! (Gettleman, 2009). He asserts that "Nairobi, Kenya's capital is a teeming city of have-nots and have-lots, so notorious for violent crime that it is often called "Nai-robbery." "But there is a new problem, or at least one that is causing new fear — kidnapping, and several recent attacks have been on children and Western women" (Gettleman, 2009). One wonders whether Nairobi is more violent than American cities like Chicago, Philadelphia, New York, and Los Angeles, to deserve this kind of negative publicity!

Furthermore, the western media reports Africa only when there is a negative incidence such as war, hunger, piracy in Somalia, displacement of populations for reasons of war, and rioting due to an electoral failure. But, they do not report, more aggressively as they do negative events, any positive development taking place in Africa like a successful election, developmental successes, and achievements that are being made daily by the African people, particularly their women entrepreneurs.

Nicholas Kristof (2012) adds that generations of Americans have learned to pity Africa. It is mainly seen as a quagmire of famine, poverty, and genocide, a destination only for a sybaritic safari or a masochistic aid mission. So here is another way to think of Africa: Africa is an economic dynamo of the 21st century. It is time to prepare for the African tiger economy. Six of the world's 10 fastest-growing economies between 2001 and 2010 were in Africa, according to The Economist Magazine. The International Monetary Fund says that between 2011 and 2015, African countries will account for 7 of the top 10 spots in the fasted growing economies in the world. Africa is not just a place for safaris or humanitarian aid. It is also a place to do business and make money.

The way many of the African Diaspora live and what they do, particularly in the USA, does not help the African image either. It oftentimes confirms what the Americans hear and read about Africa. Many of these people came to the USA with high but unmitigated expectations which were dashed because of unanticipated difficulties of doing anything worthwhile, in the USA, without being sufficiently endowed with good education and financial resources. Many of them dropped out of school because they could not afford to pay the high college and university fees prevailing in the USA. And they end up doing odd and lower rank jobs, particularly when they ran out of immigration status. In a lot of cases, they live in their ethnic communities so there is group think and little challenge among them which does not help matters particularly with their education. Some in these communities have been involved in serious crimes.

Of course, that is not to say that there are no successful Africans in the Diaspora. There are Africans in the Diaspora who are highly qualified professionals in many areas including lawyers, accountants, researchers, writers, teachers, engineers, medical doctors, nurses, management consultants, and university professors. These professionals are making huge contribution to the development of the countries in which they live and in turn make large remittances to Africa annually. For example, anecdotal data indicates that there are over 6,000 Nigerian medical doctors in the USA alone. But, the African Diaspora in these high level professions is a very small number out of over 40 million Africans in the Diaspora. The overwhelming majority have fallen on the way side and are under cover!

The negative perception of Africa is perpetuated further by the countless number of churches and charity organizations that run less than flattering commercials on Western television regarding hunger and poverty in Africa in order to raise money purportedly for hungry children in Africa. The imagery chosen for these adverts depicts African children as haggard, starving, dirty, and desperate. These images, while some may be true in some slums in Africa, are mostly exaggerated to evoke sympathy and interest to give money and most of the time they are the only images that many foreigners, particularly Americans and Europeans, have of Africa.

How attractive would the U.S. be, for business, for example, if the only images broadcast the world over was of the gang fights in Chicago, the ghettos in Philadelphia, Los Angeles, and other big cities? If the only news that came out of the U.S. was of the countless cases of pedophilia even by catholic priests and the regular murder of children in some cities. Some of these crimes exist at an alarming rate in the U.S today more so than in Africa. Such negative publicity will not project the U.S. to be the attractive and pulling country it is today. Crime, however, is not exclusive to the USA, but a global problem and wherever there is poverty and hunger. USA is a great country in countless other ways. Indeed, the same applies to Africa.

While poverty, slums, and hunger do exist in Africa, they are not the only reality of life in Africa and they are not exclusively African problems. Many truthful observers say, for example, that there are more hungry and poor people today in

India than anywhere else in the world. Therefore, it is not right that charity organizations and churches should choose to focus exclusively on the situation of hunger and poverty in Africa.

How about appealing for funds to support small-scale farmers and entrepreneurs? The image of farmers working hard, for example, in the beautiful and fertile highlands of Kenya is a reality and small businessmen and vibrant women consciously, enthusiastically, and robustly working hard in their small and well-stocked shops in Ghanaian, Senegalese, Nigerian, South African, Tanzanian, Zambian, Moroccan, Egyptian, and Rwandese cities and towns are another everyday reality in Africa. Why can't the well-oiled philanthropists like the Bill Clinton and Bill and Melinda Gates foundations change their models of operation to support and finance the development of small and microenterprises in Africa instead of supporting programs that destroy them – like a sad story described by Moyo (2009) on how provision of free mosquito nets made a mosquito net manufacturer in Senegal go out of business destroying fifty jobs in the process. Philanthropic programs to Africa are not sustainable and will not help Africa to grow. They can only help by supplementing the Africans' efforts.

Of course, the philanthropists are well intentioned, but their actions create a dependence syndrome. They destroy the development of entrepreneurs in Africa through their offerings of free mosquito nets and drugs for example. Why not support small businesses that manufacture nets to prosper and create jobs and be a sustainable source of nets? Why not support small pharmacies that store, market, and distribute drugs at a price and create jobs in the process? Why not support small-scale farmers with small irrigation projects to enable the farmers to sustainably grow their own food instead of the irregular food aid supply to Africa? A Chinese philosopher aptly and famously said once which is paraphrased here thus: "do not give me fish but teach me how to fish and I shall have and eat fish for ever instead of the only one day when you give me the fish."

There is also the case of celebrities who traverse the whole of Africa and the world treating Africans and their problems like little children who need an adult to help. Celebrities like Irish musician Bono and actor Angelina Jolie, while their intentions are good, end up painting a very bleak and negative picture of Africa in order to raise money purportedly for African causes such as hunger and disease. Their massages variously describe Africa as a basket case continent in need of a helping hand, or Africa as the poor continent in need of all the aid we can get!

These negative messages, sent far and wide by the celebrities, paint very bleak and depressing images of Africa and do not help Africa to prosper or be an attractive market for businesses, particularly in attracting the essential and desirable Foreign Direct Investments. There should be a complete paradigm shift in the actions of these well-intentioned philanthropists for Africa from charity to supporting African entrepreneurs in agriculture, commerce, and innovation to develop Africa; particularly the innovative, resourceful, and hard working African woman. Charity parse will never develop Africa. It will create a dependence syndrome. It is only the African themselves who can develop Africa, but of course, they will always need global friends, partners, and not philanthropist parse.

REFERENCES

Acemoglu, D., & Robinson, J. A. (2012). *Why nations fail: The origins of power, prosperity, and poverty*. New York: Crown Business.

AU. (2009). *Economic report on Africa 2010*. Addis Ababa, Ethiopia: AU Commission.

AUC. (2012). *AU strategic plan 2009-2012*. Addis Ababa, Ethiopia: AU Commission.

Benoni, C. (2009, December 14). I foresee 7.5 percent growth rates in Africa in 2010: African development bank (AFDB) president, Donald Kaberuka. *The East African*.

Bernstein, R., & Rasco, J. (2007, July 23). Africa, the final frontier. *Merrill Lynch Report*.

Butagira, T. (2012, March 24). Charities want Africa poor, says UK official. *Daily Nation*.

Clinton, W. J. (2011). *Back to work: Why we need smart government for a strong economy*. New York: Alfred A. Knopf.

Davidson, A. (2012, March 19). Why some countries go bust. *New York Times*.

Deng, F. M., & Zartman, W. I. (2002). *A strategic vision for Africa: The Kampala movement*. Washington, DC: The Brookings Institution.

Drucker, P. F. (1999). *Management challenges for the 21st century*. New York: Harper Business: An Imprint of HarperCollins Publishers.

EIU. (2009). African business and economic report. *The Economist Intelligence Unit*.

Friedman, T. L., & Mandelbaum, M. (2011). *That used to be us: How America fell behind in the world it invented and how we can come back*. New York: Farrar, Straus, and Giroux.

Gettleman, J. (2009, October 11). Easy money fuels rise in kidnappings in Kenya. *New York Times*.

Heifetz, R. (1994). *Leadership without easy answers*. Boston: Harvard University Press.

Heifetz, R. A., & Laurie, D. (2001, December). The work of leadership. *Harvard Business Review*. PMID:10174450.

Hope, K. R., & Chikulo, B. C. (2000). *Corruption and development in Africa: Lessons from country case studies*. London: Macmillan Press Limited.

Juma, C. (2011). *The new harvest: Agricultural innovation in Africa*. Oxford, UK: Oxford University Press.

Kamara, A. B., Bousrih, L., & Nyende, M. (2008). Growing a knowledge based economy: Evidence from public expenditure on education in Africa. *African Development Bank Economic Research working paper series*. Tunis, Tunisia: AFDB.

Karambu, I. (2012a, January 23). Kenya's growth rate to fall behind the other four East African states in the next two years: Quoting Mr. Wolfgang Fengler of the World Bank. *Daily Nation*.

Karambu, I. (2012b, February 8). Trade barriers costing Africa billions of dollars, says World Bank. *Daily Nation*.

Kempe, R. H. (1997). Development structures for Africa: The need for policy reform and good governance. *Journal of Opinion*, *25*(1).

Khanna, T., & Palepu, G. K. (2005, May). Strategies for emerging markets. *Harvard Business Review*. PMID:15938439.

Khanna, T., Palepu, G. K., & Sinha, J. (2005, June). Strategies that fit emerging markets. *Harvard Business Review*. PMID:15938439.

Khanna, T., & Pelepu, K. (1997, September-October). Why focused strategies maybe wrong for emerging markets. *Harvard Business Review*.

Kituyi, M. (2012a, January 28). A free trade road map for Africa, but who will keep their promise?. *Daily Nation*.

Kituyi, M. (2012b, June 30). Obama's strategy for Africa and the continent's reality. *Daily Nation*.

Kotler, J. P. (1990). *A force for change: How leadership differs from management*. New York: Free Press.

Kristof, N. D. (2010, June 30). Africa on the rise. *New York Times*.

Kristof, N. D. (2012, June 30). Africa on the rise. *New York Times*.

Mahajan, V. (2009). *Africa rising: How 900 million African consumers offer more than you think.* Amazon Kindle.

Mbaku, J. M. (1998). Improving African participation in the global economy: The role of economic freedoms. *Business and the Contemporary, 10*(2).

Mbaku, J. M. (2004). *Institutions and development in Africa.* Africa World Press.

McKeown, M. (2008). *The truth about innovation.* London: Prentice Hall.

Mkapa, B. W. (2009). *The role of the alumni in governance and institutional development in Africa: A public lecture at the inaugural of Makerere University Grand Alumni Re-Union.* Kampala, Uganda: Makerere University.

Mo, I. (2012). *Ibrahim African governance prize annual report, 2012.* London: Ibrahim Prize.

Mofadal, M. A. (2010, June 27). Africa faces major image problems. *Sunday Nation.*

Moyo, D. (2008). *A small price to pay: Financing Africa's infrastructure bill. Global Economics Paper No: 174.* New York: Goldman Sachs.

Moyo, D. (2009). *Dead aid: Why aid is not working and how there is a better way for Africa.* New York: Farrar, Straus, and Giroux.

Okoth, J. (2012, September 4). Experts warn insecurity could dim Africa's growth. *The Standard.*

Opanga, K. (2010, September 25). Millennium development goals must be achieved. *Daily Nation.*

Ortiz, J. (2010). The global environment through the SLEPT framework. *International Journal of Business and Globalization, 5*(4).

Ostby, G. (2004). *Horizontal inequalities and civil conflict.* Paper presented at the 13th Annual National Political Science Conference. Hurdalsjoen, Norway.

Page, J. (2008). Rowing against the current: The diversification challenge in Africa's resource-rich economies. *Global Economy Development Working Paper 29.* Washington, DC: Brookings Global Economy and Development.

Porter, M. E., & Kramer, M. R. (2011, January-February). Capitalism is under siege: Diminished trust in business is causing political leaders to set policies that sap economic growth: Business is caught in a vicious circle: The purpose of the corporation must be redefined around creating shared value. *Harvard Business Review.*

Prahalad, C. K., & Meshelkar, R. A. (2010, July-August). Innovation's holy grail. *Harvard Business Review*. PMID:20648874.

Sachs, J. (2005). *End of poverty: The economic possibilities for our times*. New York: Penguin Books.

Saltmarch, M. (2010, August 2). South Africa tries to scale up the industrial ladder. *New York Times*.

Ulimwengu. (2009). Tanzanians react to their monolithic leadership. *The EastAfrican*).

UNAIDS. (2006). *United Nations AIDS annual report*. Geneva, Switzerland: UNAIDS.

UNAIDS. (2008). *United Nations AIDS annual report*. Geneva, Switzerland: UNAIDS.

UNCTAD. (2003). *United Nations conference on trade and development annual report*. Geneva, Switzerland: UNCTAD.

United Nations. (2003). *Economic development in Africa: Trade performance and commodity dependence*. Geneva, Switzerland: UN.

Voegle, J. (2011, January 11). Agricultural and rural development, the World Bank. *New York Times*.

Williamson, P. J. (1997, September-October). Asia's new competitive game. *Harvard Business Review*.

Wood, A., & Kate, J. (2000). Why does Zimbabwe export manufactures and Uganda is not? *The Journal of Development Studies*, *37*(2). doi:10.1080/713600070.

World Bank. (1993). *The East Asian miracle: Economic growth and public policy*. New York: Oxford University Press.

World Bank. (2005). *Doing business in 2005: Removing obstacles to growth in the world*. Washington, DC: World Bank.

World Bank. (2007a). *Expanding the possible in Sub-Saharan Africa: How tertiary institutions can increase growth and competitiveness in Sub-Saharan Africa*. Washington, DC: The World Bank.

World Bank. (2009a). *Technology exports report*. Washington, DC: World Bank.

World Bank. (2009b). *Prospects for the global economy*. Washington, DC: World Bank.

World Bank. (2009c). *Remittances data, March revision*. Washington, DC: World Bank.

World Economic Forum. (2010-2011). *World competitive report 2010-2011*. Geneva, Switzerland: The World Economic Forum.

World Food Program. (2009). *World food program report*. Rome, Italy: WFP.

World Health Organization. (2006). *Annual report 2006*. Geneva, Switzerland: WHO.

Yoshino, Y. (2008). Domestic constraints, firm characteristics, and geographic diversification of firms-level manufacturing exports in Africa. *Policy Research Working Paper, 4575*. Washington, DC: The World Bank.

Chapter 10
Overcoming the Challenges of Doing Business in Africa

ABSTRACT

This chapter presents a framework and suggests specific strategies to eliminate or minimize the impact of the environmental micro-challenges when doing business in Africa. The minimization of these challenges will most likely attract increased Foreign Direct Investments to Africa. The chapter discusses twenty different policy and strategic initiatives that can make Africa an attractive business region. It also thoroughly explains how effective application of these strategies has helped other regions or countries with emerging economies such as China, India, and Brazil to grow phenomenally in the last three decades.

1. INTRODUCTION

Globally, doing business remains easiest in the high income economies of the Organization for Economic Co-operation and Development (OECD) and most difficult in Africa and South Asia (World Bank Doing Business Report, 2010). More than a billion African people, and particularly the over 900 million people, in 48 countries, in Sub-Saharan Africa, continue to present the world with its most formidable development challenges. Africa is supposedly home to 34 of the world's 48 poorest

DOI: 10.4018/978-1-4666-4570-7.ch010

countries. The average income, excluding the Republic of South Africa, Botswana, Mauritius, and Seychelles—some of the highest per capita income African countries—is only US$600 per person (ERA, 2010).

Of the 32 countries in the world with the lowest levels of human development index, 24 are in Africa, and few countries on the continent are on track to meeting many of the Millennium Development Goals (MDGs) (ERA, 2010). In contrast to other regions, in which poverty levels have declined dramatically over the past four decades, the number of poor people—living with less than US$2 a day—in Africa has increased. From 1981 to 2001—at the height of the World Bank and IMF imposed structural adjustments period—the number of Africans living in poverty almost doubled from 164 million to 314 million (Moyo, 2009).

Yet progress has been achieved since 2005, in crucial areas, and thus many scholars and commentators (Deng et al., 2002; Kamara et al., 2008), including the World Bank, have for example, called 2005 "the Year of Africa" (ERA, 2010). African economies are increasingly active in making political and institutional reforms to create a conducive, suitable, and supportive business climate. According to the ERA (2010), considerable progress has consistently occurred in the following areas:

- Gross National Income (GNI) per head has recently averaged over $1000 in Sub-Saharan Africa, ranging from slightly above $100 per head in Burundi to over $7000 in the Seychelles. This will reduce poverty. Further, pandemics such as HIV/AIDS, tuberculosis, and malaria are being contained and their negative effects on the Africa populations being permanently reversed (UNAIDS Report, 2009);
- Access to Information and Communication Technologies (ICT), while still limited, is increasing. In 2002, there were about 12 personal computers per thousand people in Sub-Saharan Africa, a rise of more than 30 percent from 2000. Internet use and mobile phone is rising rapidly in Africa, with a very high intensity penetration level (Mom Ibrahim Annual Report, 2009);
- Africa's political leadership is taking ownership of conflict resolution, good governance, and poverty reduction, at both national and regional levels, through initiatives like New Partnership for African Development (NEPAD), African Leadership Forum (ALF), and Conference on Security, Stability, Development, and Cooperation (CSSDCA) (Deng, et al., 2002);
- A substantial improvement in economic governance and ease of doing business has taken place across Africa since 2005 and African countries are some of the best reformers in the world today (ERA, 2010). And since the mid-1990s, the Gross Domestic Product (GDP) in 15 African countries grew consistently at a rate of over 6 percent per year. The African Development Bank (AFDB) anticipates that African GDP will grow at 7.5 percent in 2010 and 8.5 percent thereafter (Benoni, 2010);

- Several countries have increased exports by more than 10 percent per year - new exports in cut flowers, horticultural products, tourism, and manufactures—are reaching an increasingly a diverse set of markets in the world (ERA 2010);
- Skilled political leadership, international support, and Africans' desire for peace have led to real progress in addressing conflicts—Uganda, Rwanda, Liberia, Sierra Leon, Burundi, South Sudan, and Mozambique are examples of countries that have made real turnarounds and are now relatively stable, peaceful, and growing (Deng et al., 2002). In North Africa, the Arab Spring is changing the area and bringing democracy to countries that have been single man dictatorships for decades. However, Somalia has remained a thorn in the African flesh. The country is increasingly becoming ungovernable, insecure, and even developing a terrorist and piracy cultures.

Scholars, policy, and development experts—World Bank, IMF, African Development Bank, UNDP—and other commentators on African political and development issues (Juma, 2011; Mbaku, 2004; Deng et al., 2002) have suggested important steps and strategies that the African continent should take and strongly focus on, from many fronts, in order to successfully tackle its debilitating and inhibiting business challenges, hunger, and poverty now and in the future. These strategies include but not limited to the following:

2. EFFECTIVE LEADERSHIP AND GOVERNANCE IN THE AFRICAN ENVIRONMENT

African leaders should be focused and take pride in actually developing their countries and enriching and improving the living standards of their citizens. They should have a total approach incorporating all facets of national development—agriculture, infrastructure, education, healthcare, and sustainable in growth—and be responsible and accountable for their actions. They should accelerate regional integration and trade agreements to enlarge their market space and increase and enhance business opportunities for entrepreneurs and corporations to create employment. Employment will create wealth that is desirable to alleviate pervasive poverty and chronic hunger in the continent.

Furthermore, African leadership should develop new national constitutions and governance principles that anchor the bill of rights—that incorporates universal human rights and protocols—in their national constitutions and promote disciple in their actions. They should always adhere to their national constitutions in changing political leadership. African leadership should shun corruption in all its forms and lead to earn legitimacy nationally and globally. And they ensure national cohesion by minimizing horizontal inequalities in the country. They should create a sense of purpose and an energizing and unifying vision for their countries. They should inspire and mobilize their people to pursue the national vision to its logical conclusion.

In one of his regular presentations on leadership in East Africa, President Kagame of Rwanda has proposed three desirable and practical principles of effective leadership and strong governance in an African country like Rwanda:

In Rwanda, and as leaders, we have been guided by three main principles in this endeavor of building a stable and steadily growing country: firstly, acceptance of and building on our diversity that should no longer be seen as a threat but a powerful basis for mobilizing and uniting our citizens to build the country; secondly, consensus-building on what constitutes our common good and national interest; and thirdly, power-sharing in a participatory environment whereby the winner does not take all, but rather fosters the inclusion of all political expressions in national debate and execution of our country's development agenda and platform.

Deng et al. (2002) asserts that African leaders should legitimize themselves through responsible and accountable leadership that governs through universally acceptable norms. He explains that norms have always been important to the effective organization and functioning of human society. Norms are observed and they are broken, and both actions are the business of politics. The dramatic paradox is that, in the absence of a legislating body, norms are established and changed by the same process by which they are broken – by being tested. Like muscles, a norm is kept in shape by challenges and exercises.

Norms themselves, of course, do not prevail, since they are not actors; they are made to prevail by the actions of the parties who uphold them by sanctioning a violator in a range of ways – from words of condemnation and guidance to acts of opposition and punishment. If such reaction fails so often and the challenges to the norms succeed too often, the norm is defeated or changed. Therefore, African leaders should keep and govern by universally accepted norms—particularly by the consent of their people through regular and democratic elections—and not by the whims of the "big man" as it has happened in Africa for too long. However, this is changing although slowly. The events such as the Arab Spring in North Africa and regular democratic elections held in countries like Ghana, even in Nigeria, the purportedly most corrupt country in Africa, attest to these changes.

3. REFORMED INSTITUTIONS AND ECONOMIC FREEDOMS

Today, high levels of poverty, low quality of physical infrastructure, excessive external debt, political and bureaucratic corruption, political instability, destructive ethnic conflicts, and other ills that remain significant constraints to economic development characterize many African countries (Deng et al., 2002). Although researchers have explored the reasons for endemic poverty in Africa, few have examined the importance of institutions and lack of economic freedoms to underdevelopment in Africa (Mbaku, 1998, 2004). Unless African countries provide themselves with laws and institutions that guarantee economic freedom to promote economic development, poverty will remain pervasive. Africa will continue to operate on the periphery of the global economy. The continent will remain essentially a reservoir of raw materials for the industrialized economies and increasingly today for China and India. And a market for manufactured and high value products; a mercantile type of economic relationships under which Africa has considerably suffered for decades (Wild et al., 2008).

In their seminal book, *Why Nations Fail*, Daron Acemoglu and James Robinson (2012)—quoted in the New York Times by Thomas Friedman (2012)—argue that the key differentiators between successive and failed countries are institutions. Nations thrive when they develop "inclusive" political and economic institutions, and they fail when those institutions become "extractive" and concentrate power and opportunity in the hands of only a few. Inclusive economic institutions that enforce property rights, create a level playing field, and encourage investments in new technologies and skills are more conducive to economic growth than extractive economic institutions that are structured to extract resources from the many by the few (Friedman, 2012).

Inclusive economic institutions, are in turn supported by, and support, inclusive political institutions. The political institutions distribute political power widely in a pluralistic manner and are able to achieve political decentralization. They will also establish law and order, the foundations of secure property rights, and an inclusive market economy.

Conversely, extractive political institutions that concentrate power in the hands of a few reinforce extractive economic institutions to hold power. Countries thrive when they build inclusive political and economic institutions that unleash, empower, and protect the full potential of each citizen to be creative, to innovate, invest, and develop. The lesson of history is that you cannot get your economics right if you do not get your politics right.

Growth without the right political institutions is not sustainable because it doesn't foster the degree of "creative destruction" that is so vital for innovation and higher incomes. Sustained economic growth requires innovation, and innovation cannot be decoupled from creative destruction, which replaces the old with the new in the economic realm and also destabilizes established power relations in politics (Friedman, 2012).

Existing laws and institutions in many African countries are "extractive" and enhance the ability of bureaucrats and politicians to engage in corruption and opportunism to extract extra-legal income for them. They provide politicians and civil servants greater benefits for serving the interests and objectives of interest groups rather than those of the people. Poorly designed, weak and ineffective laws and institutions are real obstacles to economic development in Africa (Mbaku, 2004).

Furthermore, government activities in many African economies have discouraged the development of viable economic infrastructures, stunted the development of indigenous capitalism. They have slowed the emergency of a strong African entrepreneurial class that can provide "creative destruction" and as source of creativity and innovation in their economies. The government activities have created a large urban sector that depends primarily on the surplus extracted from a poorly funded and poorly organized agricultural sector; and generally impeded economic growth and development. They further impeded the agricultural sector from selling its production at market prices through the creation of poorly managed agricultural marketing boards. This further stunted economic development and enhanced poverty (Mbaku, 1998; Juma, 2011).

Although agriculture is considered central to African economies, it is always—institutionally and in policy terms—treated like other sectors, each with their own distinctive institutions and with little regard for their relationship with the rest of the economy. This view is reinforced by the traditional approach, which argues that economic transition occurs in stages that involve the transfer of capital from the agricultural sector to the industrial sector. Both the sector and stage approaches conceal the important linkages between agriculture and all the other sectors of the economy.

But, African governments, policy makers, and schools of thought should treat agriculture as having critical economic linkages and as a skill to be learned, valued, and improved upon from early childhood through adult careers instead of as a last resort for people who cannot find the resources to move to a city and get an industrial job. That way the agricultural sector will contribute greatly to African economic development to alleviate chronic hunger and poverty in the continent (Juma, 2011).

Scholars (Mbaku, 1998; Deng and William, 2002; Sachs, 2005) assert that there is much evidence to indicate that many perverse or poorly designed economic policies in the African countries, in the post-independence era, were not necessarily as a result of incompetence. But, they were deliberate efforts by opportunistic public servants and special interest groups to corruptly generate wealth for themselves, their families, and friends. These policies are reflected by poor plans, which were intentionally designed and implemented poorly by corrupt elites to exact rent from businesses and individuals. This condition pertains in most of Africa even today.

The main problem has not only been poor leadership and weak governance, but also weak and insufficient rules, non-viable institutions, and incentive systems—created by African elites—that have encouraged and rewarded, very generously, opportunistic behaviors. It is true that post-independent Africa has suffered significantly from such lack of competent, well-skilled, notionally focused, and disciplined bureaucrats and politicians. However, the overwhelming cause of Africa's poor economic performance and continued underdevelopment is the absence of efficient laws and institutions.

That is institutional arrangements that guarantee economic freedom and as a consequence, enhance productivity in the economy. The emphasis should be on providing each country with institutional arrangements that maximize the ability of entrepreneurs to engage in wealth creation and provide for peaceful co-existence of the several cleavages in each country (Mbaku, 2004).

To ensure sustainable growth and development in the African countries therefore requires the provision of the appropriate model of government. One that effectively constraints the ability of interest groups and the African elites to seize governmental structures and use them to plunder the economy for their benefit. And the government that creates and implements effective, inclusive, and sustainable institutional arrangements that include economic freedoms for long-term economic development of Africa.

According to Mbaku (1998, 2004), the basic elements of an economic freedom structure every African government should institute—as a prerequisite for effective and inclusive institutional and legal arrangements—in its economy could include the following elements:

- A stable and freely convertible currency with predictable value;
- Individual households and firms, not the government, to decide on what to produce in the economy and how, when, and where to produce it;
- Government should not be involved in discriminatory practices to provide benefits for some groups at the expense of others;
- Open the economy to international trade particularly and increasingly to regional trade;
- Ensure the presence of adequate and efficiently and effectively functioning legal, political, and economic institutions and to always protect property rights;
- Ensure a well-functioning, responsible, and fully accountable civil service;
- A well educated and health population;

- Efficiently and effectively provided public goods including infrastructure, education, healthcare, and strong environmental protection arrangements;
- An efficiently and effectively functioning banking system, capital market arrangements, and foreign exchange market.

In recent years, however, several African countries have been the greatest institutional reformers, in Africa and the world, in order to institute economic freedoms in their economies to accelerate economic development through the attraction of Foreign Direct Investments into their economies. These countries included Mauritius, South Africa, Botswana, Namibia, and Rwanda. In fact, Rwanda has been described as the fasted reformer in Africa and the world since 2005 in order to create conducive business climate to attract Foreign Direct Investment into the country (World Competitive Report, 2010-2011; World Bank Doing Business Report, 2010).

4. INCREASING COMPETITIVENESS IN THE AFRICAN ECONOMIES

In today's tough global economic environment, African governments—to grow and create employment to deal with poverty—should focus on increasing the competitive abilities and strengths of their products and services in the domestic and global markets. This will increase sales in these markets both in the short-run and the long-run (Juma 2011). The World Economic Forum has gleaned through the experiences of successfully exporting developed and emerging economies—particularly Germany, Singapore, and China, who have been leading world exporters in recent years—to develop a framework to define competitiveness, competitive economies, and pillars of competitiveness.

Competitive economies are those that have in place factors driving the productivity enhancements on which their present and future prosperity—through the successful marketing of their products and services in the domestic and global markets—is built. A competitiveness supporting economic environment can help national economies to support high incomes and ensure that the mechanisms enabling solid economic performance going into the future are in place (World Economic Forum Report, 2010-2011).

Competitiveness is the set of institutions, policies, and factors that determine the level of productivity of a country. The level of productivity, in turn, sets the sustainable level of prosperity that can be earned by the economy and produces higher levels of income of the country's citizens and a high return on the factors of production. Because the rates of return are the fundamental drivers of the growth rates of the economy, a more competitive economy is one that is likely to grow faster in the medium and long-run and bring prosperity to its citizens (World Economic Forum Report, 2010-2011).

According to the authors of the World Economic Report, 2010-2011, there are many determinants driving productivity and competitiveness—which they describe as the 12 pillars of competitiveness—in an economy and many of the pillars are nurtured by an economy itself. The African countries should ensure that they increasingly and intensively nurture these pillars in their economies as a means of producing competitive products and services for their domestic and global markets to create wealth to deal with poverty and hunger in the continent. The twelve pillars of global competitiveness are:

- Institutions, which are determined by the legal and administrative framework within which individuals, firms, and government interact to generate income and wealth in the economy;
- Infrastructure, which is critical for ensuring the efficient and effective functioning of the economy, as it is an important factor—in terms of its quality and size—determining the location of economic activities and the kinds of activities and sectors that can develop in a particular economy;
- Macroeconomics environment, which is the branch of economics in a country that focuses on the general features and processes that make up a national economy and the ways in which different segments of the economy—interest rates, inflation, fiscal balances, exchange rates, and external balances—are connected and interact and/or influence each other to stimulate the growth of the economy in terms of GDP growth. The stability of the macroeconomics environment is important for business and, therefore, it is important and vitally necessary for the overall competitiveness of an economy;
- Health and primary education, which is that health and basic education are critical and essential in economic development and in initiating systems that are necessary to improve productivity that is essential in competitive economies;
- Higher education and training, which is essential in introducing new technologies to enhance productivity and reduction of cost of production leading to the competitiveness of products and services both in the domestic and global markets;
- Goods market efficiency, which is countries with efficient goods markets are well positioned to produce the right mix of goods and services given their supply-and-demand conditions, as well as to ensure that these goods and services can be most efficiently and effectively traded in the economy and in global markets;

- Labor market efficiency, which is the criticality of the efficiency and flexibility of labor to reduce labor costs and essential equity in the business environment between women and men;
- Financial market development, which is the central role of a sound and well-functioning financial sector plays to allocate financial resources to the most productive and efficient sectors of the economy to promote fast economic development through productivity enhancement;
- Technological readiness, which is the increasing technology applications in firms' operations in order to make them efficient and effective in order for them to successfully compete and prosper. Technological readiness is measuring the agility with which the economy adopts existing and new technologies to enhance the productivity of industries, with its specific emphasis on its capacity to fully leverage Information and Communication Technologies (ICT);
- Market size, which means that the size of the market affects productivity since large markets allow firms to exploit economies of scale. The size of the market, in this case, includes export markets. There is vast empirical evidence showing that trade openness is positively associated with growth and productivity improvement, especially for countries with small domestic markets;
- Business sophistication, which means that business sophistication, is conducive to higher efficiency in the production of goods and services. This leads, in turn, to increased productivity, thus enhancing a nation's competitiveness in global and domestic markets. Business sophistication concerns the quality of a country's overall business networks as well as the quality of individual firms' operations and strategies;
- Innovation, which means that as the other pillars run into diminishing returns in production in an economy, there is need for innovation, as a pillar, to boost productivity and competitiveness. Innovation is the ability to creatively develop and apply new ideas into business operations in order to improve and increase productivity of factors of production and thus improving the quality and cost of products and services hence their increased competitiveness in domestic and global markets.

President Clinton (2011) has also suggested and essentially crystallized what he thinks are key functions of an effective government in the globalized world that will ensure the competitiveness of its firms in the global markets. He asserts thus: "I think the role of government is to give people the tools and create the conditions to make the most of out of our lives. Governments should empower us to do things we need or want to do that we can only do together by pooling our resources and spending them in large enough amounts to achieve the desired objectives."

Therefore, the most competitive and successful nations in the twenty-first century have both a strong economy and a strong and effective government. Here is a list of the functions of a successful and strong government with globally competitive corporations:

1. *National security*, including the military, intelligence agencies, diplomatic efforts and development assistance, homeland defense, federal law enforcement, border control, natural-disaster response, and the area most recently added to the list by the Pentagon and CIA, combating climate change.
2. *Assistance to those otherwise unable to fully support themselves and to provide a decent retirement for seniors*, including Medicaid, Medicare, and Social Security, aid for the disabled, food stamps, unemployment benefits, nutrition aid for newborns and mothers, and public housing.
3. *Equal access to opportunity*, including federal aid to education for low-income and disabled students, the HOPE Scholarship tax credits for college tuition costs, the student loan program, Pell Grants, work-study-payments, and job-training assistance.
4. *Economic development*, including trade agreements, financing for businesses to enter new markets; incentives to create new businesses and jobs in advanced manufacturing, clean energy, energy efficiency, and other high-growth areas; investments in basic research and development and incentives for private research and development to be done in the United States; an adequate minimum wage and support for work and childrearing, including the Family and Medical Leave Law and the child tax credit; Small Business Administration – guaranteed, microcredit, and community development loans to promising businesses that would otherwise be shut out of credit markets; financing and other support to help companies sell products made in America in other countries; and incentives to invest in areas of high unemployment and low incomes.
5. *Oversight of financial markets and institutions* to ensure transparency and honest dealing, competition, and consumer choice and to limit leverage to avoid future collapses and bailouts.
6. *Protection and advancement of public interests the market can't fix,* including clean air, clean water, safe food, safe transportation, safe workplaces, civil rights, access to affordable health care, and preservation of natural resources for the common good, including national monuments, and national forests.
7. *Providing investments,* through tax or fee revenue, for projects we all need when the costs are too great or the cost recovery period too long for the private sector to finance, including highways, airports, rails, accelerated broadband

connections, a national electric grid, and critical research and development in areas from space to advanced materials to nanotechnology and biotechnology to clean energy.

8. *A revenue collection system,* to collect taxes and issue credits and deductions deemed by congress to be in the national interest, including tax deductions for home mortgage payments, charitable giving, health-care payments, children, and many business expenses and deductions.

4.1. Clusters and Global African Competitiveness

Introduction: Porter (1998) has succinctly argued for the absolute importance of the formation of economic and industrial clusters as sources of sustainable competitive advantage and global competitiveness of nations. African nations can encourage and support the formation of economic and industrial clusters in their economies to enhance their global competitiveness. A framework for the development of clusters exists in many African countries today in the "Export Processing Zones" that they use to produce products, such as textiles, for exports under such schemes as the AGOA program.

Porter (1998), quoted herein extensively, asserts thus about the importance of clusters in an economy or country: Paradoxically, the enduring competitive advantages in a global economy lie increasingly in local things – knowledge, relationships, and motivation that distant rivals cannot match. Now that companies can source capital; goods, information, and technology from around the world, often with the click of a mouse, much of the conventional wisdom about how companies and nations compete needs to be overhauled. In theory, more open global markets and faster transportation and communication should diminish the role of location in competition.

After all, anything that can he efficiently sourced from a distance through global markets and corporate networks is available to any company and therefore is essentially nullified as a source of competitive advantage. However, if location matters less, why, then, is it true that the odds of finding an excellent mutual-fund company in Boston are much higher than in most any other place in the world? Why could the same be said of textile-related companies in North Carolina and South Carolina, of high-performance auto companies in southern Germany, or of fashion shoe companies in northern Italy?

Today's economic map of the world is dominated by what Porter (1998) calls *clusters:* critical masses—in one place—of unusual competitive success in particular fields. Clusters are a striking feature of virtually every national, regional, state, and even metropolitan economy, especially in more economically advanced nations. Silicon Valley and Hollywood may be the world's best-known clusters.

Clusters are not unique, however; they are highly typical-and there-in lie a paradox: the enduring competitive advantages in a global economy lie increasingly in local things—knowledge, relationships, motivation—that distant rivals cannot match.

Although location remains fundamental to competition, its role today differs vastly from a generation ago. In an era when competition was driven heavily by input costs, locations with some important endowment—a natural harbor, for example, or a supply of cheap labor—often enjoyed a *comparative advantage* that was both competitively decisive and persistent over time. Competition in today's economy is far more dynamic. Companies can mitigate many input-cost disadvantages through global sourcing, rendering the old notion of comparative advantage less relevant and competitive success in so many fields are geographically concentrated – whether it's entertainment in Hollywood, finance on Wall Street, or consumer electronics in Japan.

Clusters affect competitiveness within countries as well as across national borders. Therefore, they lead to new agendas for all business executives not just those who compete globally. More broadly, clusters represent a new way of thinking about location, challenging much of the conventional wisdom about bow companies should be configured, how institutions such as universities can contribute to competitive success, and bow governments can promote economic development and prosperity for its people.

What is a cluster? Clusters are geographic concentrations of interconnected companies and institutions in a particular field. Clusters encompass an array of linked industries and other entities important to competition. They include, for example, suppliers of specialized inputs such as components, machinery, and services, and providers of specialized infrastructure. Clusters also often extend downstream to channels and customers and laterally to manufacturers of complementary products and to companies in industries related by skills, technologies, or common inputs. Finally, many clusters include governmental and other institutions—such as universities, standards-setting agencies, think tanks, vocational training providers, and trade associations—that provide specialized training, education, information, research, and technical support.

The California wine cluster, for example, is an extensive complement of industries supporting both wine making and grape growing industries. It includes suppliers of grape stock, irrigation and harvesting equipment, barrels, and labels; specialized public relations and advertising firms; and numerous wine publications aimed at consumers.

Clusters affect competition in three broad ways: first, by increasing the productivity of companies based in the area; second, by driving the direction and pace of innovation, which underpins future productivity growth; and third, by stimulating the formation of new businesses, which expands and strengthens the cluster itself. A cluster allows each member to benefit from these developments as *if* it had greater scale or *as if* it had joined with others formally - without requiring it to sacrifice its flexibility.

Clusters and Productivity: Being part of a cluster allows companies to operate more productively in sourcing inputs; accessing information, technology, and needed institutions; coordinating with related companies; and measuring and motivating improvement.

Better Access to Employees and Suppliers: Companies in vibrant clusters can tap into an existing pool of specialized and experienced employees, thereby lowering their search and transaction costs in recruiting and even training. Because a cluster signals opportunity and reduces the risk of relocation for employees, it can also be easier to attract talented people from other locations, a decisive advantage in some industries. A well-developed cluster also provides an efficient means of obtaining other important inputs. Such a cluster offers a deep and specialized supplier base.

Sourcing locally instead of from distant suppliers lowers transaction costs and even overall material costs. It minimizes the need for inventory, eliminates importing costs and delays, and-because local reputation is important- lowers the risk that suppliers will overprice or renege on commitments. Proximity improves communications and makes it easier for suppliers to provide ancillary or support services such as installation and debugging. Other things being equal, then, local outsourcing is a better solution than distant outsourcing, especially for advanced and specialized inputs involving embedded technology, information, and service content.

Formal alliances with distant suppliers can mitigate some of the disadvantages of distant outsourcing. But all formal alliances involve their own complex bargaining and governance problems and can inhibit a company's flexibility. The close, informal relationships possible among companies in a cluster are often a superior arrangement. In many cases, clusters are also a better alternative to vertical integration. Compared with in-house units, outside specialists are often more cost effective and responsive, not only in component production but also in services such as training. Although extensive vertical integration may have once been the norm, a fast-changing environment can render vertical integration inefficient, ineffective, and inflexible.

Even when some inputs are best sourced from a distance, clusters offer advantages. Suppliers trying to penetrate a large, concentrated market will price more aggressively, knowing that as they do so they can realize efficiencies in marketing, economies of scale, and in service.

Working against a cluster's advantages in assembling resources is the possibility that competition will render them more expensive and scarce. But companies do have the alternative of outsourcing many inputs from other locations, which tends to limit potential cost penalties. More important, clusters increase not only the demand for specialized inputs but also their supply.

Access to Specialized Information: Extensive market, technical, and competitive information accumulates within a cluster, and members have preferred access to it. In addition, personal relationships and community ties foster trust and facilitate the flow of information. These conditions make information more transferable.

*Complementarities: A h*ost of linkages among cluster members results in a whole greater than the sum of its parts. In a typical tourism cluster, for example, the quality of a visitor's experience depends not only on the appeal of the primary attraction but also on the quality and efficiency of complementary businesses such as hotels, restaurants, shopping outlets, and transportation facilities. Because members of the cluster are mutually dependent, good performance by one can boost the success of the others and force them too to act productively and beneficial to others.

Complementarities come in many forms. The most obvious is when products complement one another in meeting customers' needs, as the tourism example illustrates. Another form is the coordination of activities across companies to optimize their collective productivity. In wood products, for instance, the efficiency of sawmills depends on a reliable supply of high-quality timber and the ability to put all the timber to use-in furniture (highest quality), pallets and boxes (lower quality), or wood chips (lowest quality). In the early 1990s, Portuguese sawmills suffered from poor timber quality because local landowners did not invest in timber management. Hence most timber was processed for use in pallets and boxes, a lower-value use that limited the price paid to landowners. Substantial improvement in productivity was possible, but only if several parts of the cluster changed simultaneously.

Logging operations, for example, had to modify cutting and sorting procedures, while sawmills had to develop the capacity to process wood in more sophisticated ways. Coordination to develop standard wood classifications and measures was an important enabling step. Geographically dispersed companies are less likely to recognize and capture such linkages. Other complementarities arise in marketing. A cluster frequently enhances the reputation of a location.

A few-Hollywood's entertainment cluster and High Point, North Carolina's household -furniture cluster are well known. Others are less familiar, such as golf equipment in Carlsbad, California, and optics in Phoenix, Arizona. A relatively small number of clusters usually account for a major share of the economy within a geographic area as well as for an overwhelming share of its economic activity that is "exported" to other locations. Exporting clusters—those clusters that export products or make investments to compete outside the local area—are the primary source of an area's economic growth and prosperity over the long run. The demand for local industries is inherently limited by the size of the local market, but exporting clusters can grow far beyond that limit.

Location in a particular field, making it more likely that buyers will turn to a vendor based there. Italy's strong reputation for fashion and design, for example, benefits companies involved in leather goods, footwear, apparel, and accessories. Beyond reputation, cluster members often profit from a variety of joint marketing mechanisms, such as company referrals, trade fairs, trade magazines, and marketing delegations.

Finally, complementarities can make buying from a cluster more attractive for customers. Visiting buyers can see many vendors in a single trip. They also may perceive their buying risk to be lower because one location provides alternative suppliers. That allows them to multisource or to switch vendors if the need arises. Hong Kong thrives as a source of fashion apparel in part for this reason.

Access to Institutions and Public Goods: Investments made by government or other public institutions—such as public spending for specialized infrastructure or educational programs—can enhance a company's productivity. The ability to recruit employees trained at local programs, for example, lowers the cost of internal training. Other quasi-public goods, such as the cluster's information and technology pools and its reputation, arise as natural by-products of competition.

It is not just governments that create public goods that enhance productivity in the private sector. Investments by companies—in training programs, infrastructure, quality centers, testing laboratories, and so on—also contribute to increased productivity. Such private investments are often made collectively because cluster participants recognize the potential for productive benefits.

Better Motivation and Measurement: Local rivalry is highly motivating. Peer pressure amplifies competitive pressure within a cluster, even among noncompeting or indirectly competing companies. Pride and the desire to look good in the local community spur executives to attempt to outdo one another. Clusters also often make it easier to measure and compare performances because local rivals share general circumstances—for example, labor costs and local market access—and they perform similar activities. Companies within clusters typically have intimate knowledge of their suppliers' costs. Managers are able to compare costs and employees' performance with other local companies. Additionally, financial institutions can accumulate knowledge about the cluster that can be used to monitor performance.

Clusters and Innovation: In addition to enhancing productivity, clusters play a vital role in a company's ongoing ability to innovate. Some of the same characteristics that enhance current productivity have an even more dramatic effect on innovation and productivity growth. Because sophisticated buyers are often part of a cluster, companies inside clusters usually have a better window on the market than isolated competitors do.

Computer companies based in Silicon Valley and Austin, Texas, for example, plug into customer needs and trends with a speed difficult to match by companies located elsewhere. The ongoing relationships with other entities within the cluster also help companies to learn early about evolving technology, component and machinery availability, service and marketing concepts, and so on. Such learning is facilitated by the ease of making site visits and frequent face-to-face contact.

Clusters do more than make opportunities for innovation more visible. They also provide the capacity and the flexibility to act rapidly. A company within a cluster often can source what it needs to implement innovations more quickly. Local suppliers and partners can and do get closely involved in the innovation process, thus ensuring a better match with customers' requirements.

Companies within a cluster can experiment at lower cost and can delay large commitments until they are more assured that a given innovation will pan out. In contrast, a company relying on distant suppliers faces greater challenges in every activity it coordinates with other organizations—in contracting, for example, or securing delivery or obtaining associated technical and service support. Innovation can be even harder in vertically integrated companies, especially in those that face difficult trade-offs if the innovation erodes the value of in-house assets or if current products or processes must he maintained while new ones are developed.

Reinforcing the other advantages for innovation is the sheer pressure—competitive pressure, peer pressure, constant comparison—that occurs in a cluster. Executives vie with one another to set their companies apart. For all these reasons, clusters can remain centers of innovation for decades and thus continually improving productivity and competition.

Clusters and New Business Formation: It is not surprising, then, that many new companies grow up within an existing cluster rather than at isolated locations. New suppliers, for example, proliferate within a cluster because a concentrated customer base lowers their risks and makes it easier for them to spot market opportunities. Moreover, because developed clusters comprise related industries that normally draw on common or very similar inputs, suppliers enjoy expanded opportunities.

Clusters are conducive to new business formation for a variety of reasons. Individuals working within a cluster can more easily perceive gaps in products or services around which they can build businesses. Beyond that, barriers to entry are lower than elsewhere. Needed assets, skills, inputs, and staff are often readily available at the cluster location, waiting to be assembled into a new enterprise. Local financial institutions and investors, already familiar with the cluster, may require a lower risk premium on capital. In addition, the cluster often presents a significant local market, and an entrepreneur may benefit from established relationships. All of these factors reduce the perceived risks of entry – and of exit, should the enterprise fails.

The formation of new businesses within a cluster is part of a positive feedback loop. An expanded cluster amplifies all the benefits described herein, and it increases the collective pool of competitive resources, which benefits all the cluster's members. The net result is that companies in the cluster advance faster relative to rivals at other locations.

Poor countries, like many of the African countries, lack well-developed clusters; they try to compete in the world market with cheap labor and natural resources. To move beyond this stage, the development of well-functioning and productive clusters is essentially important. Clusters become an especially controlling factor for countries moving from a middle-income to an advanced economy. Even in high-wage economies, however, the need for cluster upgrading is constant. The wealthier the economy, the more it will require innovation to support rising wages and to replace jobs eliminated by improvements in efficiency and the migration of standard production to low-cost areas.

Promoting and developing cluster formation in developing economies, like the African economies, means starting at the most basic level. Policymakers must first address the foundations: identifying areas of cluster location in the economy, improving education and skill levels, building capacity in technology, opening access to capital markets, and improving institutions. Over time, additional investment in more cluster-specific assets is necessary.

Government policies in developing economies often unwittingly work against cluster formation. Restrictions on industrial location and subsidies to invest in distressed areas, for example, can disperse companies artificially. Protecting local companies from competition leads to excessive vertical integration and blunts pressure for innovation that retards cluster development. African economies should devise cluster development policies in order to develop clusters in various areas in the country. Moreover, many African countries have in place facilities—the economic zones already existing in many African countries—to enable them develop successful clusters that will enhance their competitiveness in global markets.

5. ECONOMIC GROWTH

Achieving the Millennium Development Goals requires still broader and faster progress and a sharpened focus on economic development. Historically, African growth has not been sufficient to reduce poverty in Africa substantially. Despite progress in some countries, overall growth in Africa has averaged about 3 percent over the last two decades, compared to the 5 percent needed to keep the number of poor people from rising and the 7 percent or over is needed to achieve the MDG goal of halving poverty by 2015 (UN Report, 2008 and ERA, 2010).

However, the African Development Bank estimates that the African economies will grow at 7.5 percent in 2010 and 8.5 percent there-after; rather ambitious growth rates (Benoni, 2010). Still, it is possible Africa can achieve these high growth rates with efficient and effective economic management of its natural resources, increased participation in international trade, and greater regional integration in Africa (ERA. 2010). Regional integration expands markets for products and services leading to increased productivity and employment creation in the countries involved in the regional integration process. Regional integration can also expand employment opportunities as it makes it easier for people to move from one country to another for work and even earn better wages thus improving the living standards of the people in the region (Mbaku, 1998).

6. INTERNATIONAL TRADE

Low economic growth in Africa is closely linked with Africa's poor international and regional trade performance (Ghemawat, 2005). African's trade has remained highly volatile and pro-cyclical and continues to be largely determined by global economic developments. This is because of its reliance on low value agricultural products and mined minerals. From 1970 until the end of the 1990s, Africa's share of world trade dropped from 3.5 percent to 1.5 percent. That decline translates to an amount equivalent to one-fifth of the GDP of Sub-Saharan Africa, or about $70 billion annually, five times the level of development assistance during the period (Moyo 2009). However, it grew again in 2000s reaching 3.5 percent in 2008 when African merchandise trade stood at $558 billion in imports and $485 billion in exports (ERA, 2010).

The continent's merchandise trade remains undiversified, both in portfolio mix and destination. Agriculture, mining and fuel products constitute at least 80 percent of the exports. Most of these exports go to Europe and North America even though there has been a discernible shift towards Asia, especially China and India (ERA, 2010).

International trade in services has been one of the most robust areas of growth for most economies of the world spurred by rapid globalization. Unfortunately, and despite the promise that the trade holds in services, particularly in quick creation of high quality jobs, Africa's share of the global services trade has lagged behind merchandise trade. Its share of global services trade has been overtaken by merchandise trade. In 2007, for example, the continent's total services trade reached $174 billion; $76 billion being exports. There is a lot of room in export trade in services, particularly areas like tourism—where Africa has a competitive advantage—to create high value jobs to reduce poverty (ERA, 2010).

To sustain a broad-based export drive, Africa needs more efficient ports, smoother customs administration and processes, institutional and legal reforms to improve business climate, and a rehabilitated infrastructure particularly roads and railroads. Additionally, any strategy to accelerate international trade must embrace agriculture, which accounts for 70 percent of Africa's labor force and 40 percent of its exports. As mentioned earlier, expanding the contribution that international trade can make to growth in Africa also depends on effective regional integration.

African economies remain small and fragmented, with intraregional trade accounting for only about 10 percent of Africa's total trade (Wild et al, 2008 and ERA, 2010). "Open regionalism"—using regional solutions to integrate more fully into global markets—is needed to support national efforts to boost trade and economic development to eradicate pervasive poverty (Ghemawat, 2005) and also expand markets for firms to do business in Africa and thus make a desired contribution to the development of the African economies to create employment and thus deal with pervasive poverty in Africa.

7. PRIVATE SECTOR GROWTH

Africa's private sector—too long marginalized—must be given the space it needs to realize its potential as an engine for growth and job creation. The private sector includes not only a handful of large corporations involved in the mining and farming industries, but the full array of private actors in the economy. They include small enterprises, the service sector operators, and small agricultural farms in the rural areas where the largest share of the African population earns its living.

Of a total US$135 billion of Foreign Direct Investment (FDI) in 2003, only US$20.9 billion went to Africa, and more than half of that went to only three major oil-exporting countries in Sub-Saharan Africa—Nigeria, Angola, and Sudan—and oil, gas, and phosphates producers in North Africa. The FDI's into Africa were US$ 87 billion in 2008 and still the investments were concentrated in the extractive industry with 15 countries leading in this industry receiving almost 88 percent of the investment (ERA, 2010).

The challenge is to raise the capacity of African countries to attract and make good and diversified use of private investors, large and small, foreign and domestic. These investments will in turn require improvements in education, healthcare, infrastructure, elimination of institutional voids, and improved political leadership and governance. The investments will also need the application of the concept of "Smart Regulation" by African governments in the support and management of businesses in their countries (Global Competitive Report 2008-2009).

"Smart Regulation," as described in the world competitive report, is a basic concept applied to many regulatory programs that are critical to the country's competitiveness. Canada, for example, set up an External Advisory Committee on Smart Regulation (EACSR) in May 2003 to modernize the regulatory system to support an innovative and dynamic economy. United Kingdom also established Better Regulation Executive (BRE) in May 2005 to challenge existing and new legislations and simplify, improve, and even scrap existing inappropriate regulations. Singapore formed a Smart Regulation Committee (SRC) in December 2005 to improve the knowledge, awareness, and practices of regulations across the public service, too, to enhance the ability to attract foreign direct investments to Singapore more than to China (World Competitive Report, 2008-2009).

Smart Regulation is not about regulating less or more. Smart Regulations are bolts and nuts of effective independent-self-governing. It is about governments working better to serve the interests of its people and businesses: better protection, lower costs, faster and more stable and predictable regulatory processes, less overlap and duplication, more rapid alignment with global best practices and greater transparency and accountability. It means efficiency, competitiveness, and effectiveness in economic management of the economy (Grabosky 1999). It is minimizing institutional voids in an economy to enhance the business and investment climate in order to attract foreign direct investments and local entrepreneurs to the various sectors of the economy to create jobs and eliminate poverty in Africa (Mbaku 2004).

It is, therefore, not surprising, that those economies that rank best, in the World Bank's Doing Business report have instituted "Smart Regulation" ideas. They are also among the most competitive countries around the globe. In fact, 19 out of the 25 best performing economies from the World Bank's Doing Business 2008 report and 17 from the 2009 report and ranked among the 25 most competitive economies in the Global Competitiveness Report 2008-2009 are countries that have instituted smart regulations of one form or another (World Competitive Report, 2010). It is imperative, therefore, that African countries develop their form of "Smart Regulation" framework that takes into consideration of their political and economic circumstances.

8. SHARED GROWTH STRATEGIES

Economic and private sector growths alone, however, are not sufficient to reduce poverty in Africa. The growth must be fairly and equitably shared, among all segments of society in the country, to reduce income inequality. In Africa, the fortunes of the poor have changed over time and across countries, depending on the pattern of growth and external shocks. In Ethiopia and Mali, for example, the growth of household consumption by the bottom 20 percent of the population lagged behind the African mean consumption between 1981 and 2001. During this same period, in Madagascar and Ghana, consumption by the poorest 20 percent increased at a rate greater than the mean in some years and less in others (Page, 2008).

A strategy of shared growth that invests in the poor to help them to contribute to and benefit from the growth process is needed. There is an overwhelming need to develop and nurture the middle class too. The middle class enhances business growth and economic development generally in any country. America and other western economies are strong and sophisticated markets that they are today—with 70 percent of the American economy being household expenditure—because of their large and economically strong middle class population. Many democratic governments always try to deliberately nurture this economic class through a variety of fiscal and monetary policies, although many governments have difficulties to do so lately because of fiscal constraints resulting mostly from the 2008/9 world economic meltdown (ERA, 2010). Governments have been affected differently by the meltdown particularly the Euro zone countries; effects being most severe and pronounced in Ireland, Portugal, Greece, Spain, and Italy.

Policies that generate more widely shared prosperity lead to stronger and more sustainable economic growth—and that is good for everyone. The rich are better off with a smaller percentage of a fast-growing economy than a larger share of an economy that is barely moving and the poor have income to spend to stimulate the economy further. Consumer spending is one of the most important and critical engines of economic growth in any economy (Reich, 2010).

To minimize income consolidation at the top 10 percent and to have more widely shared prosperity in a country, Reich (2010) has suggested several strategies to achieve a fair income distribution in an economy. He asserts that in a country like the USA, for example, have no income tax for people earning up $ 20, 000 or minimum wage per annum and require increase of tax by several percentage points for people earning $ 250,000 and more. Secondly, ensure quantity and quality of primary and secondary education for all citizens that is subsidized by the government. Thirdly, have free university education; in return, graduates would then be required to pay back at 10 percent, annually, of their first 10 years income of full-time employment. Fourthly, have "earning insurance" to cover workers who lose their jobs for a period of more than two years. And lastly, regularly retrain workers so that they are current to the job needs in the market and ensure that they have adequate healthcare cover all the time.

In this regard, the New York Times in its April 10· 2012 editorials, when commenting on President Obama's tax reform and economic strategy in order to share growth equitably, asserted thus:

The discussion of inequality must not end up with a debate on fair taxes. To ensure that the benefits of economic growth are shared among all Americans, Washington must do a lot more to strengthen the institutions that foster broad prosperity. Those institutions include quality public education, infrastructure, universal healthcare, Social Security, affirmative action, financial regulation, and equitable minimum wage.

These institutional actions are equally important for African development and equitable sharing of benefit of growth.

9. STRATEGIES FOR POVERTY ERADICATION IN AFRICA

Poverty is the inability to afford the minimum survival requirements of living necessary—that is living on less than US$ 1.25 a day measured by a country's GDP per capita income—to afford minimum standards of food, clothing, education, healthcare, and shelter (ERA 2010). Poverty is *absolute poverty* when it quantifies the number of people who live below a fixed real poverty threshold like under US$1.25 per day as specified by the World Bank and IMF. It is a level of poverty defined in terms of the minimal requirements—below US$ 1.25 per day—necessary to afford minimal standards of food, clothing, health care, education, and shelter. Poverty is relative *poverty when it* is defined as being below some relative threshold. For example, the statement that "households with an accumulated income less than 60% of the median income are living in poverty" uses a relative measure to define poverty (AER, 2010).

According to AER (2010), poverty in Africa is substantially higher and more highly feminized than in many other developing regions of the world. The share of the population living below the US$1.25 a day threshold is as high today, at 50 percent, as it was in the 1980s before the poverty inducing structural adjustment programs by the World Bank and IMF were introduced (Moyo 2009). The poverty levels in Africa have remained stagnant despite significant improvements in growth in Africa since the beginning of the 21st century.

Therefore, to deal with poverty in Africa will require economic development strategies that strengthen the growth-employment nexus for poverty reduction. Employment is the key channel through which economic growth can result in poverty reduction in Africa. However, unemployment rates, in Africa, remain stubbornly high, in double digits in most cases. Although unemployment data in Africa are hard to come by and what is available may be unreliable, available data, however, suggest that unemployment rates averaged 27 percent among secondary school leavers and 11 percent among university leavers in 2008 (ERA, 2010).

High, sustained, and employment generating economic growth rates, combined with equitable income distribution, are necessary for growth to lead to significant poverty reduction. To achieve high rates of economic growth, therefore, there has to be better understanding of how economic growth occurs and the success factors in the countries that have recorded significant economic growth levels and reduced poverty (ERA, 2010).

Modern growth theory suggests two fundamental sources of economic growth; the rate of factor accumulation and Total Factor Productivity (TFP) growth (Aghion and Howitt, 2009; ERA, 2010). Indeed, some authors argue that the source of all economic growth is total factor productivity. Total factor productivity results from increase in technology, innovation resulting from Research and Development, and employee training leading to improved and increased employee skills. Factor accumulation includes, but not limited to, investment in physical and human capital as well as increase in the labor force (ERA, 2010).

The rate of factor accumulation depends on the rate of savings in an economy. Societies that save a higher proportion of their incomes are able to accumulate more and therefore grow at a faster pace than that of those who do not save a large proportion of their incomes (ERA, 2010). Compared with South Asia countries, which on average save and invest about 35 percent of their GDP and educate a relatively large proportion of their young people for longer periods of time and are growing fast, African countries save an average of under 20 percent of their GDP and educate a relatively low proportion of young people and are growing at a relatively slower pace than South Asian countries (ERA, 2010).

In order for African countries to accelerate economic development—to create increasing employment in order to deal with poverty—they should develop and implement the following economic development strategies (ERA, 2010; Juma, 2011):

- Accumulate factors at a faster pace than they save through increased transfers from other countries in the form of loans, aid, direct foreign investment, and Diaspora remittances;
- Use expansionary fiscal, monetary, and exchange rate policies for factor accumulation, especially of human capital and infrastructure;
- Increase domestic resource mobilization, increase total factor productivity growth through technological transfers and credible research and development efforts, institutional reforms, and expanded market access, at least to the common market levels in each region of Africa through regional integration and trade;
- Develop policies to shift growth poles from extracting natural resources to other large labor intensive sectors—and with a high employment growth elasticity—of the African economies such as agriculture, manufacturing, and

services; meanwhile ensuring there is effective inter sector linkages and to the wider economy. Successfully tackling and achieving high development in these three areas will reduce unemployment by over 70 percent and considerably reduce poverty in Africa (AER, 2010).

- Teach and educate people, particularly those in rural areas, where 70 percent of Africans live—and vigorously support them financially with market access and most importantly with productivity enhancing technologies—that they can only come out of poverty by generating and earning income from the resources that they already have and in a majority of cases their resource is land, which they should develop and manage well and scientifically to earn them increasingly sustainable income (Juma, 2011);
- As mentioned above, regionally integrate, with increased urgency, the continent's national small markets into larger markets to create opportunities for producing products and services that are globally competitive through lower cost achieved through economies of scale and improved technology. Moreover, jobs in the export industry, often, pay much better than purely domestic industry wages. Scholars (Wild et al., 2008) suggest that most of the time export industry wages are 13-28 percent more than purely domestic wages depending on the country's technological advancement and the export industry involved.

Africa is a diverse continent with diverse resources, cultures, constraints, and opportunities. Therefore, this calls for country-specific economic development and employment creation strategies that are tailored to address each country's specific needs. The strategies in each country can be implemented against the background of resource and institutional constraints and development priorities of each African country (ERA, 2010).

10. IMPERATIVES IN HEALTH AND EDUCATION IMPROVEMENTS

Central to shared growth and poverty eradication strategies, discussed above, is consistently greater investments in areas such as education, healthcare, and rural development, accompanied by greater improvements in the delivery of these services to the poor. HIV/AIDS, for example, and according to the World Health Organization, currently costs Africa 1 percent of per-capita income growth per year. Each year, nearly 1 million African pupils lose a teacher to the epidemic. Furthermore, many African children die *each* month as a result of malaria, the "silent Tsunami" (ERA, 2010).

Public intervention, which could prevent these epidemics, will have to involve a substantial effort and investment of large sums of money. Currently, health expenditures averaged only $13 per head in Sub-Saharan Africa, excluding South Africa, and were below $10 per head in 16 African countries (WHO Report, 2007). Contrast that healthcare expenditure with Europe of $ 1200 and US of $ 1000 per head respectively (WHO Report, 2007). African governments have a lot to do to improve the provision of healthcare services to their people in order to achieve the Millennium Development Goals in the area by the target date of 2015 (ERA, 2010).

In today's hyper-connected world, the rewards for countries and individuals that can raise their educational achievement levels will be bigger than ever. While the penalties for countries and individuals that do not raise their educational achievement will be harsher than ever before. There will be no personal security without good education. Likewise, there will be no national security in a country without proper and quality education (Friedman et al., 2011).

Education is key to technological and economic development of any country, more so those of Africa. In today's hyper-connected world, every African need to find what Friedman (2011) describes as their "extra." This is an individual's unique value contribution ability that makes them stand out in whatever is their field of employment. *Therefore, Average is over.*

However, educational trends in Africa are somewhat more favorable, with a steady fall in illiteracy, from 42 percent in 1997 to 35 percent in 2003 (ERA, 2010). The gross primary enrollment rate at 96 percent has recovered and now exceeds its 1980 level of 80 percent and it is expected that many African countries will achieve this particular goal in the Millennium Development Goals scheme of things (UN MDG Report, 2008). However, there needs to be more emphasis on technical education and increased research to enhance innovation and technological advancement, both of which are not only necessary to create jobs of the future, but are also necessary for Africa to be more competitive in the global job market. And in producing quality and competitive products for the global markets (ERA, 2010).

Friedman et al. (2011) assert further that to promote an effective educational system in a country, there are six interrelated elements that are necessary and must work together to achieve a successful and effective operation of the educational system. These are principles and factors that African governments should put in place to ensure continuous success of their educational systems. These factors include:

- Government and politicians that create a country's educational policy and ensure that there is an effective educational structure and effectively implement the educational policy and structure in the country. The policy and structure should include training, measuring, and evaluating teachers. The educational policy and structure should also create educational standards and how they are achieved by teachers and students. The politicians should always push to raise the national educational standards to meet the global needs of a country;

- There should be competent and capable teachers and principals who are initially sufficiently taught and trained in their teaching subject, such as math, science, and English. And in teaching methods to teach their subject and thus implement the educational system as per the national standards. The teachers and principals should be well, appropriately, and regularly trained, measured, evaluated, and correctly rewarded to make the teachers feel appreciated and to inspire excellence among teachers;
- The parents and guardians who should always be involved and demanding effectiveness of their children's education. They cannot delegate this responsibility to anyone in the educational system. The others in the educational system simply leverage the parents' efforts. Parents should always be responsible and accountable for the education of their children. Parents should create a disciplined ambition and high expectations in their children to succeed. They should provide them with necessary learning materials and emotional, motivational, and inspirational resources that the children need to continuously do well at school. Parents should have regular contacts with their children's teachers to help teachers ensure that the children do well at school as per their expectations. The goals of the parents and teachers for the success of children at school are similar; the success of children as per the educational standards, global and national standards. For example, achieving superior performance in tests such as the OECD Program for International Student Assessment (PISA) measures should be encouraged. The PISA test measures mainly how fifteen old students in several countries are being prepared for the jobs of the future. The test asks them to use their knowledge of math and science to solve real world problems and to use their reading skills to "construct, extend, and reflect on the meaning of what they have read" (Friedman, et al., 2011);
- The community, particularly neighbors, who are ready to invest in schools even though their children do not attend them. Neighbors can also help parents with the discipline of children at school by the values they reflect in the community;
- The business leaders committed to raising educational standards in their communities reflected in their hiring standards and value they attach to educational success of children in their communities;
- The students who are disciplined, motivated, and come to school prepared to learn, not texting friends and getting involved in violent acts at school and out of school. In discussing causes of educational failure in the USA today, which could be a source of concern in many other countries today too, Friedman

> (2011) states thus: The larger cause of failure in education in the USA is almost unmentionable: *shrunken student motivation.* Students, after all, have to do the work. If they are not motivated, even capable teachers may fail. Student motivation comes from many sources: *curiosity, sense of adventure, and ambition to be something real big*; *parental expectations; the desire to get into a 'good' college; inspiring or intimidating teachers; peer pressure.*

The unstated assumption of much school 'reform' in the USA is that if students aren't motivated, it's mainly the fault of schools and teachers. Wrong, Friedman said. Motivation is weak because more students (of all races and economic classes, let it he added) don't like school, don't work hard, and don't do well. In a 2008 survey of public high school teachers, 21 percent judged student absenteeism a serious problem; 29 percent cited student's apathy as a serious problem. African parents and political, business, and community leaders should ensure the motivation and discipline of African students remain high in their countries. They can ensure this by implementing some of the student's motivational strategies suggested here-in.

11. DEVELOPING INDIGENOUS COMPANIES IN AFRICA

African countries need to support the development of indigenous corporations through the vigorous support of the African entrepreneurship. The indigenous companies will leverage economic development of the African countries. They will also stabilize the African financial markets in times of global economic crisis through foreign exchange earnings, stock market stabilization, and sustenance of jobs during any global economic downturn (Williamson, 1997).

A few such companies exist in Africa that can provide a framework on which to build. They include the South African Breweries and Beverages Company, which currently operates in 29 African countries. There are also several African indigenous banks that operate regionally in Africa. Such banks include Kenya Commercial Bank of Kenya, Standard Bank of South Africa, and GT Bank and Diamond Bank both of Nigeria. Together with this pioneering group, there are African airlines such as Kenya Airways, Royal Air Morocco, South African Airways, Egypt Air, and Ethiopian Airways. These airlines link African countries to each other and connect Africa to the rest of the world. The airlines are making regional integration in Africa a reality. These African companies and flag carriers should be strengthened to increasingly go global like the Asian giants have done so that they are the African champions to support the sustainable economic development of Africa, through increased global access.

For Africa to develop faster, particularly through the usually most effective private sector development, more indigenous entrepreneurs should not only be encouraged but also supported with appropriate policies to start companies and make them competitive in the domestic and global markets. The future of African business depends highly on the African entrepreneurs and companies as it is true in Asia and other regions of the world with their global champions.

12. THE IMPORTANCE OF INVESTING IN KNOWLEDGE, SKILLS, AND INNOVATION BY AFRICAN COUNTRIES

In discussing the formula for phenomenal American success, Friedman and Mandelbaum (2011) have identified five pillars that together constitute the country's own version of a partnership between the public and the private sector to foster outstanding economic growth in the country. These pillars include:

- Providing high quality public education for more and more Americans. As technology has improved, the country has prepared people to exploit new *opportunities and* inventions – from the cotton gins, steamships, to assembly lines, to laptops, to the Internet;
- The building and continual renewal and modernization of the infrastructure – roads, rails, bridges, airports, *electricity, water*, bandwidth, fiber-optic lines, and wireless networks – so that Americans workers and firms can communicate, collaborate, *and function* efficiently and effectively and thus deliver their goods and services swiftly and cheaply to their destinations. From the beginning, governments at every level in the United States have financed the infrastructure necessary for commerce to start and flourish;
- Keeping the America's doors to immigration open so that the country is constantly adding appropriate talents that keep the country energized and having the best minds in the world to enrich American universities, start new companies, and engineer new breakthroughs from medicine to engineering;
- Government support for basic research and development, which not only increases the store of knowledge by pushing the frontiers of basic chemistry, biology, and physics, but also spawns new products, *services,* and processes that have enriched American entrepreneurs and workers; and
- The implementation of necessary regulations on private sector activity that provides safeguards against financial collapse and environmental destruction and protection of copyrights, patents, and intellectual property generally. This inspires small business and venture capitalists to start up and prosper in the country creating enriching employment in the process.

These five pillars that ensure phenomenal economic success of countries—they at least ensured American success—have definite implications for heavy investment in knowledge, skills, and innovation by a country. Therefore, in order to achieve accelerated economic development in Africa, African economies should develop and be treated as "systems of innovation" resulting from national knowledge and skills accumulation (Juma, 2011). The concept of systems offers a suitable framework for conveying the notions of parts of the economy, their interconnectedness, and their interaction, evolution over time, and emergence of novel structures that enhance development (Juma, 2011).

An innovation system can be defined as a network of organizations, enterprises, and individuals focused on bringing new products, new processes, and new forms of organization into economic use, together with the institutions and policies that affect their behavior and performance (Juma, 2011). Innovation requires acquiring and internalizing appropriate knowledge and skills.

Therefore, African countries, particularly resource-rich countries, need to invest in knowledge, skills, and innovation. Investment in these critical areas will enable the African resource-rich countries to generate constructive destruction in their economies—through imagination, creativity, and innovation—but also develop the ability to deal with the economic condition generally known as the Dutch Disease. Dutch disease results when a resource-rich country is unable to diversify its economy due to increased production costs of alternative export resulting from the rising value of its currency. This rise in value of the currency is as a result of increased demand of its natural resources in the global markets. The end result of the Dutch disease is the uncompetitiveness of the country's alternative exports and even their sales in the domestic market because imports become cheaper unless steps are taken to deal with the condition in time.

Africa needs also to invest in knowledge, skills, and innovation to enable the continent to diversify to other industries as the depletion of natural recourses increases over the coming years. The regular rise of prices of oil, minerals, and agricultural products and the expansion of new discoveries of mineral resources represent an unparalleled opportunity for Africa's resource-rich economies to transform themselves through diversification and sophistication. Yet, while some societies in the world have succeeded in harnessing natural resources for sustained increases in production, including increased economic sophistication and diversification to other industries, others have not. This is particularly true in Africa (Page, 2008).

Many resource-rich countries in Africa like Nigeria have suffered the consequences of the Dutch Disease phenomenon. Scholars further assert that if history repeats itself, after two decades output for the typical African commodity exporter will be around 25 percent lower than it would have been without the current export boom of natural resources. This makes Africa's future growth prospects highly vulnerable to the natural resource curse unless it diversifies (Page, 2008). Investment in education, knowledge, skills, and innovation will accelerate the diversification efforts and increase the chances of high economic development nurtured by other industries including agriculture (Page, 2008; Juma, 2011).

In addition, recent research on the impact of agglomeration economies on production costs and international competitiveness strongly suggests that latecomers to industrialization, such as Africa's natural resource exporters, suffer from a competitive disadvantage linked to the spatial distribution of global industry. It is far easier to expand an existing industrial agglomeration than to start a new one. These phenomena are clearly reflected in data that show Africa's mineral rich economies are lagging in key indicators of industrial dynamism (Page, 2008).

Therefore, complementary investments in education, knowledge, skills and innovation—as natural resources are depleted—offer prospects for dealing with agglomeration and achieve improved competitiveness, sophistication in the economy, and a more diversified economy in Africa's natural resources-rich and even non resource-rich African economies. Furthermore, unlike manufacturing, resource extraction is to an extent idiosyncratic, with particular problems associated with location-specific geology. These condition creates scopes for specialist knowledge of these localized features giving a country an opportunity to diversify, become more sophisticated, and in turn give local firms a comparative advantage globally (UNIDO, 2009).

One of the classic examples of this process of investment in education, knowledge, skills, and innovation—leading to economic diversification and sophistication—is oil extraction in Norway. At the time of the oil discoveries, Norway had no expertise whatsoever in the oil industry. However, the Norwegian government invested heavily over many years in building expertise. It established a national oil company, which partnered with foreign companies in order to learn from them, and it invested in specialist departments within its universities, which gradually built up both industry-wide knowledge and locally specific knowledge about deep-sea, cold-water oil exploration. Now, Norway's knowledge-based oil service industry is a major source of income in its own right and has a positive impact in other industries and businesses in the country (Page, 2008).

Resource-rich economies in Africa can undertake similar efforts to exploit and improve local knowledge. Government investment is likely to be through building up the geology, technology, and engineering departments of universities. It is clearly neither efficient nor feasible for each resource-rich country in Africa to develop such expertise. A more promising strategy is likely to be to develop a few region-wide centers—a long currently growing regional integration schemes—of excellence in mining engineering, geology, technology, tourism development, manufacturing technology, and other disciplines like agricultural sciences.

For example, Makerere University in Uganda has a long tradition of serving as a regional hub for Eastern and Central Africa and is close to a wide range of mineral discoveries (Page, 2008). Similarly, South Africa, in the SADC region, is an obvious candidate for a centre of expertise on mining technology, Nigeria for a centre on oil technology, in the ECOWAS region, and in Kenya a center of expertise for cut flower technology and tourism development in the Eastern, Central, and South African regions.

Chile shows a different way to use natural resource revenues to generate knowledge, skills, diversification, and sophistication. In the Chilean case, the knowledge was not directly linked to its main natural resource export, copper, but to a new line of business, agro-industry, in which geography and external markets played a significant role. The main driver of productivity improvements was generation and diffusion of production knowledge and skills. Close interaction between regional and national governments and the private sector helped to ensure the relevance of the knowledge and skills generated. A formal public-private partnership—the Fundacion Chile—led the effort to identify and adapt global best practices, and as the industry matured, a strong focus on research by local and national universities evolved (Page 2008). Some African natural resource exporters may find similar opportunities to generate knowledge and skills relevant to new export initiatives in agriculture or services, such as tourism, where geography, terrain, exotic wildlife, and other endowments provide a comparative advantage.

Furthermore, governments—through improvements in the investment climate and public expenditures—can mitigate the worst consequences of the Dutch disease. In the case of the investment climate and governance, Africa's resource-rich economies will need mechanisms to reduce rent seeking and improve accountability and perhaps through the use of shared growth strategies to foster better distribution of national wealth and the creation of checks and balances.

In the case of public expenditure, combining infrastructure investments with an export test in the form of an Export Processing Zone (EPZ) may help late starters to encourage the formation of internationally competitive industrial clusters. Complementary investments in knowledge and skills also offer prospects for improved competitiveness and a more diversified and sophisticated economy.

Still, there is need for increased research in Africa to improve evidence-based decision-making mechanisms. The agenda for research to support evidence-based policy making in Africa's resource-rich economies is largely an unfinished one. It ranges from the need for better understanding of the magnitude of the Dutch disease in individual economies to comparative case studies on policy and institutional innovations to detailed micro economic analyses of the benefits of increased diversity, sophistication, and agglomeration at the country level (Page, 2008).

The potential productivity enhancing benefits of investments in infrastructure, skills, and knowledge need to be quantified to support the cost-benefit analysis of proposed public expenditures. Cost-benefit analysis is an absolutely essential element of good public expenditure management in resource-rich economies. The agenda for political economy research is similarly rich: why, for example, has Botswana succeeded in converting diamonds into sustained growth while other countries in the region have largely failed? Is it through the absence of checks and balances that fosters rent seeking in resource exporters' regulatory regimes? Can national vision exercises bolster accountability and development? Successful diversification in resource-rich economies is all about making good choices, but without evidence, good choices are impossible therefore the need for research (Page, 2008).

Chile, Indonesia, and Malaysia—each a major natural resources exporter—had rising incomes and increasing sophistication of their manufacturing and export structure between 1980 and 2000. Successful diversification away from dependence on natural resources was the consequence of different, but effective, research based public policies to mitigate the impact of the Dutch disease. The contrast with Nigeria, which experienced little income growth and declining production in traditional industries of cocoa and ground nuts and therefore lack of export sophistication during the same period, is telling (Page, 2008).

The Nigerian minister of finance, Olesegun Aganga, recently said—as quoted in the BBC on line news, www.bbc.com, on September 3, 2010—that the Nigerian economy grew at 7% in the first half of 2010 and will grow by at least 10% by 2012. He does not say, however, how he arrived at such high growth rates and what happens after 2012. Nevertheless, Nigeria—the most populous and oil-rich country in Africa—can deal with its negative and dubious trade mark of being the most corrupt country in Africa and achieve this expected phenomenal economic growth by pursuing a number of approaches using its massive oil revenue.

Some of these approaches are: improving the business climate through reforms; improving governance; improving security and safety; investing heavily in quantity and quality of primary and secondary education and healthcare; investment in infrastructure and agriculture; making university education free; particularly in its volatile oil producing regions; and creating centers of excellence for research and production of high level manpower, technology, and entrepreneurs, in some of its well-known universities like Ibadan as Norway and Chile have successfully done in recent years. In that way, Nigeria can provide much needed leadership and a befitting role model in economic development of Africa (Page, 2008).

Africa can also learn from Indian experience in knowledge, skills, and innovation management. In India, researchers, universities, and businesses regularly collaborate in order to pioneer ways to do more with fewer resources to produce inexpensive products and services or create more value for less money for more people (Prahalad et al., 2010). These products and services are going global particularly to Africa and other Asian countries where they are competitively successful. Bharti Airtel, for example, is an Indian telecommunication company, that has invested over $10 billion to sell mobile phones cheaply in Africa causing serious disruptions to the business models of existing and long established mobile phone companies like Safaricom of Kenya (Daily Nation, 2010).

The Indian researchers and companies use what scholars (Phahalad et al., 2010) describe as the "Ghandhian innovation" method to enhance their competitiveness in global markets. The Ghandhian innovation methodology focuses on three key and interrelated elements about innovation:

- Disrupting existing business models to build things much more cheaply;
- Modifying organizational capabilities and business models to be able to do things much more efficiently and effectively;
- Creating or outsourcing new capabilities to enhance organizational success. The Indians always get their innovations right by:
    - Developing a deep commitment to serve the un-served;
    - Articulating and embracing a clear organizational vision, mission, goals, and objectives;
    - Setting ambitious and challenging goals and objectives to foster an entrepreneurial spirit in their organizations;
    - Accepting that constraints will always exist. They therefore develop strategies to creatively operate around the constraints;
    - Focusing on people/customers, not just shareholders and profits, in what they do always.

In discussing the knowledge acquisition, innovation, and management changes—that are relevant to Africa—that will make the USA competitive again and bring back long gone manufacturing jobs, Jeffrey Immelt (2012), GE Chief Executive Officer, states thus:

Two things are clear in today's business environment: First, outsourcing that is based only on labor costs is yesterday's business model. Secondly, every American employee can deliver competitive success – because of their ability, because of their attitude, and because they expect to deliver. Every American employee, from the factory floor to the boardroom, knows we can win. And we will win only if we are not afraid not to compete.

He continues to argue that as a country, if we want to revive USA manufacturing and regain our competitive edge, we have to execute. However, we also need confidence and the mind-set that we technologically can outperform anyone in the world. We should start by making a serious commitment to manufacturing in the USA and export.

People talk about the Darwinian nature of markets. They say that America has undergone a natural evolution from farming to manufacturing to services, as have other mature economies. However, nothing is predestined or inevitable about the industrial decline of the United States. China is growing fast because it is investing heavily in education and in technology. And has zero intention of letting up on manufacturing. We should not be afraid of that; we should be inspired by the competition.

To meet that competition, we will need a strong core of innovations and a stable financial system built around helping entrepreneurs—small and medium-size businesses—and industrial companies to succeed. We will need an update in infrastructure to support manufacturing, which the private sector can help, fund: better roads and airports, broadband capability, water and modern sewage systems, and a bigger and smarter electricity grid. Finally, we will need well-trained and motivated teams. Only the best-trained and motivated workforce will make America faster, better, and more competitive over the long term. The nation's consumers cannot lead this recovery. Business investment and exports must.

That is the imperative. However, before an imperative comes an impetus for action. We cannot do any of this if we are afraid to get in the game. We need to believe that we can design, develop, and produce here in the United States; that we can do it cost-effectively and efficiently; and that we can win. Then we need to find ways to collaborate and make the necessary investments. If we do, our workers will prove America's potential.

African countries need to have the same life-changing dreams like those held by CEO Immelt when managing their abundant raw materials from mining to final quality and globally competitive products and services through innovation and acquisition of knowledge, skills, and technology mainly through research and development.

13. DEVELOPMENT OF ENTREPRENEURSHIP IN THE AFRICAN ECONOMIES

Related to the development of the private sector, indigenous corporations, knowledge, skills, and innovation in Africa, is the critical necessity to ensure the development and nurturing sustainable growth of entrepreneurship in the Africa economies. Entrepreneurship thrives and grows in an environment rich of knowledge, skills, and innovation (Getman, 2008). In fact, entrepreneurship is synonymous to knowledge, skills, and innovation. Entrepreneurial expertise innovatively identifies, assesses, and takes advantage of emerging opportunities through the creation of new institutions and businesses. And/or upgrading the existing institutions to successfully and profitably exploit opportunities they present. Such entrepreneurial acts are essential for economic development and creation of jobs in Africa. And that way, creating a middle class for products and services in the African economies and therefore increasing business opportunities for corporations and entrepreneurs (Juma, 2011).

Meanwhile, Bwisa et al. (2012) assert that the importance of entrepreneurship to any economy need not be overemphasized. Wealth and a majority of jobs are created by small businesses started by entrepreneurially minded individuals, many of whom go on to create big national businesses. People exposed to entrepreneurship frequently express that they have more opportunity to exercise creative freedoms, higher self-esteem, and an overall greater sense of control over their own lives. As a result, many experienced and successful business people, political leaders, economists, and educators believe that fostering a robust entrepreneurial culture, in a community and or a nation will maximize individual and collective economic and social success on a local, national, and global scale.

Entrepreneurship can spur innovations, steer innovation processes, and compel the creation of an innovation-enabling environment while giving rise to and sustaining innovation systems in an economy. Entrepreneurial ventures are an embedded power that steers institutions, stimulate learning, and create or strengthen linkages that constitute the pillars of innovation systems in an economy. These systems lead to the emergence, development, and growth of small, micro, and medium enterprises that are the largest employers in many developed and emerging economies in the world today (Juma 2011). Small and Micro enterprises are the largest employer in the USA today, for example. They create 99% of the new jobs annually and hence growing a middle class that is a consumer of products and services in an economy (Wild et al., 2008).

Therefore, African economies should always create conducive business environment that nurtures the growth of entrepreneurship and indigenous capitalism to create jobs and wealth to eliminate poverty in their countries. Furthermore, the presence of successful entrepreneurs, in any African economy, will and most likely attract into the country direct foreign investments to franchise, to create joint ventures, create contractual business agreements, and to develop strategic alliances that will spur greater economic growth that will create more employment and wealth in the African economies and thus eliminate further poverty in the continent and generally attract more investments.

14. ELIMINATION OF HORIZONTAL INEQUALITIES

The elimination of horizontal inequalities in Africa can minimize insecurity and instability in the continent. The elimination of horizontal inequalities in Africa can occur in many ways. These ways include preferential educational opportunities, training, and job quotas that give preferential treatment to disadvantage groups. And at the same time ensuring that the growth of a competitive culture is not hindered in a country by this policy. The process should also include the development of entrepreneurship in the economy to create employment throughout the country (Moraa, 2006).

Malaysia can serve as a good example of a country that has put in place policies and programs aimed at reducing the conditions and processes in an economy that create horizontal inequalities. The country has achieved this by promoting general economic growth in the country, reconciliation of communities, strong attention to national cohesion, and national stability (Khanna et al., 2005).

Malaysia sees national security as inseparable from political stability, economic success, and social harmony. Comprehensive security is also essential for regional stability hence programs to achieve all these values should be put in place by the state (Deng et al., 2002). Therefore, the government of Malaysia, in the last three decades or so, has had a variety of anti-poverty policies adopted by the government that included the introduction of education and job quotas within public institutions and the introduction of credit policies that favored Malays more than ethnic Chinese. These policies went a long way in reducing the inequalities that existed between Malays and ethnic Chinese, and they significantly decreased the case for social conflict and civil strife in Malaysia (Khanna et al., 1997). The Malaysian case illustrates the fact that horizontal inequalities that have been in existence for long periods of time require deliberate, systematic, and long-term policies in order for them to be sufficiently eliminated.

It is important to note that elimination of inequalities was not only between major Malaysian ethnic groups—the Chinese and Malays—but it was also targeted between Malaysian indigenous businesses and foreign businesses as described by the former Malaysian Prime Minister, Seri Mahathir Mohammad. He put it this way in 1996 in a speech given in Bangkok: "But for the right and the ability to regulate the economy in favor of locals in certain areas, while allowing and even providing incentives for foreign investment in other areas, it is doubtful that Malaysia would be as prosperous as it is today.... Without these powers to give unequal treatment, it is likely that Malaysia will be another basket case" (Williamson, 1997). These policies enhanced Malaysia's economic growth averaging 6 percent GDP growth per annum in the last three decades. Interestingly too, Malaysia was the most successful Asian country in tackling the serious events resulting from 1997 Asian financial and economic meltdown (Khanna et al., 2005).

Ghana achieved more or less the same results of ensuring security and stability in the country. This has been reflected in the last three peaceful transitional elections held in the country. They achieve the elimination of horizontal inequalities by devolving and delegating leadership and governance to the communities as described by former Ghanaian president Jerry John Rawlings. He put it this way in a speech he gave in 2006 at the University of Witwatersrand, in South Africa, on "African leadership and governance" (Daily Nation, 2006): "The Provisional National Defense Council, which I chaired from January 1982 to January 1992, recognized that we had to somehow translate the traditional communal spirit into a meaningful participatory democracy in which every stakeholder genuinely felt that he or she could make a difference. Although we were belabored with external pressures to quickly concoct a new constitution, form political parties, and hold national elections we said "No" even at the risk of being described as a military dictatorship. We wanted to begin at the grassroots in order to evolve a system in which our people felt a genuine ownership of governance. To do so, we had to take the considerable risk of initially calling on the people themselves, without any guidelines, to form community and workplace committees to rekindle the spirit of communal participation...We then provided structured guidelines and funding for these localized groups to focus on practical projects....in terms of planning, budgeting, implementing, and monitoring local development within the districts."

Kenya is also dealing with its horizontal inequalities—that are believed to have resulted in violence in its 2007 presidential elections—in its unique and far reaching ways and actions. Extensive individual/personal and property ownership rights have been incorporated in its recently approved—in a national referendum—constitutional framework and dispensation. Furthermore, the new constitution also devolves economic development, political, and decision-making powers to the 47 newly constituted county governments. The devolution will also include the annual provision of 15 percent of central government revenues to the county governments (Kenya Constitution promulgated on August 27, 2010), in addition to the Constituent Development Fund (CDF), and Local Authority Transfer Fund that have been in place in that order. These power and resource distribution arrangements are expected to deal with perceived discrimination in the old constitution and usher in a period of seriously needed national reconciliation and cohesion and hopefully accelerated economic development to tackle pervasive and chronic poverty in the country (Deng et al., 2002).

15. ROLE OF THE INTERNATIONAL COMMUNITY

Africa is the major test of the international community's determination to defeat global poverty (Moyo, 2009). This can only be accomplished through a strong partnership, led by Africans and supported by the international community. Here, too, are some positive signs. Net aid to Sub-Saharan Africa rose about 40 percent in 2003, because of higher bilateral and multilateral flows. As of July 2004, 11 countries had reached Heavily Indebted Poor Countries (HIPC) debt relief decision points and 12 had reached completion points. Total debt service relief represented about $43 billion, and pro-poor expenditures had begun to increase in most of the countries (Moyo, 2009). However, much remains to be done; on a per-capita basis. The development assistance at $37 in 2009 is still below its level in 1992 of US$40 (World Bank's Country at a Glance Report, 2009).

Nevertheless, it is important to note that aid did not succeed in the African development in the last fifty years. It engendered corruption in many countries of Africa (Moyo, 2009). Therefore, any new aid to Africa should be targeted, geared toward leveraging local resources, and closely monitored to ensure transparency and accountability in order to meet its intended goals and objectives (Abrams, 2009).

16. COMPENSATION TO AFRICA BY THE IMF AND WORLD BANK FOR THE 1980S/90S STRUCTURAL ADJUSTMENTS PROGRAM FAILURES

Africa has massively suffered over the centuries through debilitating events that have kept the continent backward that it is today. These events include slavery, colonization, and, in recent times, externally imposed and misguided policies and programs, like the structural adjustments of the 1980s/90s by the IMF and World Bank.

During slavery, millions of able-bodied Africans were transported to the various parts of the world mainly and more intensively beginning the mid 17th century to the second half of the 19th century. In North America alone, it is estimated that over ten million Africans came into the continent between 1640 and 1840, twenty years before the end of slavery in 1965 (Larson, 2004).Slavery depleted Africa of its strongest men and women who could have made a big difference in its development endeavors. These Africans came and laid a strong and firm economic foundation for the USA for example.

Twenty years after the end of slavery in 1885, in the infamous Berlin Conference, Africa was partitioned and colonized and its abundant raw materials exploited over the years by the European nations. The continent was divided into small states for the purpose of ownership by various occupying powers. They also applied divide and rule policies among the various ethnic communities in the countries they governed. Because of these divisive policies, it was difficult for these states to form viable nations later at independence. And it also has been almost impossible to bring Africans together to trade and form larger and viable markets to produce competitive products and services using their abundant raw materials and in order to compete in a globalized world.

Many African countries became independent in the 1960s. Almost twenty years after independence, beginning the 1980s to the beginning of the new Millennium, 2000, the IMF and the World Bank imposed a set of externally, poorly conceived, and unsustainable structural adjustment programs on the African countries. These poorly designed and implemented programs—focused on African macroeconomic policies—investable impoverished Africa over the years whenever they were applied. Scholars (Moyo, 2009) have estimated that the programs left Africa poorer than at the beginning of the programs, meaning that Africa would have been economically far better than it is today were it not for these programs, assuming that the development rates and momentum of the 1970s was maintained and continued.

Anecdotal data and commentators further indicate that the African GDP would have been twice what it is today—that is two trillion US dollars by 2000—had it not been for the destructive effects of the structural adjustment programs by the IMF and World Bank. The former IMF managing director, Camdessus (2000), concurs that the structural adjustment programs were excessive, severe, and mostly not appropriate for the various African economies when he states that "I obliged those African countries seeking IMF help for development to submit to major macroeconomic surgery when six aspirins could have brought the same results to these countries" (Stiglitz, 2003).

Therefore, many African people think and believe that the IMF and World Bank should compensate Africa for hindering and sabotaging African development because of their poorly conceived and inappropriate policies and advice in the 1980's/1990's (Stiglitz, 2003). I think IMF and World Bank have an obligation to compensate Africa and should do so with at least $1 trillion paid over 10 years. The money should be shared among African countries using their population numbers at the beginning of the year 2000. The money paid to the African countries should be spent on key development areas including education, research and technology, infrastructure, agriculture, healthcare, and the environment, to enhance African development to deal with current chronic poverty and hunger in the continent, a lot of it instigated by IMF and World Bank structural adjustment programs for over almost decades.

17. PERFORMANCE CONTRACTS

In many African countries, written contracts between employees and the employers are becoming commonplace (Keeler, 2010). A performance contract is an agreement between an employee and his/her superior. It specifies the job profile and responsibilities of an employee with deadlines and how often the employee should be evaluated by the manager to determine the achievement of the job targets specified in the performance contract.

These contracts are increasingly becoming very popular in Africa. They cover all levels of management, including the Chief Executive Officer and the board of directors, in a private Corporation, and senior executives in ministries of government, including the ministers and their principal secretaries (Moyo, 2009).

Performance contracting practices have their origin in Peter Drucker's (1994) management by objectives and constructive destruction of organizations concepts. These contracts should enhance performance when they are tied up to performance management models such as the Balanced Scorecard framework—developed by Kaplan and Morton in 1992—with individualized implementation of the scorecard indicating the performance elements of finance, customer, process, and innovation (Kaplan et al., 1992).

It is anticipated that the effective application of performance contracting, and of the Balanced Scorecard—as a planning, implementation, and evaluation tool—in particular, will improve quality of work performance in Africa. They will achieve cost improvement; increase the quality of customer service, and eventually competitiveness—of organizations—in the market and quality service delivery to the public by public institutions.

18. ROLE OF THE AFRICAN MEDIA IN CHANGING THE AFRICAN IMAGE

One of the biggest challenges in the quest for image change is that image is invisible. The bull of image cannot be grabbed from its horns. Image is imprinted in the unconsciousness of the person. This in turn affects one's decision whether he/she is a politician, businessman, journalist, activist, ordinary citizen, or an NGO official. A bad image makes the viewer see only one slice of reality. He/she sees only the empty part of the cup. This is definitely true of the African image in the world today (Mofadal, 2010).

The Africa media should correct and positively promote the dented African image in the world. They should come out of their coons and national borders to sell Africa positively to the world audiences. They have that obligation and noble duty. The African media should come to the international stage to promote African business opportunities and challenges of doing business in Africa and how to mitigate these challenges, both in the short-term and long-term.

One way of doing this is to run documentaries, on Africa, in their systems and collaborate with foreign media to air and project or show these documentaries in their countries. They should focus on the North American and European media and possibly in the Chinese, Brazilian, and Indian media. They should get financial support from the African Union and their individual governments to develop and air these documentaries.

On a reciprocal basis, the African editors should regularly write appropriate articles and documentaries to appear in the foreign press. Again, the focus should be on daily papers such as the *New York Times, Washington Post*, and the *Times of London*, the *Le Monde* in France, and weekly magazines like the *BusinessWeek* and *Time* in the USA, and the *Economist* in the UK, and similar papers and magazines in Germany, Eastern Europe, and Asia.

In every newspaper or magazine, they should engage prolific and respected writers and columnists like Paul Krugman, Thomas Friedman, David Brook, and Nicholas Kristof, all of the New York Times. These venerable writers and commentators regularly write stimulating, a lot of times supportive, and informative articles on various countries particularly those of South America, Eastern European, Asian countries, and today on the Arab Spring. They hardly do anything on Africa unless it is a seriously negative event, like the recent electoral problems in Ivory Coast, hunger in the horn of Africa, and the Arab Spring in North Africa. Nicholas Kristof confirms this as he stated, in his recent column in the New York Times, on Africa in general and Lesotho in particular:

All in all, though, Africa is becoming more democratic, more technocratic, and more market-friendly. Yet, Americans are largely oblivious to the idea of Africa as a success story. One of the problems with journalism—that is supposed to inform them—is that we focus on disasters. We cover planes that crash, not those that take off. In Africa, that means we cover famine in Somalia and genocide in Sudan, terrorism in Nigeria and warlords in Congo. Those are important stories—deserving more attention, not less—but they can also leave a casual reader convinced that all of Africa is lurching between genocide and famine. So that's why I decided to start this win-a-trip journey in a delightful country like Lesotho that just had a democratic change of power. Its streets are safe, and it is working on becoming one of the first countries in the world with an electric grid that is 100 percent reliant on renewable energy. It's a symbol of an Africa that is rising.

19. ROLE OF THE AFRICAN UNION (AU)

AU should also play its rightful role in the process of changing the African image by having the AU chairman to make statements of policy and generally what AU is doing to promote doing business in Africa and economic development generally. On a regular basis, the chairman should tour major Western and Asian countries to promote Africa. Other countries like China, India, and Japan do it regularly. Whenever, for example, a new Chinese president, Indian and Japanese prime ministers come to power, for the first time, their first duty is to visit the USA, Europe, and even Africa, to promote their countries with their leading business partners. It is not business as usual for them! Why should it be for Africa?

AU should also appoint and post professional and competent – not some political failures from some African country and who do not have any understanding of globalization and political, social, business, and economic issues of Africa – as ambassadorial staff posted to major capitals in Europe, the Americas, and Asia to promote Africa on a permanent basis. It will be costly to change the extremely negative perceptions on Africa held in the world, particularly in the Western and Asian countries—that are major sources of private investments and development aid to Africa—but it will be worth trying and the returns will be enormous to the African continent in the future, more so in generating at least tourism business for many African countries.

Many African countries have a competitive advantage in tourism business because of their rich history, artifacts, beautiful geographic terrains, beautiful beaches, and rich wild life diversity. Some scholars have estimated that if African countries, like Kenya and Ghana, consistently received, one million American tourists annually—American tourists are great spenders—for five years, the countries will be middle income countries with $10,000 per capita income from $ 1200 it is today in five years (Sachs, 2005). A big jump in the wealth of the people indeed and a huge business opportunity for entrepreneurs!

20. LEARNING FROM INDIAN AND CHINESE EXPERIENCES

It is common knowledge today that China and India, as large emerging economies, have had phenomenal economic growth in the last three decades. What is their secret that has ensured their tremendous growth and has made them the "factories" and technology centers of the world?

The first obvious factor is that these countries are the largest markets in the world today. This fact makes them attractive to multinational corporations seeking new manufacturing sites to produce low cost and globally marketed competitive products. The countries are also markets in which corporations sell their products and services to create new value for their stakeholders at home (Juma, 2011). China has the largest population today in the world followed by India. There are over 1.3 billion and over 1.2 billion Chinese and Indians respectively. Moreover, scholars (Prahalad et al., 2010) estimate that China and India together will have 2 billion to 3 billion consumers, with a $ 5000 per capita income, in the next decade. Africa can attain the same status through increased regional integration and trade.

The second factor is that, during the last three decades or so, China and India have consistently reformed and liberalized their business environments. They have undertaken reforms in their economies to make it easier and cheaper to start and do business in these countries. For example, for nearly a half a century, India was a closed economy wedded to socialism. Its sudden embrace of reforms in the 1980s stimulated high levels of economic growth and trade as well as an enormous inflow of foreign direct investments into the country (Prahalad et al., 2010).

India began embracing reforms and the free market economy in the 1980s and stepped up the pace of change in 1991 when the country faced a financial crisis. From mid-1991 onwards, India became part of the wave of market reforms, joining China, the Soviet Union, Eastern Europe, and Latin America in their globalization process (Sachs, 2005). Those changes tremendously increased economic growth and made possible the rise of technology and low cost companies like Infosys and Wipro. These companies focused on providing services cheaply for American and European corporations (NY Times, 2009). Therefore, both China and India are some of the lowest cost and business friendly destinations for global companies in the world today (NY Times, 2009) that Africa can learn from.

Meanwhile, Indian businessmen and investors have praised and vividly described how important the changes in the Indian business environment and climate have been important to recent and phenomenal development of the Indian economy. For example, Vivek Wadhwa, a former technology entrepreneur who now researches on innovation asserts that the "climate for start-ups in India is a lot better today than it was a few years ago. It should continue to improve in part because companies like General Electric have hired tens of thousands of engineers and technologists in

India to work in research and development. Once they have been working on these projects for a few years, they will outgrow the companies that they are working for. They will hook up with those entrepreneurs that failed on previous start-up attempts and create new companies. Many Indian universities have also started entrepreneurship programs and classes to enhance the changes in the Indian economy as the destination for outsourcing businesses in high technology businesses" (Prahalad and Meshelkar, 2010).

Paranipe states that another change that may augur well for the Indian economy is that early this decade, the Indian market was too small and isolated to make it very lucrative for businesses to develop products there, so most technology companies focused on selling services to the West. "That has changed dramatically because the Indian market has become bigger. In the last eight years, the size of the Indian economy has roughly doubled along with the importance of foreign trade and innovation. And this, of course, must be something to envy, fear, and marvel about India and its economy and innovative prowess" (Prahalad and Meshelkar, 2010).

The third learning experience is that China and India rank high in the world ease of doing business index and therefore, they are the largest recipients of, not only foreign direct investments, in the last five years, but also the greatest recipients of remittances from their nationals in the Diaspora (World Competitive Report, 2010-2011). In the case of India, remittances provide a very large source of foreign exchange to finance critical imports such as oil or even food. So the remittances have a huge impact at the macroeconomic level. But at the individual and household levels, the impact is even more striking because for a lot of poor people, remittances are usually all they have (UN Remittances Report, 2009). Out of $304 billion world remittances in 2007, India—the largest recipient—received $ 27 billion ($46.4 billion in 2008) and China received $25.7 billion in 2007 (UN Remittances Report, 2009).

Lastly and most importantly is the fact that India and China have considerably improved their education and literacy levels in the last three decades or so leading to an increasingly skilled and innovative workforce. India literacy level is 80% and that of China is 90%. The countries have also put a lot of recourses into higher education, technology and IT training in order to attract outsourcing and manufacturing jobs into their countries to create wealth and reduce poverty. All these investments in education and jobs and wealth creation—in China and India—have domino effects in their economies (Juma, 2011). For example and according to the USA Department of Commerce 2009 Report, in 2009, China led in the high technology exports achieving $381 billion of exports in the world followed by the USA which exported $231 billion in the same period.

The World Bank describes high-technology exports as "products with high R&D intensity, such as in aerospace, computers, pharmaceuticals, scientific instruments, *ITC services,* going green and electrical machinery." These are all fields in which the

United States prides itself, and the U.S. remains in first place in the pharmaceutical industry. Despite this, China has beaten America in the high technology exports since the World Bank began collecting data on this category in 2005. Between 2005 and 2008, Chinese high-tech exports increased by78%, relative to a mere 21% by the U.S. over the same period (World Bank High Technology Export Report, 2009).

Furthermore, anecdotal data indicate that India and China incur a lot of resources to educate their nationals in American universities. The graduates go back, not only to manage their national economies, but also become entrepreneurs and small business owners using knowledge, skills, and experiences gained in the American business environment. The businesses started by these returning students become incubators of indigenous entrepreneurship that become big employers in the two countries and national business champions of tomorrow.

These are some of the areas that Africa should learn from India and China and focus on in order to be an attractive business destination. The changes should include creating bigger markets through regional integration. Many individual African countries' markets are too small to attract foreign businesses. Therefore, there is an urgent need, as discussed in chapter five above, to expand the African products and services markets, through increased regional integration, at least to the common market levels. But, the East African Community became a common market in June, 2011. The other African regions are either at free trade area or custom union levels of the regional integration process, but steadily progressing to higher schemes of regional integration.

African countries should also coordinate the African Diaspora better to encourage it to increase their remittances to the continent. There are 40 million Africans in the Diaspora that can generate resources for the development of Africa. These are valuable resources that can make a difference in the development of individual African countries particularly those with a large number of nationals in the Diaspora (ERA, 2010). For example Kenya—one of the leading African recipients of Diaspora remittances in Africa—had $ 1.588 billion of remittances in 2008, Uganda had $ 849 million, Rwanda had $ 51 million, and Tanzanian, the biggest country in East Africa, had $ 14 million in remittances (UN Report, 2009).

Other countries such as Ghana, Nigeria, Egypt, and South Africa, with large numbers of nationals in the Diasporas, have much higher remittances annually. One way African countries can enhance the inflow of these remittances is by having a Diaspora department, in the home country, to develop and coordinate the remittances policies of the Diaspora. Countries like Mali are said to have such departments and/ or ministries already (EIU, 2009).

African nations should also invest more in education to produce sufficient numbers of talented and innovative workers to enable the continent to be competitive in the global markets particularly in attracting manufacturing and outsourcing businesses.

African numbers in high education and research cohorts are dismally low and need considerable enhancement as discussed earlier. Africa must invest more money in tertiary and university education, as India and China, have done, in recent years. These investments have contributed to their phenomenal economic growth and in attracting increasing foreign direct investments (EIU, 2009).

Furthermore, African countries can work with American and European universities, like India and China are anecdotally said to be doing today, in order to increase the number of African students admitted to these universities. *For example, there were 160,000 Chinese students in American universities against 20,000 American students in Chinese universities in the year 2011-2012 (Shambaugh, 2013).* The African countries can also encourage America and European universities—through appropriate educational policies—to open campuses in Africa, either independently, or in collaboration with the African universities. Indian, China, and other Asian countries' universities are known to have these collaborative arrangements today that help these countries to acquire high level of educational cohorts necessary to achieve high technological advancement and phenomenal economic growth (Mpaka, 2011).

REFERENCES

Abrams, J. J. (2009, May 11). 10 questions: The Liberian president's new memoirs. *Time*.

Bajaj, V. (2009, December 8). In India, anxiety over the slow pace of innovation. *New York Times*.

Barboza, D. (2010, August 15). China passes Japan as the second-largest economy in the world. *New York Times*.

Benoni, C. (2010, December 14). I foresee 7.5 percent growth rates in Africa in 2010: African development bank (AFDB) president, Donald Kaberuka. *The East African*.

Bwisa, M. H., & Nafukho, F. M. (2012). *Learning entrepreneurship through indigenous knowledge*. Nsemia Publishing Company.

Clinton, W. J. (2011). *Back to work: Why we need smart government for a strong economy*. New York: Alfred A. Knopf.

Corden, W. M. (1982). *Booming sector and Dutch disease: Economic survey and consolidation. Oxford Economic paper*. Oxford, UK: Oxford University Press.

Corden, W. M., & Neary, J. P. (1984). Booming sector and de-industrialization in a small open economy. *The Economic Journal*, 92.

Cullen, J. B., & Parboteeah, P. K. (2008). *Multinational management: A strategic approach* (4th ed.). Thompson South-Western.

Deng, F. M., & Zartman, W. I. (2002). *A strategic vision for Africa: The Kampala movement*. Washington, DC: The Brookings Institution.

EIU. (2009). African business and economic report. *The Economist Intelligence Unit*.

ERA. (2010). *Economic report on Africa*. Addis Ababa, Ethiopia: AU Commission.

Friedman, T. L. (2012, March 31). Why nations fail. *New York Times*.

Friedman, T. L., & Mandelbaum, M. (2011). *That used to be us: How America fell behind in the world it invented and how we can come back*. New York: Farrar, Straus, and Giroux.

Immelt, J. R. (2012, March). The CEO of GE on sparking American manufacturing renewal. *Harvard Business Review*.

Juma, C. (2011). *The new harvest: Agricultural innovation in Africa*. Oxford, UK: Oxford University Press.

Kamara, A. B., Bousrih, L., & Nyende, M. (2008). Growing a knowledge based economy: Evidence from public expenditure on education in Africa. *African Development Bank Economic Research working paper series*. Tunis, Tunisia: AFDB.

Kaplan, R. S., & Norton, D. (2005, July-August). The balanced scorecard: Measures that drive performance. *Harvard Business Review*. PMID:10119714.

Kaplan, S. R., & Grossman, S. A. (2010, October). The emerging capital market for nonprofits. *Harvard Business Review*.

Keeler, D. (2010, November). Kenya: Rebirth of a nation. *Global Finance*.

Khanna, T., Palepu, G. K., & Sinha, J. (2005, June). Strategies that fit emerging markets. *Harvard Business Review*. PMID:15938439.

Khanna, T., & Palepu, K. (1997, September-October). Why focused strategies maybe wrong for emerging markets. *Harvard Business Review*.

Larson, K. C. (2004). *Harriet Tubman: The portrait of an American hero, bound for the promised land*. New York: Random House Publishing Group.

Markides, C. C. (1997, November-December). To diversify or not to diversify. *Harvard Business Review*. PMID:10174800.

Mbaku, J. M. (1998a). Emerging trade blocks and the fortune of African participation in the world economy. *Journal of Economic Integration*, *10*(2).

Mbaku, J. M. (1998b). Improving African participation in the global economy: The role of economic freedoms. *Business and the Contemporary, 10*(2).

Mbaku, J. M. (2004). *Institutions and development in Africa*. Africa World Press.

Meyer, C., & Kirby, J. (2010, April). Leadership in the age of transparency. *Harvard Business Review*. PMID:20402054.

Mofadal, M. A. (2010, June 27). Africa faces major image problems. *Sunday Nation*.

Mom, I. (2009). *Performance of the African leadership*. The East African.

Moraa, G. (2006). *Eliminating horizontal inequalities in post conflict northern Uganda: Tackling the neglected dimensions of the humanitarian crisis in northern Uganda*. (Unpublished Master's Thesis). Seton Hall University, South Orange, NJ.

Moyo, D. (2009). *Dead aid: Why aid is not working and how there is a better way for Africa*. New York: Farrar, Straus, and Giroux.

Page, J. (2008). Rowing against the current: The diversification challenge in Africa's resource-rich economies. *Global Economic Development Working Paper 29*. Washington, DC: Brookings Global Economy and Development.

Parboteeah, P. K. (2008). *Multinational management: A strategic approach* (4th ed.). Thompson South-Western.

Porter, M. E. (1998, November-December). Clusters and the new economics of competition. *Harvard Business Review*. PMID:10187248.

Prahalad, C. K. (2005). *The fortune at the bottom of the pyramid (BOP), eradicating poverty through profits: Enabling dignity and choice through markets*. Philadelphia: Wharton School Publishing.

Prahalad, C. K., & Meshelkar, R. A. (2010, July-August). Innovation's holy grail. *Harvard Business Review*. PMID:20648874.

Rawlings, J. J. (2006, January 6). Africa will progress, the devil is the type of leaders it gets. *Daily Nation*.

Reich, R. B. (2010, September 2). How to end a great recession. *New York Times*.

UN Remittances. (2009). *World remittances report, 2009*. New York: UN.

Sachs, J. (2005). *End of poverty: The economic possibilities for our times.* New York: Penguin Books.

Shambaugh, D. (2013). *China goes global: The partial power.* Oxford, UK: Oxford University Press.

Stewart, W. H. Jr, Watson, W. E., Carland, J. C., & Carland, J. W. (1998). A proclivity for entrepreneurship: A comparison of entrepreneurs, small business owners, and corporate managers. *Journal of Business Venturing*, 14.

Stiglitz, J. (2003). *Globalization and its discontents.* New York: W. W. Norton and Company.

Stiglitz, J. (2010). *Free fall: American free markets and the sinking of the world economy.* New York: W. W. Norton and Company.

UN MDG. (2008). *United Nations millennium development goals report.* New York: UN.

UNAIDS. (2009). *United Nations annual AIDS report.* Geneva, Switzerland: United Nations.

UNIDO. (2009). *Industrial development report, 2008/2009.* Geneva, Switzerland: United Nations Industrial Development Organization.

United Nations. (2003). Economic development in Africa: Trade performance and commodity dependence. In *Proceedings of the United Nations Conference on Trade and Development (UNCTAD).* Geneva, Switzerland: UN.

United Nations Economic Commission on Africa (UNECA) and African Union Commission. (AUC). (2010). *Economic report on Africa.* Addis Ababa, Ethiopia: UNECA/AUC.

WHO. (2007). *World health report, 2007.* Geneva, Switzerland: WHO.

Wild, J. J., Wild, K. L., & Han, J. C. Y. (2008). *International business* (4th ed.). Upper Saddle River, NJ: Pearson.

Williamson, P. J. (1997, September-October). Asia's new competitive game. *Harvard Business Review.*

World Bank. (2007). *Expanding the possible in sub-Saharan Africa: How tertiary institutions can increase growth and competitiveness.* Washington, DC: The World Bank.

World Bank. (2009a). *Prospects for the global economy*. Washington, DC: The World Bank.

World Bank. (2009b). *Remittances data, March revision*. Washington, DC: The World Bank.

World Bank. (2009c). *Technology exports report, World Bank technology exports report*. Washington, DC: World Bank.

World Bank. (2009d). *World Bank's country at a glance report*. Washington, DC: World Bank.

World Bank. (2010). *Doing business in the world in 2010: Removing obstacles to growth*. Washington, DC: The World Bank.

World Economic Forum. (2008). *World competitive report 2010-2009.* Geneva, Switzerland: The World Economic Forum.

World Economic Forum. (2011). *World competitive report 2010-2011*. Paper presented at the World Economic Forum. Geneva, Switzerland.

Chapter 11
Summary and Conclusion

ABSTRACT

Chapter eleven summarizes the book's message and focus. It makes concluding remarks on emerging business opportunities, market entry, competitive strategies, and foreign direct investments in the continent. It further states the compelling imperatives of doing business in Africa today.

1. SUMMARY

Since the early 1990s, developing countries, including African countries, have been and still are the fastest-growing economies and markets in the world for most products and services (Palepu et al., 2005). Africa has been growing and continuous to grow at an average of 5% per annum. This a great opportunity for consumer products and services.

Global corporations and companies can lower their operating costs by setting up businesses, particularly manufacturing facilities, selling and service centers in Africa, a continent characterized by relatively inexpensive skilled labor and trained managers, abundant environmental resources, an increasingly growing middle class, and an improving business climate. Many African countries have realized not only the importance but the critical necessity of reforms in their economies. Therefore, there is increasing political and institutional reforms by many African countries in order to attract direct foreign investments and to stimulate the growth of indigenous entrepreneurship (Mbaku, 2004; Moyo, 2009).

DOI: 10.4018/978-1-4666-4570-7.ch011

Africa is composed of a set of regionalizing and low cost emerging markets that are developing fast. The African Development Bank estimates that Africa will grow on average at 7-8 percent per annum into the foreseeable future (Benoni, 2010). There are over 700 million literate Africans with an increasing average per capita income and purchasing power parity per capita both estimated to grow at 5 percent per year in the coming decades. There is also a growing business opportunity for consumer products and services in these developments.

There are many opportunities of doing business in Africa, by global companies, that include the use of the growing regional markets made up of countries with a lot of similarities in language, legal, administrative, and political systems and exploitation of abundant environmental resources in various African countries. The African currencies are convertible to the dollar and to the other major currencies such as the Yen, the Euro, and the Sterling Pound, within a well functioning capital market and banking system, allowing for effective international financial transactions. African populations are becoming increasingly literate with a strong and growing demand for IT and IT related services like mobile phones and Internet services.

The challenges of doing business in Africa include poverty and its related destabilizing insecurity and instability, an underdeveloped infrastructure, institutional voids, poor leadership, weak governance, poor African image, almost insurmountable healthcare problems; particularly HIV/AIDS and malaria pandemics, and corruption. Many African governments are reforming their institutions, including mechanisms to ensure social and political stability. Therefore, an ambitious and obsessive management with a well-articulated strategic intent can easily exploit the emerging and existing opportunities that include abundant environmental and increasingly creative human resources that Africa offers to create value for their organizations and stakeholders.

Furthermore, any firm wishing to enter the African market should carefully study the institutional context of each country and region of Africa to be able to make a decision in which country/region to enter first. Empirical data indicate that firms that take the extra initiative to carefully study and understand the institutional context differences and similarities between countries and regions are likely to choose the best markets to enter, select optimal entry and competitive strategies, and will make the most out of operating in emerging African markets (Khanna, 2005).

2. CONCLUSION

Africa is the continent of the future, with great emerging business opportunities. Therefore, any company that wishes to be and remain competitive globally ought to have a footing in Africa sooner than later. This will give the company a first-mover and incumbent advantages. Incumbency and first-mover advantages enable a firm to develop a sustainable competitive advantage, both of which enhance its barriers to entry. Africa is the last frontier in global business and in creating increasing value for global and domestic companies' stakeholders. According to anthropologists and social societies, Africa is the origin of man (Diamond, 1998). The continent will be the last frontier in creating wealth for mankind in the 21st century.

REFERENCES

Benoni, C. (2010, December 14). I foresee 7.5 percent growth rates in Africa in 2010: African development bank (AFDB) president, Donald Kaberuka. *The East African*.

Diamond, J. (1998). *Guns, germs, and steel: The fates of human societies*. New York: W. W. Norton and Company.

Khanna, T., Palepu, G. K., & Sinha, J. (2005, May). Strategies for emerging markets. *Harvard Business Review*. PMID:15938439.

Mbaku, J. M. (2004). *Institutions and development in Africa*. Africa World Press.

Moyo, D. (2009). *Dead aid: Why aid is not working and how there is a better way for Africa*. New York: Farrar, Straus, and Giroux.

Palepu, G. K., & Khanna, T. (2005, May). Strategies for emerging markets. *Harvard Business Review*.

Compilation of References

Abrams, J. J. (2009, May 11). 10 questions: The Liberian president's new memoirs. *Time*.

Acemoglu & Robinson. (2012). *Why nations fail: The origins of power, prosperity, and poverty*. New York: Crown Business.

Adler, N. J., & Gundersen, A. (2007). *International dimensions of organizational behavior* (5th ed.). Thomson Southwestern.

AFDB. (2008). *African economic development: The bank's annual report*. Tunis, Tunisia: AFDB.

AFDB. (2010). *African development bank (AFDB) annual economic report*. Tunis, Tunisia: AFDB.

AFDB. (n.d.). Retrieved from http.//www.afdb.com

AGOA. (2009). *AGOA annual report*. Washington, DC: Department of Commerce.

Andrews, K. (1980). *The concept of corporate strategy* (2nd ed.). Dow-Jones Irwin.

Annan, K. (1999). Peace and development: One struggle two fronts. *Address to the World Bank Staff*. Washington, DC: DANCE. Retrieved from http://www.un.org/News/Press/docs/1999/19991019.sgsm7187.doc.html.

Annan, K. (1999). *Peace and development: One struggle two fronts*. Retrieved from http://www.un.org/News/Press/docs/1999/19991019.sgsm7187.doc.html

AU. (2009). *Economic report on Africa 2010*. Addis Ababa, Ethiopia: AU Commission.

AU. (2012). *African union strategic plan 2009-2012*. Addis Ababa, Ethiopia: AU.

AUC. (2012). *AU strategic plan 2009-2012*. Addis Ababa, Ethiopia: AU Commission.

AUC. (2012). *The commission strategic plan, 2009 – 2012*. Addis Ababa, Ethiopia: AU Commission.

Bajaj, V. (2009, December 8). In India, anxiety over the slow pace of innovation. *New York Times*.

Balfour, F. (2009, June 8). The surprising strength of South East Asia. *Business Week*.

Barboza, D. (2010, August 15). China passes Japan as the second-largest economy in the world. *New York Times*.

Barney, B. J. (1986). Organizational culture: Can it be a source of sustained competitive advantage? *Academy of Management Review*, *11*(3).

Barney, B. J. (1991). Firm resources and sustained competitive advantage. *Journal of Management, 17*(1). doi:10.1177/01492063 9101700108.

Barney, B. J. (1997). *Gaining and sustaining competitive advantage*. Reading, MA: Addison-Wesley Publishing Company, Inc..

Barney, J. H. (2002). *Gaining and sustaining competitive advantage* (2nd ed.). Upper Saddle River, NJ: Pearson International Education.

BBC. (2010). Retrieved from www.bbc.com.

Benoni, C. (2009, December 14). I foresee 7.5 percent growth rates in Africa in 2010: African development bank (AFDB) president, Donald Kaberuka. *The East African*.

Bernstein, R., & Rasco, J. (2007, July 23). Africa, the final frontier. *Merrill Lynch Report*.

Bharadwaj, S. G., Varadarajan, P. R., & John, F. (1993). Sustainable competitive advantage in service industries: A conceptual model and research propositions. *Journal of Marketing*, 57.

Black, J. S., & Morrison, J. A. (2010, September). A cautionary tale for emerging market giants: How ethnocentric leadership in corporate japan knocked its companies off the world stage. *Harvard Business Review*.

Breemer, I. (2005, June). Managing risk in an unstable world. *Harvard Business Review*.

Brown, K. (1996). *Goodwives, nasty wenches, and anxious patriarchs: Gender, race, and power in colonial virginia*. Chapel Hill, NC: University of North Carolina Press.

Bungay, S. (2011, January-February). How to make the most of your company's strategy: The art of translating top management's aspirations into concrete action on the ground. *Harvard Business Review*.

Business Week. (2009). Retrieved from http://www.businessweek.com/.

Butagira, T. (2012, March 24). Charities want Africa poor, says UK official. *Daily Nation*.

Bwisa, M. H., & Nafukho, F. M. (2012). *Learning entrepreneurship through indigenous knowledge*. Nsemia Publishing Company.

Calestous, J. (2011). *The new harvest: Agricultural innovation in Africa*. Oxford, UK: Oxford University Press.

Campbell, A., & Alexander, M. (1997, November-December). What is wrong with strategy? *Harvard Business Review*. PMID:10174797.

Chandler, A. D. (1962). *Strategy and structure: Chapters in the history of the American industrial enterprise*. Cambridge, MA: Massachusetts Institute of Technology Press.

Chan, K. W., & Renee, M. (2005). *Blue ocean strategy: How to create uncontested market space and make the competition irrelevant*. Boston: Harvard Business School Press.

Chironga, M., Leke, A., & van Wamelen, A. (2011). *Checking the next growth market: Africa*. Boston: Harvard Business School Publishing in partnership with the Economist Intelligence Unit of the Economist Magazine.

Clinton, W. J. (2011). *Back to work: Why we need smart government for a strong economy*. New York: Alfred A. Knopf.

Collins, J. (2009a, May 25). How the mighty fall. *Bussiness Week*.

Collins, F. J., & Porras, I. J. (1996, September-October). Building your company's vision. *Harvard Business Review*.

Collins, J. (2001). *From good to great: Why some companies make the lip to greatness and others do not*. Brown Herron.

Collins, J. (2009b). *How the mighty fall*. New York: Harper Collins Publishers Inc..

Copeland, M. J., & Schuster, C. P. (2006). *Global business practices: Adapting for success*. Washington, DC: Thomson.

Corden, W. M. (1982). *Booming sector and Dutch disease: Economic survey and consolidation. Oxford Economic paper*. Oxford, UK: Oxford University Press.

Corden, W. M., & Neary, J. P. (1984). Booming sector and de-industrialization in a small open economy. *The Economic Journal*, 92.

Crowder, B. (2011). *Choices and consequences*. Our Daily Bread.

Cullen, J. B., & Parboteeah, P. K. (2008). *Multinational management: A strategic approach* (4th ed.). Thomson Southwestern.

Cutter, S. (1993). *Living with risk*. New York: Routledge.

Daily Nation . (2009). Retrieved from www.nationmedia.com.

Davidson, A. (2012, March 19). Why some countries go bust. *New York Times*.

Day, G. S., & Wensley, R. (1988). Assessing advantage: A framework for diagnosing competitive superiority. *Journal of Marketing*, 52.

Deng, F. M., & Zartman, W. I. (2002). *A strategic vision for Africa: The Kampala movement*. Washington, DC: The Brookings Institution.

Diamandis, P. N., & Kotler, S. (2012). *Abundance: The future is better than you think*. New York: Free Press.

Diamond, J. (1998). *Guns, Germs, and Steel: The Fates of Human Societies*. New York: W. W. Norton and Company.

Drucker, P. F. (1994, September-October). The theory of the business. *Harvard Business Review*.

Drucker, P. F. (1999). *Management challenges for the 21st century*. New York: Harper Business: An Imprint of HarperCollins Publishers.

Dyer, J. H., Prashant, K., & Harbir, S. (2004, July-August). When to ally and when to acquire. *Harvard Business Review*. PMID:15241957.

EE. (1999). *American history*. Encarta Encyclopedia.

EIU. (2009). African business and economic report. *The Economist Intelligence Unit*.

EIU. (2009). African economic report. *The Economist Intelligence Unit*. Retrieved from http://viewswire.eiu.com/index.asp.

ERA. (2009). *Economic report on Africa*. Addis Ababa, Ethiopia: AU Commission.

ERA. (2010). *Economic report on africa*. Addis Ababa, Ethiopia: African Union Commission.

EX-IM Bank. (2009). *World investments by EX-IM bank report*. Washington, DC: The Export and Import Bank of America.

Frankel, J., & Rose, A. (2000). *An estimate of the effects of currency unions on growth*. Unpublished.

Frederick, B. (2009, June 8). The surprising strength of South East Asia. *Business Week*.

Friedman, T. L. (2011, October 1). How did the robot end up with my job? *New York Times*.

Friedman, T. L. (2012, March 31). Why nations fail. *New York Times*.

Friedman, T. L. (2005). *The world is flat: A brief history of the 21st century*. New York: Farrar, Straus, and Giroux.

Friedman, T. L., & Mandelbaum, M. (2011). *That used to be us: How America fell behind in the world it invented and how we can come back*. New York: Farrar, Straus, and Giroux.

Garter, J. (1997, September-October). Troubles ahead in emerging markets. *Harvard Business Review*.

Gekonge, M. (2006). *Eliminating Horizontal Inequalities in Post Conflict Northern Uganda: Tackling the Neglected Dimensions of the Humanitarian Crisis in Northern Uganda. (Unpublished Master's Research Project)*. South Orange, NJ: Seton Hall University.

Gettleman, J. (2009, October 11). Easy money fuels rise in kidnappings in Kenya. *New York Times*.

Ghemawat, P. (2010). Finding your strategy in the new landscape. *Harvard Business Review*. Retrieved from http://hbr.org/2010/03/finding-your-strategy-in-the-new-landscape/ar/1.

Ghemawat, P. (2001, September). Distance still matters: Hard realities of global expansion. *Harvard Business Review*. PMID:11550630.

Ghemawat, P. (2005). Regional strategies for global leadership. *Harvard Business Review*. PMID:16334585.

Ghemawat, P. (2010, March). Finding your strategy in the new landscape. *Harvard Business Review*.

Giddens, A. (2002). *The transformation of intimacy*. Stanford, CA: Stanford University Press.

Gitman, L. J., & McDaniel, C. (2005). *Future of business* (5th ed.). Thomson South-Western.

Greenwald, B., & Khan, J. (2005, September). Strategy is local. *Harvard Business Review*. PMID:16171214.

Hamel, G. (2002). *Leading the revolution*. New York: Plume (Penguin Books).

Hamel, G., & Prahalad, C. K. (1989, May-June). Strategic intent. *Harvard Business Review*. PMID:10303477.

Hamel, G., & Prahalad, C. K. (1990, May-June). The core competence of the corporation. *Harvard Business Review*.

Hamel, G., & Prahalad, C. K. (1994). *Competing for the future*. Boston: Harvard Business School Press.

Hamel, G., & Välikangas, L. (2003, September). The quest for resilience. *Harvard Business Review*. PMID:12964393.

Han, J. C. Y., Wild, J. J., & Wild, K. L. (2008). *International business* (4th ed.). Upper Saddle River, NJ: Pearson.

Hansen, P. C. (2013, January 1). *Compendium*. Working Group on American Investment in Africa.

Harry, K., & Alexander, M. (2009, December). When you shouldn't go global. *Harvard Business Review*.

Hart, B. H. L. (1967). *Strategy*. New York: Basic Books.

Hax, A. C., & Wilde, D. L. II. (1999, Winter). The delta model: Adaptive management for a changing world. *Sloan Management Review*.

Heifetz, R. (1994). *Leadership without easy answers*. Cambridge, MA: Harvard University Press.

Heifetz, R. A., & Laurie, D. (2001, December). The work of leadership. *Harvard Business Review*. PMID:10174450.

Henderson, B. (1983). The anatomy of competition. *Journal of Marketing*, 47.

Henderson, B. D., & Zakon, A. J. (1983). The concept of strategy and the growth-share matrix in corporate growth strategy. In Albert, K. J. (Ed.), *The Strategic Management Handbook*. New York: McGraw-Hill.

Henisz, W. J., & Zelner, B. A. (2010, April). The hidden risks in emerging markets. *Harvard Business Review*.

Hill, C. W., & Jones, G. R. (2001). *Strategic management theory* (5th ed.). New York: Houghton Mifflin Company.

Hoffman, P. N. (2000). An examination of the sustainable competitive advantage concept: Past, present, and future. *Academy of Marketing Science Review*, 4.

Hofstede, G., & Hall, E. T. (1980). *Culture: Consequences: International differences in work-related values*. Beverly Hills, CA: Sage.

Holiday, C. (2001, September). Sustainable growth, the DuPont way. *Harvard Business Review*.

Hope, K. R., & Chikulo, B. C. (2000). *Corruption and development in Africa: Lessons from country case studies*. London: Macmillan Press Limited.

Horton, L. E., & Horton, J. O. (1999). *African-american history. Encarta Encyclopedia*. Redmond, WA: Microsoft.

Hunt, S. D., & Morgan, R. M. (1995). The comparative advantage: Theory of competition. *Journal of Marketing*, 59.

IFC. (2009). *The bottom of the pyramid (BOP) report, 2009*. Washington, DC: IFC.

ILO. (2009). *Global employment trends*. Geneva, Switzerland: ILO.

IMF. (2009). *2009 regional economic outlook, Sub-Saharan Africa*. Washington, DC: IMF.

Immelt, J. R. (2012, March). The CEO of GE on sparking American manufacturing renewal. *Harvard Business Review*.

Juma, C. (2011). *The new harvest: Agricultural innovation in africa*. Oxford, UK: Oxford University Press.

Kagame, P. (2009, May 30). Regional integration, an interview. *Daily Nation*.

Kamara, A. B., Bousrih, L., & Nyende, M. (2008). Growing a knowledge based economy: Evidence from public expenditure on education in africa. *African Development Bank Economic Research Working Paper Series*. Abidjan, Cote d'Ivoire: African Development Bank.

Kamau, S. (2012, February 11). African diaspora to boost investment in Africa. *The East African*.

Kaplan, R. S., & Norton, D. (2005, July-August). The balanced scorecard: Measures that drive performance. *Harvard Business Review*. PMID:10119714.

Kaplan, S. R., & Grossman, S. A. (2010, October). The emerging capital market for nonprofits. *Harvard Business Review*.

Karambu, I. (2012a, January 23). Kenya's growth rate to fall behind other East African states in the next two years: Quoting Mr. Wolfgang Fengler of the World Bank. *Daily Nation*.

Karambu, I. (2012b, February 8). Trade barriers costing Africa billions of dollars, says World Bank. *Daily Nation*.

Karel, C., & Ingemar, D. (1993). Rivalry, strategic groups, and firm profitability. *Strategic Management Journal*, 14.

Kasperson, J. X., & Kates, R. W. (1983). Comparative risk analysis of technological hazards: A review. *Proceedings of the National Academy of Sciences, 80*.

Keeler, D. (2010). Kenya: Rebirth of a nation. *Global Finance*. Retrieved from http://www.globalfinance.gr/page/.

Kempe, R. H. (1997). Development structures for Africa: The need for policy reform and good governance. *Journal of Opinion, 25*(1).

Khanna, T., & Palepu, G. K. (2005, May). Strategies for emerging markets. *Harvard Business Review*. PMID:15938439.

Khanna, T., Palepu, G. K., & Sinha, J. (2005, May). Strategies for emerging markets. *Harvard Business Review*. PMID:15938439.

Khanna, T., & Palepu, K. (1997, September-October). Why focused strategies maybe wrong for emerging markets. *Harvard Business Review*.

Kim, C. W., & Mauborgne, R. (2004, October). Blue ocean strategy. *Harvard Business Review*. PMID:15559577.

Kim, W. C., & Mauborgne, R. (2005). *Blue ocean strategy: How to create uncontested market space and make the competition irrelevant*. Boston: Harvard Business School Press.

Kim, W. C., & Mauborgne, R. (2009, September). How strategy shapes structure. *Harvard Business Review*.

Kisiang'ani, E. (2007). The lies about jomo kenyatta and kenya. *The Standard*. Retrieved from http://www3.standard.com/net/public/Individuals.

Kituyi, M. (2012, January 28). A free trade road map for Africa, but who will keep their promise?. *Daily Nation*.

Kituyi, M. (2012b, June 30). Obama's strategy for Africa and the continent's reality. *Daily Nation*.

Kotler, J. P. (1990). *A force for change. How leadership differs from management*. New York: Free Press.

Kristof, N. D. (2010, June 30). Africa on the rise. *New York Times*.

Lafrance, R., & Schembri, L. (2002). *Purchasing-power parity: Definition, measurement, and interpretation*. Ottawa, Canada: International Department, Bank of Canada.

Larson, K. C. (2004). *Harriet tubman: The portrait of an american hero, bound for the promised land*. New York: Random House Publishing Group.

Lymbersky, C. (2008). *Market entry strategies: Texts, cases, and readings in market entry management*. Laboratory Press.

Lynch, R. (2000). *Corporate strategy*. London: Pitman Publishing.

Mahajan, V. (2009). *Africa rising: How 900 million african consumers offer more than you think*. Upper Saddle River, NJ: Pearson Prentice Hall.

Manning, P. (1990). *Slavery and African life: Occidental, oriental, and African slave trades*. New York: Cambridge University Press.

Marcelo, G. (2012, February 10). CobWeb of obstacles that make Africa unable to trade with itself. *Daily Nation*.

Markides, C. C. (1997, November-December). To diversify or not to diversify. *Harvard Business Review*. PMID:10174800.

Mbaku, J. M. (1998). Improving African participation in the global economy: The role of economic freedoms. *Business and the Contemporary, 10*(2).

Mbaku, J. M. (1998). Emerging trade blocks and the fortune of african participation in the world economy. *Journal of Economic Integration, 10*(2).

Mbaku, J. M. (2004). *Institutions and development in africa*. Trenton, NJ: Africa World Press.

McClelland, D. C. (1987). *Human motivation*. New York: Cambridge University Press.

McGahan, A. M. (2004, October). How industries change. *Harvard Business Review*. PMID:15559578.

McGrath, M. (2012, April 20). 'Huge' water resource exists under Africa. *BBC World Service*.

McKeown, M. (2008). *The truth about innovation*. London: Prentice Hall.

Meyer, C., & Kirby, J. (2010, April). Leadership in the age of transparency. *Harvard Business Review*. PMID:20402054.

Mintzberg, H. (1973). *The nature of managerial work*. New York: Harper and Row.

Mintzberg, H. (1979). *The structuring of organizations*. Englewood Cliffs, NJ: Prentice Hall.

Mintzberg, H. (1987, July-August). Crafting strategy. *Harvard Business Review*. PMID:10280177.

Mintzberg, H. (1988, Summer). Crafting strategy. *The McKinsey Quarterly*.

Mintzberg, H. (1994). *The rise and fall of strategic planning*. New York: Basic Books.

Mintzberg, H., Ahlstrand, B., & Lampel, J. (1998). *Strategy safari: A guided tour through the wilds of strategic management*. New York: The Free Press.

Mintzberg, H., & Hames, A. W. (1985). Of strategy delivered and emergent strategy. *Strategic Management Journal, 6*(3). doi:10.1002/smj.4250060306.

Mintzberg, H., & Quinn, J. B. (1988). *The strategy process*. Harlow, MA: Prentice-Hall.

Mkapa, B. W. (2009). *The role of the alumni in governance and institutional development in Africa: A public lecture at the inaugural of Makerere University Grand Alumni Re-Union*. Kampala, Uganda: Makerere University.

Mofadal, M. A. (2010, June 27). Africa faces major image problems. *Sunday Nation*.

Mo, I. (2012). *Ibrahim African governance prize annual report, 2012*. London: Ibrahim Prize.

Mom, I. (2009). *Performance of the African leadership*. The East African.

Moraa, G. (2006). *Eliminating horizontal inequalities in post conflict northern Uganda: Tackling the neglected dimensions of the humanitarian crisis in northern Uganda.* (Unpublished Master's Thesis). Seton Hall University, South Orange, NJ.

Morley, W., Klepp, S. E., & Smith, B. G. (2005). *The unfortunate: The voyage and adventures of william morley, an indentured servant.* University Park, PA: Pennsylvania State University Press.

Moyo, D. (2008). *A small price to pay: Financing africa's infrastructure bill. Global Economics Paper No: 174.* New York: Goldman Sachs.

Moyo, D. (2009). *Dead aid: Why aid is not working and how there is a better way for Africa.* New York: Farrar, Straus, and Giroux.

Mutsa, C., Acha, L., & van Wamelen, A. (2011). *Checking the next growth market: Africa.* Boston: Harvard Business School Publishing.

NSE. (2010). *Nairobi stock exchange annual report.* Nairobi, Kenya: NSE.

OAU. (1963). *Organization of african union charter.* Addis Ababa, Ethiopia: OAU.

OECD. (2008). Definition. In *The OECD Benchmark Definition of Foreign Direct Investment* (4th ed.). Paris: OECD.

Okoth, J. (2012, September 4). Experts warn insecurity could dim Africa's growth. *The Standard.*

Opanga, K. (2010). Millennium development goals must be achieved. *Daily Nation.* Retrieved from http://www.nation.co.ke/.

Ortiz, J. (2010). The global environment through the SLEPT framework. *International Journal of Business and Globalization, 5*(4).

Ostby, G. (2004). Horizontal inequalities and civil conflict. In *Proceedings of the 13th Annual National Political Science Conference.* Hurdalsjoen, Norway: SEAS Press.

Page, J. (2008). Rowing against the current: The diversification challenge in Africa's resource-rich economies. *Global Economic Development Working Paper 29.* Washington, DC: Brookings Global Economy and Development.

Palepu, G. K., & Khanna, T. (2005, May). Strategies for emerging markets. *Harvard Business Review.*

Parboteeah, P. K. (2008). *Multinational management: A strategic approach* (4th ed.). Thompson South-Western.

Pearce, J., & Robinson, R. (1997). *Strategic management: Strategy formulation, implementation, and evaluation.* Upper Saddle River, NJ: Prentice Hall.

Porter, M. (1990). *Competitive advantage of nations model.* Retrieved from www.valuebasedmanagement.com

Porter, M. E. (1980). *Competitive strategy: Techniques for analyzing industries.* New York: Free Press.

Porter, M. E. (1985). *Competitive advantage: Creating and sustaining superior performance.* New York: The Free Press.

Porter, M. E. (1986). *Competitive strategy.* Boston: Harvard Business School Press.

Porter, M. E. (1990). *The competitive advantage of nations*. New York: Free Press.

Porter, M. E. (1996, November-December). What is strategy? *Harvard Business Review*.

Porter, M. E. (1998, November-December). Clusters and the new economics of competition. *Harvard Business Review*. PMID:10187248.

Porter, M. E. (2001, March). Strategy and the internet. *Harvard Business Review*. PMID:11246925.

Porter, M. E. (2007). *Global competitiveness: Implications for Kenya*. Nairobi, Kenya: Harvard Business School: Strathmore Business School.

Porter, M. E., & Kramer, M. R. (2011, January-February). Capitalism is under siege: Diminished trust in business is causing political leaders to set policies that sap economic growth: Business is caught in a vicious circle: The purpose of the corporation must be redefined around creating shared value. *Harvard Business Review*.

Porter, M. E., & Kramer, M. R. (2011a, February). Business is caught in a vicious circle. *Harvard Business Review*.

Porter, M. E., & Kramer, M. R. (2011b, February). The purpose of the corporation must be redefined around creating Shared Value. *Harvard Business Review*.

Porter, M. E., & Kramer, M. R. (2011b, January). Diminished trust in business is causing political leaders to set policies that sap economic growth. *Harvard Business Review*.

Porter, M. E., & Rivkin, J. W. (2012, March). The looming challenge to U.S. competitiveness. *Harvard Business Review*.

Powell, C. (2012). *It worked for me: In life and leadership*. New York: HarperCollins Publishers.

Prahalad, C. K. (2005). *The fortune at the bottom of the pyramid (BOP): Eradicating poverty through profits: Enabling dignity and choice through markets*. Philadelphia: Wharton School Publishing.

Prahalad, C. K., & Hamel, G. (2005, July-August). Strategic intent. *Harvard Business Review*.

Prahalad, C. K., & Meshelkar, R. A. (2010, July-August). Innovation's holy grail. *Harvard Business Review*. PMID:20648874.

Pralahad, C. K., & Hamel, G. (1989, July-August). Strategic intent. *Harvard Business Review*.

Rasco, J., & Bernstein, R. (2007, July 23). Africa, the final frontier. *Merrill Lynch Report*.

Rawlings, J. J. (2006, January 6). Africa will progress, the devil is the type of leaders it gets. *Daily Nation*.

Reich, R. B. (2010, September 2). How to end a great recession. *New York Times*.

Ross, S., & Agiesta, J. (2012). Survey finds racial views have not improved since 2008. *The Philadelphia Inquirer.* Retrieved from http://philly.newspaperdirect.com/epaper/viewer.aspx.

Rozakis, L. (2007). *Schauni's quick guide to writing great research papers* (2nd ed.). New York: The McGraw-Hill Companies Inc..

Rumelt, R., & Lippman, S. (1982). Uncertain imitability. *Journal of Economics*, 13.

Sachs, J. (2006). *End of poverty: The economic possibilities for our times*. New York: Penguin Books.

Saltmarch, M. (2010, August 2). South Africa tries to scale the industrial ladder. *New York Times*.

Schuster, C. P., & Copeland, M. J. (2006). *Global business practices: Adapting for success*. Atlanta, GA: Thomson.

Shambaugh, D. (2013). *China goes global: The partial power*. Oxford, UK: Oxford University Press.

Singh, J. V., & Aaron, R. (2005, December). Getting off shoring right. *Harvard Business Review*.

Sjöberg, L. (1991). *Risk perception by experts and the public: Risk research report no. 4*. Stockholm, Sweden: Center for Risk Research.

Slovic, P. (1997). Perception of risk. *Science*. PMID:3563507.

Slywotzky, A. J., & Drzik, J. (2005, April). Countering the biggest risk of all. *Harvard Business Review*. PMID:15807041.

Smart, S. B., Megginson, W. L., & Gitman, L. J. (2007). *Corporate finance* (2nd ed.). Thomson Western.

Srivastava, R., Shervani, T., & Fahey, L. (1998). Market-based assets and shareholder value: A framework for analysis. *Journal of Marketing*, 62.

Ssomogerere. (2002). Financial sector restructuring under the structural adjustment programs and economic program in uganda. *A policy paper.*

Stalk, G. Jr, & Lachenauer, R. (2004, April). Hardball: Five strategies for trouncing the competitions. *Harvard Business Review*. PMID:15077367.

Stewart, F. (2000). *Policies towards horizontal inequalities in post-conflict reconstruction*. Oxford, UK: Queen Elizabeth House.

Stewart, W. H. Jr, Watson, W. E., Carland, J. C., & Carland, J. W. (1998). A proclivity for entrepreneurship: A comparison of entrepreneurs, small business owners, and corporate managers. *Journal of Business Venturing*, 14.

Stiglitz, J. (2003). *Globalization and its discontents*. New York: W. W. Norton and Company.

Stiglitz, J. (2010). *Free fall: American free markets and the sinking of the world economy*. New York: W. W. Norton and Company.

Straziuso, J. (2012, October 7). Africa sees hotels rise with its economic gains. *The Philadelphia Inquirer*. Country Forecast. (2009, November). Sub-Saharan Africa regional overview. *The Economist Intelligence Unit*.

Stulz, M. R. (2009, March). Ways companies mismanage risk. *Harvard Business Review*.

Suarez, F., & Lanzolla, G. (2005, April). Half-truths of first-mover advantage. *Harvard Business Review*. Editor. (2009, May 11). An interview with the Liberian President. *Time*.

Tarun, K., & Krishna, P. G. (2005, May). Strategies for emerging markets. *Harvard Business Review*.

The Africa Guide. (2005). Map of Africa, 2005. Retrieved from www.africaguide.com.

The Daily Bread. (2011, December). [The Daily Bread.]. *Galatians, 6, 7*, 9–10.

The East African . (2010) Retrieved from www.nationmedia.com.

Thompson, A. (2006). *Crafting and executing strategy: The quest for competitive advantage: Concepts and cases*. AIPI Publishers.

Tregoe, B., & Zimmerman, J. (1980). *Top management strategy*. New York: Simon and Schuster.

Ulimwengu. (2009). Tanzanians react to their monolithic leadership. *The East African*).

UN MDG. (2008). *United Nations millennium development goals report*. New York: UN.

UN Remittances. (2009). *World remittances report, 2009*. New York: UN.

UNAIDS. (2006). *United Nations AIDS annual report*. Geneva, Switzerland: UNAIDS.

UNAIDS. (2008). *UNAIDS annual health report, 2008*. Geneva, Switzerland: UNAIDS.

UNAIDS. (2009). *United Nations annual AIDS report*. Geneva, Switzerland: United Nations.

UNCTAD. (2003). *International trade report*. New York: United Nations Trade and Development Report.

UNCTAD. (2003). *The African growth opportunity act (AGOA): A preliminary assessment report prepared for the United Nations Conference on Trade and Development*. New York: UNCTAD.

UNCTAD. (2003). *United Nations conference on trade and development annual report*. Geneva, Switzerland: UNCTAD.

UNCTAD. (2008). *United Nations conference on trade and development annual report, 2008*. New York: UNCTAD.

UNCTAD. (2009). *UNCTAD world investment report*. New York: UNCTAD.

UNIDO. (2009). *Industrial development report, 2008/2009*. Geneva, Switzerland: United Nations Industrial Development Organization.

United Nations Economic Commission on Africa (UNECA) and African Union Commission. (AUC). (2010). *Economic report on Africa (ERA) 2010*. New York: UNECA/AUC.

United Nations Economic Commission on Africa (UNECA) and African Union Commission. (AUC). (2010). *Economic report on Africa*. Addis Ababa, Ethiopia: UNECA/AUC.

United Nations. (2003). Economic development in Africa: Trade performance and commodity dependence. In *Proceedings of the United Nations Conference on Trade and Development (UNCTAD)*. Geneva, Switzerland: UN.

USA Department of Commercial. (2009). *Annual 2009 report*. Washington, DC: US Government.

Vanhonacker, W. R. (2004, April). When good Guanxi turns bad. *Harvard Business Review*.

Voegle, J. (2011, January 11). Agricultural and rural development, the World Bank. *New York Times*.

Wachira & Mureithi. (2013). Coming soon, Kenya's greatest and largest water dam. *Daily Nation*. Retrieved from http://www.nation.co.ke/.

Wang, J. Y. (2007). What drives China's growing role in Africa. *IMF working paper 07/211*. Washington, DC: IMF.

Wang, M., Garner, J. F., & Silver, V. (2008). GEMs equity strategy: Sub-saharan africa: Improved fundamentals priced near term. *Morgan Stanley*. Retrieved from http://www.morganstanley.com/.

Wang, M., Garner, J. F., & Silver, V. (2008). *GEMs equity strategy: Sub-saharan africa. Improved Fundamentals Priced Near Term*. New York: Morgan Stanley.

WEF. (2011). *The world economic forum report*. Davos, Switzerland: The World Economic Forum.

Wernerfelt, B. (1984). A resource-based view of the firm. *Strategic Management Journal*, 5.

WHO. (2007). *World health report, 2007*. Geneva, Switzerland: WHO.

Wild, J. J., Wild, K. L., & Han, J. C. Y. (2008). *International business* (4th ed.). Englewood Cliffs, NJ: Pearson.

Wild, J. J., Wild, K. L., & Han, J. C. Y. (2008). *International Business* (4th ed.). Upper Saddle River, NJ: Pearson Hall.

Williams, J. R. (1992, Spring). How sustainable is your competitive advantage? *California Management Review*. doi:10.2307/41167422.

Williamson, P. J. (1997, September-October). Asia's new competitive game. *Harvard Business Review*.

Wong, E. (2009, December). China's export of labor faces scorn. *New York Times*. Retrieved from http://www.nytimes.com/.

Wood, A., & Kate, J. (2000). Why does Zimbabwe export manufactures and Uganda is not? *The Journal of Development Studies*, *37*(2). doi:10.1080/713600070.

World Bank. (1993). *The East Asian miracle: Economic growth and public policy*. New York: Oxford University Press.

World Bank. (2005). *Doing business in 2005: Removing obstacles to growth in the world*. Washington, DC: World Bank.

World Bank. (2007). *Expanding the possible in sub-Saharan Africa: How tertiary institutions can increase growth and competitiveness*. Washington, DC: The World Bank.

World Bank. (2007). *World economic report, report by the world, 2007*. Retrieved from www.bbc.com

World Bank. (2009a). *Prospects for the global economy*. Washington, DC: The World Bank.

World Bank. (2009a). *Technology exports report*. Washington, DC: World Bank.

World Bank. (2009b). *Remittances data, March revision*. Washington, DC: The World Bank.

World Bank. (2009d). *World Bank's country at a glance report*. Washington, DC: World Bank.

World Bank. (2010). *Doing business in the world in 2010: Removing obstacles to growth*. Washington, DC: The World Bank.

World Bank. (n.d.). Retrieved from http://data.worldbank.org

World Economic Forum. (2008). *World competitive report 2010-2009*. Geneva, Switzerland: The World Economic Forum.

World Economic Forum. (2011). *World competitive report 2010-2011*. Paper presented at the World Economic Forum. Geneva, Switzerland.

World Food Program. (2009). *World food program report*. Rome, Italy: WFP.

World Health Organization. (2006). *Annual report 2006*. Geneva, Switzerland: WHO.

Yoshino, Y. (2008). Domestic constraints, firm characteristics, and geographic diversification of firms-level manufacturing exports in Africa. *Policy Research Working Paper, 4575*. Washington, DC: The World Bank.

Zelner, B. A., & Henisz, W. J. (2010, April). The hidden risks in emerging markets. *Harvard Business Review*.

About the Author

Christopher Gekonge has had a long, interesting, and fruitfully checkered career. He went to school in Africa, Britain, and Canada, and he is also a CPA in Kenya, a holder of MBA, Strategic Management, and diplomas in Finance Administration and Supply Chain Strategy, both from Britain, a certificate in Aviation Management from McGill University, Montreal, Canada, where he was taught "Principles of Management" by the Canadian and internationally recognized management Guru, Professor Henry Mintzberg. Christopher is an experienced lecturer, professionally qualified financial analyst, and administrator. He worked—for 32 years—in various industries in Kenya including the civil service, as a senior manager, and as a management consultant and small businesses and micro enterprises consultant and counselor and more recently as an adjust professor in global business and researcher on doing business in Africa in the USA. He has researched and published articles on various areas of management and strategy in a referenced journal in Kenya, and he has traveled widely in Africa and the world, particularly in Europe, the Americas, and Asia, including China and India, thus gaining firsthand business knowledge in Africa and the world. Christopher Gekonge currently lives in the USA where he has taught management and global strategy as an adjunct lecturer of management and global strategy at Syracuse University, NY, and Organization and Management Lecturer at Herkimer County Community College, upstate New York. In addition, while he was at Syracuse University, he had several outreaches to the chamber of commerce of Central NY to talk about doing business in Africa. Christopher Gekonge is currently a researcher and consultant with Doing Business in Africa Inc., in Philadelphia, PA. Doing Business in Africa Inc. is a non-profit organization that focuses on research and doing business in Africa. The organization does research and makes organizations and students aware of business opportunities in Africa and on how to enter Africa and exploit these opportunities.

Index

K

L

M

N

O

P

R

S

T

U

V

W

Y

Lightning Source UK Ltd.
Milton Keynes UK
UKOW05n1829250816

281531UK00011B/109/P